OXFORD LEGAL PHILOSOPHY

Series Editors: Timothy Endicott, John Gardner, and Leslie Green

Allowing for Exceptions

OXFORD LEGAL PHILOSOPHY

Series Editors: Timothy Endicott, John Gardner, and Leslie Green

Oxford Legal Philosophy publishes the best new work in philosophically oriented legal theory. It commissions and solicits monographs in all branches of the subject, including works on philosophical issues in all areas of public and private law, and in the national, transnational, and international realms; studies of the nature of law, legal institutions, and legal reasoning; treatments of problems in political morality as they bear on law; and explorations in the nature and development of legal philosophy itself. The series represents diverse traditions of thought but always with an emphasis on rigour and originality. It sets the standard in contemporary jurisprudence.

ALSO AVAILABLE IN THE SERIES

The Ends of Harm
The Moral Foundations of Criminal Law
Victor Tadros

Corrective Justice
Ernest J. Weinrib

Conscience and Conviction
The Case for Civil Disobedience
Kimberley Brownlee

The Nature of Legislative Intent
Richard Ekins

Why Law Matters
Alon Harel

Imposing Risk
A Normative Framework
John Oberdiek

Allowing for Exceptions

A Theory of Defences and Defeasibility in Law

Luís Duarte d'Almeida

OXFORD
UNIVERSITY PRESS

OXFORD
UNIVERSITY PRESS

Great Clarendon Street, Oxford, OX2 6DP,
United Kingdom

Oxford University Press is a department of the University of Oxford. It furthers the University's objective of excellence in research, scholarship, and education by publishing worldwide. Oxford is a registered trade mark of Oxford University Press in the UK and in certain other countries

First Edition published in 2015

Published in the United States of America by Oxford University Press
198 Madison Avenue, New York, NY 10016, United States of America

British Library Cataloguing in Publication Data
Data available

Library of Congress Control Number: 2014950250

ISBN 978–0–19–968578–3

Cover image: *Le Défenseur* (c. 1860) by Honoré Daumier. Superstock/Glowimages.com

To my father, and to the memory of my mother

Series Editors' Preface

Recent work in the philosophy of criminal law has given renewed prominence to the distinction between offences and defences. Unconvinced that this is merely a technical distinction drawn for the purpose of allocating burdens of proof as between the parties to criminal proceedings, several theorists have attempted to establish that the distinction is rooted in the general theory of responsibility, and that it has significance beyond the criminal law. In this fascinating work, Luís Duarte d'Almeida joins those who deny that the distinction is merely a technical one. He also agrees that it has a significance reaching well beyond the criminal law, extending into the whole theory of rules and exceptions in practical reasoning. But he argues that all this is nonetheless compatible with an understanding of the distinction that ties it very closely to the theory of proof.

The first moves of Duarte d'Almeida's book lay the foundation for these claims by retrieving some ideas from H.L.A. Hart's early (and later disowned) arguments about the role of defences in law and morality. Duarte d'Almeida's sophisticated reworking of these ideas provides the groundwork for his original account of the more general distinction between rules and exceptions. He shows how this view casts new light on several issues and problems, including the notion of the burden of proof and the distinction between offences and defences in criminal law.

Luís Duarte d'Almeida thus reconnects the local concerns of criminal law theory and the theory of legal proof with wider problems in philosophy of law. He also speaks to lawyers. The book is highly original and highly critical of some prevailing dogmas, yet it also reminds us that sometimes the traditional legal analysis of a problem can give the best clues in the search for a philosophical understanding.

T.A.O. Endicott
J. Gardner
L. Green

Acknowledgments

My greatest debt of gratitude in writing this book is to John Gardner, who supervised the D.Phil. thesis out of which the book has grown. Generous and stimulating guidance is only one among the many things for which I thank him. I am also very grateful to many friends and colleagues for helpful comments and discussions. José de Sousa e Brito has been a gentle teacher and a patient critic. Pedro Múrias, who read many versions of several chapters, and Benjamin Spagnolo, who read at least one version of each chapter, both gave me extensive remarks and corrections. At different stages I profited from exchanges with Eugenio Bulygin, Andrea Dolcetti, James Edwards, Sebastián Figueroa, Leslie Green, Matthew Grellette, Daniël Hogers, José Juan Moreso, Nicola Muffato, Maribel Narváez Mora, Diego Papayannis, Frederick Schauer, Fábio Shecaira, Richard H. S. Tur, José António Veloso, Fred Wilmot-Smith, and Hugo R. Zuleta; and the final draft was greatly improved by Alex Flach's expert suggestions. I am equally grateful to Antony Duff and Timothy Endicott, my doctoral examiners, for instructive feedback on the original thesis; to audiences in Barcelona, Bahía Blanca, Belo Horizonte, Buenos Aires, Cambridge, Frankfurt, Girona, Lisbon, Milan, Oxford, and Hamilton, Ontario, where versions of several chapters were presented over the past few years; and to Celia Davis for excellent research assistance. And I am especially beholden to the Edinburgh Legal Theory Group for organizing, and to the Edinburgh School of Law for supporting, a one-day workshop on the penultimate version of the typescript. Many thanks to all who participated, and especially to Andrew Cornford, James Edwards (again), Guy Fletcher, Martin Kelly, Alex Latham, Euan

MacDonald, Cláudio Michelon, Nick Treanor, and Neil Walker; their comments led me to revise and expand several passages, and to correct some mistakes, when preparing the final version.

I enjoyed exceptional research conditions both as a Junior Research Fellow at Churchill College, Cambridge, and as a Research Fellow in Legal Philosophy at the University of Girona; I am grateful to these institutions, to Matthew H. Kramer, and to Jordi Ferrer. I also acknowledge the support provided by the Portuguese Foundation for Science and Technology,[1] by the University of Lisbon, and by University College, Oxford.

Chapter 3 incorporates (with several changes) material previously published as 'A Proof-Based Account of Legal Exceptions' (2013), *Oxford Journal of Legal Studies* 33: 133–68; and Chapter 8 includes (again with changes) arguments first presented in '"O Call Me Not to Justify the Wrong": Criminal Answerability and the Offence/Defence Distinction' (2012), *Criminal Law and Philosophy* 6: 227–45. These materials are used with the kind permission of Springer and the Oxford University Press.

[1] Grant SFRH/BD/44394/2008, financed by POPH–QREN–Type 4.1–Advanced Training, co-funded by the European Social Fund and by national MCTES funds (2008–2011).

Contents

Thucydides wrote of people who made rules and followed them. Going by rule they killed entire classes of enemies without exception. Most of those who died felt, I am sure, that a terrible mistake was being made, that, whatever the rule was, it could not be meant for them. 'I!—': that was their last word as their throats were cut. A word of protest: I, the exception.

Were they exceptions? The truth is, given the time to speak, we would all claim to be exceptions. For each of us there is a case to be made. We all deserve the benefit of the doubt.

But there are times when there is no time for all that close listening, all those exceptions, all that mercy. There is no time, so we fall back on the rule. And that is a great pity, the greatest pity. That is what you could have learned from Thucydides.

J. M. Coetzee, *Age of Iron* (1990)

'Sorry, sir, no exceptions. Where would we be if we began making exceptions? Soon everyone would want to be an exception, and then there would be no rules left, would there?'

J. M. Coetzee, *The Childhood of Jesus* (2013)

'What about here?' she says. She leans over his shoulder and stabs a finger at the text. Her hand is tiny, her skin mottled; on the third finger is a diamond in an extravagant setting. 'Where it says *Notwithstanding the aforesaid*.'

'It says that if you can demonstrate financial distress you are entitled to apply to the trust for support.'

'What about *notwithstanding*?'

'It means that what is stated in this clause is an exception to what has been stated before and takes precedence over it.'

'But it also means that the trust cannot withstand my claim. What does *withstand* mean if it doesn't mean that?'

'It is not a question of what *withstand* means. It is a question of what *Notwithstanding the aforesaid* means. You must take the phrase as a whole.'

She gives an impatient snort. 'I am hiring you as an expert in English, not as a lawyer,' she says. 'The will is written in English, in English words. What do the words mean? What does *notwithstanding* mean?'

A madwoman, he thinks. *How am I going to get out of this?*

J. M. Coetzee, *Summertime* (2009)

PART I
Defeasibility in Question

1

The Irreducibility Thesis

1.1 Introduction

You find yourself in a court of law, accused of having hit someone. What can you do to avoid conviction? You could simply deny the accusation: 'No, I didn't do it.' But suppose you *did* do it. You may then give a different answer. 'Yes, I hit him', you grant, 'but it was self-defence'; or 'Yes, but I was acting under duress.' To answer in this way—to offer a 'Yes, but . . .' reply—is to hold that your particular wrong was committed in exceptional circumstances. Perhaps it is true that, as a rule, wrongdoers ought to be convicted. But in your case the court should set the rule aside. You should be acquitted.

Within limits, the law allows for exceptions. Ordinarily, courts apply general law to individual cases. Generality is not only a defining feature of a legal system. It is also a valuable one. Without general norms—without rules—law would be unable to perform its action-guiding function. Yet not all individual cases are equitably decided on the ground of previously identifiable norms. Some cases are irregular, displaying exceptional features that would make it unjust to decide them in strict accordance with the applicable rules. Indeed, no rule-maker, however wise or careful, can anticipate and take into account the full range of possibly relevant exceptions. The lingering prospect of exceptional cases poses a quandary for legislative authorities. Should courts be allowed to set aside the relevant legal rules when faced with exceptional turns of events? When does justice trump the certainty that comes with the application of general norms?

In legal systems everywhere, courts do sometimes enjoy a power of this sort. At least when dealing with certain kinds of cases, judges are authorized to take into consideration exceptional circumstances, and to decide accordingly. Or so we tend to think. In fact, the line between what counts as an exception and what as part of a rule is harder to draw than it seems. The picture sketched in the first paragraph is deceptively clear. If the court heeds your claim that you acted in self-defence and acquits you, does that not show that the relevant 'rule' is not really the rule that wrongdoers ought to be convicted, but the rule that wrongdoers *who do not act in self-defence* ought to be convicted? And if 'No' and 'Yes, but. . .' answers both amount to a denial that this fully spelled-out rule is satisfied in your case, perhaps they are not that different after all.

Then again, how could that be right? How can the negation of an exception be itself part of the relevant rule? Are exceptions not necessarily 'external', as it were, to the rules *to which* they are exceptions? And don't we think that whether some consideration is an exception or a rule-element can make a practical difference? Doesn't it make sense to hold that in principle it should be for the defendant to carry the burden of proving the occurrence of some exception, rather than for the claimant or prosecutor to prove its non-occurrence? So how *is* the distinction between exceptions and ordinary rule-elements—whose proof should clearly be up to claimants and prosecutors—to be drawn? How, to put it more generally, is the role of exceptions in judicial decision-making to be understood?

This important question was first isolated and addressed by H. L. A. Hart more than six decades ago, in his 1949 essay 'The Ascription of Responsibility and Rights'. Take the simple example, adapted from Hart's, of a judge having to decide whether to instruct a defendant to pay damages for breach of contract. A decision of this sort will usually depend on the verification of certain 'positive conditions', as Hart called them: at least two parties, offer, acceptance, consideration, and so on, together with the circumstances constitutive of the contractual breach itself. Yet such conditions, claimed Hart (1949: 175), 'although necessary, are not always sufficient'. Why not? Because there will be a number of exceptions or 'defences'—duress, misrepresentation, lunacy, and many others—that, should they happen to emerge, 'defeat' the plaintiff's claim. Those necessary conditions are therefore only also sufficient if no such defeating circumstance happens to be present. So, Hart

(1949: 174) reasoned, the possibility to raise an exception in court implies that no set of sufficient conditions for correct judicial decisions can be specified: 'any set of conditions may be adequate in some cases but not in others'.

Hart's piece ignited a lively discussion. Some believed that although his actual arguments were unconvincing, Hart's thesis was correct. He understood, they said, that legal reasoning is non-monotonic: conclusions of law derived from a given set of premises are not necessarily preserved when that set is expanded. We may want to say, for example, that whoever kills another human being is, as a matter of law, guilty of murder; and we want to be able to combine this statement of a putative legal rule with the statement that some person A killed another human being, and derive the conclusion that A is guilty of murder. But then we also want to say that self-defence counts as an exception in this context, and so that whoever kills another human being in self-defence is not, as a matter of law, guilty of murder. Yet we don't think that the statements 'whoever kills another human being is guilty of murder' and 'whoever kills another human being in self-defence is not guilty of murder', understood literally as universal statements, are both true relative to the same legal system. So it has seemed to many theorists that Hart was right: we shouldn't take our statements of legal rules to specify sufficient conditions for the corresponding consequences. Others, however, insist that Hart was wrong. For defeating circumstances, they say, can be restated as negative conditions and incorporated into the applicable legal rules. An accurate statement of the rule on murder, for example, really should include a clause stating that the killing is *not* done in self-defence. So there is no reason to think that exceptions prevent us from stating sufficient conditions of the relevant legal effects.

Sixty-five years on, interest in the subject has only grown. 'Defeasibility'—the word, too, was Hart's proposal—has become a central issue in jurisprudence. But the debate generated by Hart's essay has not yet been satisfactorily settled, and the notion of an exception has proved surprisingly difficult to explain. The field remains divided between those—the non-deductivists, as we may call them—who adopt a non-monotonic approach to the representation of legal rules, and those—the incorporationists—who believe that, in spite of all appearances, exceptions or defences are reducible to negative rule-elements.

The problem is that neither approach is satisfactory. At least when the admissible defences can all be listed in advance of any actual case—and Hart was concerned with decision-making contexts in which such closed catalogues of exceptions can be identified—there seems to be no reason why sufficient conditions of (correct) judicial decisions cannot be specified. And more generally, shouldn't we be wary of letting go so easily of the thought that conclusions of law can be presented as following deductively from some combination of statements of legal rules and statements of the corresponding facts?

As for the incorporationist strategy—the strategy of embedding, in the rule's antecedent, the negation of the disjunction of the admissible exceptions—it has the correlative disadvantage of failing to do justice to the equally attractive idea that there *is* an important distinction to draw between exceptions and the negation of ordinary rule-elements, between 'Yes, but . . .' and 'No' answers to claims and charges. For it would seem that even in contexts in which a closed catalogue can be found, exceptions are never properly understood as negative parts of the applicable rules. After all, as I said, we think of them as exceptions *to* the relevant rules. It is true that exceptions as well as negative rule-elements both indicate circumstances whose presence will bring about an effect of the same kind: both make it legally incorrect for courts to issue judicial decisions of certain types. Thus a murder conviction is legally correct only in the absence of self-defence, and likewise a conviction of rape is correct only in the absence of consent on the part of the purported victim. Yet we think of self-defence in murder as a defence or exception, and we don't similarly think of consent as a defence or exception in rape.[1] Rather, we think of the *absence* of consent in a case of rape as an element of the corresponding criminal offence. There seems to be some relevant difference in the way in which exceptions (or their absence) and negative rule-elements bear on the correctness of judicial decisions. And this is a difference that the incorporationist strategy fails to accommodate.

So each of the two approaches appears to lack, and indeed to reject, precisely what the other provides. I seek in this book to overcome this persistent

[1] It is of course a contingent matter whether the negation of some given fact x is classified by law as an offence-element, or x is classified as a defence instead. It is only because self-defence is typically classified as a defence in murder in contemporary legal systems, and lack of consent as an element of the offence of rape, that I am able to use these as examples. Fletcher (1978/2000: 698–707) suggests that 'it may be preferable to treat consent to sexual contact as ground for exculpating incriminating conduct'; but his arguments unwarrantedly conflate the claim that sexual penetration is prima facie wrongful, and the claim that sexual penetration should be thought of as a discrete criminal offence. On this point see Dempsey and Herring (2007: 470–1).

dilemma, which is, I think, the product of several interconnected and widespread mistakes. I offer in Part II an account of defeasibility—I call it the 'proof-based' account—that seeks to reconcile the seemingly conflicting intuitions that we have about exceptions. But the topic of defeasibility has ramifications well beyond general jurisprudence and into different areas of substantive and procedural law. And here, too, there are widespread opinions concerning the status and procedural role of legal 'defences'—opinions held by theorists, lawyers, and lawmakers—that will have to be called into question. Take the issue of the relation between legal defences and the allocation of probative burdens. The received picture is that (a) the classification of some relevant fact as a defence (rather than an ordinary offence-element or rule-element) will normally guide us in determining who should carry the corresponding burden of proof, though (b) claimants and prosecutors sometimes carry the burden of proving the absence of defences, and (c) defendants do not necessarily carry the burden of proving defences, though they normally carry an 'evidential' burden of making defences a 'live issue' in the procedure.

We will see that this picture, familiar as it may be, is wrong. It misconceives both our actual practices and the notion of a legal defence. One goal of this book is to challenge the way in which lawyers commonly think about legal defences and the interplay of claims or accusations and answers in procedural contexts. If the book's core theses are sound, then one conclusion is that the orthodox view of the relation between legal defences and the allocation of burdens of proof gets things exactly backwards. Another conclusion is that some mainstream accounts of defences in specific domains of the law—including the standard conception of the relation between defences and offences in criminal law which I discuss in Part III—stand in need of revision.

We start, though, by revisiting Hart's views on our topic. His essay was the first sustained attempt to give an account of the role of exceptions in judicial decision-making. It generated a great deal of commentary, inscribed 'defeasibility' in the catalogue of main topics in philosophy of law, and secured Hart the Oxford Chair of Jurisprudence.[2] The essay was misguided in many respects, and Hart would come to retract it.[3] Still, it leaves a curious impression. Hart seemed to be on to something: constantly chasing an intuitively appealing but as yet diffuse and slippery thought about

[2] At least according to him: see Sugarman (2005: 276).

[3] See Hart (1968/2008: v).

exceptions in law—but a thought that appears to reveal itself as false or self-contradictory or otherwise untenable as soon as one tries to pin it down or give it an accurate formulation.

I want to begin by trying to capture that elusive thought. In this chapter we re-examine some aspects of Hart's argument, and reconstruct the actual thesis—the 'irreducibility thesis', as I propose to label it—that he ought to have adopted. It is not a thesis that Hart succeeded in articulating. Nor is it a thesis that contemporary discussions of exceptions and defeasibility in law have pursued to any extent. But we will see that the irreducibility thesis is both correct and worth defending. It expresses an insight that no theory of exceptions can afford to disregard.

1.2 Hart on Defeasible Concepts

Hart's essay was not primarily concerned with the topic of exceptions. It was concerned with the concept of a human action. His 'main purpose' was

> to suggest that the philosophical analysis of the concept of a human action has been inadequate and confusing, at least in part because sentences of the form 'He did it' have been traditionally regarded as primarily descriptive whereas their principal function is what I venture to call *ascriptive*, being quite literally to ascribe responsibility for actions much as the principal function of sentences of the form 'This is his' is to ascribe rights in property.[4]

Hart's account of action came to be known as 'ascriptivism'. He was particularly interested in what he took to be a peculiarity of our 'usage of verbs of action',[5] and he focused on simple sentences in which a verb of action φ is used to say of some person that she φ-ed. How did his argument run? Suppose that on the strength of some facts that we observe, we say that 'Smith hit her'. But then 'on investigating the facts' we come to learn, for example, that the hitting was accidental (because 'she got in his way while he was hammering in a nail'); or that it was done in self-defence ('she was

[4] Hart (1949: 171).
[5] Hart (1949: 192).

about to hit him with a hammer'); or that Smith was 'forced . . . by a bully'; or that Smith is mad; or—you get the picture.[6] That would lead us to withdraw or revise our initial attribution. We would now hesitate to say 'He did it' without qualification. Yet the initial facts—the actual hitting—remain unchallenged. That shows, according to Hart (1949: 186), that our initial judgement was no mere description of those initial facts. Otherwise why should we want to withdraw it? 'On the contrary', he claims,

> saying 'He hit her' is . . . an ascription of liability justified by the facts; for the observed physical movements of Smith's body are the circumstances which in the absence of some defence, support, or are good reasons for the ascriptive sentence 'He did it'.[7]

But Hart's case for ascriptivism was made obliquely. He proposed first to pay attention to the law, and specifically to 'the formal statements of claim, the indictments, the admissions, the judgments, and the verdicts which constitute so large and so important a part of the language of lawyers':

> [T]he logical peculiarities which distinguish these kinds of sentences [ie 'ascriptive' sentences of the form 'He did it'] from descriptive sentences or rather from the theoretical model of descriptive sentences with which philosophers often work can best be grasped by considering certain characteristics of legal concepts, as these appear in the practice and procedure of the law[.][8]

What specifically interested him is what he called the 'defeasible character of legal concepts'—a notion that can be 'illustrated in detail from the law of contract'.[9] I have mentioned this example already, but the passage is worth quoting in full:

> When the student has learnt that in English law there are positive conditions required for the existence of a valid contract, *i.e.*, at least two *parties*, an *offer* by one, *acceptance* by the other, a *memorandum* in writing in some cases and *consideration*, his understanding of the legal concept of a contract

[6] Hart (1949: 189–91).
[7] Hart (1949: 190).
[8] Hart (1949: 171–2).
[9] See Hart (1949: 174, 181).

is still incomplete . . . For these conditions, although necessary, are not always sufficient and he has still to learn what can *defeat* a claim that there is a valid contract, even though all these conditions are satisfied. That is, the student has still to learn what can follow on the word 'unless' which should accompany the statement of these conditions. This characteristic of legal concepts is one for which no word exists in ordinary English. The words 'conditional' and 'negative' have the wrong implications, but the law has a word which with some hesitation I borrow and extend: this is the word '*defeasible*' used of a legal interest in property which is subject to termination or '*defeat*' in a number of different contingencies but remains intact if no such contingencies mature. In this sense then, contract is a defeasible concept.[10]

To challenge a claim in contract by raising a 'defence' or 'exception' is to do 'something quite different' from denying the facts that ground the claim to begin with:

[T]he accusations or claims upon which law courts adjudicate can be challenged or opposed in two ways. First, by a denial of the facts upon which they are based (technically called a traverse or joinder of issue) and secondly by something quite different, namely, a plea that although all the circumstances are present on which a claim could succeed, yet in the particular case, the claim or accusation should not succeed because other circumstances are present which bring the case under some recognised head of exception, the effect of which is either to defeat the claim or accusation altogether or to 'reduce' it, so that only a weaker claim can be sustained.[11]

Analogously,

the sentence 'Smith hit her' can be challenged in the manner characteristic of defeasible legal utterances in two distinct ways. Smith or someone else can make a flat denial of the relevant statement of the physical facts, 'No, it was Jones, not Smith'. Alternatively . . . any of a vast array of defences can be pleaded by Smith or his friends which, though they do not destroy the charge altogether, soften it, or, as lawyers say, 'reduce' it.[12]

[10] Hart (1949: 175–6).
[11] Hart (1949: 174).
[12] Hart (1949: 190).

The 'concept of a human action', then—claimed Hart—is, like the legal concept of contract, a 'defeasible concept':

[O]ur concept of an action . . . is fundamentally not descriptive, but ascriptive in character; and it is a defeasible concept to be defined through exceptions and not by a set of necessary and sufficient conditions whether physical or psychological.[13]

By the time that Hart disowned his essay, two decades later, it was 'widely agreed', as Joel Feinberg observes, that

Professor Hart's analysis [of action sentences], although it contains insights of permanent importance, still falls considerably short of the claims its author originally made for it. Yet, characteristically, there appears to be very little agreement over which features of the analysis are 'insights' and which 'mistakes'.[14]

Hart himself appears to have always thought that his essay did contain 'some things which were quite useful and true'.[15] But here I am not primarily concerned with the merits and flaws of his account of action (though I will occasionally return to some of his non-legal examples). I want to focus on his views on exceptions and 'defeasible concepts'.

Hart's main claim is meta-theoretical. He sees himself as addressing the 'theorist bent on providing a general definition' of some given concept.[16] The claim is that when the definiendum happens to be a 'defeasible concept', the 'theoretical model' with which theorists 'traditionally' work—the model of a 'definition in terms of a set of necessary and sufficient conditions' is 'logically inappropriate'.[17] So Hart endorses the following thesis:

(T1*) Defeasible concepts cannot be defined in terms of a set of necessary and sufficient conditions.[18]

13 Hart (1949: 189).
14 Feinberg (1965: 119).
15 See Sugarman (2005: 276).
16 Hart (1949: 177).
17 Hart (1949: 171–2, 179).
18 This particular formulation is my own (as is the choice of '(T1*)' to label it); but see Hart (1949: 173, 175 n 2, 189) for passages to the same effect.

This is not to say that no statement of the relevant conditions can be given at all. Hart himself identifies the necessary elements that have to be in place in a case of contract. But what we then need, he proposes, is to couple the statement of these necessary elements with the conjunction 'unless', followed by the list of available defences.[19]

With (T1*), however, Hart misstates his actual point. (T1*) is formulated as a claim about the definition of concepts of a certain kind. But Hart's reasons for endorsing (T1*) have nothing directly to do with the explanation or definition of concepts. Consider again his main example. Why should CONTRACT be said to be a 'defeasible' concept? Hart is concerned with the 'actual procedure of the courts', and particularly with 'the judge's function . . . in a case of contract'.[20] His point regards the specification of the conditions under which a judicial decision for the plaintiff can be said to have been correctly issued. He wants to claim that the fact that the plaintiff's claim is 'defeated' if a valid defence or exception emerges shows that 'any set of conditions may be adequate in some cases but not in others' for the judge to decide for the plaintiff. This is the argument behind (T1*). But then why is (T1*) articulated as a thesis about concepts?

The answer is that Hart also seems to think that the judge's 'function' in a case of contract is to decide whether 'there is' a valid contract (or whether 'on the facts before him a contract does or does not exist'), 'applying' the concept of a contract or a valid contract.[21] Hart speaks as if there is no distinction to draw between (a) the problem of identifying the conditions on which, in a case of contract, the judge's decision for the plaintiff depends, (b) the problem of supplying an answer to the question 'What is contract?', and even (c) the problem of identifying the meaning of 'contract'.[22] That is why he refers to cases in which a defence is present as cases in which 'the concept [of a contract] may not be applied or may only be applied in a weakened form'.[23] Hence the language in which (T1*) is formulated.

But Hart's equivalence is obviously problematic. It is far from clear that the problem of identifying the conditions under which a judge

[19] Hart (1949: 175).

[20] Hart (1949: 178, 182).

[21] Hart (1949: 172–3, 178, 182–3).

[22] See Hart (1949: 173–4, 181).

[23] Hart (1949: 174).

should decide for the plaintiff in a case of contract is adequately construed as a problem concerning the definition, application, or meaning of 'contract' (or of 'valid contract') or indeed of any other term or concept. This presentational worry, however, does not prevent us from grasping and discussing the substance of Hart's (T1*) thesis. The substance of (T1*) is the claim that we cannot specify a set of necessary and sufficient conditions for a judge to decide for the plaintiff in a case of contract and any similar cases in which a certain decision or judgment depends on the non-emergence of defeating circumstances. I will refer to this claim as '(T1)':

> (T1) No set of necessary and sufficient conditions of a correct judgment *J* can be specified when the correctness of *J* depends on the non-emergence of defeating circumstances.

We shall have to return to the relations between legal defences and questions regarding application or meaning of legal concepts, and thus to the relation between (T1) and (T1*).[24] For now, however, let us concentrate on (T1).

1.3 The Irreducibility Thesis

So is the claim in (T1) correct? We saw that Hart's argument for it relies on a distinction between two kinds of circumstance that bear on how judges should decide any given case. On the one hand, we have elements required by the law as necessary conditions of a decision for the plaintiff.[25] These are circumstances whose individual presence must be established if the decision is to be correctly made. On the other hand, we have those circumstances—defences—that bring the case 'under some recognised head of exception'.[26] In cases in which no defence emerges, the plaintiff will succeed if those necessary elements are all established. But when any one of the admissible defences is successfully raised, the plaintiff's claim will be defeated, and the judge should decide for the defendant. Does that warrant Hart's conclusion that it is impossible to specify a set of necessary and always sufficient conditions for a judge to correctly decide for the plaintiff?

[24] See section 2.3.

[25] Hart (1949: 175).

[26] Hart (1949: 175).

There is one natural objection to (T1). If Hart is right about how defences operate, then why can't we simply say that the absence of each one of the admissible defences is itself a necessary condition of the judgment? This charge that (T1) is falsified by Hart's own line of argument was voiced by J. L. Mackie:

[I]s there really no set of necessary and sufficient conditions for such things as contract and action? From what Hart himself says, it would appear that there is such a set. There are certain positive features—let us call them A and B—which are necessary and, in the absence of a defence, sufficient for a contract. There are various defences which would defeat the claim that there is a contract—let us call them K, L, M, N. Then if this is the complete range of defences, the complex term $A\ B\ \overline{K}\ \overline{L}\ \overline{M}\ \overline{N}$ is the necessary and sufficient condition of contract.[27]

This is what I referred to as the 'incorporationist' account of defences. It says that the negation of each of the admissible exceptions is itself a condition of a correctly issued decision for the plaintiff. The fact that Hart does not discuss the incorporationist strategy—which, if sound, undermines (T1)—might lead us to suppose that he was not really committed to (T1), but only to the weaker claim that

(T2) No set of necessary and sufficient *positive* conditions of a correct judgment *J* can be specified when the correctness of *J* depends on the non-emergence of defeating circumstances.

This was G.P. Baker's suggestion. Baker thought that Hart's thesis that defeasible concepts cannot be defined in terms of necessary and sufficient conditions

rests on a distinction between positive and negative conditions. Absence of a defence should not be seen as a positive condition whose satisfaction is sufficient for the application of a defeasible concept, whereas, presumably, definition *per genus et differentiam* proceeds by stipulating a positive condition for something to fall within a genus itself determined by a positive condition.[28]

[27] Mackie (1955: 32).

[28] Baker (1977: 32–3). See also Baker's claim that unless it is 'possible to distinguish positive and negative properties', Hart is unable 'to defend his thesis that non-satisfaction of the "unless" clauses linked with a defeasible concept cannot be represented as a *positive* condition for its application': Baker (1977: 49, emphasis added). Baker's critique retains, of course, as does Mackie's, Hart's language of 'definitions' and 'concepts' and their 'application', which

If so, Hart was on the wrong track. 'It is far from clear', as Baker (1977: 33) says, 'that there is any intelligible way to segregate conditions into negative and positive ones.'

But this reading that ascribes to Hart only the feeble and tedious (T2) is unwarranted. Hart does occasionally refer to defeating circumstances as '*negative* examples showing where the concept may not be applied'. He also sometimes refers to those elements 'required for the existence of a valid contract' as '*positive* conditions'.[29] But that the latter are 'positive' elements—in the sense that the term with which any such condition is described denotes the occurrence (rather than the non-occurrence) of certain events or circumstances—is a purely contingent feature, having to do only with the example at hand. What matters is that those elements are 'required'—not that they happen to be 'positive'. It is irrelevant for his (T1) claim that in a case of contract the list of required elements—'at least two *parties*, an *offer* by one, *acceptance* by the other, a *memorandum* in writing in some cases and *consideration*'[30]—contains only 'positive' items. His catalogue of defences in contract, furthermore, is ostensibly not restricted to 'positively' described circumstances.[31]

Rather, the relevant distinction to draw is that between those facts—positive or negative—that *have* to be 'present', as Hart (1949: 174) puts it, for a claim in contract to succeed; and the 'quite different' set of facts—positive or negative—which, *if* present, bring the case 'under some recognised head of exception' and thereby defeat the plaintiff's claim, but which do not otherwise affect the claim's likelihood of success.

Let me refer to the former as '*P*-facts', and to the latter as '*D*-facts'. This is a crucial contrast to which we will return in later chapters. But for now the point is that this contrast doesn't map onto any distinction between positive and negative conditions. Both *P*-facts and *D*-facts can be either positive or negative. So Baker's reading of (T1) is not to be adopted. Differently from what Baker suggests, what motivates the claim that defeasible concepts are undefinable *per genus et differentiam* is not the thought that this

is the language of (T1★). But nothing turns on that; their arguments hold *mutatis mutandis* against (T1) as well.

29 Hart (1949: 174, emphases added).

30 Hart (1949: 174–5).

31 See Hart (1949: 175–6) for his list of the 'principal' defences 'with which an otherwise valid claim in contract can be met'. One item on the list is 'non-disclosure of material facts'.

method of definition proceeds by stipulating 'positive' conditions only; it is the thought that definition *per genus et differentiam* proceeds by stipulating necessary and always sufficient conditions.

Nor would Hart have granted Mackie's point. Hart offers no actual argument against the incorporationist strategy; but he rejects it nonetheless. He explicitly considers the view that a definition of defeasible concept like CONTRACT could be constructed by 'specifying as the necessary and sufficient conditions of contract, consent and other positive conditions and the negation of the disjunction of the various defences'; and he says that this 'could, of course, be done'—but 'vacuously'.[32] If 'he admits this', Mackie (1955: 32) wonders rhetorically, 'what is he denying?' The question rests on a false assumption. What Hart's adverb conveys is his unwillingness—with or without good reason—to endorse the incorporationist strategy.

Some very simple formulations will help us to see the relevant point more clearly. What Hart is denying is that we should adopt the following scheme (which I will immediately explain) to represent the material conditions under which a judge correctly decides for the plaintiff in a case of contract:

(A) It is correct to decide for the plaintiff if and only if (P and *not-D*).

By a 'correct' decision, what I mean is a decision that the court is both legally authorized and legally required (or at least permitted) to issue in the case. I use 'P' to stand for the conjunction (P_1 and P_2 and . . . P_n) of those circumstances whose presence is required for it to be correct for the court to decide for the plaintiff. These are the circumstances I have proposed to call 'P-facts'. As to 'D', it stands for the disjunction (D_1 or D_2 or . . . or D_n) of any one of the admissible defeating circumstances (or 'D-facts'). '*Not-D*' is just an abbreviated way of writing 'it is not the case that D'. So what the scheme in (A) says is that a decision for the plaintiff is correct if and only if *all* the relevant P-facts are the case, and *no* D-fact is the case.

As I said, Hart rejects the scheme in (A). What he suggests instead is that the statement of the relevant P-facts co-occurs with the word 'unless', followed by the list of admissible defences. So he proposes

[32] This remark is found in a footnote which is absent from the original version of Hart's essay, but silently made its way into a 1951 reprint: see Hart (1951: 152).

that we adopt something like the following scheme, which says that a decision for the plaintiff is correct whenever *P* is the case, *unless* some *D*-fact is the case:

(B) If *P*, then it is correct to decide for the plaintiff, unless *D*.

The fact that Hart rejects (A), though not (B), as 'vacuous' confirms that he opposes the reduction of defences to 'negative' conditions in yet a different sense of the adjective. He denies that *that no D-fact is the case* is itself aptly represented as a condition of a correctly issued judgment for the plaintiff (whether or not each of the admissible *D*-facts $D_1, D_2, \ldots D_n$ happens to be 'positively' defined). He must therefore intend to endorse a stronger thesis than Baker's (T2).[33] He must deny that *D*-facts can adequately be accounted for in terms of—that *D*-facts can be explanatorily reduced to—necessary conditions, either positive or negative, of correct judicial decisions.

So let us single out and attribute to Hart—even though he never articulates it as such—the following claim, meant to capture the idea that he diffusely expresses by saying that 'contract' (for example) is 'irreducibly defeasible'.[34] I will call it the *irreducibility thesis*:

(T3) Defeating circumstances are not reducible to necessary conditions of correct judgments.

1.4 Two Questions

Two questions can now be taken up for discussion. The first is whether (T3), the irreducibility thesis, is right. The second is how it relates to (T1).

The answer to the former question would appear to be negative. Hart's endorsement of the irreducibility thesis seems to rely on the

[33] Actually, Baker's use of the 'positive'/'negative' distinction is equivocal. But in attributing to Hart the claim that absence of defeating circumstances cannot be represented as a *positive* condition, Baker suggests that the difference between *that* claim and the stronger claim that absence of defeating circumstances cannot be represented as a necessary condition *at all* (that is, either as a *positive* or a *negative* necessary condition) is a difference that Hart recognizes as relevant, and which underlies his main claim on defeasibility. It is this suggestion that I contest.

[34] Hart (1949: 176).

assumption that *D*-facts are fundamentally distinct from *P*-facts—fundamentally distinct, that is, from those 'necessary' elements whose presence is required for the judge correctly to issue a judgment for the plaintiff. Hart does not deny that if any of the relevant *P*-facts happens not to be present the judge ought to decide against the plaintiff. But he explicitly rejects the converse thought that cases in which the judge ought to decide against the plaintiff—cases in which 'contracts are held not to exist', as he puts it—'"must" be cases in which some necessary condition' of the plaintiff's success is 'absent'.[35] For he thinks, as we saw, that defences proper—*D*-facts—amount to 'something quite different' from a denial of the relevant *P*-facts.[36] The problem is that in the absence of any further supporting argument, this sounds not merely wrong but indeed self-contradictory—which was Mackie's point. If the presence of any one of the admissible *D*-facts prevents a certain decision from being correctly issued, is it not then forcibly the case that the absence of *D*-facts is a necessary condition of the correctness of such a decision, and that the presence of a *D*-fact amounts precisely to the absence of a necessary condition? Baker has a similarly compelling objection: 'if there are', as Hart acknowledges, 'any *necessary* conditions for the existence of a contract', then, says Baker, 'there are *sufficient* conditions for there not being a contract':

> The statement that there is no contract between *A* and *B* is an application of the term 'contract', albeit a negative one. Therefore it is incoherent to explain defeasibility by stating that there are only necessary and normally sufficient conditions, but never sufficient conditions, for the *application* of a defeasible concept. If there are no sufficient conditions for its application, there cannot be any necessary conditions either.[37]

Let me add to this collection of demurrals by noting that given that according to Hart *P*-facts are to be counted as necessary conditions, his own proposed 'unless'-formulation—the scheme, given above as (B), with which adequate definitions of defeasible concepts are, he says, to be constructed—can in fact be shown to imply the very

[35] Hart (1949: 183).

[36] Hart (1949: 174).

[37] Baker (1977: 34). Once again this objection, though cast in the language of 'concepts', translates straightforwardly as a point about the conditions of correctly issued judicial decisions.

formulation—formulation (A)—that he purports to reject as 'logically inappropriate'.[38] Here are (A) and (B) again:

(A) It is correct to decide for the plaintiff if and only if (*P* and *not-D*).
(B) If *P*, then it is correct to decide for the plaintiff, unless *D*.

(B) entails, on the one hand, that if the relevant *P*-facts are present and no *D*-facts emerge, the judge will rightly decide for the plaintiff:

(i) If *P* and *not-D*, then it is correct to decide for the plaintiff.[39]

But (B) also seems to imply, by virtue of the meaning of the word 'unless', not only that

(ii) If *D*, then (if *P*, it is *not* correct to decide for the plaintiff),

but also that if some defeating circumstance happens to be present, then whether or not it is the case that *P*—that is, as we might also put it, even if it is the case that *P*—the correct decision to issue is a decision for the *defendant*. The presence of a *D*-fact, in other words, is a sufficient condition for it to be *incorrect* to decide for the plaintiff:

(iii) If *D*, then it is *not* correct to decide for the plaintiff.

From (iii), in turn, it follows that the absence of defences is necessary for a decision for the plaintiff to be correct:

(iv) If it is correct to decide for the plaintiff, then it must be true that *not-D*.

Equally required, according to Hart, is the presence of the relevant *P*-facts, which he explicitly classifies, as we have seen, as 'necessary' conditions:[40]

(v) If it is correct to decide for the plaintiff, then it must be true that *P*.

It follows, from (iv) and (v), that the *conjunction* of all the relevant *P*-facts and the absence of defences is itself necessary for the plaintiff to succeed:

(vi) If it is correct to decide for the plaintiff, then it must be true both that *P* and that *not-D*.

[38] Hart (1949: 179).
[39] My formulations are meant solely to convey the relevant points with sufficient clarity; I abstain from commenting on how our natural language conditionals ought ultimately to be interpreted.
[40] Hart (1949: 180).

But then from (vi) and (i) we derive

(A) It is correct to decide for the plaintiff if and only if (*P* and *not-D*),

which is, of course, what Hart meant to reject.

It is no wonder that Hart failed to persuade most of his critical readership. To be sure, there are theorists who think that Hart was correct in adopting (T1). As I mentioned already, they credit Hart with the insight that legal reasoning is non-monotonic. The fact that a judge will correctly decide for the plaintiff when all the required *P*-facts—and nothing else—are present establishes that the occurrence of such *P*-facts is enough in that instance for the plaintiff to succeed. But when some defeating circumstance, some *D*-fact, happens also to be present, this conclusion is no longer derivable—it is no longer correct to decide for the plaintiff—and consequently the required *P*-facts cannot be deemed sufficient. For this reason, quite a few authors have come to believe that no adequate account of legal defences can be given that does not call into question the very applicability of classical logic to the representation of legal reasoning.[41] They would therefore subscribe to a claim along the lines of (T1); and indeed Hart's essay is often named in the literature as a forerunner of this non-monotonic approach.[42]

But those who argue that Hart was wrong seem to have a stronger case. They could agree, of course, that an interesting and difficult problem might arise from the possibility of so-called 'implicit' exceptions—exceptions that cannot be identified and stated as such in advance and independently of any actual case.[43] But it is clear, as I said, that Hart was concerned with 'explicit' exceptions only.[44] And explicit exceptions, of which a closed list can be given, are unproblematic. Explicit exceptions, just like Mackie said, can simply be restated as negative conditions—but as conditions nonetheless, or as elements of conditions—as part of the

[41] For a clear presentation, see Alchourrón (1993: 63–9).

[42] See Freeman (1991: 139–49); Sartor (1994: 192); Loui (1995); Chesñevar and others (2001: 339); Prakken and Vreeswijk (2002: 229); Sartor (2005: 76); Stelmach and Brożek (2006: 49–51).

[43] The distinction between 'explicit' (or 'express') and 'implicit' defeasibility was introduced in MacCormick (1995: 99–100). We shall see in Chapter 5 that these labels are misleading.

[44] That 'explicit' exceptions were Hart's 1949 topic is exegetically plain. Open-endedness in the definition of 'legal concepts' is mentioned only in passing and immediately contrasted with defeasibility, which Hart introduces as '*another* [noteworthy] characteristic' of legal concepts: Hart (1949: 174, emphasis added). For further evidence, consider the way in which the catalogue of defences in contract is alluded to (1949: 175 n 2); or sentences

relevant rules. In fact, in the contemporary literature on defeasibility, this incorporationist strategy is widely accepted: something like the formulation in (A) is commonly adopted as an apt scheme for the display of explicit defences.[45]

I side with those who are unconvinced by Hart's claims. But against the endorsers of the incorporationist strategy, I do share Hart's insight—even though he failed to provide even the beginning of an argument to support it—that the reduction of defences to necessary conditions fails to properly represent them *qua* defences. It is part of my project in this book to bridge this argumentative gap, and to provide the necessary *pars construens* by offering a novel account of defeasibility in law. I shall argue later on that there is a version of (T3)—a version of the irreducibility

such as 'in the case of crime, as in contract, *it is possible to compile a list* of the defences or exceptions with which different criminal charges may be met': see Hart (1949: 175 n 2, 179, emphasis added); or the explicit reference (1949: 192) to the fact that 'our actual criteria for qualifying [ie defeating] "He did it", though multiple and heterogeneous, *are capable of being stated* with some precision' (emphasis added); or the already mentioned footnote, added to a 1951 reprint of his essay, in which Hart asserts that a formula embedding, as one of its elements, the 'negation of the conjunction of the various defences' *could* 'of course' be provided—something he wouldn't say if he were not considering *closed* lists of defences (Hart 1951: 152). Notice, moreover, that no mention of open-endedness is made in connection with his discussion of the defeasibility of 'the concept of a human action': unlike defeasibility, open-endedness is presented as a specifically *legal* topic connected with some features of judicial decision-making: see Hart (1949: 173). It is only in *The Concept of Law*—a book in which his main 1949 theses are no longer defended—that Hart specifically addresses the different issue of exceptions 'not exhaustively specifiable in advance': see Hart (1961/2012: 139). Commentators who miss the point include Boonin (1966: 372, 374–5); Lucas (1977); Howarth (1981: 35–8); Jori (1985: 163); Luzzati (1990: 152, 156); Pintore (1990: 12–5, 18); Stavropoulos (1996: 54); Bayón (2000: 163); Guastini (2012: 190); Mendonca (2012: 202); and Rodríguez (2012: 94–5). But compare, correctly, Helm (1968: 173–5); Martin (1987: 119); Nino (1987: 19); or Bix (2012: 193).

[45] See Nakhnikian (1957: 26), on the 'formal' equivalence of 'P-conditions' and 'negated D-conditions'; Moore (1981: 238); Martin (1987: 119–20); Susskind (1987: 196); Alchourrón (1991); Bayles (1992: 12); Tur (1993: 214–15); MacCormick (1995: 100); Rodríguez (1997: 85–6, 97–8); Atria (2001: 124–5, 137–8); Tur (2001a: 359–60, 367); Pérez Bermejo (2009: 21); or Waluchow (2012: 260). Compare Holdcroft (1969: 323, 329); Wang (2003: 17–8); and Stavropoulos's erroneous move from the (substantially correct) remark that the 'very defeating power of [defeating] circumstances is testimony to their relevance to the concept', to the conclusion that the non-occurrence of defeating circumstances must form part of the set of the corresponding 'concept's conditions of application' (which set the occurrence of a defeating circumstance gives us 'occasion' and reason to 'revise'): Stavropoulos (1996: 62–5). In *The Concept of Law*, Hart himself maintained that if some overriding factor can be identified as an exception, it can then be 'reduced to [the general] rule': see Hart (1961/2012: 134, 139). The presuppositions of this widespread approach will be more fully considered in Chapter 5.

thesis—which is correct, and hence that the commonly adopted scheme in (A) is to be rejected.

The second of the questions mentioned at the beginning of this section concerned the relation of (T3) and (T1). Hart believes that the former implies the latter. It is 'owing to the defeasible character of the concept' of a contract, as he puts it, that any 'statement of the conditions in which contracts are held to exist', 'though it would express the necessary and sometimes sufficient conditions for the application of "contract", could not express conditions which were always sufficient'.[46] This means that he takes the impossibility of defining 'contract' 'by specifying the necessary and sufficient conditions for its application', to be a consequence of the concept's 'defeasible' character.[47]

My view is that, on the contrary, (T1) does not follow from (T3), and moreover that (T1) is actually false. If this is right, it will at the same time disprove those who believe that Hart was wrong because they think that (A) gives us a satisfactory scheme, and those who believe that Hart was right because they think that (T1) is correct.

But I don't want to get ahead of myself. Before we can assess whether (T1), in particular, is right or wrong, we need to acquire a sounder grasp of the claim it purports to convey—and indeed a clearer picture of the problem of defeasibility in law. That is the purpose of Chapter 2.

[46] Hart (1949: 181).

[47] Hart (1949: 174).

2

The Issue of Defeasibility

2.1 Two Notions of Defeasibility

Two notions of defeasibility are often confused. One tracks the non-final character of some of our decisions and judgments. The other regards the relation between the presence or absence of defeating circumstances and the correctness of certain (final or non-final) decisions and judgments. It is on this second notion that a theory of exceptions should concentrate—or so I argue in this chapter.[1]

What are these two notions? We can begin to distinguish between them by paying closer attention to one of Hart's examples of a 'defeasible' ascription of responsibility: the simple example, described in Chapter 1, of an accusation—made on the strength of some facts we have observed—that someone hit someone else. 'Smith hit her', we say. But then we come to learn more about what happened, and realize that our original accusation needs to be qualified. Now we would no longer say—not *sans phrase*—that 'Smith hit her'. We would say instead (suppose) that 'He hit her in self-defence.' Our first judgment would otherwise have 'remain[ed] intact'.[2] But faced with the

[1] My aim is to arrive at a clearer understanding of what I take to be the core jurisprudential problem of defeasibility in law. I am not concerned with the many other senses in which the term 'defeasibility' has in fact—sometimes for no good reason—come to be employed in the literature. Rodríguez and Sucar (1998: 151) identify and discuss *eleven* senses in which 'defeasibility can be predicated in connection with the law' (my translation); see also Hage (2003: 222–6); Brożek (2004: 24–41); Hage (2005: 8–15); Chiassoni (2012: 160–80); and Duarte d'Almeida (2014b).

[2] Hart (1949: 175, 193).

defeating circumstance of self-defence, we must modify our judgment; we must 'judge again'.[3]

2.1.1 *Defeasibility* qua *Non-Finality*

Hart's example is meant to illustrate the defeasibility of that first judgment, that 'Smith hit her', by contrast with the second, qualified judgment, that 'He hit her in self-defence'. What is the relevant feature of the initial judgment, the feature by virtue of which it counts as an instance of a defeasible judgment? It would appear to be the fact that it is open to being 'challenged' (as Hart is fond of saying), and eventually retracted or replaced—'defeated'—in the context and for the purpose it is made. This is an extra-legal example, and when we make such judgments as 'private individuals', Hart remarks, we

> are not in the position of a judge whose decision is authoritative and final, but who is required only to deal with the claims and defences actually presented to him. In private life, decisions are not final, and the individual is not relieved, as the judge often is, from the effort of inquiring what defences might be pleaded.[4]

It seems, then, that a defeasible judgment is a non-final one, a judgment vulnerable to challenge or impugnation. Can this notion be articulated in more detail? Hart's example incorporates a chronological element. There is an initial point in time at which, on the grounds of 'merely the physical facts' observed, we judge that 'Smith hit her'. But additional information may become available at some further moment, and it may be that in view of this new, expanded body of information, we should now 'refus[e] to say "He did it" without qualification'.[5] So with this chronological element in mind, let me suggest a simple scheme of analysis that will help to clarify several points that Hart's cursory account of this and other examples does not fully capture.

I will say that the correctness of decisions or judgments of the kind that Hart has in mind is to be assessed relative to both (a) a given body of information, however described (for example, 'all the relevant information available at the moment the judgment is made'); and (b) a

[3] Hart (1949: 193).
[4] Hart (1949: 193).
[5] Hart (1949: 192).

given point in time. I use 'T_1' and 'T_2' to stand for the two moments implicitly referred to in the example. We may thus say that a token of 'Smith hit her' is a correct judgment at T_1, though not at T_2; and that at T_2 the appropriate judgment to make would instead be a token of 'Smith hit her in self-defence'.

Hart says that the judgment made at T_1 will have to be qualified at T_2 in view of the new, expanded body of information. This is not quite right. It suggests that at T_2 that first judgment will somehow *become* an incorrectly made one. In fact we have two distinct judgments, both correct relative to the moment at which they are made and the information then available. The judgment that 'Smith hit her' was, and remains, correct, even if some defeating circumstance has later emerged. But Hart's abbreviated manner of speech is quite naturally employed if at T_1 and T_2 the object as well as the purpose of both judgments happens to coincide. Such a coincidence is clearly presupposed in the example. It is only on the diachronic assumption that at T_2 we are still concerned with the very same object as at T_1, and that we are concerned with it for the same reason or purpose, that in a different (and looser) sense of the term we may also say, as Hart does, that our initial judgment 'no longer remains' correct. We stay open to replacing it with a different judgment. Our initial judgment is not, as Hart says, a final one.

Both in the legal domain and in the non-institutional domain of decisions made in private life, our judgments may and often do remain open to reassessment in this sense. In both domains, to put it differently, given any judgment J_1 made at some moment T, there is nothing extraordinary about the possibility that if at some moment T_{+1} a change in the relevant body of information has taken place—which means that the modified set B_2 is not coextensive with the initial set B_1—another judgment J_2 is made which, in so far as it coincides or overlaps in object and purpose with J_1, will replace it in the same decision-making context. T_{+1} may be either a specific point in time purposefully scheduled in advance or, more commonly, any contingent moment at which new information happens to become available.

But finality, too, can be present in everyday decision-making as well as in the law. Hart is wrong to say that in private life decisions are not final, and that our position 'as private individuals' is in this respect qualitatively different from that of a judge. For whatever reason, one may simply not remain open, come what may, to the possibility of reassessment beyond some point in time T_n—which will thus be the moment at which one is to make one's final judgment, or the moment at which a previously made judgment becomes final.

The suggestion that a 'defeasible' judgment is *ipso facto* not final is one that Hart's paper repeatedly conveys. He says that the phenomenon of defeasibility can best be grasped 'by examining the distinctive ways in which legal utterances can be challenged', and it is *always* claims, accusations, criminal charges, allegations, and the sort—as opposed to the court's rulings, in so far as these are assumed to be final—that he mentions as being susceptible to 'defeat' in the legal domain.[6] He is not interested, of course, in just any factor that may ground successful opposition to a claim or an accusation. Nor can he really be concerned, to be precise, with *claims* in contract, or *accusations* in criminal cases, in or of themselves. Claims and accusations, like judicial decisions, are complex procedural acts. The act of making an accusation—a charge—in a case of crime, for example, is a compound that typically includes, but is not reducible to, the claim or judgment that someone φ-ed. The procedural act of submitting a claim in contract is a comparably complex act, of which the judgment (or 'claim' in the ordinary sense) that there is a valid contract between plaintiff and defendant is but a constituent, if prominent, part. And surely it is with these constituent acts that Hart is concerned when he focuses on cases of crime or contract. His references to the defeat of claims and accusations must be synecdochic; these complex acts are *themselves* very often final. For while the claim or judgment whose defeasibility is at stake in a criminal case—the claim that someone committed a crime—is typically not a final one (reassessment of *that* issue will be undertaken at a later point in the process), the accusation of which such judgment is a part is normally (though not necessarily), *qua* complex act, the final act of its kind to be made in the course of the criminal process. Nor, as I said, does the topic under Hart's consideration encompass *all* possible factors that may lead to the reassessment and replacement of non-final judgments. The topic does not even include all those factors having to do with

[6] See Hart (1949: 175, 187, 193). He alludes to the circumstances that may 'defeat [a given] *claim* or *accusation* altogether' (1949: 174, emphasis added); to the contingencies that 'can defeat a *claim* that there is a valid contract' (1949: 175, emphasis added); to 'defences [. . . that] serve to defeat or weaken a *claim* in contract' (1949: 176, emphasis added); to 'defences with which an otherwise valid *claim* in contract can be met' (1949: 178, emphasis added); to the circumstances 'which would if present defeat the *accusation* [in criminal procedure]' (1949: 180, emphasis added); to 'exceptions or defences which can defeat *claims* or *accusations*' (1949: 182, emphasis added).

modifications of the body of available information. Hart is concerned only with the terminating or modifying effects of the emergence of circumstances of a particular sort. He is concerned only with defeating circumstances—with defences.

This notion of a defeasible judgment—or, as I shall label it to underscore its intrinsic connection with non-finality, a 'defeasible$_{NF}$' judgment—may be articulated along the following lines:

> *Defeasible$_{NF}$ judgment.* For any given judgment J_1 made at some moment T on the grounds of a given body of information B_1, J_1 is a defeasible$_{NF}$ judgment if, and only if, the possibility remains for a new judgment J_2 (overlapping with J_1 in object and purpose) to be made, and to replace J_1 in the same decision-making context, if at some moment T_{+1} the relevant body of information has changed in such a way that B_2, the modified body of information, mentions the occurrence of a defeating circumstance.

2.1.2 *Defeasibility Proper*

Outstanding as this dimension of non-finality may be, there is a further distinction to draw in connection with Hart's exemplar ('Smith hit her') of a defeasible judgment. The distinction is not immediately apparent, but the elementary scheme just introduced will assist us in bringing it to light.

Observe, first, that it is a contingent matter whether the body of information at T_2 differs from that available at T_1. Consider the following variant of Hart's example:

> *Variant 1*: On investigating the facts, we come to find no more information than we had at T_1.

Given the coincidence of the two bodies of information, in *Variant 1* the correct judgment at T_2 will coincide in content with the one made at T_1. Both will be tokens of the *un*qualified judgment that 'Smith hit her'. That first judgment, in Hart's abbreviated phrase, 'remains intact', because no defeating circumstances have meanwhile 'matured'.[7] But this thought, too, can be unpacked in clearer terms. It means that the correct judgment to make at T_2 is the unqualified 'Smith hit her' because B_2, the body of information then available (and to which such a judgment is relative) includes no mention of defeating circumstances. It means, more

[7] Hart (1949: 175).

precisely, that for the unqualified judgment to be correctly made at T_2 it has to be the case both (a) that B_2 includes reference to the occurrence of the relevant facts—the facts of the actual hitting; and (b) that it does not include reference to the occurrence of any of the admissible defeating circumstances.[8]

Now if in *Variant 1* the correct judgment to make at both moments would be a token of the unqualified 'Smith hit her'; and if both judgments are to be assessed as correctly or incorrectly made relative to the bodies of information available at the time of their making; then for the unqualified judgment to be correctly made at T_1 it must also be the case both that B_1 includes reference to the occurrence of the relevant facts, and that it does *not* include reference to the occurrence of any of the admissible defeating circumstances. Consider another variant of Hart's example:

> *Variant 2*: We are from the very beginning—that is, straight from T_1—in possession of not only the information which *in Hart's example* is the information then available, but also of the information which *in Hart's example* becomes available only after further investigation of the facts.

Here the appropriate judgment to make at T_1 would clearly be not the unqualified 'Smith hit her', but the judgment that 'Smith hit her in self-defence'. This shows, to repeat, that in the original version of Hart's example, the conditions that make it correct at T_1 to judge unqualifiedly that 'Smith hit her' must include the fact that the body of information then available, B_1, to which the judgment is relative, includes no reference to the occurrence of any defeating circumstance.

So we can draw a contrast between instances in which the correct judgment to make on the grounds of the relevant body of information is the judgment that 'Smith hit her', and instances in which the proper judgment to make is the qualified one. In Hart's versions of the example, these two scenarios occur, respectively, at T_1 and T_2. But the chronological distinction is irrelevant for the purposes of the contrast. At T_2 a defeating circumstance is present that renders inappropriate (that 'defeats') the unqualified 'Smith hit her' and calls instead for the judgment that 'Smith did it in self-defence'. But as *Variant 2* illustrates, this could just as well have been the scenario at T_1 if we had had access to the relevant information from the beginning. By the same token, what

[8] B_2 could, of course, still differ from B_1 in including, for example, additional information corroborating the already established facts of the hitting.

makes the unqualified judgment the appropriate one to make (in Hart's version of the example) at T_1 is not simply that the facts of the hitting happen to be present, but also that B_1 includes no mention of any defeating circumstance—which is exactly what would have rendered the unqualified 'Smith hit her' appropriate at T_2 if, as in *Variant 1*, our investigations happened to have brought in no new relevant fact.

Two distinctions, then, rather than just one, are simultaneously at play in Hart's example. One—defeasibility$_{NF}$, defined in section 2.1.1—concerns the question whether, at any given moment T, the correct judgment to make is a final or a non-final one. The other concerns the question whether, at any given moment T, the correct judgment to make is the unqualified 'Smith hit her', or rather the qualified 'Smith hit her in self-defence'. It is true that the former distinction is more conspicuous, given how the example is set up. But it is the latter, I suggest, that lies at the core of our interests. This second notion—I will label it 'defeasibility$_P$' (for defeasibility *proper*)—may be given the following working definition:

> *Defeasible$_P$ judgment.* For any kind of judgment J, tokens of which are in each case to be made relative to some body of information B, J is defeasible$_P$ if, and only if, there is a class of defeating circumstances D_1, D_2, . . . D_N such that no token K of J is correctly issued if the body of information to which K is relative mentions the occurrence of some D.

There is nothing preventing any token defeasible$_P$ judgment from being also a final one, and thus from *not* being a defeasible$_{NF}$ judgment. Defeasibility$_{NF}$ and defeasibility$_P$ are independent properties. It is no coincidence, however, that in his example Hart focuses, distractingly, on a defeasible$_P$ judgment which is also not a final one. It is the consequence of his inability to pin down his own object of interest, and to articulate its relevant characteristics.

Hart's conflation of defeasibility$_P$ and defeasibility$_{NF}$ is patent in many passages of his essay. I have already noted how he explicitly associates defeasibility to the 'ways in which legal utterances can be challenged',[9] and how it is never final judicial decisions, but claims and accusations, that he refers as susceptible to being 'defeated'. These references are to aspects of defeasibility$_{NF}$, not defeasibility$_P$. On the other hand, he also wants to say that defeasibility is a characteristic of *concepts* (of legal concepts in general, 'as these appear in the practice and procedure of

[9] Hart (1949: 175).

the law',[10] of the concept of contract,[11] of our concept of action[12]); his account of the phenomenon of defeasibility, presented mainly with regard to judicial decisions made 'upon the claims and defences actually [and thus already] made and pleaded before him',[13] focuses not on the possibility of the future emergence of defeating circumstances, but instead on the relation between the decision and the circumstances that presently support it;[14] and he does occasionally stress that defeasible judgments are correctly made only 'in the absence of some defence'.[15]

It should now be clear, despite Hart's equivocations, that non-finality—defeasibility$_{NF}$—must be peripheral to what should interest us about the issue of defeasibility. I remarked in section 2.1.1 that Hart is not concerned with the full range of circumstances that may possibly bring about the retraction of a non-final judgment. He is concerned only with the emergence of those circumstances he refers to as 'defences'. We have also learned that the effect brought about by these circumstances is in no way conditional on the fact that they emerge only after some particular judgment (susceptible to future 'defeat') has already been made. What matters about duress, lunacy, or misrepresentation in contract, for example, has nothing to do with the moment at which they may happen to come to the decision-maker's attention. What matters is rather that these circumstances are admitted *as defeating circumstances*, and thus that they constrain the corresponding judgments in a peculiar, distinctive way. What matters is that in contract, the judgment for the plaintiff is a defeasible$_P$ judgment. That any correctly made defeasible$_P$ judgment happens to be only one of a succession of similarly purposed judgments is—just like its particular place in any such series (first, last, or somewhere in between) or its final character (which is independent of insertion in any series)—immaterial.[16]

Judgments of this sort, then—defeasible$_P$ judgments—are the proper focus of our interest. These are judgments that are correctly made only if no defeating circumstances are present (present, of

[10] See Hart (1949: 172, 173, 174, 175, 178, 181, 187).

[11] Hart (1949: 175, 178, 181).

[12] Hart (1949: 177, 188–9).

[13] Hart (1949: 182).

[14] Hart (1949: 182–3).

[15] See Hart (1949: 186, 187, 190).

[16] That Hart's paper superficially conveys the contrary impression has led some commentators to claim, mistakenly, that his main concern was with such 'procedural' matters. Hart's conflation of defeasibility$_P$ and defeasibility$_{NF}$ is probably the reason why Bruce Chapman,

course, at the time of their making). *That* is the distinctive feature of such judgments. That is the feature that leads Hart to say that 'any set of conditions may be adequate in some cases but not in others' for such judgments to count as correctly issued, the feature for which he coins the adjective 'defeasible'.[17]

Nowhere is Hart's confusion more evident, in fact, than in his choice of the adjective 'defeasible' to refer to judgments of the kind he purports to discuss. At the level of its ordinary meaning, the word suggests that a judgment is defeasible only if it remains vulnerable to challenge and substitution—'subject to termination'[18]—at some further point in time. Given that in his examples Hart deals almost invariably with non-final judgments and decisions, his use of 'to defeat' and its cognates does not immediately strike us as awkward. Once the confusion is dissolved, however, the unwarranted connotations of these terms spring up, and we would naturally hesitate to apply them in connection with defeasible$_P$ judgments. We wouldn't employ the participle 'defeated', for instance: the consequence of the presence of a defeating circumstance is that *no* token of the defeasible$_P$ judgment is to be properly made—not that some previously made judgment comes now to be 'defeated'. Nor would we simultaneously apply 'defeasible' *and* 'undefeated' to the same token judgment, even though any correctly made token of a defeasible$_P$ judgment, depending as it does on the fact that no defeating circumstance is present, is for that very reason 'undefeated'.

But our definition of defeasibility$_P$ is, of course, a stipulation. 'Defeasibility' and 'defeasible' have become stock terms in jurisprudence, and the unwelcome undertones of Hart's terminological option are not sufficient reason to coin new words. In any case, the differentiating indices are no longer necessary. Instead of using 'defeasibility$_{NF}$' and

for example, asserts that 'what Hart had in mind' in denying that the absence of defeating conditions is aptly characterized as a 'necessary condition [. . .] for the concept's proper use' was 'the theoretical ploy which would accommodate defeasibility *in one step*'; 'for Hart', says Chapman, defeasibility is 'an essentially sequenced idea, where the different legal norms, with their offsetting effect, are only admitted into the decision making calculus in a certain order of priority': the 'path-dependent nature of defeasibility [. . .] allows it to make sense of the complicated structure of pleadings and presumptions, as well as shifting burdens of proof, that are characteristic of legal arguments in a case': see Chapman (1998a: 450–1); Chapman (1998b: 1508–9); Chapman (1998c: 323); or Chapman (2012: 403–5). See also Hall's objection in Hall (1966: 21); and Epstein (1973: 559–60).

17 Hart (1949: 174).

18 Hart (1949: 175).

'defeasible$_p$', I shall from now on employ the bare terms to refer to the sort of judgments that, as I have argued, form the actual object of our theoretical interest.

2.2 Defences and Exceptions

'Defence', too, is for more than one reason a misleading term to employ in connection with defeating circumstances. It is a multiply ambiguous term. First, it is sometimes used, particularly in the legal domain, with a wider scope than usual: it is used as a general label applying to any circumstance whose verification enables a defendant to oppose a claim or accusation, securing a favourable decision. In criminal law, for example, the term 'defence', in this broad sense, encompasses such diverse circumstances as unfitness to plead and diplomatic immunity, as well as the denial that the constitutive elements of the offence are verified.[19] In our discussion, however, as I have noted, we are concerned only with a particular kind of circumstance; we are concerned with 'defences' in the strict sense.

But the term 'defence' is ambiguous not merely with regard to its scope, but also with regard to its object. It can be used on the one hand to refer to a class of *facts* whose presence in a given decision-making context brings about (or should bring about) the effect of preventing a defeasible judgment or decision from being correctly issued. The fact, in murder, that a killing was done in self-defence is a defence in this first sense. Yet 'defence' can also be used to refer to a characteristic way of bringing such facts to the attention of decision-makers in the course of the legal process. Thus a person charged with murder may choose to bring forth, *as* a defence in this second sense—as a defence *to* the criminal charge—the fact that she acted in self-defence. So the term 'defence' carries the suggestion that the relevant circumstances, if they are to constrain the corresponding decision or judgment, have actually to have been put forth by someone in their capacity

[19] See Duff (2007: 179–81, 263); compare Campbell (1987: 74–6); Robinson (1997: 11–12); Gardner (2004: 141).

as a defendant, and as a means of opposing a claim or answering a charge made against them.

This is a suggestion we want to avoid. It is true that in the legal domain judges are often bound to decide, as Hart (1949: 182) observes, 'upon the claims and defences actually made and pleaded before him, and not on those which might have been made or pleaded'. But that has no bearing on the issue of defeasibility. The actual manner by which we may come to acquire the relevant information is immaterial. (In Hart's own 'Smith hit her' example, for instance, it is 'on investigating the facts' that we come to know about the occurrence of some relevant defeating circumstance.) The constitution of the body of information to which any given judgment is relative may be governed and constrained by many different sorts of rules. Rules determining the inadmissibility of evidence obtained in certain ways, for example, or rules to the effect that information about facts of a certain kind will be admitted only if adduced by a given procedural party, are rules that negatively delimit the body of information on which the court can appropriately rely. In non-institutional, everyday contexts such as that of Hart's example, there are usually no similar constraints. But such issues are of no consequence for the topic of defeasibility and the characterization of defeasible judgments. What matters here, as our definition of defeasibility$_{P}$ makes clear, is the sort of *facts* that are present or absent from the body of information to which any given judgment is relative, not what counts in each case as a well-formed body of information.

There are, moreover, interesting connections between these two senses of 'defence'—between procedural defences and defeating circumstances—and it will prove convenient to have different terms at our disposal with which to designate them. So I will normally reserve 'defence' to refer to those objections, counterclaims, or replies put forth by whoever is confronted, in the legal field or otherwise, with claims or accusations—that is, I will normally use 'defence' in its procedural sense—and when alluding to the relevant *facts* I shall adopt and primarily employ 'exception'. For stylistic variety, 'defeating circumstance' will also do; and of course I will continue to make use of the equivalent notion of a '*D*-fact', which was introduced (together with the notion of a *P*-fact) in section 1.3.

2.3 Defeasibility and the Application of Legal Concepts

So now recall, from Chapter 1, these three theses:

(T1*) Defeasible concepts cannot be defined in terms of a set of necessary and sufficient conditions.

(T1) No set of necessary and sufficient conditions of a correct judgment *J* can be specified when the correctness of *J* depends on the non-emergence of defeating circumstances.

(T3) Defeating circumstances are not reducible to necessary conditions of correct judgments.

(T1*) was Hart's claim on defeasibility. (T1) is my attempt at capturing the substance of (T1*) while avoiding the language of 'concepts' and their 'application'. (T3) is what I proposed to call the *irreducibility thesis*. The suggestion is in all three cases that the peculiar kind of constraint imposed by defeating circumstances upon judicial decisions is not explainable in the standard terms of necessary and sufficient conditions. I said at the end of Chapter 1 that I believe that (T1) is wrong, but also that there is a version of (T3) that captures a crucial thought about exceptions. The account that I begin to develop in Chapter 3 will enable us to see why that is. First, however, there is one point about the notion of defeasibility still in need of clarification. How plausible is it to construe the 'defeasibility' of any given judicial decision, as Hart does with (T1*), as an issue about the application or even the meaning of legal concepts or concept-terms?

In order to answer this question, let us once again turn to the legal domain, and to Hart's main example: contract. It should be obvious that meaning of 'contract' was not Hart's subject. His claims about contracts are offered merely as illustrations of the topic that concerns him—defeasibility. (T1*) has nothing to do with any particular predicate. It is not a claim about contract. Nor is it a claim about trespass, or duty to supply, or about the concept of action, to cite some of Hart's other examples of 'defeasible concepts'. (T1*) is a claim about 'defeasible concepts' *in general*, a claim that will be applicable to contract only if and in so far as contract happens to be, in the relevant sense, a defeasible concept. Notice, also, that although the term 'defeasibility' (or rather, the adjective 'defeasible') is introduced in Hart's paper with a stipulated meaning, Hart uses it to capture what he takes to be a familiar, well-known feature of the workings of the law. That defeasibility *is* at play in the legal domain is taken by Hart to be indisputably true; so much so that instead of providing an explicit characterization of the notion, he finds it sufficient simply to refer his readers to what happens in a case of contract. His example, of course, cannot be meant to imply that defeasibility is necessarily at play in all conceivable legal cases of contract; the point must be that defeasibility is a feature typically to be found in such cases. And what matters, at any rate, cannot be that they are cases of *contract*—nor indeed that they are *legal* cases—but simply that in such cases defeasibility happens to be at play. So Hart's example, properly understood, is not strictly speaking that of a case of contract. It is that of a case of contract in which defeasibility happens to be at play.

With this in mind, let us turn to our question, which is in fact threefold. I noted in section 1.2 that Hart very often characterizes the judge's 'function' in a case of contract as that of having to decide whether 'there is' or 'there exists' a contract.[20] Is he right, we must then ask, to hold that such a 'function' is aptly described by saying that the judge is to make a decision of the form 'there is an *x*'? If so, are we justified in thinking that this '*x*' is to be interpreted as 'contract'? And would that establish, as Hart seems also to believe, that defeasibility bears on the meaning of 'contract'?

All three queries, I will now suggest, are to be answered negatively. Let us at first grant *arguendo* that Hart is at least on the right track when he characterizes the judge's function in a case of contract as that of making a decision or judgment of the form 'there is an *x*'. So let us take the second and third queries first: how plausible is it to maintain that in a case of contract, '*x*' stands for 'contract'?

2.3.1 *Defeasibility: Not About Meaning*

We can begin by noting that 'contract', a general, abstract term, is ill-suited to the purpose of describing the actual content of any one judicial decision in the sort of cases that interest Hart. There are many types and subtypes of contract, each one dependent on its own set of *P*-facts, and possibly subject to its own set of defeating circumstances. Strictly speaking, no judge decides that *there is a contract*; if one grants that the 'there is an *x*' scheme is suitable for the description of judicial

20 Hart (1949: 172–3, 182–3).

decisions in contract, then what one ought to say is rather that the judge decides that there is (for example) a *contract for sale*, a *tenancy agreement*, a *charter-party*, and so on.[21] One ought to say, to put it differently, that a judge in a case of contract makes a decision of the form 'there is a CONTRACT', taking 'CONTRACT' here as a symbol (rather than a name) to be replaced, in each case, by the actual name of the relevant kind or sub-kind of contract: a symbol whose range of adequate interpretations will be the range of objects that can, in spite of their possibly different features, be brought together as members of the general class of contracts. (In what follows I shall use 'CONTRACT', thus notated, in this way.) This point, which Hart fails to notice,[22] is a relatively minor one. But even if we charitably take his claims about the meaning of 'contract' to refer instead to particular interpretations of 'CONTRACT'—to refer, that is, to the meaning of the name or expression designating the relevant type of contract in each case—several other issues remain in need of clarification.

Indeed, insistent as Hart's references to the concept of 'contract' may be,[23] and although he asserts that 'the judge is literally deciding that on the facts before him a contract does or does not exist',[24] there is another way of describing the judge's 'function' which Hart seems to employ just as naturally, if less often. It is to say that a judge has to decide 'whether there is or is not a *valid* contract'.[25] Yet, if one uses both modes of descriptions interchangeably—as Hart does[26]—'contract' must take a different meaning in each case. A 'valid contract' in this second mode of description is the equivalent of a 'contract' in the first; an 'invalid contract' the equivalent of 'not a contract'. In that first mode of description, of course, the term 'contract' (or, rather, the relevant interpretation of 'CONTRACT' in the particular case) must apply

[21] This is not to say that there can be no commonality of *P*-facts and/or defeating circumstances between contracts of any two given types. Nor am I suggesting (of course) that judges would not simply *say* in any particular case that 'there is a contract', omitting the pertinent qualifications. The point is rather that defeating circumstances will bear in each case on whatever type or types and subtypes of contract may be in issue, and not (or at any rate not necessarily) on the more abstract general notion of a contract.

[22] Save for an isolated and casual reference to a judge's decision 'that on the facts which he has found there is a *contract for sale* between A and B'—Hart (1949: 172, emphasis added)—the general noun 'contract' is the one that Hart invariably employs.

[23] Hart (1949: 173–5, 178).

[24] Hart (1949: 182).

[25] Emphasis added; see Hart (1949: 174–5, 182).

[26] He describes the plaintiff's claim, for example, both as the claim that 'there is a contract' and as the claim that 'there is a valid contract': see Hart (1949: 175, 177).

whenever the relevant *P*-facts are present, whether or not any defeating circumstance also happens to be present. If we write this as '$\text{CONTRACT}_{\text{P}}$', then the claim made by the defendant who raises a defence is not that no $\text{CONTRACT}_{\text{P}}$ was concluded or 'exists'. What a defendant who raises a defence thereby claims is that such a $\text{CONTRACT}_{\text{P}}$ is not (or is not to be recognized as) *valid* in the context or for the purpose of the particular judicial decision to be made.[27] But if one chooses instead to refer to those *P*-facts as elements that are sufficient for a CONTRACT to 'exist' only if no defences emerge, one will then be using 'CONTRACT' to mean that there is a *valid* $\text{CONTRACT}_{\text{P}}$. This can be marked out as '$\text{CONTRACT}_{\text{V}}$'. In so far as Hart holds that defeasibility affects the meaning of (particular interpretations of) 'CONTRACT', then he is not concerned with the meaning of interpretations of 'CONTRACT' in the context and for the purposes of some particular decision. He is concerned with the meaning of interpretations of '$\text{CONTRACT}_{\text{V}}$', not of '$\text{CONTRACT}_{\text{P}}$'.[28]

These remarks are sufficient to cast doubt on the suggestion that defeasibility in a case of contract does bear on the meaning of (interpretations of) 'CONTRACT' (let alone upon the meaning of 'contract') in this sense of '$\text{CONTRACT}_{\text{V}}$'. That any given decision that there is a $\text{CONTRACT}_{\text{V}}$ happens to be 'defeasible' in the relevant sense is, as pointed out at the beginning of this section, a contingent matter: but then how could defeasibility affect what any given interpretation of '$\text{CONTRACT}_{\text{V}}$' *means*? Suppose, however, that one were willing to go along with the dubious hypothesis that any given interpretation of '$\text{CONTRACT}_{\text{V}}$'—any given interpretation, that is, of 'valid $\text{CONTRACT}_{\text{P}}$'—has a different meaning according to whether a decision in a case of contract happens to be dependent on the non-emergence of defeating circumstances. Now, clearly even within the same legal system it is quite possible that for different purposes, the set of admissible

[27] Compare Stoljar (1959: 353–6); MacCormick (1995: 102); and Atria (2001: 138–9 and n 7).

[28] Notice how Hart's exposition trades on this ambiguity, for example, in the following passage (about 'will', rather than 'contract'): 'What should we say of the sentence written in my diary that "My father made his will yesterday" if it turns out that since it was not witnessed and he was not domiciled in Scotland the courts refuse to recognise it as a will [?] Is the sentence in my diary false? We should, I think, hesitate to say it is; on the other hand, we would not repeat the sentence after the court's decision is made'; see Hart (1949: 184). If the sentence is taken to mean that the father made a *valid* will, then there is no reason why we should hesitate to say that indeed it is false. If, in turn, the sentence states simply (without implying anything about legal validity) that the father made a will, there is no reason why we wouldn't now repeat it.

defences may vary, and consequently that the conditions under which the same set of *P*-facts will be recognized a valid CONTRACT$_P$ will also vary. To maintain that defeasibility bears on concept-meaning, one would need to defend that, given the same interpretation of 'CONTRACT', 'CONTRACT$_V$' would *mean* different things in each such context—which cannot be right.

Hart's unwarranted projection of defeasibility onto concept-meaning stems from his resolve to describe a judicial decision for the plaintiff in a case of contract as a decision that 'there is' or 'exists' a (valid) CONTRACT. As the set of conditions on which the judge's decision for the plaintiff depends encompasses the non-emergence of defeating circumstances, one would correspondingly say that if some such circumstance does emerge, then the judge will have to conclude that 'there is' *no* (valid) CONTRACT. So if one takes *D*-facts as well as *P*-facts to affect whether or not it is correct to decide that *there is* a (valid) CONTRACT, the 'applicability' of '(valid) CONTRACT' really does turn on whether *D*-facts (as well as *P*-facts) are present or absent; and hence (so the underlying reasoning seems to run) defeasibility affects the meaning of '(valid) CONTRACT'.

But this last step is unwarranted. Hart's mistake here is that he treats 'valid' (or 'valid contract') as a one-place predicate. When discussing whether it is possible to state the necessary and sufficient 'conditions for the existence of a valid contract', he apparently assumes that such a 'definition of contract' would take the form 'There exists a valid CONTRACT$_P$ iff . . .', or '*X* is a valid CONTRACT$_P$ iff . . .'.[29] But any such sentence of the form '*X* is a valid CONTRACT$_P$' is either elliptical or ill formed. 'Valid CONTRACT' is a many-place predicate: any CONTRACT can properly be said to be 'valid'—or any *X* can be said to be a 'valid CONTRACT'—only relative to a given system of norms *Y* and perhaps a given context or purpose of assessment *Z*. So we have to deal with sentences of the form '*X* is a valid CONTRACT$_P$ in *Y* for purpose *Z*'. Accordingly, Hart's query about the possibility of stating the necessary and sufficient 'conditions for the existence of a valid contract' would have to be rendered as a question about the viability of a definition of the form '*X* is a valid CONTRACT$_P$ in *Y* for purpose *Z* iff . . .' (or, if we take variable *X* to range only over CONTRACTS$_P$, '*X* is valid in *Y* for purpose *Z* iff . . .'). The point, again, is that in different systems and

[29] Hart (1949: 174, 177).

for different purposes the set of relevant 'conditions' may (and typically will) vary. Hence any given CONTRACT$_P$ may happen to be valid in some system and not in others, or, within the same system, valid for some purpose but not for others. In all cases, however—whatever the set of relevant conditions—the meaning of the term 'valid CONTRACT$_P$' (as well as the meaning of the general terms 'contract' and 'valid contract') remains, of course, exactly the same. A change in validity conditions does not affect the meaning of 'valid contract'. It affects only (or may affect) which contracts count as valid in which system.

2.3.2 Defeasibility: Not About Concepts

Nor, at any rate, is the judge's 'function' in each particular case of contract adequately described (as, for the sake of argument, section 2.3.1 conceded) as that of applying the concept of a valid contract—or indeed as that of applying any concept at all.

The legally stipulated consequence of the fact that all relevant *P*-facts are present and no *D*-fact emerges is (at least in paradigmatic cases of contract) that there is some state of affairs that the judge is both authorized and required to enforce, prescribe, or bring about. The judge may be legally required to instruct the defendant to pay compensatory damages for breach of contract; to grant an injunction; to order the specific performance of some contractual obligation; and so on.

There is in each case of contract, of course, *some* decision to be reached by the judge. But that decision—this is my point—is aptly and fully described by reference to whatever state of affairs she is legally empowered to prescribe or enforce when all *P*-facts are present and no *D*-fact emerges. The judge's normative position, in other words, is comprehensively described in a conditional statement that *if* the relevant *P*-facts are present and no relevant *D*-facts emerge, *then* the judge is to decree or bring about a given state of affairs. It is true that Hart would deny that any such sufficient condition could be formulated whenever defences are at play. That is the claim that thesis (T1)—as opposed to thesis (T1*)—is meant to capture; and (T1) is a thesis whose correctness we are yet to assess. But *that* is a completely different issue from the one we are addressing in the present section. The issue we are presently addressing concerns the apt representation or description of the content of the judge's eventual decision. It concerns the *consequent*, not the antecedent, of the conditional statement of the judge's normative position in a case of contract. And the simple point that I am now pressing is that that normative position—of being authorized and required to enforce or prescribe a given state of affairs—is not tantamount to (or describable as) that of having to make any decision or judgment of the form 'there is an *x*', or having to 'apply' any given concept *x*. Judicial rulings—amounting as they do, after all, to performance of certain actions in an official capacity, and namely to the issuance of individual norms—cannot be adequately characterized in terms of any 'Is there an *X*?' question whose answer it is the judges' 'function' to provide.

What the judge in some sense 'applies'—should one wish to use this sort of language at all[30]—is the *rule* that authorizes and requires her to issue a given judgment for the plaintiff when all *P*-facts are present and no *D*-facts emerge. And clearly it is the structure of such a rule that constitutes the real object of Hart's interest. His concern is with the set of conditions on which the correctness of certain judicial decisions or judgments depends. His concern, more precisely, is with *defeasible* judicial decisions or judgments, in the sense of the adjective clarified in section 2.1: with judgments, issued or to be issued, the correctness of which depends on the absence of exceptions. But the fact that Hart erroneously describes such decisions by speaking of decisions or judgments 'whether there is or is not a valid contract' misleads him both to frame the issue of defeasibility as if it were essentially connected to the 'application' of concepts, and to articulate his own main claim on defeasibility as a claim about the conditions for such 'application'.

Here is a perhaps clearer way of making my present point. I have disentangled what I take to be the two autonomous premises on which Hart's main claim on defeasibility rests: first, that no set of necessary and always sufficient conditions can be specified for any given defeasible judicial decision to count as rightly made; second, that defeasible decisions can be described as being decisions to the effect that 'there is an *x*', and thus as decisions or judgments applying the concept of an *x*. From the conjunction of these two premises, the conclusion does follow that no set of necessary and always sufficient conditions can be specified for a decision that there is an *x* (or for the application of the concept of an *x*). This is how Hart chooses to

[30] I discuss in Chapter 5 this non-fundamental language of legal 'rules' and their 'applications'.

phrase his views, as captured in the language of (T1*). But now that we have learned that that second premise is unwarranted, this conclusion is left unsupported.

Our reconstruction has also made clear that the nub of Hart's views on defeasibility lies in that first premise, not in the second. And the first premise corresponds to the thesis that I proposed to articulate as (T1). So we can now more rigorously restate it as the thesis that

> (T1') The circumstances on which the correctness of a defeasible decision depends cannot be specified by a set of necessary and sufficient conditions.

Applied to defeasible judicial decisions in contract—applied, that is, to any judicial decision to be made in a case of contract in which defeasibility happens to be at play—(T1') yields no necessary claim about the meaning, the definition, or the application of 'contract', 'valid contract', or any other term or concept.

Hart's joint commitment to those two premises leads, perhaps inevitably, to further puzzles. One thing he claims is that

> since the judge is literally deciding that on the facts before him a contract does or does not exist, and to do this is neither to describe the facts nor to make inductive or deductive inferences from the statement of facts, what he does may be either a *right* or a *wrong* decision or a *good* or *bad* judgment and can be either *affirmed* or *reversed* and (where he has no jurisdiction to decide the question) may be *quashed* or *discharged*. What cannot be said of it is that it is either *true* or *false*, logically necessary or absurd.[31]

This is true, of course—though trivially so. We are focusing on the conditions on which judicial decisions depend, and judicial decisions—judgments, rulings—are simply not the sort of things we would conceive of as having truth values. (This is the case whether or not 'defeasible concepts' happen to be involved. One wonders whether the point is worth making at all.) In any event, Hart needs to be able to reconcile this contention that a judicial decision is not a 'descriptive statement'—and particularly his (sound) resistance to reducing judicial decisions to descriptions of any set of facts brought before the judge—with his (unwarranted) use of the sentence 'there is a (valid)

[31] Hart (1949: 182).

contract' to describe the content of such a decision. In order to do so, he would need to maintain that this sentence (or any given interpretation of 'there is valid CONTRACT$_P$') is not truth-apt. But that would not be a very plausible view, and indeed Hart never brings himself to endorse it. On the contrary, he finds it important to stress that 'it would be a misunderstanding of the judicial process' to maintain that the parties are 'merely treated *as if* there was a contract'. 'There *is* a contract', he emphatically insists.[32] Each of Hart's two premises, in short, seems to falsify the other.

It might perhaps be countered that even if a judicial decision to award damages for breach of contract, for example, cannot be said to be equivalent to (and thus exhaustively describable as) a decision that 'there is' a valid contract, it is nonetheless the case that the former in some sense presupposes the latter—that the judge who decides to award damages for breach of contract must take the corresponding contract to be valid—and so that Hart would not have been wholly mistaken in characterizing the judge's 'function' as that of having to say or decide 'whether there is or not a valid contract'. Would this be a pertinent objection? It concedes that the phrase 'there is a valid contract' does not aptly describe the consequent of the conditional formulation with which the judge's position can in principle be stated. That phrase must then suitably describe (the objection seems to assume) the antecedent of that conditional formulation, or part thereof. But is that the case? As just noted, the natural rendition of this conditional formulation would state that *if* all the relevant *P*-facts are present and all the relevant *D*-facts absent, the judge is to issue a judgment for the plaintiff, which judgment amounts to the prescription or enforcement of some state of affairs. What then is the relation between the claim that there is a valid contract (in the relevant decision-making context, and

[32] Hart (1949: 182). It is true that Hart says that the sense in which there 'is' a contract is 'the timeless sense of "is" appropriate to judicial decisions'. But this claim has the ring of an ad hoc attempt to both have and eat his philosophical cake: in so far as the claim allows for the truth-aptness of the proposition that there is a valid contract, it is inconsistent with his reasons for endorsing (T1*). Hart's endorsement of (T1*) is linked to his view that no set of facts brought before a judge can ever descriptively amount to, or imply, or make it the case (in conjunction with the relevant legal rules), that there is a (valid) contract. Such facts, he insists, can only be said to 'support' (Hart 1949: 172, 181, 183, 185, 187, 189), never to entail (Hart 1949: 183), the conclusion that there is a valid contract. Yet if 'there is a valid contract' can at all be true, then there is no reason why it cannot be made true by facts 'brought', as Hart says, 'to [the judge's] attention', in combination with the relevant rules.

for the purpose of the corresponding judgment) and the claim that the relevant *P*-facts are present and the relevant *D*-facts absent? One possible answer might be that the claims are equivalent; that it is the case both that

(1) If all *P*-facts are present and all *D*-facts absent, then there is a valid contract,

and that

(2) If there is a valid contract, then all *P*-facts are present and all *D*-facts absent.

But the conjunction of (1) and (2) does not adequately capture the relation between (a) the statement that *P*-facts are present, and *D*-facts absent, in a case of contract, and (b) the statement that 'there is' a valid contract. It would seem to be a contingent matter whether (2), in particular, is true. We can easily think of a defendant who is willing to grant that a contract was *validly* concluded, but claims—by invoking an exception, a *D*-fact—that some legal consequence which would otherwise be duly enforced is nonetheless *not* to be enforced by the judge in that particular case.

Indeed, plaintiffs do not simply claim that 'there is a valid contract'. That is normally not what brings them to court. What a plaintiff will rather claim is (for example) that there is a valid contract *and* that it has been breached *and* that as a consequence she incurred some damage, and so on. They claim that the conditions are present that require the court to enforce or decree a given state of affairs (for instance, by instructing the defendant to pay damages). In order to avert this consequence, correspondingly, the defendant does not have to deny that a contract was validly performed. She may instead deny that the contract was breached, or simply allow both that there was a valid contract and that she breached it, but raise a *D*-fact which, she claims, prevents the judge from correctly requiring her to pay damages.[33]

Moreover, and importantly, we can now see that the relevant *P*-facts on which the success of the plaintiff's claim depends are neither necessarily nor typically restricted to those facts—offer, acceptance,

[33] The fact that the contract was '"frustrated" by a fundamental and unexpected change of circumstance' included in Hart's catalogue of defences—see Hart (1949: 176)—would seem to lend itself to this interpretation.

consideration—that could plausibly be taken to be definitional of either 'contract' or 'valid contract'. In most any plausible example, Hart's list of 'required' conditions would have to be expanded. In the example just given, the fact that the contract has been breached is a *P*-fact as much as the fact that the contract was validly made. It wouldn't be possible, therefore, to characterize the available defences in contract as amounting to denials that there is a (valid) CONTRACT.

At this point the rejoinder might still be set forth, I suppose, that even though it may well be that as a stand-in expression, 'there is a (valid) CONTRACT' does not suitably capture the combination of the presence of all the relevant *P*-facts and the absence of all the relevant *D*-facts in a case of contract, there will surely be *some* term or concept *X*—or at the very least that we must be able to coin one—that allows us comprehensively to refer to the entire antecedent of the relevant defeasible decision. The corresponding statements of type (1) and type (2) would then, it seems, necessarily hold:

(1a) If all *P*-facts are present and all *D*-facts absent, then there is an *X*.
(2a) If there is an *X*, then all *P*-facts are present and all *D*-facts absent.

The immediate reply would be that even if this were the case, we would still have good reason to do away with the language of 'concept'-application in the context of our topic. We would have good reason, that is, not to frame our discussion of defeasibility in law by saying either that the judge decides that 'there is' an *X*, or that the judge 'applies' the concept of an *X*. Why? Because even if there is some concept *X* such that 'there is an *X*' is equivalent to (and thus interchangeable with) 'all *P*-facts are present and all *D*-facts are absent', the fact remains that what interests us is the possibly peculiar way in which judicial decision-making is affected by the presence or absence of *D*-facts. So our topic is more clearly and suitably laid down and addressed if we make use of the 'all *P*-facts are present and all *D*-facts are absent' phrase, which explicitly separates the (supposedly different) kinds of relevant facts that interest us, than if we employ an indiscriminating 'there is an *X*' formulation. For the purposes of our inquiry, the antecedent of the conditional formulation with which the judge's normative position is putatively to be stated is always more helpfully represented with an unpacked formulation like

(3) If all *P*-facts are present and all *D*-facts absent, then the judge is to issue a decision for the plaintiff

than with a compressed formulation like

(4) If there is an *X*, then the judge is to issue a decision for the plaintiff.

Indeed, although Hart's (T1*) claim would commit him to reject (3)—and thus also to reject the conjunction of (1a) and (2a)—it would not require him to reject (4) if '*X*' is specifically introduced as a term that simply stands for the antecedent (whatever it may be) of the judge's decision. So even if we were to grant that a 'there is an *X*' formulation could always be found that would fittingly stand in for, and comprehensively restate, the antecedent of any correctly issued defeasible decision, we would still have good reason to proceed with our inquiry without having to appeal to the language of 'concepts' and their 'application', from which there is nothing to be gained. And that is exactly what I will now do.

2.4 Agenda

Let us take stock. The discussion in this chapter has given us a clearer understanding of the issue of defeasibility. It has also enabled us to render Hart's main claim on defeasibility—which in Chapter 1 was given a preliminary articulation—in a more precise way. With our stipulation in hand that a judgment or decision is aptly called 'defeasible' if and only if its correctness depends on the non-emergence of exceptions, we saw that Hart's main claim can more fittingly be restated as the claim that

(T1') The circumstances on which the correctness of a defeasible decision depends cannot be specified by a set of necessary and sufficient conditions.

The claim I have called the *irreducibility thesis* may now be also slightly rephrased as follows:

(T3') Exceptions are not reducible to necessary conditions of defeasible decisions.

It is time to follow through with my announced argumentative programme. I said that there is a version of (T3') that is correct. I also said that (T1') not only does not follow from (T3'), but is in fact false. To establish these two points we need to grasp the notion around which our entire discussion gravitates—the notion of an exception. After all it was by reference to it that our definition of a defeasible judgment was articulated. So the notion of an exception is our basic notion, our primary explanandum. We need an account of exceptions. That is what I will now try to offer.

PART II
Defeasibility in Theory

3

The Proof-Based Account

3.1 Preliminaries

We face a dilemma. We have seen that the following claim has very little going for it:

(T1') The circumstances on which the correctness of a defeasible decision depends cannot be specified by a set of necessary and sufficient conditions.

This was my rendition of a thesis first set forth by H. L. A. Hart and endorsed today by a number of theorists. We can identify necessary conditions of defeasible decisions, they say, but not conditions that are always sufficient. This view falls prey to what I called the 'incorporationist' objection. The incorporationist objection says that (T1') is self-contradictory. A 'defeasible' judicial decision, by definition, is a decision that is correctly issued only in the absence of exceptions. But if the presence of an exception is sufficient to prevent a certain judicial decision from being correct, then the absence of exceptions is a necessary condition of the correct decision. If duress is a valid defence in contract, then absence of duress is a necessary condition for the judge to decide for the plaintiff. That means that we can incorporate the conjunction of the negations of each admissible exception in our specification of the conditions of defeasible decisions. So there is nothing preventing us from specifying their sufficient conditions. Not, at least, when a closed list of exceptions can be given—as in the cases that Hart and others are concerned with. Therefore (T1') is false.

This is a forceful objection. But the incorporationist account of exceptions also leaves something to be desired. Indeed, it is dissatisfaction with the incorporationist account that draws some theorists towards theses like (T1'). What is the cause of such dissatisfaction? Recall, from Chapter 1, the following scheme, which adopts the incorporationist strategy for representing the conditions of a defeasible decision in a case of contract:

(A) It is correct to decide for the plaintiff if and only if (*P* and *not-D*).

Here, to briefly recapitulate, '*P*' stands for the conjunction (P_1 and P_2 and . . . P_n) of those elements whose presence is required for the judge's decision, and '*D*' stands for the disjunction (D_1 and D_2 and . . . D_n) of the admissible exceptions. In the terminology of this book, facts of the former kind are called '*P*-facts', and facts of the latter kind are called '*D*-facts', 'defeating circumstances', or simply 'exceptions'. To say that a decision or judgment is legally correct is to say that it is both (a) legally authorized, and (b) legally required or at least permitted.

As scheme (A) makes visible, the incorporationist approach treats the conjunction of all the relevant *P*-facts and the non-occurrence of any *D*-fact not merely as a necessary condition, but also as a sufficient condition of it being correct to decide in a certain way. In what regards their logical status, then, *P*-facts and *D*-facts are treated as equivalent kinds: incorporationists recognize no difference between a *negative P*-fact and the *negation* of a *D*-fact. That is a trait of the incorporationist approach. Incorporationists think that the distinction between '*P*-facts' and '*D*-facts' is a spurious distinction. This is not a point about contract; it is a general point about exceptions in law. So in the field of criminal law, for example, incorporationists think that—in the words of one prominent endorser, Glanville Williams—there is 'no intrinsic difference between the elements of an offence and an exception (or defence) to that offence':[1]

> [A] rule that is subject to an exception is only partly true if it is stated without the exception . . . The exception is, rationally regarded, part and parcel of the rule. Hence looking for the line between a rule and an exception is, to use the proverbial simile, like looking in a dark room for a black cat that isn't there. There are no characteristic features of exceptions: 'exceptions' are merely linguistic constructs. Since they lack any specific definition, the negative of an element of an offence can be regarded as an exception, and the negative of an exception can be regarded as an element of the offence.[2]

1 Williams (1988: 277).

2 Williams (1988: 278). Given that 'all the exceptions (or defences) can be stated in negative form as part of the offence, instead of as something outside the offences', the 'offence

The problem for incorporationism is that there does seem to be something about defeating circumstances that tells against equating them with *P*-facts. We tend to think that a defendant who denies that the relevant *P*-facts are present is doing 'something quite different', as Hart (1949: 174) remarks, from a defendant who, granting the relevant *P*-facts, offers a defence instead. There *is*, we think, a distinction to be drawn between plain 'No' and 'Yes, but . . .' replies to claims and charges.

Hart believed that we could do justice to this distinction by adopting a scheme like (B) rather than a scheme like (A):

(B) If *P*, then it is correct to decide for the plaintiff when *P*, unless *D*.

We saw in Chapter 1, however, that this is unworkable. Given Hart's classification of *P*-facts as 'necessary' conditions, (B) collapses back into (A). But he was right to resist the pull to explain *D*-facts in terms of *P*-facts. And this unease with the incorporationist move is what lies behind what I called the *irreducibility thesis*:

(T3') Exceptions are not reducible to necessary conditions of defeasible decisions.

I agree with the incorporationists that (T1') is false. But I think that the incorporationists' own reduction of exceptions to necessary conditions fails to properly represent exceptions. I think that (T3'), or at any rate a version of (T3'), is true.

On the other hand, I am reluctant to go along with those theorists who, endorsing (T3'), and wanting to substantiate the thought that there is an important difference between the ways in which *D*-facts and *P*-facts constrain judicial decisions, maintain that judicial reasoning proceeds non-monotonically. According to this picture—the 'non-deductivist' picture, as I called it in Chapter 1—conclusions of law correctly derived from a given set of premises are not necessarily preserved when this set is expanded. In a civil case, for example, given a set of premises affirming all and only the relevant *P*-facts, we are warranted in concluding, 'defeasibly', that it is correct for the court to decide for the plaintiff. Here our conditional premise

package' consisting of 'the offence elements and the negative of defences' is, Williams says, an 'indivisible whole': absence of self-defence is 'a negative element of the crime, just as the woman's non-consent is a negative element of rape'. See Williams (1988: 278–9), and also Williams (1982: 237–9 and 247–9).

could be thought of simply as 'If *P*, then it is correct to decide for the plaintiff'. But when to that original set of premises we add a premise affirming the occurrence of a *D*-fact, the conclusion that the plaintiff should succeed no longer follows. The correct judgment to issue is now a judgment for the defendant. So should this lead us to revise our original conditional ('If *P*, then it is correct to decide for the plaintiff') along the lines suggested by the incorporationists (that is, as 'If *P* and *not-D*, then it is correct to decide for the plaintiff')? No it shouldn't, say the non-deductivists. Rather, we should hold on to that original conditional—which tracks an important link between *P*-facts and legal conclusions—but take it to specify something weaker than a sufficient condition of a decision for the plaintiff.

This non-deductivist picture is rightly opposed to the explanation of *D*-facts in terms of standard necessary conditions of correct decisions. It assigns different statuses to *P*-facts and *D*-facts. It supports (T3'). But there is no conclusive reason to prefer the non-deductivist picture to the incorporationist one. For the non-deductivist account, too, comes at a cost. It comes at the cost of abandoning the otherwise appealing thought—which the incorporationist account preserves—that for any legally correct decision or conclusion of law, it should be possible to come up with some combination of statements of law and statements of fact that deductively justifies that conclusion. And at least in those cases in which an exhaustive catalogue of exceptions can be identified, it must be possible to specify sufficient conditions of correct defeasible decisions.

That is why we face a dilemma. The incorporationist and the non-deductivist accounts are incompatible. But neither is satisfactory. What is needed is an account of exceptions that, like the non-deductivist account, vindicates the irreducibility thesis—(T3')—while managing, like incorporationism, to conclusively reject (T1').

I begin in this chapter to develop such an account. In this and Chapters 4–6, I seek to offer a complete account of defeasibility in law. I call it a 'proof-based' account, for reasons that will be evident. The account is first introduced in section 3.2 for scenarios in which only so-called 'explicit' exceptions are allowed: scenarios in which an exhaustive catalogue of the admissible exceptions can be compiled in advance of any particular decision. In sections 3.3 and 3.4, I deal with some immediate objections to which the proof-based account may conceivably give rise. A restatement of the irreducibility thesis is given, together with a summary of the main results thus far, in section 3.5. Slightly more complex scenarios are then considered in section 3.6, where I offer some refinements to the proposed account. In Chapter 4, I discuss at length the connections between the proof-based account and the legal doctrine of the burden of proof, before expanding the scope of inquiry to address, in Chapters 5 and 6, the more difficult issue of so-called 'implicit' exceptions.

3.2 Introducing the Proof-Based Account

The problem with both (A) and (B) is that these formulations do not allow us to capture in a sufficiently discriminatory manner the way in which defeasible decisions are made to depend on the fact that no exception 'is present' or 'matures'.[3]

In the context of judicial decision-making we cannot simply say that a given circumstance *X* is 'present' if it is the case that *X*, and 'absent' if it is not the case that *X*. 'Presence' and 'absence' of relevant circumstances depend rather on whether any such circumstance may be said to have been established or ascertained—or 'proved', the term I will favour—in accordance with certain rules and procedures. Given that any circumstance *X* may be either proved or not proved, and that the same can be said of its negation, we have for any given *X* the following four possibilities:

A. *X* is proved.
B. *Not-X* is proved.
C. *X* is *not* proved.
D. *Not-X* is *not* proved.

Now the notion that some circumstance or set of circumstances *P* has to be 'present' for it to be correct to decide for the plaintiff may easily be cast in terms of it being necessary that *P* be proved, as in (1):

(1) It is correct to decide for the plaintiff only when *P is proved*.

The notion, however, that some defeating circumstance *D* has to be 'absent'—or not to 'mature'—for the plaintiff to succeed admits two competing readings. It suggests, of course, that if *D is proved*, the

[3] These were Hart's terms: see Hart (1949: 174–5, 179).

judge will be prevented from ruling for the plaintiff. This is formulation (2),

(2) If *D is proved*, then it is *not* correct to decide for the plaintiff,

from which it follows that

(3) It is correct to decide for the plaintiff only if it is *not proved that D*,

or, in other words, that it cannot be simultaneously the case that it is *proved that D* and yet the plaintiff is entitled to succeed.[4]

But keep in mind that '*proved that D*' can be denied not only externally ('*not proved that D*') but also internally ('*proved that not-D*'). So there are two candidate readings of the notion that for a judgment for the plaintiff to be correct it is necessary that no exceptions be 'present' or 'mature'. One is the reading just mentioned and formulated as (3). The other is (4):

(4) It is correct to decide for the plaintiff only if it is *proved that not-D*.

The first reading, reading (3), says that for the plaintiff to succeed it is necessary that the *occurrence* of *D* be *not proved*. The second reading, reading (4), says that for the plaintiff to succeed it is necessary that the *non-occurrence* of *D* be *proved*.

Clearly, it is the former reading that adequately captures exceptions. This is, as a matter of fact, how defeating circumstances behave in cases like the ones we have been considering. While the court cannot, for instance, award compensatory damages for breach of contract when some *D*-fact is proved (as stated in (2)), such a judgment does not depend on the *non*-occurrence of defeating circumstances actually being *proved*. As stated in (5), the fact that it hasn't been *proved* that *no* exceptions occurred does not prevent the judge from correctly ruling for the plaintiff:

(5) It is *not* the case that *that not-D is not proved* prevents a correct decision for the plaintiff.

The implication is that

(6) A correct decision for the plaintiff does not depend on *not-D* being proved,

[4] Throughout most of this chapter, I adopt the simplifying assumption that only one level of exceptions is admitted. I discard this assumption in section 3.6.

or, in other words, that (4) is false.

For the plaintiff to succeed, however, it does have to be the case that *no* exception has been proved. This—which is what formulation (3) is meant to capture—is the right way to render the more diffuse idea that defeating circumstances have to be 'absent', or not to 'mature'. We may thus represent with (7) the thought that for the plaintiff to succeed it is necessary *both* that *P*-facts be present and that no exceptions 'mature':

(7) A correct decision for the plaintiff depends both on it being *proved that P* and on it *not being proved that D*.

This in turn makes clear that the *presence* of *P*—that is, the fact that *P is proved*—is never enough for the plaintiff to succeed. What *will* suffice is the conjunction of it being *proved that P* and *not proved that D*:

(8) If *P is proved* and it is *not proved that D*, then it is correct to decide for the plaintiff.

And from (7) and (8) it follows that:

(9) It is correct to decide for the plaintiff if and only if (*P is proved* and it is *not proved that D*).

This allows us to understand both why Hart was right to reject the scheme in (A)—which reads, remember, 'It is correct to decide for the plaintiff if and only if (*P* and *not-D*)'—and why he was unable to improve on it. The point is that the notion that some circumstance or set of circumstances *P* must be present for a given decision to be correct is, in the context of our discussion, to be understood as the requirement that *P* be *proved*. This is not to say that *P*—the circumstance (or the group of circumstances) *P* itself—is a necessary condition of the correct decision. It is to say that it has to be the case that *P* be *proved*, not that it has to be the case that *P*.[5]

Hart conflates the two notions: the notion, on the one hand, that some circumstance *P must be present* for a given judgment to be correct, and, on the other hand, the notion that *P* is a *necessary condition* of such a judgment being correct. That is why he says that those elements that must be present for a judge to correctly rule

[5] As commonly used in the context of legal decision-making—and thus in the sense that matters for our discussion—the verb 'to prove' is not a factive.

for the plaintiff in a case of contract—two parties, offer, acceptance, consideration, etc—are 'required' or 'necessary' elements.[6] The confusion then extends to his odd suggestion that the conjunction of these elements is *sometimes* sufficient for the correct judgment for the plaintiff, a suggestion implied by his assertion that such elements are 'not always sufficient'.[7] Hart's argument here is that when no exceptions 'mature' *nothing else but P* needs to be present for the court to rule for the plaintiff. But he confuses the idea of something being a sufficient condition with the idea of something being *all that needs to be present* for the plaintiff to succeed. It is true that all that needs to be present is *P*. What needs to be present is what needs to be established or proved, and nothing else apart from *P* has to be proved for the court to rule for the plaintiff. But this does not mean that *that P is proved* is ever sufficient for the court to rule for the plaintiff. It means only that no other element on which the court's ruling depends has the structure 'proved that . . .' And we have seen that *that P is proved*, although necessary, is not a sufficient condition for a correct judgment. It also needs to be the case that it is *not proved that D*. Hart's mistake, then, lies in confusing the 'presence' of circumstances relevant for a correct judgment with the verification of conditions necessary and/or sufficient for a correct judgment. In short, he erroneously conflates '*X* is *all* that has to be proved' with '*X* is a sufficient condition'; and '*X has* to be proved' with '*X* is a necessary condition'.

So even though Hart rightly finds the scheme in (A) inadequate, his confusion causes him to misunderstand his reasons for doing so. He correctly resists the suggestion, which is conveyed by (A), that both *P* and *not-D* have to be *present* for a judgment for the plaintiff to be correctly issued. But his equivocation leads him nevertheless to accord *P* the status of a *condition* of a correctly issued judgment. He is thereby prevented from saying, as he should have, that in all cases, *P* is all that has to be present for the judgment to be correct. He would have taken this to mean that *P* is a sufficient condition of the correct judgment, which sounds decidedly wrong whenever

[6] Hart (1949: 174).

[7] Hart (1949: 175).

some defeating circumstance does 'mature'. But given that he is led to treat *P* as a condition (a necessary condition) of the correct judgment, his denial that *P* is sufficient in cases in which a defence 'matures' has the result that the non-occurrence of defeating circumstances must also be conceived as a *condition* of the correct judgment.

With this confusion dissolved, however, we are now able to reconstruct Hart's refusal of (A) as the claim, formulated in (10), that it is *not the case* that both *P* and *not-D* have to be present—have to be *proved*—for the plaintiff to succeed:

(10) It is *not* the case that (it is correct to decide for the plaintiff if and only if (it is *proved that P* and it is *proved that not-D*)).[8]

In turn, the formulation above given as (9) conveys precisely what Hart would seem to have in mind but was incapable of articulating by means of his 'unless'-formulation (that is, formulation (B): 'If *P*, then it is correct to decide for the plaintiff, unless *D*').[9] (9) captures both the idea that if some defeating circumstance is 'present' the judge is to decide against the plaintiff, and the idea that when no defeating circumstance 'matures' *all* that has to be proved is *P*.

[8] Compare Hart's partly confused recourse to 'the practice of the law' in search of support for his point: 'no party attempting to enforce a contract', he says, 'is required to give evidence that [there are no defences];' and 'though in special cases where some person in a fiduciary position seeks to enforce a bargain with the person in relation to whom he occupies that position, the onus lies upon him to prove that no influence was, in fact, exerted', 'even here the proof consists simply in the exclusion of those facts which ordinarily constitute the defence of undue influence, though the onus is in such cases by exception cast on the plaintiff': Hart (1949: 178).

[9] L. Thorne McCarty was one of very few commentators to remark that Hart's resistance to the suggestion that the 'necessary and sufficient conditions of contract' could be stated 'by specifying as the necessary and sufficient condition of contract, consent and other positive conditions and the negation of the disjunction of the various defences'—see Hart (1951: 152)—can be explained by distinguishing between two senses in which the 'negation of the disjunction of the various defences' may be interpreted. But McCarty's suggestion is that the distinction to be drawn is between two kinds of negation: the strong negation of classical logic (which, in his reading, Hart would have rejected), and the weaker, non-monotonic negation-as-failure (which allows us to infer *not-X* from failure to prove *X*): McCarty (1991: 4–7). For reasons that the present and the following chapters make clear, I find this neither an apt reconstruction of Hart's views, nor, more importantly, an adequate account of explicit exceptions.

3.3 Substantive Representations of Exceptions

3.3.1 Exceptions and Substantive Legal Rules

You may resist my suggestion that the judge's decision is conditioned not by what positive and negative circumstances *are* the case, but rather by what circumstances are and are not *proved* to be the case. Does this suggestion not run counter to our common assumptions regarding matters of proof?

It does seem to be widely accepted that, as Jordi Ferrer puts it,

> what must be proved in court depends on the factual hypotheses with which legal norms associate certain consequences. Thus what must be proved in the legal process is the proposition asserting the occurrence of such facts, so that the corresponding legal consequence can be applied.[10]

According to this view, proof is an activity primarily and instrumentally directed at ascertaining the factual antecedents of 'substantive' legal rules (as they are sometimes called). I have doubts as to the soundness of this received approach. I would tend instead—generally speaking—to side with Kelsen's view that the relevant condition in a case of murder, for example, is not the fact of murder itself, but the ascertainment of that fact in court:

> [T]he legal rule does not say: 'If a certain individual has committed murder, then a punishment ought to be imposed upon him'. The legal rule says: 'If the authorized court in a procedure determined by the legal order has ascertained, with the force of law, that a certain individual has committed a murder, then the court ought to impose a punishment upon that individual'.[11]

The natural rejoinder to Kelsen is to acknowledge that there are, of course, 'procedural' rules that require judges to decide on the basis

[10] Ferrer Beltrán (2005: 49, my translation). For similar remarks see Wróblewski (1973: 161–2); Wróblewski (1975: 168–74); Jackson (1983: 88); Bulygin (1985: 163); Wróblewski (1992: 131–7); Taruffo (1992: 45–7, 65, 67–70, 74–7, 80–4); Jackson (2004: 124–30); Ferrer Beltrán (2006: 308–9); Ho: (2008, 5–6, 10–11, 68–9); or Roberts and Zuckerman (2010: 108).

[11] Kelsen (1960/67: 239–40). See also Kelsen (1944a: 46–7); Kelsen (1944b: 217–18); Kelsen (1945: 135–6); Kelsen (1979/91: 128–30, 140–1, 243–4, 413–4); and my disclaimer in n 24 below. Compare Sánchez Brígido's and Seleme's 'truth-less' (M)-model of the justification of judicial decisions in Sánchez Brígido and Seleme (2001).

of what has been proved, but to insist that it remains the case that the substantive rules have the actual facts, not their proof, in view. Eugenio Bulygin, for example, has insisted that judges are under 'the duty to base judicial decisions on true statements of fact'.[12] It is true that the need to reach an 'authoritative' decision 'based on evidence produced in a limited time-span' may lead to a ruling that, based as it may be 'on a false statement of fact', is nevertheless 'lawful or valid', and produces 'all legal effects'. But such a decision remains 'erroneous or incorrect' in one important sense, says Bulygin, for the legal process 'purports to determine the truth', and the judge is 'under an obligation to search' for it:

> [T]he rule of criminal law—contrary to Kelsen's opinion—stipulates the duty to punish those who have committed murder and not those of whom the judge says they have committed murder.[13]

This substantive rule of criminal law 'constitutes the standard of correct and incorrect judging', and this is a standard that judges can fail to meet. After all, 'facts are what they are and not what judges and other officials say they are': 'there is no legal murder besides the natural one, and no facts whatsoever are created by a judge or a jury declaring that [for example] Tom killed Peter'.[14]

According to this view, then, propositions affirming the occurrence of the relevant facts are seen to operate as premises in legal reasoning, and taken to constitute the object proper of legal proof; and rules about proof are accordingly conceived of as determining the conditions under which any such proposition may be accepted as true, and incorporated as a premise in the judge's or the decision-maker's argument.[15]

But this popular view is problematic. By characterizing the supposed level of 'substantive' rules in terms of rules that establish how judges ought to decide, it implies that when a relevant proposition is proved but false, or true but disproved, the judge

12 Bulygin (1995: 23).

13 Bulygin (1994: 19–20); Bulygin (1995: 21–2).

14 Bulygin (1995: 20, 22–3). For similar or related arguments, see also Alchourrón and Bulygin (1992: 13–16), and the discussion of the contrast and relation between what they call the 'primary [or 'subject'] system' and the 'secondary [or 'judge'] system' in Alchourrón and Bulygin (1971: 153–5).

15 See Bulygin (1995: 30–2); Ferrer Beltrán (2005: 31, 96–7); Ferrer Beltrán (2006: 308); Ferrer Beltrán (2007: 29–30).

will infringe a legal duty. If a decision made in accordance with what has been proved (as stipulated in the applicable 'procedural' rules) is admittedly to be acknowledged as 'lawful or valid', then, as Bulygin points out, that decision can only be judged as erroneous or incorrect by a standard of evaluation that is 'external to the legal process'.[16] Is this still a standard of *legal* correctness in any useful sense of the term? This is a debated issue. Kelsen's view was that it is not: 'If it is said: "A court ascertained that a certain individual committed a certain murder, although 'in reality' this individual did not commit it"', writes Kelsen (1960/67: 239-40), 'this means that the court ascertained the existence . . . of a fact, which according to the opinion of individuals legally not competent to ascertain this, did not exist.' 'From the point of view of a legal order', however,

> only *one* opinion can be decisive. Which one, must be determined by the legal order. This opinion is expressed in the court decision. It alone is legally relevant, the opinions of all others are irrelevant.[17]

Bulygin's criticism of Kelsen's conclusion that 'it makes no sense to discuss the correctness of a final judicial decision'[18] is meant to convey the opposite idea, that a judicial decision based on false premises is *legally* incorrect:

> Kelsen is wrong when he says that there is only one opinion that is legally relevant, viz. the decision of the judge, and that all other opinions are legally irrelevant. The non-official statements of law can show—if true—that a judicial decision, though lawful, is incorrect, because it is based on a false statement of fact . . . The standard of correctness of judicial decisions is truth and truth does not depend on official statements of a court.[19]

But then Bulygin has to simultaneously defend two conflicting claims. One is the claim that

[16] Bulygin (1994: 19–20); Bulygin (1995: 21).

[17] Kelsen (1960/67: 240). Compare MacCormick's remarks on 'truth-certifying procedures'—a notion introduced in Bańkowski (1981: 265–6)—in MacCormick (1992: 189–90), where he observes that 'the legal system admits of no other truth of the relevant matter, whatever the relative strengths of the reasons for believing and for disbelieving *p* in the first place'; and MacCormick (2005; 72–5).

[18] Bulygin (1994: 21); Bulygin (1995: 22).

[19] Bulygin (1995: 24).

[i]f a jury has decided that the [false] sentence 'Dimitri [Karamazov] killed his father' has been proved in court, then the judge is under the obligation to sentence Dimitri to imprisonment, because there is a norm that prescribes that judges ought to sentence to imprisonment those persons who have been found guilty of murder. So the judge has the duty to issue an individual norm sentencing Dimitri.[20]

Yet he also holds, as we saw, that the 'rule of criminal law . . . stipulates the duty to punish those who have committed murder and not those of whom the judge says they have committed murder'.[21] So Bulygin's characterization leads to the unwelcome result that whenever a mismatch exists between what is proved and what is actually the case, the judge will necessarily infringe a legal obligation. If the judge fulfils her legal duty 'to sentence to imprisonment those persons who have been found guilty of murder', she will have breached the 'rule of criminal law' requiring that convictions be based on 'true statements of fact'.[22] This counter-intuitive conclusion suggests that Bulygin's reconstruction is not to be accepted.[23]

My remarks are not intended as anything close to a definitive argument against any possible version of the dominant view.[24] The

[20] Bulygin (1995: 24). See also Bulygin (2003: 246)—'the procedural rules do not merely indicate under which circumstances the judge can convict a suspect, but establish an obligation to punish him'—or Bulygin (1985: 162–3)—asserting that the 'law of procedure', as contrasted with 'substantial' penal laws, imposes upon the judge an 'obligation' to sentence Karamazov to prison.

[21] Bulygin (1995: 22).

[22] Bulygin (1995: 22–4). For a different take on this debate see Jackson (1998: 246–52).

[23] Ferrer suggests that Caracciolo's distinction between two senses of the phrase 'judicial decision' can help explain our 'contradictory feelings' about the matter. The phrase can designate either the institutional *act* of issuing an individual ruling, or the content of the ruling itself (that is, the issued *norm*) which is the 'result' of that act: see Caracciolo (1988: 41–2). This distinction, says Ferrer, allows us to 'consider as unjustified, for example, [the *norm*-content] that someone is condemned for a crime she did not commit and, at the same time, consider the *act* or decision to condemn her as correct or justified (in the light of the available evidence)': Ferrer Beltrán (2006: 310, emphasis added); see also Comanducci (2010: 125–6). But Ferrer's suggestion is misguided. Caracciolo's distinction (which contrasts an act with the specific result whose occurrence is definitional of that very act) leaves no conceptual room for the possibility that a judicial decision be justified *qua* act but not also justified *qua* normative result—as Caracciolo (1988: 46) himself points out. At any rate, Ferrer is trying to solve a non-existent problem. To offer an account of the justification of judicial decisions *qua* acts is to offer a complete account of the justification of judicial decisions. There is nothing left to explain or reconstruct. For a model that does not allow for the possibility that a judicial decision can count as justified *qua* act but not *qua* norm, see Sánchez Brígido and Seleme (2001: 292).

[24] I should also make clear that I do *not* endorse Kelsen's view—at least it seems to be his view—that it is the court's actual *decision or claim that some relevant fact is proved* that is the

discussion, as I read it, seems to turn on the theoretical fruitfulness of admitting of a strand of 'substantive' formulations parallel to the 'procedural' one;[25] and I do not mean to deny that, for some carefully stated explanatory purpose, reference to the occurrence (rather than the proof) of the facts described in the relevant propositions may be an apt way of accounting, at a more basic level, for the function of the 'procedural' rules that instruct judges to decide on the grounds of what is proved and not proved. The objection presented in the previous paragraphs might then be avoided. It bites only against those variants of the dominant view which (like Bulygin's) maintain that it is also in terms of 'substantive' norms that we are to think about which judicial decisions are legally authorized, permitted, or required. My present claim, however, would remain intact. For my claim is not that it is not theoretically fruitful to posit a substantive representation of defeating circumstances. My claim is that no adequate substantive representation of defeating circumstances can be articulated at all. So even if we were to grant, for the sake of argument, that the supposed 'substantive' correlates of, for example, (11P) or (12P),

(11P) If it is *proved that P* and *proved that not-D*, then it is correct to decide for the plaintiff;

(12P) If it is *proved that P* and *proved that D*, then it is correct to decide for the defendant,

criterion of what *is* legally proved. There are rules about legal proof, admissible evidence, standards of proof, and so on, that judges are required to apply: rules that determine what facts count as legally proved in what contexts. And of course, judges (or fact-finders more generally) may fail to apply these rules correctly. They may declare that some fact is proved when according to the relevant rules it should *not* be considered proved, or vice versa. Any judgment they issue on such grounds will therefore be mistaken—*legally* mistaken. Such a judgment may still be legally valid. The judge who issues it may be exercising a valid power. These judgments will then hold unless and until they happen to be repealed. But the fact that a judgment is legally valid does not mean that it is legally correct; for a correct judgment—as I use the adjective in this book—is one that is *both* legally valid (that is, legally authorized) and legally permitted (whether or not it is also legally required). A judge who issues a judgment based on a mistaken assessment of what facts are legally proved will be validly exercising a power that she is nonetheless legally required not to exercise under such circumstances. So I agree with Bulygin (1995: 22) that the rule of criminal law does not simply stipulate the duty to punish 'those of whom the judge *says* they have committed murder'. What I disagree with is his claim that the rule of criminal law stipulates the duty to punish 'those who *have* committed murder'.

[25] See Silving (1947: 648–54).

would be, respectively, (11S) and (12S),

(11S) If *P* and *not-D*, then it is correct to decide for the plaintiff;
(12S) If *P* and *D*, then it is correct to decide for the defendant,

there is no adequate 'substantive' formulation with which to represent (13P) below. There is no formulation, that is, in which both *P* and *D* (or their respective negations) can figure as elements of the relevant norm-conditions:

(13P) If it is *proved that P* and *not proved that D*, then it is correct to decide for the plaintiff.
(13S) ?

Once again to stress the relevant point, given that *not proved that D* is compatible with *not proved that not-D*—a factual proposition and its negation can both be simultaneously not proved—neither *D* nor *not-D* could be indicated as the supposed fact whose occurrence would in some way, at the 'substantive' level, correspond to the 'procedural' situation in which it is *not* proved that *D*. A rule that makes the correctness of a given decision depend on the fact that a given proposition *X* is *not* proved cannot be grounded or justified simply by reference to the truth or falsehood of *X*.[26]

3.3.2 A Note on Evaluative Exceptions

What about evaluative exceptions—for example, the defence that a contract was made for *immoral* purposes, or that it *unreasonably* restrains the freedom of trade, to quote from Hart's own list[27]—whose application requires decision-makers to form views about normative rather than purely natural or empirical matters? It may seem dubious that circumstances so described can strictly speaking be the object of legal *proof*. So can the proof-based account accommodate them?

It can. The thought that motivates the proof-based account is that the difference between the fact that (for any element *X*) *not-X is ascertained* and the fact that *X is not ascertained* is the key to understanding the common distinction between defences (in the sense of exceptions, of *D*-facts) and negative elements. So the account can accommodate the possibility that in any given decision-making context the

[26] I discuss further aspects of the idea of a 'substantive' norm and its relation to the notion of a 'substantive' issue in Duarte d'Almeida (2014c) and (2015a).

[27] See Hart (1949: 176).

ascertainment of some relevant circumstance is not, or not solely, what we might strictly call a matter of 'proof'. Besides, the decision-maker's evaluative judgments will still be judgments made on the basis of the non-normative facts established by the available evidence, and in relation to these the distinction between what is and is not strictly proved will continue to apply. Take the fact that a contract was made for immoral purposes, and consider the difference between instructing courts to rule for the plaintiff (a) unless on the basis of the available evidence the court judges the contract to have been made for immoral purposes, or (b) only if on the basis of the available evidence the court judges the contract *not* to have been made for immoral purposes. In (a), the fact that the contract was made for immoral purposes is a *D*-fact. If evidence is adduced for whatever non-normative facts would support the judgment of immorality, the correct judgment to issue will be a judgment for the defendant. In (b), in turn, the fact that the contract's purpose was *not* immoral must be established if the judge is to correctly decide that the contract is valid. In (b), therefore, that fact is a (negative) *P*-fact.[28] So it makes no difference for the proof-based account that in examples like this, the term 'established' cannot be taken to be synonymous with 'proved'. The distinction between *P*- and *D*-facts is preserved irrespective of the presence of evaluative terms in the description of facts of either sort.

It should also be noted, more generally, that this is not a worry that the proof-based account needs to deal with in any detail. The sense in which I use the term 'fact' should raise no more suspicion than the sense in which in traditional, 'substantive' representations of conditional legal rules, the rule's antecedent may be said to contain a description of the relevant 'facts'. These facts—which according to the traditional view, too, are meant to constitute the object of proof—are not necessarily empirical or non-evaluative facts; indeed, they are exactly the

[28] Tur (2001a) seems to think that no 'value facts' can (or should?) figure as (what I call) *P*-facts; he insists that 'value terms' should figure only in 'unless'-clauses describing (what I call) *D*-facts. I cannot see why this should be so: Tur's claim seems descriptively false, and normatively implausible. By his own standards, in fact, given that he endorses the incorporationist view according to which 'unless'-clauses can always be restated in the form of negative conditions—see Tur (1993: 214) and Tur (2001a: 358)—any 'value fact' could accordingly be recast as a negative *P*-fact. Moreover, if a circumstance *X* counts as *D*-fact relative to a given judgment for the plaintiff, then *X* will normally count as a *P*-fact relative to the corresponding judgment for *the defendant*. This is not to deny that the use of 'evaluative' terms by legislators may be particularly apt in connection with exceptions: see Moreso (2001); Moreso (2004: 58–60); Moreso (2009: 63–6); and Moreso (2012: 234–6).

same facts the proof-based account deals with. Whatever difficulties may be involved in explaining the precise sense in which evaluative facts can be said to be 'ascertained' or 'proved', they are not difficulties that specifically affect the proof-based account of exceptions.

3.4 '*Probanda*' and '*Non-Refutanda*'

But perhaps I am jumping to conclusions. In a couple of well-known articles, Giovanni Sartor notes that traditional representations of legal norms cannot accommodate exceptions, and that this is due to a failure to appreciate that absence of exceptions does not have to be ascertained. But he still thinks that there is a way of representing legal norms that assigns the status of elements of norm-conditions both to what I have called *P*-facts and to defeating circumstances. He thinks, that is, that we can give a substantive representation of exceptions, in the sense in which I have been using the adjective.

Let me explain why Sartor's account does not quite work. I begin by summarizing his views.[29] The 'usually proposed' formalization of conditional legal norms can be rendered as

(14) E **if** A_1 **and** . . . **and** A_n,

in which 'E' stands for a given legal effect, the literals 'A_1', . . . 'A_n' stand for the elements of the norm's antecedent, and the conjunction 'A_1 **and** . . . **and** A_n' expresses a sufficient condition. There is a 'fundamental aspect' of conditional norms, Sartor says, that this formulation does not capture. Formulation (14) fails to distinguish between 'two ways in which a fact can occur in a norm condition', and, as a consequence, 'does not explicate the use of those norms in the derivation of legal conclusions'.[30] 'For the judges to declare a certain legal effect', argues Sartor, 'the ascertainment of all elements of a total legal condition producing the effect is not necessary'.[31] 'Some elements' are indeed 'elements to be proved' or ascertained. As for some others, however, it suffices that they are not refuted: it suffices that their complements are 'not ascertained'. Sartor calls elements of the former

[29] See Sartor (1991b); Sartor (1993), which is identical to Sartor (1995); and compare Gordon's earlier claims on rules and exceptions in Gordon (1987: 232), and Gordon (1988: 118–19). Gordon's views are restated in Gordon (1995).

[30] Sartor (1991b: 155); Sartor (1993: 282–3).

[31] Sartor (1991b: 155); Sartor (1993: 283).

kind '*probanda*', and elements of the latter kind '*non-refutanda*'.[32] His point is that the difference between these two 'categories' of elements must be made explicit in the representation of conditional norms. He uses the symbols '⟨' and '⟩' to bracket *non-refutanda*, and offers the following as his rendition of the structure of conditional norms:

(15) E **if** A_1 **and** . . . **and** A_i **and** $\langle A_j \rangle$ **and** . . . **and** $\langle A_n \rangle$.

Here 'the A_1, . . . A_i are *probanda* (elements to be ascertained, for the legal condition to be satisfied) and the $\langle A_j \rangle$, . . . $\langle A_n \rangle$ are *non-refutanda* (elements not to be refuted, for the legal condition to be satisfied)'.[33]

This 'partition of the elements of the antecedent into the two categories' is meant to track 'the role of each element in the derivation—or rather, in the justification—of the effect of the norm':

> [T]he derivation of a legal effect can be considered justified, in a certain justification context, if the effect is the consequent of a norm (accepted in that context) whose antecedent is satisfied. And a norm condition must be considered satisfied if every *probandum* contained in that norm antecedent has been derived [eg by means of 'empirical evidence'] in the accepted justification context, and no *non-refutandum* included in that antecedent has been refuted.[34]

The claim, then, is that the distinction between *probanda* and *non-refutanda* is necessary for the proper representation of exceptions. Sartor illustrates this with two provisions of Italian civil law, related to one another as rule and exception, which he formalizes as follows:

(16) $\mathbf{r}_1$: x is liable for the damage d derived from the fact f **if**
x has accomplished f by fault **and**
f has caused the unjust damage d.

$\mathbf{e}_1$: x is **not** liable for the damage d derived from the fact f **if**
x has accomplished f in self-defence.[35]

[32] This is the terminology used in Sartor (1993); in Sartor (1991b: 155, 157), the former are called 'principal facts', and the latter 'secondary facts'.

[33] Sartor (1993: 283).

[34] Sartor (1993: 284).

[35] Sartor (1993: 294).

The usual treatment of exceptions seeks to avoid the potential contradiction between $\mathbf{r}_1$ and $\mathbf{e}_1$ by incorporating the complement of the exception-fact[36]—which complement is the fact that *f* was *not* accomplished in self-defence—as a condition of the rule to which the exception-fact constitutes an exception, as in (17R):

(17R) *x* is liable for the damage *d* derived from the fact *f* **if**
x has accomplished *f* by fault **and**
f has caused the unjust damage *d* **and**
x has **not** accomplished *f* in self-defence;

(17E) *x* is **not** liable for the damage *d* derived from the fact *f* **if**
x has accomplished *f* in self-defence.[37]

But what a satisfactory representation really requires, says Sartor, is that the complement of the exception-fact be incorporated in the antecedent of the rule *and* classified as a *non-refutandum*, as in (18R):

(18R) *x* is liable for the damage *d* derived from the fact *f* **if**
x has accomplished *f* by fault **and**
f has caused the unjust damage *d* **and**
⟨*x* has **not** accomplished *f* in self-defence⟩;

(18E) *x* is **not** liable for the damage *d* derived from the fact *f* **if**
x has accomplished *f* in self-defence.[38]

Why does this matter? What makes the usual approach in (17R) inadequate and 'fundamentally erroneous', Sartor (1993: 295–6) says, is that it 'allow[s the] conclusion to be derived only when the premises set contains the assertion that the fact has not been accomplished in self-defence'. His representation in (18R), in turn, allows 'liability to be derived even when there is no information about the existence (or the inexistence) of a situation of self-defence'.[39] For an example, suppose that 'during a quarrel with her husband' Mary has thrown against him 'a valuable piece of pottery'.[40] Sartor represents this as the conjunction of two facts:

[36] An *exception-fact* is defined as the condition of an *exception-provision*: see Sartor (1993: 293). In this example, the exception-fact is the fact that *f* has been accomplished in self-defence.

[37] See Sartor (1993: 295–6).

[38] See Sartor (1993: 294–5, 300).

[39] Sartor (1993: 296).

[40] Sartor (1993: 294).

f_1: *Mary* has accomplished *DishThrow* by fault;
f_2: *DishThrow* has caused the unjust damage *DishBreak*.

If we represent our rule as in (17R), then 'nothing is derivable' (as Sartor puts it) from the combination of that rule and these two facts. The reason nothing is derivable is that 'we have no information' about the rule-condition that requires that '*x* has **not** accomplished *f* in self-defence'. By contrast, Sartor's proposed representation—(18R)—allows, he says, the correct outcome. If we combine (18R) with f_1 and f_2, 'we can derive that Mary is liable'.[41] So there is, Sartor (1993: 294) says, 'a strict connection between the norms whose condition contains *non-refutanda* and the combinations of rules and exceptions': '[e]ach combination of rules and exceptions can be translated into an equivalent set of norms containing *non-refutanda*, and *vice versa*'.

This is Sartor's proposal in a nutshell. Is it right? I do not think it is. It does not give us, I will now argue, an adequate representation of exceptions, and is mistaken or confused in more than one respect.

For convenience, let me translate what Sartor presents as the 'usual' representation of exceptions, the one in (17), as well as his own, in (18), into the following formulations:

Usual representation

(U1) If *P* and *not-D*, then *E*;
(U2) If *D*, then *not-E*.

Sartor's representation

(S1) If *P* and ⟨*not-D*⟩, then *E*;
(S2) If *D*, then *not-E*.

We have just seen that Sartor's grounds for rejecting *Usual representation* is the fact that it allows effect *E* to be derived 'only when' our factual premises include the assertion that *not-D*.[42] And from (U2) it does follow that (U3),

(U3) If *E*, then *not-D*,

[41] Sartor (1993: 296–7).
[42] Sartor (1993: 296).

which is exactly what Sartor means to oppose. Yet does the very same not follow from (S2) as well? It would seem that it does.[43] Sartor, however, would presumably want to allow only (S3):

(S3) If *E*, then ⟨*not-D*⟩.

And if we ask ourselves how to restate (S3) in fully informal terms, an important ambiguity emerges concerning Sartor's very notions of a *probandum* and a *non-refutandum*.

Before I expand on this point, recall that Sartor's concern is with how norms are used 'in the derivation of legal conclusions'. How does one 'derive' a legal conclusion? By applying the respective legal norm, Sartor (1993: 283) says, to the facts of the case. The derivation of a legal conclusion, that is, articulates two kinds of premises: a set of rules (or, more precisely, of statements of rules), and a matching set of facts (or statements of facts) satisfying the rule or rules' conditions. With this in mind, then, let us take Sartor's (S1) rule, and ask ourselves what the facts of the case must be in order to derive conclusion *E*.

One possible answer would be that the facts of the case are *P* and *not-D*. For the facts of the case are (one might plausibly reason) the facts with which some legal consequence is associated in a legal norm; and the facts described in the antecedent of (S1) are *P* and *not-D*. That one of these is deemed a *probandum* and the other a *non-refutandum* does not affect their common status as factual elements with which the effect is associated. But that would mean that for the derivation of *E* to be justified, both *P* and *not-D* would have to be incorporated as premises in the judge's reasoning. And this cannot be right. By Sartor's own lights,[44] *not-D* can only be introduced as a premise if *it is ascertained that not-D*—and that is precisely what is *not* needed if *D* is an exception. (That *D* is an exception, in turn, is what Sartor means to signal by bracketing and marking its complement, *not-D*, as a *non-refutandum*: '⟨*not-D*⟩'.) It is only *P* that must be ascertained.

So it seems that we should instead say that *P* exhausts the set of the relevant facts of the case, and thus that for the effect *E* in (S1) to be

[43] At least given Sartor's explicit treatment of what he calls 'perfect conditional norms' as connecting legal effects to sufficient conditions: see Sartor (1993: 282). (In the formal non-monotonic model of legal reasoning presented in the 'Appendix' to Sartor (1993), in turn, legal norms are represented as inference rules: see Sartor (1993: 308, 309 n 20). But what motivates this interpretation is the supposed need to accommodate non-monotonicity by allowing that it can be simultaneously the case that *E* if *P*, that *P*, and yet that not *E*.)

[44] See Sartor (1993: 304, 307); and Sartor (1991b: 156).

derived, a single factual premise is required—a premise affirming *P*. This is indeed the approach Sartor takes. In the example of Mary, remember, Sartor says that we can derive the conclusion that *Mary is liable* from the combination of the (18R) rule and facts $\mathbf{f}_1$ and $\mathbf{f}_2$.[45] The corresponding result for (S1) would therefore be that *E*, the effect, could be derived from the single factual premise affirming *P*. But this, too, cannot be right. The following derivation does not seem valid:

(19) (S1) If *P* and ⟨*not-D*⟩, then *E*
P
∴ *E*

Or, to put things differently: if, in order to derive *E* from (S1), *P* were the single required factual premise, ⟨*not-D*⟩ would be rendered superfluous or argumentatively inert. But that seems odd, given not only that ⟨*not-D*⟩ is represented as an element in the antecedent of (S1),[46] but also that ⟨*not-D*⟩ appears in Sartor's account to be a necessary condition of *E*. In other words, ⟨*not-D*⟩ would be a necessary condition of *E* which would not have to be satisfied in order for *E* to be derived. Clearly, something is wrong.[47]

The root of the problem lies, as I hinted, in an ambiguity concerning Sartor's distinction between *probanda* and *non-refutanda*. This pair of terms can be seen to mark not one, but two different contrasts, both of which appear to be simultaneously and indistinctly at play in Sartor's account of exceptions.

Probanda are sometimes defined as those elements—positive or negative, it makes no difference[48]—that 'must be ascertained . . . for *the conditioned effect to be derived*': as elements, that is, whose ascertainment is *necessary* for *E* to be derived. A matching definition is offered of *non-refutanda* as those elements that 'must not be refuted for the conditioned effect to be derived'; that is, as elements whose

[45] See the text accompanying n 41.

[46] See also Sartor (1993: 300): '*probanda* . . . *i.e.* . . . the facts whose ascertainment compels us to derive the effect *under the condition* that the complement of no *non-refutandum* included in the same total antecedent is ascertained' (emphasis added).

[47] Another way of putting this: given that the conjunction (*P* and ⟨*not-D*⟩) occurs in (S1) as a sufficient condition of *E*, then, according to Sartor's own account, *that* condition must itself be a *probandum* or a *non-refutandum*. The fact that the condition is not bracketed suggests that we would need to take *it* as a *probandum*. But surely the ascertainment of (*P* and ⟨*not-D*⟩) must require something more than the ascertainment of *P*.

[48] Sartor (1993: 291–2).

non-refutation is *necessary* for E to be derived.[49] Call this his 'first' definition.

On other occasions, however, Sartor says something quite different. He defines *probanda* as the elements whose ascertainment is necessary for 'the satisfaction of the legal condition', and likewise refers to *non-refutanda* as elements 'not to be refuted, for the legal condition to be satisfied'.[50] Call this his 'second' definition.

While the meaning of this second definition is not entirely clear, the two definitions are not equivalent; and Sartor seems more often than not to favour the second over the first. To see this, consider (S1) again:

(S1) If P and ⟨*not-D*⟩, then E.

Here, says Sartor, P occurs as a *probandum*, and *not-D* (as the brackets around it are meant to indicate) as a *non-refutandum*. But (S1) neither states nor implies that in order for E to be derived it is necessary that P be ascertained, nor that it is necessary that *not-D* not be refuted. What (S1) indicates is that the conjunction (P and ⟨*not-D*⟩) is a sufficient condition of E, not a necessary one. So when Sartor says that in (S1), P and *not-D* occur respectively as *probandum* and *non-refutandum*, he cannot be using the terms in the sense of what I called his 'first' definition. He seems instead to be alluding to a difference in structure between both kinds of elements. But how, precisely, are we to understand the contrast here? Or consider (S3)—the formulation that, as we have seen, actually differentiates Sartor's view from the traditional one:

(S3) If E, then ⟨*not-D*⟩.

Here *not-D* seems to occur as a *non-refutandum* in both senses at the same time. On the one hand, it occurs bracketed as ⟨*not-D*⟩, and so it counts as a *non-refutandum* in the second sense—the same sense in which it counts as a *non-refutandum* in (S2). On the other hand, it also occurs as a necessary condition of E. What are we to make of this?

What Sartor seems to wish to point out with (S1) is, I suppose, that in order for E to be derived it is *sufficient* that P *be proved* and *not-D be not refuted*. If this is what he means, I certainly agree. But then, clearly, this idea cannot be accommodated by his proposed representation. For

[49] Sartor (1993: 298).

[50] Sartor (1991b: 155); Sartor (1993: 283).

in this case the bracketed '⟨*not-D*⟩' would be translatable as '*not refuted that not-D*', and '*P*' as '*P is proved*', yielding the statement in (L1):

(L1) If *P is proved* and it is *not refuted that not-D*, then *E*.

Given that to 'refute' a circumstance *X* means to *prove not-X*, (L1) is the same as

(L1b) If *P is proved* and it is *not proved that not-not-D*, then *E*,

and thus the same as

(L1c) If *P is proved* and it is *not proved that D*, then *E*,

which is in turn materially identical to the formulation above introduced, in section 3.2, as (8), and signifies that the elements of the norm's condition are not—*pace* Sartor—the facts that *P* and *not-D*, but rather the facts that *P is proved* and *not-D is not refuted*.

Likewise, what (S3) apparently intends to capture is that it is *necessary* that *not-D* is not refuted for the consequence to be derived. But in this case what we get is (L2):

(L2) *E* only if it is *not refuted that not-D*,

which again suggests that '⟨*not-D*⟩' is to be translated as '*not refuted that not-D*'. So again, I agree that (L2) is formulated along the right lines. It is the same as

(L2b) *E* only if it is *not proved that not-not-D*,

and thus the same as

(L2c) *E* only if it is *not proved that D*,

which is materially identical to the formulation above introduced, in section 3.2., as (3). But this shows that, contrary to Sartor's claims, the necessary condition is not that *not-D*, but that it is *not refuted that not-D*.

We can now see just why the second of the senses in which Sartor employs the '*probandum*'/'*non-refutandum*' pair seems puzzling. It is doing no relevant work. For in (L1) the combination of the facts that *P is proved* and that it is *not refuted that not-D* is a sufficient condition of *E*—making it somewhat redundant to say that for *that* condition to be satisfied it is 'necessary' that *P* be ascertained, and misleading to employ the Latin gerundive at all.

The ambiguity in Sartor's use of the '*probanda*'/'*non-refutanda*' contrast can now be brought out more clearly by noting that:

(a) on this 'second' reading just mentioned, a fact *X* is a *probandum* when *proved that X* is (an element of) a condition of a legal consequence *E*, and a *non-refutandum* when *not refuted that X* is (an element of) a condition of a legal consequence *E*; while
(b) on the reading corresponding to what I called the 'first' definition, a fact *X* is a *probandum* when *proved that X* is a necessary condition of a legal consequence *E*, and a *non-refutandum* when *not refuted that X* is a necessary condition of a legal consequence *E*.

To sum up this section, I could agree—at this stage in our discussion: we shall have to refine these claims—that, provided that we restrict our attention to examples in which no further levels of exceptions are admitted, the complements of defeating circumstances are *non-refutanda* in sense (b) and not merely in sense (a). If a fact *X* is an exception relative to a given decision or judgment *Y*, then the fact that it is *not refuted that not-X*—or, which is the same, the fact that it is *not proved that X*—is a necessary condition for *Y* to be correctly issued. In other words, the fact that *X is proved* is sufficient for *Y not* to be correctly issued. My point, though, is that neither '*probanda*' nor '*non-refutanda*' can function as terms designating conditions (or elements of conditions) in norm-antecedents. These terms do designate facts—factual circumstances—but those facts are not the relevant elements or conditions. The relevant elements or conditions are instead the facts that *it is proved that P* and that it is *not proved that D*. And *these* facts are neither *probanda* nor *non-refutanda*. They are just plain facts, the occurrence of both of which will satisfy the antecedent.[51]

3.5 First Conclusions

Sartor's mistake, we can now see, is the same as Hart's. Both understood that it is *not the case* that both *P* and *not-D* have to be 'present'—have to be ascertained—for a defeasible judgment to be correctly

[51] See also Bayón (2001: 332–3). There is in Sartor's papers yet another source of equivocation concerning the notions of a *probandum* and a *non-refutandum*. Sartor sometimes refers to *non-refutanda* as elements whose non-refutation is *sufficient* for the 'satisfaction of the legal condition': see Sartor (1993: 283). We are now able to understand this as an attempt to

issued. So both correctly rejected the traditional view of exceptions, as expressed in our formulation (A):

(A) It is correct to decide for the plaintiff if and only if (*P* and *not-D*).

But both seem to have confused the notion of a circumstance that *has to be present* or ascertained with the notion of a necessary condition, and the notion of *all* the circumstances that have to be ascertained with the notion of a sufficient condition. Both are thus committed, however unwillingly, to the misguided idea that a substantive representation of exceptions can be provided. Both affirm (or are unable to deny) that the absence of defeating circumstances is to be understood as a necessary condition of a correctly issued defeasible judgment. I have argued that this is wrong—and thus that the *irreducibility thesis*, (T3'), is indeed correct:

(T3') Exceptions are not reducible to necessary conditions of defeasible decisions.

But (T1'), Hart's thesis that

(T1') The circumstances on which the correctness of a defeasible decision depends cannot be specified by a set of necessary and sufficient conditions,

was at the same time shown to be false. For as we saw in section 3.2, we could give the following as a statement of the relevant necessary and sufficient conditions:

(9) It is correct to decide for the plaintiff if and only if (*P is proved* and it is *not proved that D*).

In fact, (T3') is correct in *both* those senses of the phrase 'necessary conditions' that we have been able to discern. What the foregoing discussion shows is not only that *D*-facts are never aptly represented as conditions, positive or negative, of judicial decisions. That is really not a specific point about *D*-facts: it is equally true of *P*-facts. What our discussion also shows is that in the context of judicial decision-making, *D*-facts behave very differently from *P*-facts. They behave very differently, that is, from those facts that, because their presence can

express the idea that, all else being equal, a norm-antecedent including *not refuted that not-X* as an element, is logically 'weaker' (and thus, in a sense, *less* demanding or encompassing) than a norm-antecedent including *proved that not-X* instead.

be said to be *required*, Hart mistook for necessary conditions. And it is in *this* sense of the phrase 'necessary conditions' that (T3') emerges as a distinct and significant thesis about exceptions—the thesis that *D*-facts cannot be explained in terms of *P*-facts. So we can finally dispel this ambiguity by restating our *irreducibility thesis* in more fully explicit terms:

(T3") *D*-facts are not reducible to *P*-facts.

The confusion just mentioned is also what underlies the widespread approach—discussed in section 3.3—which mistakes the object of judicial proof for the factual premises of judicial reasoning, and from which the hypothesis inevitably arises that legal reasoning is non-monotonic. To see this, consider a case in which it is both *proved that P* and *not proved that* any defeating circumstance *D* occurred. Given that here the correct judgment to issue is a judgment for the plaintiff, those theorists willing to equate the set of acceptable factual premises with the set of proved propositions will be led to think that such a judgment is associated solely with the verification that *P*. So *P* will appear to be a sufficient condition:

(20) If *P*, then it is correct to decide for the plaintiff.

But if at some further moment in the procedure it happens to be the case that an exception *D* is *proved*, the indisputable result is that the plaintiff should *not* succeed, which will be represented as

(21) If *P* and *D*, then it is *not* correct to decide for the plaintiff.

This cannot but yield the non-monotonicity thesis, since the consequent in (21) is the negation of the consequent in (20), and $\{P, D\}$, the corresponding set of premises in (21), is a superset of $\{P\}$, the set of premises in (20).[52]

Sartor, too, is naturally led to this result. He says, as we have seen, that from (18R) together with facts $\mathbf{f}_1$ and $\mathbf{f}_2$—that is, from the set of premises $\{(18R), \mathbf{f}_1, \mathbf{f}_2\}$—'we can derive that Mary is liable'.[53] 'Nevertheless', he says, 'if the further premise' is added that

[52] Hence the conditional in (20) will no longer be interpretable as specifying a *sufficient* condition. Rather, *P* will be said in some sense to *support*, or to be 'in the absence of other claims' a good *reason* for—but not to 'imply'—the consequent: see Hart (1949: 183, 186, 188–90); it is passages like these that give some credence to the claim that Hart was arguing in his paper in favour of a non-monotonic account of judicial reasoning.

[53] See the text following n 40.

$\mathbf{f}_3$**:** *Mary* has accomplished *DishThrow* in self-defence,

with the result that our set of premises is now {(18R), $\mathbf{f}_1$, $\mathbf{f}_2$, $\mathbf{f}_3$}, then 'the conclusion that Mary is liable is no longer derivable since the complement of the *non-refutandum* . . . results ascertained by fact $\mathbf{f}_3$, and therefore the condition of the norm is no longer satisfied'.[54] Sartor thus holds the view that

> [i]n the case of norms whose antecedent contains *non-refutanda*, non-monotonicity occurs whenever we pass from a premises set satisfying all *probanda*, and not disproving any *non-refutandum*, to a larger premises set in which a *non-refutandum* is disproved.[55]

We already know why this is wrong. The ascertainment of $\mathbf{f}_1$ and $\mathbf{f}_2$ is insufficient to satisfy the applicable rule if the *non-ascertainment* of $\mathbf{f}_3$ is also made a condition of the legal effect in (18R). The relevant set of premises would have to be rendered as {(18R), $\mathbf{f}_1$, $\mathbf{f}_2$, $\langle \mathbf{f}_3 \rangle$}, with the consequence that the ascertainment of $\mathbf{f}_3$ would not be aptly characterized in terms of the addition of 'further' premises or information: {(18R), $\mathbf{f}_1$, $\mathbf{f}_2$, $\mathbf{f}_3$} is simply not a superset of {(18R), $\mathbf{f}_1$, $\mathbf{f}_2$, $\langle \mathbf{f}_3 \rangle$}. There is nothing puzzling about the fact that different legal consequences happen to be attached to any two given sets of premises such that neither is a superset of the other. Nor does any need arise for a non-monotonic account of the corresponding reasoning from the premises to the conclusion. Of course, {$\mathbf{f}_1$, $\mathbf{f}_2$, $\langle \mathbf{f}_3 \rangle$}, which Sartor's account seems to require, makes little sense as a representation of any set of factual premises. Sartor is prevented from adequately accounting for the justification structure of 'defeasible' decisions by his insistence on representing as elements of norm-conditions the circumstances he calls *probanda* and *non-refutanda*. (This insistence reflects his endorsement of the common notion that judicial decisions 'must be justified . . . only on the basis of knowledge collected in the proceeding', and that the set of 'premises' that 'can legitimately be used to ground' a judicial conclusion includes only, besides 'the legal norms applicable to the case', the '*ascertained* facts'.[56]) The proper rendering of the relevant sets of

[54] Sartor (1993: 297).

[55] Sartor (1993: 296). See also Sartor (1991b: 159–60); and compare Sartor (1991a: 96); Sartor (1994: 189–90); Prakken and Sartor (2004: 123); or Sartor (2008: 31–2).

[56] Sartor (1993: 304, 307).

factual premises in this case would rather be {*proved that* $\mathbf{f}_1$, *proved that* $\mathbf{f}_2$, *not proved that* $\mathbf{f}_3$} and {*proved that* $\mathbf{f}_1$, *proved that* $\mathbf{f}_2$, *proved that* $\mathbf{f}_3$}; and the reconstruction of the relevant rules would have to display *these* facts—not the facts ascertained or not ascertained, but rather the facts *about* what has and has not been ascertained—as elements of norm-conditions:

(22) **If** it is *proved that x* has accomplished fact *f* by fault **and** it is *proved that f* has caused the unjust damage *d* **and** it is *not proved that x* has accomplished *f* in self-defence [= it is *not refuted that x* has *not* accomplished *f* in self-defence], **then** the judge will correctly hold *x* liable for the damage *d* derived from *f*;

(23) **If** it is *proved that x* has accomplished fact *f* by fault **and** it is *proved that f* has caused the unjust damage *d* **and** it is *proved that x* has accomplished *f* in self-defence, **then** the judge will *not* correctly hold *x* liable for the damage *d* derived from *f*.

In short, my proposal so far might be articulated as follows. A fact *X* is an exception relative to a decision or judgment *J* if (a) the fact that *X* is ascertained is sufficient to prevent *J* from being correct, and (b) the ascertainment of *not-X* is not necessary for *J* to be correct. Or, in slightly more precise terms: *P*-facts are facts whose ascertainment is necessary for a given judgment *J* to count as correctly issued; *D*-facts are facts whose ascertainment is both (a) sufficient to prevent *J* from counting as correctly made; and (b) not inconsistent with any *P*-fact.[57]

But there is still some fine-tuning to do.

3.6 Refinements

As I noted in passing at several points, our discussion so far has focused on simplified scenarios in which no second-level exceptions—no

[57] This (b)-clause is a provisional qualification, which will become unnecessary when we have looked more closely, in Chapter 4, into the meaning of 'proved'. The clause is meant to signal not only that the negation of a *D*-fact is not *itself* a *P*-fact, but also that no fact *M* (eg a criminal defendant's mistake of fact) is properly classified as a *D*-fact if *M* is such that even though the specific ascertainment of *not-M* is not, as such, required for *Y*, the ascertainment of *M* is nonetheless incompatible with some *P*-fact (eg the *P*-fact that the defendant acted intentionally).

exceptions *to* exceptions—are admitted. This restriction allowed me to present the proof-based account with as few distractions as possible. Nor was this my only simplifying assumption: in the examples we have considered I have assumed not only that no second-level exceptions are admitted, but also that for any defeasible decision or judgment *J*, only *one* set of relevant *P*-facts can be identified. Of course, neither assumption matches what is most often the case in our legal systems. Many levels of exceptions (possibly, in fact, infinite levels) are ordinarily allowed: and it may be that several, alternative sets of *P*-facts—together with their corresponding and possibly distinct sets of exceptions—are associated with the same decision-type.

Why do I now mention this? Because these two assumptions lie behind my rounding-up claims, made at the end of the previous section, that *P*-facts are facts, proof of which is *necessary* for a given decision to be correctly made, and that *D*-facts are facts, proof of which is *sufficient* for a given decision *not* to be correctly made. These claims are rhetorically vivid, I think, and in the end they carry the main message across. But in fact they overstate the relevant point. They are not strictly true of the more complex scenarios in which those two simplifying assumptions happen not to hold. At this stage, however, the picture can be safely complicated, and my claims restated, in order to show that (and how) the proof-based account accommodates less simple hypotheses.

Let us begin with *P*-facts. I will say—before offering some clarifying examples—that a given set of factual propositions (P_1, P_2, . . . P_n) is a '*P*-set' relative to a given decision-type *J* if and only if there is a sufficient condition—call it '*S*'—of it being correct to issue any token decision *K* of that type, such that it is simultaneously the case that:

(a) *that* (P_1 and P_2 and . . . and P_n) *is proved* is an element of *S*;
(b) there is no other fact (that is, no fact other than P_1 and P_2 and . . . and P_n) whose proof is an element of *S*; and
(c) *S* is not superfluous (that is, there is no sufficient condition S_2 of it being correct to issue decision *K*, such that S_2 is satisfied whenever *S* is satisfied, but not vice versa).

The notion of a *P*-set is thus relative to some given decision-type *J* and to some given sufficient condition *S* of it being correct to issue decisions of that type. I will now also define a *P*-fact as any fact that is a member of a *P*-set.

For some examples, assume that in our legal system the fact that *someone intentionally killed someone else* is such that when that fact is proved and no exceptions are proved, courts are required to convict and sentence the killer to 15 years in prison. Assume, additionally, that the only admissible exception in murder is self-defence. Relative to our legal system, then, the following two statements are true:

(1) If it is *proved that* A intentionally killed B and it is *not proved that* the killing was done in self-defence, then the court is required to convict and sentence A to 15 years in prison.
(2) If it is *proved that* A intentionally killed B and the sky is blue and it is *not proved that* the killing was done in self-defence, then the court is required to convict and sentence A to 15 years in prison.

The point is that if (1) is true, then (2)—whose antecedent includes the antecedent in (1)—is also true. Though the condition in (2) *is* a sufficient condition, it is a superfluous condition—it is a *more than sufficient* condition. Now clearly we do not want to say that the fact that the sky is blue is a *P*-fact in murder, and we want our definition of a '*P*-fact' to reflect this. The third clause in the proposed characterization above, clause (c), is designed to play that role. So the set {A intentionally killed B, the sky is blue}, which—though it passes the tests in (a) and (b)—does not pass the test in (c), is not a *P*-set relative to the decision to convict and sentence someone to 15 years in prison. (And neither, for another example, is the set {A intentionally killed B, the killing was *not* done in self-defence}.) The set {A intentionally killed B}, in turn, *is* a *P*-set (and the fact that A intentionally killed B is a *P*-fact) relative to the decision to convict and sentence someone to 15 years in prison.

This characterization does a better job of capturing the relevant notion, and is (as it should be) compatible with there being several *P*-sets relative to the same decision-type *J*. For there may be several alternative non-superfluous sufficient conditions of correct decisions of that type, and relative to each of them it may be possible to identify a particular *P*-set. (Hence it is only when there is just one *P*-set relative to *J*—and when there is no other sufficient condition—that it will be strictly true that the proof of *P* is *necessary* for a decision of type *J* to be correct.[58])

[58] Otherwise, all that can be said is, redundantly, that the proof of *P* is necessary for the satisfaction of the non-superfluous sufficient condition *S*, of which 'proved that *P*' is an element; recall the discussion that preceded n 51.

One possibility is that in the same system relative to which (1) above is true, it is also true, let us say, that

(3) If it is *proved that* A intentionally damaged B's property and it is *not proved that* the damage was necessary to avoid a greater damage, then the court is required to convict and sentence A to 15 years in prison.

The relevant decision in (3) has the same content as that in (1). Relative to such decision, then, both {A intentionally killed B} and {A intentionally damaged B's property} can be counted as *P*-sets. And even when no such completely unrelated groups of cases exist, it may be that two or more partially coincident *P*-sets can be identified relative to the same decision—as will instantly be made clearer—whenever more than one level of exceptions is allowed.[59]

Given this characterization of *P*-facts, exceptions can now be defined by saying that a fact *D* is an exception, relative, simultaneously, to (i) a given decision-type *J*, (ii) some given *P*-set *P* of *J*, and thus also to (iii) a non-superfluous sufficient condition *S* of a correct type-*J* decision, which condition has the fact that *the facts in P are proved* as an element, if and only (a) *that D is proved* prevents the satisfaction of *S*, and (b) *D* is not inconsistent with the facts in *P*.[60]

So if *D* is an exception relative to some decision of type *J* and some *P*-set of *J*, then *that not-D is proved* is not a necessary condition of a correctly made decision of that type. But it is not necessarily the case that *that it is not proved that D* is a necessary condition of such a decision. It does not have to be the case, in other words, that *that D is proved* is sufficient for the decision *not* to be correct. For there may

[59] Think again of our murder example, and suppose now that the fact that *the killer intentionally provoked the victim's attack in order to be able to claim self-defence* is a (second-level) exception *to* the (first-level) exception of self-defence. Then the following will be a true statement identifying a non-superfluous condition: 'If it is *proved that* A intentionally killed B and it is *proved that* A intentionally provoked an attack by B in order to be able to claim self-defence, the court is required to convict and sentence A to 15 years in prison.' Hence both {A intentionally killed B} and {A intentionally killed B; A intentionally provoked an attack by B in order then to be able to claim self-defence} will be, relative to the decision to convict and sentence a killer to 15 years, *P*-sets.

[60] *D* is inconsistent with the facts in *P* when it is the case either that *not-D* is an element of *P* (and therefore part of what has to be proved for *S* to be satisfied), or that *D* is such that (even though the specific ascertainment of *not-D* is not an element of *P*) the ascertainment of *D* is nonetheless incompatible with some fact in *P*. This again is a provisional qualification that will no longer be required once the meaning of 'proved' has been further clarified, as it will be in Chapter 4.

well be other sufficient conditions compatible with the fact that *D* is proved—which is the case, as I said, when exceptions *to* exceptions are allowed.

Summing up, we may now—in plainer terms—say the following. Those facts whose ascertainment features as an element of some non-superfluous sufficient condition *S* of a correctly issued decision *J*, are, relative to both *J* and *S*, '*P*-facts'. '*D*-facts'—exceptions—are facts whose ascertainment (a) prevents the satisfaction of *S*; and (b) is not inconsistent with any *P*-fact. And so we also finally come to see that our *irreducibility thesis* (T3")—restated in section 3.5 as the thesis that *D*-facts are not reducible to *P*-facts—does not really depend on *P*-facts counting as 'necessary conditions' in *any* sense of the expression. The irreducibility thesis holds whether or not, for any given defeasible decision *J*, only one *P*-set can be identified.

This chapter was concerned only with so-called 'explicit' exceptions. (The proof-based account can also satisfactorily explain 'implicit' exceptions, but that is an issue to be addressed in Chapters 5 and 6.) Explicit exceptions, we saw, are facts (like self-defence in murder) that can be identified *as* exceptions—as *D*-facts—as a matter of general law, independently and in advance of any particular case. A closed list of explicit exceptions can therefore always be provided. But this does not mean that in scenarios in which only explicit exceptions are admitted, the number of exception-*levels* is necessarily finite. That is because there can be exceptions capable of applying an unlimited number of times. Think, for example, of an exception described along the lines of 'a subsequent agreement is made by the parties to the effect that the previous agreement is no longer binding'.[61] A 'substantive' representation of exceptions—like the one decried in section 3.3—would be unable, it seems, to accommodate this phenomenon. Given that in substantive representations, the occurrence or non-occurrence of *each and every* one of the admissible lower-level exceptions would have to be incorporated (as an element) in *each* norm-antecedent, it would be impossible to formulate sufficient conditions of correct decisions in scenarios with an infinite number of exception-levels. This counter-intuitive result is avoided by the proof-based account, which deals satisfactorily with such hypotheses. Even in a system that allows for an infinite number of exception-levels, the proof-based account makes it possible to formulate sufficient conditions by 'stopping', as it were, at any arbitrarily chosen level.

[61] I owe this point to Pedro Múrias.

But now there is another issue to consider. Does the proof-based account always match the way in which legal exceptions operate? Is the account not potentially falsified by the way in which the probative burdens relative to defeating circumstances may happen to be allocated in any given jurisdiction? This question—or rather the set of objections that it may be taken to encapsulate—is the object of Chapter 4.

4

Exceptions and the Burden of Proof

4.1 Three Objections

The proof-based account faces a set of possible objections based on what many see as a distinctive feature of exceptions: their connection to the allocation of burdens of proof in legal proceedings. An objector might grant that in a case of contract—one of my working examples—the plaintiff bears at first only the burden of proving what I have been calling '*P*-facts': offer, acceptance, consideration, and so on, as well as any other facts that ground the plaintiff's specific request. It is then up to the defendant to raise any exception. And if the defendant fails to discharge this burden, prompting an unfavourable decision, then it can be said that *P* is all that needs to be proved for the plaintiff to succeed. So my objector could agree that the formulation I introduced in Chapter 3 as (13P) adequately captures this scenario:

(13P) If it is *proved that* *P* and *not proved that* *D*, then it is correct to decide for the plaintiff.

But there are three related reasons, my objector might say, why I must be wrong in suggesting that a formulation like (13P) is always an apt rendition of the sufficient conditions of defeasible decisions, and thus that it is never the case that the *absence* of exceptions—*D*-facts—must be proved.

First, I seem to be disregarding that if the defendant succeeds in bringing an exception into issue, it then becomes the plaintiff's (or, in a criminal case, the prosecutor's) job to *disprove* the exception.[1] Here (13P) seems no longer to apply. So my claim that it is *always* the case that *P* is all that needs to be proved for a plaintiff or prosecutor to succeed is mistaken.[2]

Second, I also appear to ignore that the defendant's 'burden' relative to exceptions—a burden that comes into play if the relevant *P*-facts have been proved—is usually quite different from the burden carried by plaintiffs or prosecutors relative to *P*-facts. The defendant's burden in a criminal case, for example, is normally not a burden of proof. It is a mere evidential burden. To discharge it, it is sufficient that the occurrence of any one of the available exceptions be made a 'live issue' in the procedure.[3] So it is incorrect to hold—as I do: it follows from (13P)—that when *P* is proved, the plaintiff (or prosecutor) will fail only if some exception *D* is actually proved.

Finally, am I not forgetting that however common it might be for the law to burden defendants with the proof of exceptions in some contexts, this is by no means a necessary arrangement? Isn't it possible for the law to instruct judges to decide for the defendant unless *not-D* is proved, thereby making it the plaintiff's or the prosecutor's burden to prove *not-D* from the very beginning? Is this point not abundantly illustrated in English criminal law by the fact that statutory 'reverse onus' clauses—clauses placing on defendants the burden of proving defences—are regarded as *exceptions* to the common law principle, stated in *Woolmington*,[4] that 'it is the duty of the prosecution to prove the prisoner's guilt'?[5] Does this not show that, as a rule at least, the defendant in a criminal case carries no burden of proof in respect of defences?[6] So there is nothing about exceptions that mandates, in and of itself, any particular distribution of the burden of proof. The allocation of burdens between procedural parties is a matter of justice

[1] See eg Williams (1988: 279–80); Finkelstein (1999: 160–1); Duff (2007: 198, 206–7); Ashworth and Horder (2013: 116).

[2] Even if we restrict our discussion to scenarios with just one level of exceptions, as for the sake of simplicity I will now continue to do.

[3] See eg Roberts and Zuckerman (2010: 227–30).

[4] In the well-known 'golden thread' passage by Viscount Sankey LC: see *Woolmington* v *DPP* [1935] AC 462 (HL) at 481–2.

[5] Explicit reverse onus clauses are normally counted as the 'second' exception to *Woolmington*. The 'first', acknowledged in *Woolmington* itself, is 'the defence of insanity'; implicit reverse onus clauses are the 'third'. See Zuckerman (1976: 402–26); Roberts and Zuckerman (2010: 265–72).

[6] See Williams (1988: 262–3).

and policy—not of logic.[7] I must be wrong to claim that the burden of proving exceptions always and necessarily falls on the defendant.

There is a superficial appeal to this group of rejoinders. Unfortunately, as I argue in this chapter, they all rest on a cluster of very common equivocations. I start by exploring, in sections 4.2 and 4.3, the very notion of a burden of proof. I move on to address, in section 4.4, the first two of those three objections. In section 4.5, I develop my analysis of probative burdens; and the third objection is discussed in section 4.6.

4.2 The Burden of Proof: Problems with the Received View

The received view on the notion of a burden of proof goes hand-in-hand with the common picture, discussed in section 3.4, according to which legal consequences are primarily attached—in 'substantive' rules—to facts whose existence is independent of what is proved in court. Indeed, endorsers of that common picture would say—against my proposed account—not only that it is the doctrine of the burden of proof that explains the function of rules like (13P), but also that the doctrine itself can only be understood in light of their view of legal rules. To see this, consider once again the following schemes of the two 'substantive' rules which—according to the common picture—might be said to govern a case of contract:

(11S) If *P* and *not-D*, then it is correct to decide for the plaintiff.
(12S) If *P* and *D*, then it is correct to decide for the defendant.

My objectors could agree that neither of these rules offers any guidance about how a judge should decide a case of contract when the relevant propositions of fact are neither proved nor disproved. A judge cannot directly resort to any of the two rules if neither *D* nor *not-D* is proved. Yet the court still needs to reach a decision, either for the plaintiff or for the defendant. The law must therefore determine what that

[7] A similar objection is pressed in Wang (2003: 77) against Sartor (1993). See also Campbell (1987: 85); Schauer (1991a: 875 n 13), remarking that 'the burden of proving the non-applicability of [an] exception' may be placed either on the state (or the plaintiff) or on the defendant; Rodríguez and Sucar (1998: 147 n 27); Finkelstein (1999: 160); Tadros (2005: 104); the comparative notes in Ho (2011: 6–10); or Goudkamp (2013: 41).

decision should be; and the only way of doing that is by means of some rule or rules *other* than the substantive rules in (11S) and (12S). So it is true, my objectors could grant, that substantive rules are not sufficient. We need further rules. But the role of these further rules is to indicate which of those two substantive rules should eventually be applied. More precisely, the role of these further rules is to allocate to one of the procedural parties the risk that a given proposition of fact is uncertain.[8] This risk can be allocated either way. So the law in some contexts *may* be—as in my formulation (13P)—that when *P* is proved but neither *D* nor *not-D* is proved, the judge should decide for the plaintiff:

> (13P) If it is *proved that P* and *not proved that D*, then it is correct to decide for the plaintiff.

The effect of a rule like (13P) is that when *D* is uncertain—when neither (11S) nor (12S) can be directly relied on—the judge should decide *as she would* under (12S): she should decide as if *not-D* were proved; she should decide for the plaintiff. The effect of a rule like (13P), then, say the endorsers of this common view, is simply to make the defendant, rather than the plaintiff, bear the risk that *D* is uncertain. And to allocate such a risk is to impose, upon the defendant, the 'burden' of proof relative to *D*.[9]

So the received view is that the rules by which burdens are allocated are *secondary* rules.[10] They are rules that deal with the hypothesis of uncertainty by remitting the judge to one of the two primary, substantive rules at play. The relation between the two kinds of rules can be conceptualized in different ways. Some theorists say that secondary rules allocating burdens of proof operate as 'default'-rules.[11] Some suggest that the allocation of the burden of proof relative to a proposition *X* should be characterized as a presumption—displaceable only by the proof of the contrary—that *not-X* is the case.[12] Others propose to represent the secondary rules

[8] This is not *psychological* uncertainty. To say that *X* is 'uncertain' means simply that neither *X* nor *not-X* is proved, and proof need not be characterized in a psychological sense.

[9] For the classic references, see Thayer (1928: 353–89); Wigmore (1940: 270–84); and Rosenberg (1965: 5–11). See also James (1961: 47); Jeffries and Stephan (1979: 1329–30); Belton (1981: 1216–17); Taruffo (1992: 222–3); Múrias (2000: 19–34); Roberts (2005: 187–90); and Roberts and Zuckerman (2010) 59–60, 224–6.

[10] See eg Alchourrón (1991); Rodríguez and Sucar (1998: 146–7); Bayón (2001: 332); Rodríguez (2002: 393, 397, 399); and Moreso and Rodríguez (2010: 25).

[11] Compare eg Ashford and Risinger (1969: 172–3); Carnota (1995: 156); Rodríguez and Sucar (1998: 148); Bayón (2001: 330, 332); Brożek (2004: 146-7); and Sartor (2005: 496).

[12] See eg Duff (2005: 131).

as 'negation-as-failure' inference rules, whereby 'it is not the case that *P*' is inferred from the fact that *P* has not been proved.[13] But the underlying idea is always the same. It is the idea that the function of these rules is to be understood in terms of their relation to the primary, substantive rules, which are the ones that the judge ends up applying—deciding *as if* the antecedent of one or the other were satisfied.[14]

I think this common picture is mistaken. Observe, first, that there is no reason why the consequent of a rule like (13P)—a rule whose antecedent is 'If it is *proved that P* and *not proved that D*. . .'—must necessarily be either that the judge should decide for the plaintiff or that she ought to decide for the defendant. The law might simultaneously determine that, if *P is proved*, then . . .

(i) . . . if *not-D is proved*, then the judge should decide for the plaintiff;
(ii) . . . if *D is proved*, then the judge should decide for the defendant;

and

(iii) . . . if *D is uncertain* (that is, if neither *D* nor *not-D* is proved), then the judge should decide in some *other* way (different both from what would count as decision for the plaintiff and from what would count as a decision for the defendant).[15]

Notice that provision (iii) is a way of dealing with the hypothesis that *D* is uncertain. So it performs the same function as a provision that instructed the judge to decide cases in which *D* is uncertain *as* she would *if* either (i) or (ii) were true. But in (iii) the judge is required to 'suppose', 'assume', or 'presume' nothing. There is no proposition *X* such that it can plausibly be said that (iii) requires the judge to decide *as if X* were the case.[16] In (iii), the judge is simply instructed to decide in a certain way, on the condition that *D* is uncertain. So there is no 'primary' rule relative to which (iii) could plausibly be deemed 'secondary'. Nor do we need to posit

[13] See the discussion in Prakken (2001: 264).

[14] See also Giesen (2009: 50, 53).

[15] The stock illustration of a scenario like (iii)—a scenario, that is, in which an ad hoc judgment is to be issued if some relevant proposition of fact happens to be uncertain—must be the one provided by Solomon's biblical judgment (in *Kings* 1:3) of having the disputed baby cut in two, absent sufficient evidence that it was the son of either of the women claiming to be its mother. See Múrias (2000: 99); Roberts and Zuckerman (2010: 224).

[16] See Ullman-Margalit (1983: 147–50).

or imagine any such rule in order to grasp and explain the function of a rule like (iii). Endorsers of the received view are wrong to claim that the allocation by law of the risk of uncertainty must involve presumptions, assumptions, or fictions.[17]

Moreover, the fact that we can make sense of a rule like (iii) without these notions suggests that they are dispensable with regard to (i) and (ii), too. Indeed, even when the effect attached to the hypothesis that a given proposition *X* is uncertain *coincides* with the effect attached to the hypothesis that *X* is proved (or that *not-X* is proved, as the case may be), it is misleading to refer to that first effect by saying that the judge is being instructed to decide 'as if' *X* (or 'as if' *not-X*) was proved. Such a description would gloss over the difference between (iv) and (v):

(iv) If *P is proved* and *D is uncertain*, the judge should decide for the plaintiff.

(v) If *P is proved* and *D is uncertain*, the judge should decide as if *not-D* were proved.

To see more clearly why this matters, suppose a scenario in which (i) is the case: if *P* is proved, then if *not-D* is also proved, the judge should decide for the plaintiff. In that scenario, *both* (iv) and (v) could be described as instructing the judge to decide 'as if' *not-D* was proved. But (iv) and (v) are solutions of different kinds. While (iv) establishes that if *D* is uncertain, the judge is to decide for the plaintiff, (v) establishes (blankly, as it were) that the hypothesis that *D* is uncertain is to be decided *in the same way* as the hypothesis that *D* is proved—whatever *that* decision may be. Nonetheless, both (iv) and (v) provide solutions for the hypothesis that *D* is uncertain. In the common idiom, both allocate the corresponding 'risk' of uncertainty. Thus it is a mistake to postulate any intrinsic connection between the allocation of 'burdens' of proof, on the one hand, and, on the other, the establishment of presumptions, assumptions, fictions, and so on, *even when* the effect attached by law to the hypothesis that a proposition *X* is uncertain happens to be 'the same' as the effect attached to either one of two hypotheses in which *X* is *not* uncertain.

[17] If we were to ask whether it is the plaintiff or the defendant who in a scenario like (iii) would bear the burden of proof relative to *D*, would the correct answer not be '*both*'?

4.3 Making Better Sense of the Notion

The notion of a 'burden' of proof can be further clarified in several respects. The way this metaphorical 'burden' is usually referred to suggests that it amounts to some sort of subjective legal position: it suggests that burdens of proof belong to the same family as duties, rights, powers, liabilities, and so on. These 'burdens' are said to take a certain action-type φ as their content, and sentences to the effect that some procedural party 'has' (or 'carries', or 'bears') the burden of φ-ing are deemed well formed. The burden of proof is even sometimes defined as an *obligation* of some procedural party to prove a certain proposition of fact.[18] This general picture, however, is inaccurate in at least three ways.

4.3.1 Burdens and Obligations

A first, minor point is that there is of course no legal obligation proper for any procedural party to 'discharge' her 'burden'. There is only instrumental reason to do so, given the parties' procedural goals and their commitment to the success of their claims or charges, and given, also, the risk of failure attached to the fact that some relevant proposition *X* happens *not* to be proved. The party is 'burdened' with the proof of *X* in the sense that she had better make sure that the body of admitted evidence includes enough information to establish *X* to the relevant standard of proof.

4.3.2 Burdens and Proof

Second, the common assumption that what a party's procedural 'burden' requires of her is (in all cases) that she ensure that some proposition is *proved* is also unfounded. Think about the contexts in which it is sensible to say that a procedural party is burdened with the proof of some proposition *X*. These are contexts in which the law determines that, if *X* happens *not* to be proved, that party will fail. So consider a legal provision of the following sort:

(24) If *P is not proved*, then it is *not* correct to decide for the plaintiff.

[18] See eg Tapper (2010: 121, 124).

What a provision like (24) determines is that *P must be proved* for the plaintiff to succeed: (24) entails that

(25) It is correct to decide for the plaintiff only when *P is proved*.

So we can say that a provision like (24) 'burdens' the plaintiff with the proof of *P*; (24) makes it true that the plaintiff had better make sure there is enough evidence to establish *P* to the relevant standard of proof. But notice that this talk of burden-'bearing' is but a vivid way of expressing the redundant thought that unless the necessary conditions on which a party's procedural success depends are met, she will fail.[19] This alone does not give us reason to abandon this popular terminology. But we should be wary of the related suggestion that a party's burden is always and only one of positively proving something—that is, a burden of ensuring that a given proposition *be established* to the satisfaction of the relevant standard of proof. This suggestion is mistaken. To see the point, let us come back to the conjunction of (11P), (12P), and (13P):

(11P) If it is *proved that P* and *proved that not-D*, then it is correct to decide for the plaintiff.

(12P) If it is *proved that P* and *proved that D*, then it is correct to decide for the defendant.

(13P) If it is *proved that P* and *not proved that D*, then it is correct to decide for the plaintiff.

This set, and (13P) in particular, cannot be said to impose upon the defendant the burden of proving the occurrence of any exception. For it does *not* follow from (11P), (12P), and (13P) that

[19] And by the way: how apposite, really, is it to say that by imposing these burdens the law is 'allocating' or 'distributing' between the parties the *risk* that some relevant proposition of fact is *uncertain*? This vocabulary wrongly suggests that there is such a thing as a pre-existent risk of uncertainty that it is the law's task to somehow allocate or distribute. But in so far as there is any risk at all involved for the burdened party, this risk is the *product*—rather than the object—of the law's chosen solution. It is *by* determining, say, that a given party will not succeed unless a given proposition *X* is proved that the law *creates* for that party the relevant risk. Nor is this a risk that *X* is *uncertain*. A risk of uncertainty relative to *X* would be a risk associated to the fact that neither *X* nor *not-X* is proved. But this is not the risk that any given party is made to bear as a consequence of a particular allocation of the burden of proof. The burdened party's risk must rather be the risk that a given proposition *X* is *not proved*—for it is in that case that that party will fail—and this is a risk that materializes equally when *X* is uncertain (ie when neither *X* nor *not-X* is proved) and when X *is proved* (and therefore not uncertain at all).

(26) It is correct to decide for the defendant only when it is *proved that D*.

In other words, the conjunction of (11P), (12P), and (13P) does not imply that unless *D is proved*, the plaintiff will succeed. The conjunction of (11P), (12P), and (13P) is consistent with

(24') If *P is not proved*, then it is correct to decide for the defendant,

and where (24') is adopted, (26) cannot be true. If the fact that *P* is *not proved* suffices—as it typically does—for the defendant to succeed, then it is not necessary that any exception be proved for the plaintiff to fail.

So it would be wrong to claim—at least *sans phrase*—that the conjunction of (11P), (12P), and (13P) *burdens* defendants with the proof of exceptions. What does follow from (13P) is that

(27) If it is *proved that P*, then (if it is *not proved that D*, then it is correct to decide for the plaintiff).

In other words, (13P) can be said to impose upon the defendant the burden of proving exceptions *if P is proved*.

An endorser of the common view might want to say at this point that in a case like this, the defendant's burden emerges only *if and when* the plaintiff has proved that *P*. The plaintiff (or prosecutor) would have discharged the burden of proof, which would then—but only then—'shift' to the defendant.

This idea that burdens 'shift' back and forth is also very popular. But it too is mistaken. Why? For one, if the burden imposed upon a party is to ensure that there is enough evidence to establish some proposition to a given standard of proof, then no burden can be said to have been adequately 'discharged' except in view of the full, final body of admitted evidence on which the fact-finder—judge or jury—is to decide what has and has not been proved. But consider also that (13P) implies that when no exception is proved, the defendant's success relies on it *not* being proved that *P*:

(28) If it is *not proved that D*, then it is only correct to decide for the defendant if *P is not proved*.

The point is this. If we are to say that *when P is proved*, (13P) imposes upon defendants the 'burden' of ensuring that *D is proved*, then by the same token we also have to say that when *D is not proved*, (13P) imposes upon defendants the 'burden' of ensuring that *P* is also *not proved*. For what (13P) means is that the defendant's success depends on it not being *simultaneously* true that *P is proved* and that *D is not proved*. What the defendant needs to ensure, in other words, is that either *P* is not proved, *or D* is proved:

(29) It is correct to decide for the plaintiff only when (either *P is not proved* or it is *proved that D*).

Given that this disjunction ('either *P is not proved* or it is *proved that D*') is a necessary condition of the defendant's success, the 'risk' that defendant bears is in fact the risk that *that* disjunctive condition is not true—it is the risk that neither disjunct is verified. So her 'burden', if we want to use this language, cannot be said to be a burden of *proof*, a burden of ensuring that some proposition is eventually *proved*. Her burden is rather one of ensuring that either *D* is proved, or *P* is *not* proved.

A parallel picture can, of course, be drawn on the plaintiff's (or the prosecutor's) side in ordinary scenarios. It is the case not only that

(25) It is correct to decide for the plaintiff only when *P is proved*,

but also that

(30) If it is *proved that D*, then it is *not* correct to decide for the plaintiff,

and so that

(31) It is correct to decide for the plaintiff only when (*P is proved* and it is *not proved that D*).

The plaintiff's 'burden', accordingly, is to ensure *both* that *P* is proved *and* that no exception is proved; this conjunction is a necessary condition of the plaintiff's success.

So we should resist the common suggestion that when dealing with these 'burdens' we are dealing only with requirements to ensure that certain propositions be *proved*. A procedural party's burden is relative to the conditions on which her success depends, and these may include the fact that certain propositions be *not proved*.

4.3.3 Discharging the Burden

Finally, the idea that there is something that a party must actually *do* to 'discharge' her burden is also confused. Whether a party's burden requires her to adduce any evidence in favour of some proposition—or in fact to perform any action at all—is a contingent matter of procedural tactics dependent on factors extraneous to the content of the burden itself. There can be cases in which there is nothing that a defendant tactically needs to do to ensure that *P* is not proved—and thus to ensure that the disjunction which it is her burden to make true ('either *P is proved* or *D is proved*') becomes true. (Of course, in the face of the evidence adduced by the plaintiff or prosecutor, the defendant may find it advisable to offer counter-evidence to ensure that *P* is not finally proved.) Similarly, although the defendant who attempts to meet her burden by ensuring that the second disjunct is true will normally have to offer evidence of some exception, there can be cases in which no such effort is required: for example, if the fact-finder has by other admissible means come into contact with evidence to the same effect (that is, if such evidence can be admitted even if it was not the 'burdened' party who adduced it; rules about the admissibility of evidence are independent of the way in which burdens are allocated).

The same holds for plaintiffs or prosecutors. Their burden is, in a sense, a 'heavier' one: while either '*P is not proved*' or '*D is proved*', taken separately, is a sufficient condition for a defendant to succeed, a plaintiff's success depends on it being the case *both* that *P is proved* and that *D* is *not proved*. Furthermore, plaintiffs and prosecutors are typically required to actively offer some evidence for *P*. But notice, first, that this may be all they have to do to ensure that both conjucts are true (suppose, for example, that no evidence for *D* has been offered by the defendant or otherwise accepted by the court); and, second, that it may also be that the rules that govern the admissibility of evidence allow the court, when determining whether *P* is proved, to rely on evidence not adduced by the plaintiff or the prosecutor—in which case it might be possible for a plaintiff or prosecutor to meet the burden without adducing any evidence at all.

4.4 Defences, 'Proof', and Evidential Burdens

We are now in a position to return to the group of three objections—identified in section 4.1—to the proof-based account of legal exceptions. In this and section 4.5, I deal with the first two objections. The third will be addressed in section 4.6.

4.4.1 *The First Objection*

The first objection—that I ignore that if a defendant successfully brings the occurrence of an exception into issue, it will fall to the plaintiff or prosecutor to *disprove* it—can now be quickly dismissed.

It is true that the prosecutor's or the plaintiff's burden is not only to ensure that *P* is proved. My account does not suggest otherwise. Nonetheless it is also true that *P* is *all* that has to be proved for the plaintiff or prosecutor to succeed.[20] For their burden, as we saw, is to ensure both that *P is proved* and that *D is not proved*. Now to ensure that this burden is satisfied, all they are tactically required to do, initially, is to adduce evidence for *P*. And if and when the defendant offers evidence of some exception *D*, the plaintiff or prosecutor will be tactically required to offer counter-evidence to ensure that no exception is eventually proved. But they never have to *prove*—to ensure the *proof* of—the actual *absence* of any exception *D*. What *has* to be proved for the plaintiff or prosecutor to succeed is, at all times, that *P*. It's just that *that P is proved* is never a sufficient condition of their success; it also has to be the case—again at all times—that *D* is *not proved*.

4.4.2 *The Second Objection*

The second objection was to my claim that when *P* is proved, proof of *D* is a necessary condition of the defendant's success. This claim must be wrong, the objection goes, because the burden imposed on the defendant may be a mere *evidential* burden rather than a burden of *proof* relative

[20] I denounced in Chapter 3 the mistake of confusing this with the claim that *P* is sufficient for the plaintiff or prosecutor to succeed. A confusion of the same kind is made by those who hold that—as Prakken (2001: 254) puts it—'allocations of the burden of proof make the reasoning defeasible'. For similar claims, though differently qualified, see Prakken (1997: 272); Brożek (2004: 29, 145–50); Brożek (2005: 71–4); Hage (2005: 15-23); Sartor (2005: 77, 532, 732); Prakken and Sartor (2007: 97); Brożek (2008: 145); or Sartor (2012: 130).

to the occurrence of any exception. But as we will now see, this commonly drawn contrast, too, is unsubstantiated.

For the purposes of discussion, I shall focus on Roberts' and Zuckerman's recent and representative account of the distinction in the field of criminal law. Having first drawn attention to the '"legal" or "persuasive" or "probative" burden'—the burden of *proof* proper—as 'the simplest device for allocating the risk of error in litigation',[21] Roberts and Zuckerman go on to write the following:

> The burden of production [that is, what is normally called the 'evidential' burden] imposes a lesser obligation [than the probative burden], to adduce sufficient evidence to make any given contention a live issue in the trial. In contrast to the probative burden, the burden of production does not require the proponent to establish any particular degree of confidence in the adjudicator's mind. The proponent simply has to persuade the adjudicator that the issue is worth considering in arriving at judgment; hence the notion of 'passing the judge' on a particular issue. A further procedural consequence of satisfying the burden of production in criminal proceedings is that, once an issue has been successfully introduced into the trial, the judge is usually obliged to deal with it during his summing-up to the jury at the close of proceedings—another sense in which the successful proponent has 'passed the judge' in relation to a particular issue. The 'evidential burden of proof' of popular imagination is, strictly speaking, a solecism, because the evidential burden does not require the proponent actually to *prove* anything in the sense of convincing the fact-finder of the truth of any fact in issue.[22]

This corresponds to the way in which the distinction between the two kinds of burden is usually drawn.[23] Two confusions, however, underlie the apparent plausibility of the contrast.

4.4.2.1 'Proof' The contrast seems to rest on an equivocation about the meaning of the term 'proof' (and its cognates) in the context of the legal process. In ordinary, everyday discourse, the claim that a proposition X has been 'proved' carries the suggestion that some particularly demanding standard has been met, such that the occurrence

[21] Roberts and Zuckerman (2010: 226).

[22] Roberts and Zuckerman (2010: 227–8).

[23] For other recent statements, see Tapper (2010: 121–4)—affirming (at 121) that 'discharge of . . . the evidential burden proves nothing'—and (with notes on the history of the distinction) Stumer (2010: 8–19).

of *X* has been established with a degree of probability close to certainty. But the claim that a given proposition has been *legally* proved carries no such connotation. In the legal context, the applicable standard may require much less than certainty or absence of 'reasonable doubt' as to the occurrence of the relevant facts. Indeed, the standard imposed for the proof of what I refer to as '*P*-facts' is usually different from (and considerably more demanding than) the one required for the establishment of exceptions. While in the former case absence of reasonable doubt, or something to similar effect, is a commonly accepted standard, proof of defeating circumstances normally requires no more, and often requires less, than their establishment on the balance of probabilities.

Of course, Roberts and Zuckerman would not disagree with these remarks, which are consistent with their own characterization of the notion of proof. For example, they describe the burden of proof as 'requiring the proponent to prove his case to a *specified degree of probability*': the allocation of such a burden is the product of a 'decision rule providing that the court will vindicate and enforce a claimant's right only if constitutive facts are proved by the claimant to a *specified degree of probability*'.[24] Notice that this probability-based account of legal proof does not conflate probative judgments with naked judgments of probability. When discussing the admissibility of evidence, Roberts and Zuckerman draw a distinction between judgments of mere (or 'logical') relevance, and judgments of '*legal* relevance' relative to any item of evidence.[25] 'For fact *x* to *prove* fact *y*', they say, '*x* must establish *y*'s existence to some accepted normative standard of proof'; but mere 'logical' relevance 'does not require proof, but only that the existence of *y* be rendered more or . . . less probable by *x*':

> To the question 'How much more (un)likely must *x* render *y* for *x* to be judged relevant to *y*?' the logically correct response must be '[to] any [degree] at all'. If the probability of *y* is one-in-ten-million (p(y) = 0.0000001) and proof of *x* increases that probability by the minuscule amount of another one-in-ten-million, to (p(y)=0.0000002), *x* is relevant to *y*.[26]

[24] Roberts and Zuckerman (2010: 226, emphases added).

[25] See Roberts and Zuckerman (2010: 96–109).

[26] See Roberts and Zuckerman (2010: 100–1).

'Logical' relevance is therefore, 'as it were, one-dimensional: *x* is either relevant to *y*, or it is irrelevant'.[27] 'Legal relevance', on the other hand, is 'a two-dimensional concept, introducing the dimension of quantum which merely logical relevance lacks'.[28] It 'requires, not merely a determination that the evidence affects the probability of some fact in issue, but also that the evidence has sufficient weight, or probative value, to be worthy of admission'.[29] So if a given judgment about the admissibility of an item of evidence is made to depend on an assessment of *legal* relevance, then that judgment is in the proper sense a 'probative' one—it is a judgment about the 'probative value' of an item of evidence, an assessment of whether the applicable 'admissibility standard' has been met. A judgment of proof is, in other words, a 'probability+' judgment. It is a judgment of probability *to a given degree*. Not that any numerical expression of the relevant standard is actually required:

> Since assessments of probabilities in everyday naturalistic contexts—including the criminal trial—cannot be expressed in precise numerical terms, the law is obliged to work with fairly rough-and-ready estimates of confidence levels. English law classically adopts two standards: proof on the balance of probabilities and proof beyond a reasonable doubt.[30]

But here is the worry. If this account of proof is adopted, then in what sense can we say—as Roberts and Zuckerman do at the end of the passage quoted at the beginning of section 4.4.2—that the probative burden requires the proponent to '*prove* [some]thing *in the sense of convincing* the fact-finder of the truth of [a certain] fact in issue'?[31] This cannot be taken to suggest that no fact can ever be proved unless the fact-finder is *convinced* of its truth. Otherwise it wouldn't be possible for proof on the balance of probabilities to count, as it often does, as a standard of *proof* in the strict sense.[32] For what proof on the balance of probabilities requires, as Roberts and Zuckerman point out, is 'that the probability of the proponent's

[27] Roberts and Zuckerman (2010: 101).
[28] Roberts and Zuckerman (2010: 104).
[29] Roberts and Zuckerman (2010: 104).
[30] Roberts and Zuckerman (2010: 226).
[31] Roberts and Zuckerman (2010: 228, emphasis added).
[32] Not to mention that the mere fact that probative assessments are always relative to a body of evidence constituted in accordance with certain admissibility rules—which opens the possibility that fact-finders be *psychologically* convinced of the truth of some relevant

contention being true is at least marginally greater than the probability of the opponent's counter-claim being true'.[33] There is a great distance between the establishment that the probability of a given fact is greater than 0.5, and certainty or conviction that that fact occurred.[34]

But perhaps with their reference to the fact-finder's being 'convinced of the truth' of a certain fact, Roberts and Zuckerman mean simply that the degree of probability required by any given standard of proof can be conceived of, as the passage just excerpted suggests, in terms of confidence 'levels'. They do assert that

> [a] belief in the truth of a proposition can be held with varying degrees of confidence. Legal rules are therefore needed to establish, not only the allocation of the probative burden, but also the requisite *standard* of proof, that is to say, the level of confidence which the evidence has to produce in the trier of fact.[35]

It seems, then, that their reference to the fact-finder's 'conviction' of the truth of the fact in issue—or to a proponent's burden of adducing 'enough evidence to produce a certain degree of *assurance in the mind* of the fact-finder'[36]—is simply an allusion to the fact that in order for the proposition in issue to count as 'proved', the applicable standard of proof needs to be met, and thus that the required degree of probability needs to be verified.

facts that are however *not* established by the admitted evidence—is sufficient to rule out any psychological account of legal proof, even when 'beyond a reasonable doubt' is the applicable standard. The question that fact-finders must answer is not whether they *are* convinced of the relevant propositions on the basis of the body of admitted evidence, but whether a reasonable person *would*, on the basis only of the admitted evidence, be certain of those propositions, or whether it can be said that the body of admitted evidence establishes their probability beyond a given degree, and so on. On the topic, see Bolding (1960: 12–17); Wróblewski (1989: 12–15); Cohen (1991); and Cohen (1992: 117–25).

[33] Roberts and Zuckerman (2010: 226–7).

[34] There *is* room for discussion of a fact-finder's persuasion in the proper sense, of course, if the object of persuasion is taken to be the fact that *the applicable standard has been met*. But that is not what Roberts and Zuckerman and others invariably mean when they lightly speak of legal proof in terms of persuasion. (Sometimes there are felicitous slips of the pen: Tapper speaks, on one occasion, of the 'trier of fact after assessing the evidence' '*believ[ing] it proved* that the fact had occurred'; see Tapper 2010: 154, emphasis added.) For a clear-headed critique of the 'subjective account' of probative standards, and a defence of 'objective standards', see Laudan (2006: 52–3, 63–88, 107).

[35] Roberts and Zuckerman (2010: 226).

[36] Roberts and Zuckerman (2010: 226, emphasis added).

This, in turn, clarifies two points. First, there is no intrinsic connection between the meaning of the term 'proved' and any given standard of proof. Roberts and Zuckerman (2010: 226) point out, as we saw, that proof on the balance of probabilities and proof beyond a reasonable doubt are classically adopted standards in English law. But any stipulated degree of probability n, high or low, could in principle be made (by law) a probative standard in some given context—and any fact whose probability were shown to be $\geq n$ would then count as proved in that context.

The second point is that for any of the formulations with which we have been working in this chapter, such as, say,

(27) If it is *proved that P*, then (if it is *not proved that D*, it is correct to decide for the plaintiff),

one should really substitute, for the term 'proved', the applicable standard of proof in the relevant contexts. Moreover, the applicable standards may vary according to the proposition at stake: it could be, for example, that in some context the resulting formulation would look something like

(27') If *necessarily, a reasonable person would, on the basis of the available evidence, be certain of P*, then (if *the probability of D on the basis of the available evidence is* ≤ 0.5, it is correct to decide for the plaintiff).

4.4.2.2 The Evidential Burden A second source of possible confusion in Roberts and Zuckerman's characterization of the evidential burden concerns their reference to the proponent's need to 'pass the judge' on a particular issue. In any legal process, there will come a moment when the final body of admitted evidence has to be assessed to determine whether the relevant facts are ultimately established to the satisfaction of the applicable standards. Before that moment comes, however, there may be other points at which judgments of a similar character will also have to be made. In the criminal process, for example, as Roberts and Zuckerman remark,

> there are two intermediate stages, between the prosecution's opening statement and the judge's summing-up, at which the judge may have to decide whether the cumulative weight of the prosecution's evidence is sufficient to warrant submitting the case to the jury's consideration. At the end of the prosecution's case, and before being called to mount a positive defence, the accused may submit that there is no case to answer.

This 'half-time motion' asserts that the prosecution's evidence, taken at its highest, could not be regarded by any reasonable jury as constituting proof beyond reasonable doubt . . . Later, after both parties have presented their cases before the judges but before the judge sums up to the jury, an equivalent test of evidential sufficiency may be applied to the entire body of evidence.[37]

The point of these midway assessments (to be carried out, in this case, by the judge) is to determine whether certain issues should be introduced into the trial and brought to the ultimate fact-finder (in this case, the jury). Such assessments are nonetheless *probative* in the same sense in which the jury's final finding is a probative one. They are assessments of whether a given body of evidence establishes certain facts to a given standard or degree of probability.[38] And that means that the corresponding burdens of *proof* will necessarily be in play.

The relevant burden here is *not* that of bringing a given fact into issue or of introducing it into the trial.[39] It is rather *because* no relevant fact *X* will be brought into the trial, and included in the judge's summing-up to the jury, *unless* at some intermediate procedural moment *T* the body of adduced evidence establishes *X* to a given degree of probability, that the party whose interest it is to have *X* brought into trial is burdened *with the proof* of that fact at *T*.[40]

The prosecution's burden at this stage involves ensuring that the body of adduced evidence establishes their case (or, rather, the *P*-facts of their case) *beyond a reasonable doubt* (or, if there is a difference, that the evidence is such that no reasonable jury would entertain a doubt about the *P*-facts of the prosecution's case). This is not surprising: the prosecution's burden at this stage mirrors its ultimate burden of ensuring that certain facts are established beyond a reasonable doubt on the basis of the evidence brought to the jury. What about the defendant? If the issue of whether some

[37] Roberts and Zuckerman (2010: 79).

[38] Compare Zuckerman (1976: 403 n 5).

[39] The contrary is sometimes asserted: see, for example, Stumer (2010: 16–17).

[40] It is a mistake to say, as Williams (1977a: 156) does, that 'the evidential burden governs what the judge *does*, in leaving the question to the jury or withdrawing it from them; the persuasive burden governs what he *says*, in directing the jury how they are to reach their verdict'. In so far as the evidential burden can be said to govern what the judge does, the persuasive burden must be said to govern what the *jury* does.

defeating circumstance occurred is to be brought into the trial and included for consideration by the jury, then the defendant 'has to persuade the adjudicator', as Roberts and Zuckerman say, that that proposition 'is worth considering in arriving at judgment';[41] the defendant has 'to adduce sufficient evidence to make any given contention a live issue in the trial'.[42] This is the sort of burden that is normally called 'evidential'. But when is it properly discharged? When is an issue 'worth considering'? When is evidence sufficient to make an issue a '*live* issue'? These are opaque expressions, but one thing is clear. To make an issue a 'live issue' is to establish something beyond its mere possibility. To make an issue a 'live' one is to establish it to *some* degree of probability, to meet a certain standard. It is, therefore, to *prove* it, in the precise sense that was clarified a few paragraphs ago, in subsection 4.4.2.1.

Roberts and Zuckerman do not attempt to explain what a 'live issue' is, but they do say at one point—commenting on why there may be good reason for it to be the case that 'the fact that the accused is unable to discharge the burden of adducing evidence to support a particular defence conclusively settles that issue against the accused'—that 'perhaps the accused acted in self-defence, after all, but lacks any evidence to *prove* it'.[43] My claim is that that is exactly what the defendant must do to secure an acquittal when she is unable to undermine the evidence for the relevant *P*-facts. The defendant must *prove* the occurrence of a defeating circumstance. If indeed it is true that in order to secure an acquittal, the defendant needs, as Robert and Zuckerman say, to 'produce evidence which could, if believed, create a reasonable doubt that she might have acted in self-defence',[44] then the burden that the defendant bears is a burden of *proving* self-defence. At any one of those procedurally intermediate assessments, then, the defendants' burden is—just like the prosecutors'—a reflection of their final burden relative to *D*-facts.[45] It is the burden of establishing some defeating circumstance to a certain degree of probability—a degree of probability such that it becomes a 'live issue'.

41 Roberts and Zuckerman (2010: 228).
42 Roberts and Zuckerman (2010: 228).
43 Roberts and Zuckerman (2010: 229, emphasis added).
44 Roberts and Zuckerman (2010: 229).
45 See the interesting diagrammatic representations in McNaughton (1955: 1382–91).

The conclusion is that there is no distinction to draw—save for a mere distinction of degree—between 'evidential burdens' and 'burdens of proof'. But the objection that we are now discussing (the second objection to the proof-based account) depends on the contrary assumption. Therefore the objection fails.[46]

Notice also that it is can be misleading to say that the defendant needs to 'create a reasonable doubt that she might have acted in self-defence', or, more generally, that 'the accused needs to establish a reasonable doubt that he might be innocent in order to secure an acquittal'.[47] One does not generally speak of creating a reasonable *doubt* that there *might* have been self-defence unless the fact-finder would otherwise have reason to believe, beyond a reasonable doubt, that *there was not* self-defence. Rather, what the defendant needs to do is ensure that evidence is adduced such that it would *prevent* any reasonable person from believing in the non-occurrence of self-defence—whether or not (this is the point) there is otherwise any evidence at all to believe, to any extent, in the non-occurrence of self-defence. Hence with the adequate substitutions for the participle 'proved', our formulation (27) is more clearly rendered as:

(27") If *necessarily, a reasonable person would, on the basis of the available evidence, be certain of P*, then (it is correct to decide for the defendant only if *necessarily, no reasonable person would, on the basis of the available evidence, be certain of not-D*).

[46] It is sometimes suggested that the evidential and probative burdens may 'go together' or 'diverge' on any given issue: see Roberts and Zuckerman (2010: 228–9, 244); or Tapper (2010: 128–30). This equivocates between two readings of the phrase 'evidential burden'. Taken to refer to the probative standard just discussed, there is no question of 'divergence': for any proposition *X* whose *proof* is a condition of a party's success, the burden of ensuring that *X* is proved is placed on that party, and *X* must be established to the satisfaction of the relevant standard. Sometimes, however, the phrase 'evidential burden' is improperly employed to refer to the need, discussed above, to 'pass the judge', and bring some fact into issue, at some intermediate procedural moment prior to the ultimate assessment of the admitted evidence. In that case, however, there can be no question of convergence: *both* parties will carry that 'burden'—whatever the standard required for the issue to be brought into trial.

[47] See Roberts and Zuckerman (2010: 229, 247), and remarks to the same effect in Tapper (2010: 152–3).

4.5 Developing the Analysis

Before discussing the third objection, I want to develop the account of legal proof and probative burdens proposed in the previous sections. For it may look as if my analysis is simply not in line with how the law actually works, and with how legal agents—lawyers, courts, lawmakers—understand and employ the relevant notions.

It is true that there are all sorts of legal materials with which my account *seems* to be at odds.[48] For example, here is an extract from section 118 ('Defences') of the Terrorism Act 2000:

118 Defences

(1) Subsection (2) applies where in accordance with a provision mentioned in subsection (5) it is a defence for a person charged with an offence to prove a particular matter.
(2) If the person adduces evidence which is sufficient to raise an issue with respect to the matter the court or jury shall assume that the defence is satisfied unless the prosecution proves beyond a reasonable doubt that it is not.

It would seem that my analysis fails to account for this provision. Another random example: the Australian Criminal Code Act 1995 determines in Part 2.6, Division 13, the following:

13.1 Legal burden of proof—prosecution

(1) The prosecution bears a legal burden of proving every element of an offence relevant to the guilt of the person charged.
(2) The prosecution also bears a legal burden of disproving any matter in relation to which the defendant has discharged an evidential burden of proof imposed on the defendant.
(3) In this Code:
legal burden, in relation to a matter, means the burden of proving the existence of the matter.

[48] I am grateful to James Edwards and Euan MacDonald for pressing me on this point, and for several apparent counter-examples to my proposed account.

Another, from the Draft Criminal Code for Scotland:

5 Proof in criminal proceedings

(3) The prosecution need not prove the absence of any defence or exception unless there is evidence relating to the defence or exception which is sufficient to raise a reasonable doubt as to guilt.
(4) Where there is such evidence it is for the prosecution, unless legislation provides otherwise in relation to a particular matter, to prove the absence of the defence or exception beyond reasonable doubt.

The courts, too, seem to second the view that 'it is certainly true that once a defence such as duress is left to the jury then it is for the Crown to *disprove* it to the criminal standard'.[49] In *Lambert*, Lord Steyn affirms that

In *R v Whyte* (1988) . . . the Canadian Supreme Court rejected an argument that as a matter of principle a constitutional presumption of innocence only applies to elements of the offence and not excuses. Giving the judgment of the court Dickson CJC observed (at 493):

> The real concern is not whether the accused must disprove an element or prove an excuse, but that an accused may be convicted while a reasonable doubt exists. When that possibility exists, there is a breach of the presumption of innocence. The exact characterisation of a factor as an essential element, a collateral factor, an excuse, or a defence should not affect the analysis of the presumption of innocence. It is the final effect of a provision on the verdict that is decisive. If an accused is required to prove some fact on the balance of probabilities to avoid conviction, the provision violates the presumption of innocence because it permits a conviction in spite of a reasonable doubt in the mind of the trier or fact as to the guilt of the accused.

I would adopt this reasoning.[50]

And many more such examples could easily be produced. How can they possibly be accommodated under this chapter's account of legal proof?

To show that my proposed characterization of legal proof and probative burdens does not, in fact, get the law wrong, let me press the analysis one step further. I shall also anticipate and dismiss a few other possible objections that the account may have prompted.[51]

[49] *Bianco* [2001] EWCA Crim 2516 (emphasis added).
[50] *R* v *Lambert* [2002] 2 AC 545.
[51] Here I am grateful to Alex Latham and Nick Treanor, who raised several of these objections.

4.5.1 *The Scope of 'Proved'*

I suggested at the end of both sections 4.4.2.1 and 4.4.2.2 that in formulation (27), which I had first formulated as

(27) If it is *proved that P*, then (if it is *not proved that D*, it is correct to decide for the plaintiff),

the references to '*proved that P*' and '(*not*) *proved that D*' should be replaced with descriptions of the relevant standards of proof. If the example is to track what is commonly the case in the criminal process, let us assume that the standard for *P* is proof beyond a reasonable doubt (which I proposed to read as 'necessarily, a reasonable person would, on the basis of the available evidence, be certain of *P*'), and that the standard for *D* is that of raising a reasonable doubt that the exception *might* have occurred (which I proposed to read as 'necessarily, no reasonable person would, on the basis of the available evidence, be certain of *not-D*'). So we get:

(27") If *necessarily, a reasonable person would, on the basis of the available evidence, be certain of P*, then (it is correct to decide for the defendant only if *necessarily, no reasonable person would, on the basis of the available evidence, be certain of not-D*).

We also saw that standards like 'beyond a reasonable doubt' can be understood as expressions of probability levels: they define the minimum degree of probability to which the available evidence must establish a given fact. Such standards cannot always be accurately translated into numerical terms; but let us suppose for the sake of argument that proof beyond a reasonable doubt amounts to a probability of at least 99%. This will enable me to highlight two important points. Consider the following statement (where '*F*' stands for some proposition of fact):

(α) On the basis of the available evidence, the probability that *F* is ≥ 99%.

The first point to emphasize is that to say that (α) is true (in some decision-making context) is *not* to say that *X* has been *proved* (in that decision-making context), in the legal sense of the word 'proved'. That is because for a fact *F* to be proved—in the legal sense of the word—is for the available evidence to establish *F* to some legally predetermined standard of probability. Now some fact-types are such that *that the probability of a token of the type is established, on the basis of the available evidence, to a given standard* features as an element (a non-superfluous element) in a condition of correct judicial decisions of a certain kind. These are the facts I have called '*P*-facts'. And some fact-types are such that *that no token of the type is established on the basis of the available evidence to a given standard* features as an element (a non-superfluous element) in a condition of correct judicial decisions of a certain kind. These are what I have called '*D*-facts'.

So the fact that someone killed someone else is a *P*-fact relative to a judicial decision to convict someone of murder, for example, *because* the establishment of a killing to the satisfaction of a certain degree of probability is a condition of a correct conviction. If 'beyond a reasonable doubt' is the relevant standard, then (since we are assuming that this can be numerically translated as 'at least 99% probable') we can say that the decision to convict person A of murder is correct only if the following is true:

(β) On the basis of the available evidence, the probability that *A killed another person* is ≥ 99%.

So (β) has to be true in order for the conviction to be correct. But—again—to say that (β) is true (in this decision-making context) is not the same as saying that the fact that A killed another person is *proved* (in that context), or that it is *proved beyond a reasonable doubt*. If true, yes, (β)—or any statement assigning a definite probability of 99% or more to the fact that *A* killed another person—will *make it true* that the fact that A killed another person is *proved*. But that is because the fact that A killed another person is a fact, the establishment of which to a given standard (which standard is satisfied by a probability of at least 99%) is a condition of a correct conviction in that context. It is only because the fact that A killed another person *is a P-fact* in this context, that (β) makes it true that the killing is *proved*. In a decision-making context in which the killing was not a *P*-fact (or a *D*-fact), (β) might still be true: but it would not in that context amount to the *proof*—in the relevant sense—of anything.

If this is not clear, imagine that it happens to be true in some murder case that

(γ) On the basis of the available evidence, the probability that *A killed another person on a Wednesday* is ≥ 99%.

That (γ) happens to be true (as it may well be) in a decision-making context does not allow us to say that the fact that A's killing was done on a Wednesday has been *proved* in that context. Nor does it allow us to say, strictly speaking, that it has *not* been proved. *That the killing was done on a Wednesday* is a fact relative to which there is no point in saying either that it *has* or that it *has not* been proved. For, again, a fact can be said to be proved (or not), in the legal sense of the notion, only by reference to some standard of proof legally set for it—and there is simply no standard of proof set for the ascertainment of the fact that the killing was done on a Wednesday.[52] *That a killing was done on a Wednesday* is, from the point of view of the law, immaterial for the decision; it is not an operative fact in murder (though it is possible, as I said, that its likelihood *is* established to any degree of probability, which in turn may be instrumental in assessing whether or not some operative fact has or has not been proved).

There are two alternative ways of putting this more rigorously. One would be to say that 'proved' and 'not proved' are only properly predicated of material or operative facts: facts whose ascertainment to some legally determined standard bears on what the correct decision is in a given decision-making context. In that case, immaterial facts, although their probability on the basis of the available evidence can be very high, can be neither 'proved' nor 'not proved'. Alternatively, we could stipulate that *to say that some fact F is proved* in some decision-making context is not simply to say that on the basis of the available evidence, the probability of *F* is established to some (given) degree, however high. Rather, to say that *F* is 'proved' (in some decision-making context) is to say that (a) as a matter of law, the fact *that the probability of (a token of) F is established, on the basis of the available evidence, to a given standard S*, is a fact that bears on what the correct decision is (in that context); and moreover that (b) a token of *F* has indeed been established to standard *S* on the basis of the available evidence.

This second way of putting things, unlike the first, would allow us to predicate 'not proved' of immaterial facts. That is because immaterial facts would never be proved (and so would always be 'not proved') since they would always fail to satisfy clause (a). Material facts, in turn, which by definition always satisfy clause (a), would be 'proved' if they also satisfied clause (b), and 'not proved' otherwise.[53]

52 To see this from another angle, just ask yourself when—ie under what conditions—this fact would count as 'proved' in a case of murder.

53 When is clause (a) satisfied? In any of these two scenarios: when (a1) the ascertainment of a token of *F* to standard *S* is an element in a condition of the correct decision; and when (a2) the non-ascertainment of a token of *F* is an element in a condition of the correct decision. In the first case, again, we have what I call '*P*-facts'; in the second, '*D*-facts'.

In the context of our discussion, this second way of presenting these matters seems less helpful than the first. We are not concerned with the distinction between material and immaterial facts; we are concerned with the distinction between two kinds of material facts: *P*-facts and *D*-facts. Moreover, the second way of putting things obscures to some extent the difference between facts that are not proved because they simply *cannot* be proved (since there is no corresponding standard of proof to begin with) and facts that are not proved because the corresponding standard has not been met. So it seems preferable to keep things clear, and to restrict the use of 'proved' and 'not proved' to the domain of facts that *can* be either proved or not proved: the domain of material facts.

If we adopt this terminology, then instead of saying that *P*-facts are facts, the *proof* of which is an element in a condition of the correct decision, and that *D*-facts are facts, the *absence of proof* of which is an element in a condition of the correct decision, we can now say, more rigorously, that *P*-facts are fact-types, *the ascertainment of tokens of which, on the basis of the available evidence, to a given standard of probability*, is an element in a condition of the correct decision; and that *D*-facts are fact-types, *the non-ascertainment of tokens of which, on the basis of the available evidence, to a given standard of probability*, is an element in a condition of the correct decision. Again: it is *because* their (non-)ascertainment to a given standard is an element in a condition of the correct decision that such facts can now *be* either proved or not proved. That they *are* *P*-facts or *D*-facts is therefore a precondition of us saying that tokens of *P* or *D* can be either proved or not proved.

4.5.2 *Legal Proof and Complementary Assignments of Probability*

These remarks also enable me to be clear about another important point. For any fact *F*, statements of each of the two following forms are equivalent:

(α_1) On the basis of the available evidence, the probability that *F* is $\geq n\%$.

(α_2) On the basis of the available evidence, the probability that *not-F* is $\leq 100 - n\%$.

So the two following statements, for example, are equivalent:

(β_1) On the basis of the available evidence, the probability that *A killed another person* is $\geq 99\%$;

(β_2) On the basis of the available evidence, the probability that *A did not kill another person* is ≤ 1%.

We saw in section 4.5.1 that in a murder case, in which the fact that a person killed another is a *P*-fact, the truth of (β_1) will make it true that the killing is *proved* to the standard of being at least 99% likely (which was how, for the sake of argument, I proposed to translate the standard of proof 'beyond a reasonable doubt'). So given that (β_1) is equivalent to (β_2), should we not also say that the truth of (β_2) will make it true that *that A did not kill another person* is also *proved*—to the standard of being at most 1% likely? If the occurrence of the killing is, say, 99.6% likely; and if that is the same as saying that the non-occurrence of the killing is 0.4% likely; and if this makes it the case that the occurrence of the killing is proved to the standard of being ≥ 99% likely; then is it not also the case that the non-occurrence of the killing is proved to the complementary standard of being ≤ 1% likely?

The answer is negative. The first thing to stress is that (as we also saw in section 4.5.1) since (β_1) does not by itself amount to *proof* of the fact that A killed another person, (β_2), which is equivalent to (β_1), also cannot by itself amount to *proof* of anything. (β_2) would only amount to proof of the fact that A did *not* kill another person if it were the case that as a matter of law the fact that *A did not kill another person* were a fact, the ascertainment of which to some standard *S* (which (β_2) would supposedly meet) would bear on the decision whether to convict *A* of murder. But that is not the case. There is no such standard.

The second thing to note is that there *could not* even be such a standard (that is, a standard of being *at most* 1% likely). The point may not be immediately apparent. Given that there is unquestionably a standard for the proof of the killing (the standard of being at least 99% likely), why do we not automatically get a converse or complementary standard (of being at most 1% likely) for the proof of the negation of the killing? The answer is that the complement of a standard of proof is not itself another standard of proof. A standard is a minimum threshold that has to be met: it can be either met or not; but the complement of a threshold is not itself another threshold that has to (or even can) be met.

So (β_2) does not make it true at all that *that A did not kill another person* is proved to any supposed standard of being at most 1% likely. What (β_2) *does* make true—precisely because it is the equivalent of (β_1)—is what (β_1) also makes true: namely, that the fact that *A killed another person* is proved to the relevant standard. That is why, though we may sensibly say that in a murder case the prosecutor has to prove—carries the 'burden' of proving—the killing to the relevant standard, we do not and would not sensibly say that the defendant has to prove the absence of the killing to any putative converse standard.

Indeed, what we mean when we say that the prosecution has to prove the killing is, as discussed in section 4.2, that unless (β_1)—or, equivalently, (β_2)—is true, the prosecution will not succeed. This means that in order for the defendant to win—in order for the judge to acquit—(β_1) has to be false. But for (β_1) to be false—or for (β_2) to be false, which is the same—it does not have to be the case that the available evidence establishes the non-occurrence of the killing to any degree of likelihood (and particularly that it establishes the non-occurrence of the killing to be *more* than 1% likely). For the negation of (β_1) is not

($\sim\beta_1\star$) On the basis of the available evidence, the probability that *A killed another person* is $< 99\%$,

which is equivalent to

($\sim\beta_2\star$) On the basis of the available evidence, the probability that *A did not kill another person* is $> 1\%$,

but rather

($\sim\beta_1$) It is not the case that on the basis of the available evidence, the probability that *A killed another person* is $\geq 99\%$,

which is equivalent to

($\sim\beta_2$) It is not the case that on the basis of the available evidence, the probability that *A did not kill another person* is $\leq 1\%$.

In other words, (β_1) is false if there is no available evidence either way about whether or not the killing occurred. (($\sim\beta_1\star$) implies ($\sim\beta_1$), but the reverse is not true.) So there is no particular degree of likelihood to which the non-occurrence of the killing has to be established in order for (β_1) to be false—which is to say, there is no *standard* for the proof of the non-occurrence of the killing. And that means that the non-occurrence of the killing is not a fact that can at all be *proved* in this decision-making context. It can be shown to be more or less likely, of course, on the basis of the available evidence: and if the available evidence shows the non-occurrence of the killing to be more than 1% likely, then that will also falsify (β_1); but that will not amount to *proof* of anything.

4.5.3 'Disproving' Defences

There is a similar point to be made with regard to *D*-facts. Let us now suppose that in a case of murder, self-defence—a *D*-fact—will count as proved if it is shown to be more than 1% likely to have occurred.[54] Thus the judge should acquit if (δ_1) is true:

> (δ_1) On the basis of the available evidence, the probability that *A acted in self-defence* is $>$ 1%.

But (δ_1) is equivalent to (δ_2):

> (δ_2) On the basis of the available evidence, the probability that *A did not act in self-defence* is $<$ 99%.

So again: does this equivalence not show that whenever self-defence—a *D*-fact—is proved (to the standard of being more than 1% likely), then, necessarily, the *absence* of self-defence is also proved (to the complementary standard of being less than 99% likely)? And does that not invalidate this book's proposed account of exceptions, according to which it is *never* the case that the absence of self-defence has to be proved in order for a murder conviction to be correct? If I agree that the prosecutor's job or 'burden' is to ensure that the available evidence does *not* show self-defence to be more than 1% likely, must I not by implication agree that it is the prosecutor's burden to ensure that the available evidence shows the fact that A did *not* act in self-defence to be at least 99% likely, and therefore that the prosecution must *prove*—and indeed prove *beyond a reasonable doubt* (a standard, remember, which for the sake of argument

[54] Shown *on the basis of the available evidence* to be more than 1% likely to have occurred. General statistical correlations between types of *P*-facts and types of *D*-facts (eg that 5% of all intentional killings are done in self-defence), even if they are common knowledge, are not the sort of information that fact-finders are typically allowed to rely on. The worry is not that such information has not been formally adduced as evidence by either prosecution or defence, since courts and fact-finders may (and indeed cannot but) avail themselves of some background knowledge when assessing the evidence that has been adduced. The worry is that this is merely statistical evidence, rather than evidence that pertains to the individual case.

I have proposed to translate in terms of a fact being ≥ 99% likely)—that self-defence did *not* take place?

Here too the answer is 'No', but there are two issues that can be separately emphasized. The first is once again that anyone who thinks that the fact that self-defence has *not* been proved (to some given standard) implies that its absence *has* been proved (to some putatively complementary 'standard') wrongly takes the negation of (δ_1) to be

($\sim\delta_1\star$) On the basis of the available evidence, the probability that *A acted in self-defence* is ≤ 1%,

when in fact its negation is

($\sim\delta_1$) It is not the case that on the basis of the available evidence, the probability that *A acted in self-defence* is > 1%.

The relevant point here is that ($\sim\delta_1$) does not entail the following (which is equivalent to ($\sim\delta_1\star$), but allows us to put things more clearly):

($\sim\delta_2\star$) On the basis of the available evidence, the probability that *A did not act in self-defence* is ≥ 99%.

Nor does ($\sim\delta_1$) entail that the available evidence must establish the absence of self-defence to *any* degree of probability at all: there may simply be no evidence either way. That is exactly the mark of exceptions: they are *relevant* facts—material, operative facts—that may nevertheless remain 'uncertain' in the precise sense that there may be no evidence either way.[55]

This is, with regard to exceptions, a reiteration of the point made in section 4.5.2 with regard to *P*-facts. But at this stage the following objection could be raised—a version of the first of the three objections to the proof-based account of exceptions discussed in this chapter. It may be true that if there is no evidence either way as to the occurrence of the exception, then the exception—self-defence, for example—is neither proved nor disproved. But *if* the defendant has at some point offered evidence that does establish that the exception is more than 1% likely—and if *that* is the standard for self-defence to count as proved—then in order to secure a conviction the prosecutor must offer further evidence that *decreases* this probability to at most

[55] We can also say, as I occasionally do, that exceptions can remain uncertain in the sense that it may be that neither the exception nor its negation is *proved*. As we now see, however, this statement is not quite precise. The reason that it is possible that neither an exception nor its negation is proved is that although (a) the exception itself can be *either* proved or not

1%. But necessarily, offering evidence that decreases a likelihood of more than 1% that there was self-defence is the same as offering evidence increasing the likelihood of the non-occurrence of self-defence to at least 99%. And what that means is that the prosecution will have to show *beyond a reasonable doubt* that self-defence did *not* occur. So they *do* have to disprove self-defence. Therefore I cannot be right that exceptions are facts that *never* have to (and indeed never can) be disproved. Or so this version of the first objection goes.

To deal with this objection it is not enough for me to point out (as I have in section 4.5.1) that generally speaking the prosecution will succeed if the relevant *P*-facts are proved and no *D*-fact is proved. Nor would it be sufficient to reply that once the defendant has offered evidence of the occurrence of the exception, the prosecution could simply undermine the reliability of that evidence (instead of adducing further evidence decreasing the overall likelihood of the occurrence of the exception), thereby restoring the body of available evidence to the state of there being no reliable evidence either way as to the occurrence of the exception. For my objector could insist that we can think of cases in which it is either not open (for whatever reason) to the prosecution to do that, or cases in which the defendant's evidence simply *is* reliable. And then the prosecution would clearly have to offer evidence showing that the absence of self-defence is at least 99% likely—and thus to disprove self-defence beyond a reasonable doubt—in order to secure a conviction.

But our present discussion allows me now to point out that my objector would be confusing

proved (exceptions are, we could say, 'proof-apt' facts), (b) its negation *cannot* strictly speaking be proved: it is not the sort of thing that can be either proved *or* not proved, for there simply is no corresponding standard of proof in place. But the assertion that the absence of exceptions *does not have to* be proved can wrongly be taken to suggest that it *may be* that the absence of exceptions is proved. So the idea that the absence of exceptions does not 'have' to be proved—in order for some given defeasible decision to be correct—is more rigorously rendered by saying that the decision is not dependent on the available evidence showing the non-occurrence of the admissible exceptions to any degree of probability. Exceptions are facts for which there is a legally determined standard *S* such that *if S is met* the defeasible decision is no longer correct; the decision depends on *S* not being met. But that *the absence of self-defence in murder is established to some given standard* is not something on which the conviction depends. The law does not require it as a condition of correctness, and that is the sense in which the absence of self-defence does not *have* to be proved. And to say this is, after all, the same as simply saying that the absence of self-defence *is not a P-fact*.

(δ_3) On the basis of the available evidence, the probability that *A did not act in self-defence* is ≥ 99%

with

(δ_4) It is *proved* (to the standard of being at least 99% likely) that *A did not act in self-defence.*

We already know why these two statements are not synonymous. A sentence like (δ_3) may well be true without amounting to *proof* in the legal sense of the corresponding facts. That is because, once again, unless there is, for any given fact, a standard of proof—a threshold—the satisfaction of which bears on what the correct decision is, there is simply no question of that fact being either 'proved' *or* 'not proved'.[56] So (δ_4) *cannot* be true even though (δ_3) may evidently be true in any murder case. Moreover, precisely because (δ_3) and (δ_4) are not the same, the following are also not the same:

(ε_1) In order to win, the prosecutor has to ensure that (δ_3) is true;
(ε_2) In order to win, the prosecutor has to ensure that (δ_4) is true.

In the kind of example we have been discussing—the example that my objector wants to press against the proof-based account—(ε_1) is indeed true. If the defendant has offered reliable evidence that effectively shows self-defence to be more than 1% likely—which by hypothesis meets the relevant standard of proof—then the prosecutor does have to make sure (by offering further evidence to that effect) that in the end the body of available evidence shows that the probability that the killing was *not* done in self-defence is ≥ 99%. This is true, but it by no means invalidates the proof-based account of exceptions. For what the proof-based account of exceptions implies is not that (ε_1) cannot be true, nor that it is never true. What the proof-based account implies is that (ε_2) cannot be true.

Notice, moreover, that the reason that (ε_1) will be true in the sort of example we have been discussing is that the defendant has offered evidence showing self-defence to be more than 1% likely. *Given this fact*, the only way the prosecution can meet its actual burden—which as we saw in section 4.2 is the burden of ensuring both that all relevant *P* facts are proved, and that no *D*-fact is proved—is by offering evidence that shows the non-occurrence of self-defence to be at least

[56] See n 55.

99% likely. But this is something the prosecution *has* to do only in the instrumental sense of 'having to do'. To repeat: *given the fact* that the defendant has offered reliable evidence for the occurrence of self-defence, the prosecution's only *means* of discharging its burden is to offer evidence showing the non-occurrence of self-defence to be at least 99% likely. Thereby they do more than show that the probability of self-defence is at most 1%; that they do automatically. They also *make it false* that self-defence has been proved—and that is, at all times, part of their legal burden (of their 'burden' proper).

Here is yet another way of putting this. We saw that the 'burden' carried by the prosecution at all stages is the burden of ensuring that it is true both that (a) all *P*-facts are proved to the satisfaction of some standard S_1; and that (b) no *D*-fact is proved to the satisfaction of standard S_2. Now consider: when is this second clause true? The answer is that the second clause is true when it is the case *either* that (b_1) there is simply no evidence either way concerning the occurrence of *D*-facts, *or* that (b_2) if there *is* evidence concerning the occurrence of *D*-facts, the evidence does not establish the occurrence of *D*-facts to standard S_2. In the sort of example we have been discussing, (b_1) is no longer a live option for the prosecution. Therefore the only means of making sure that (b) is true is to make sure that (b_2) is true. In this sort of example, the only means of discharging the burden—the legal burden—of ensuring that *no D-fact is proved to the satisfaction of standard S_2* is by giving evidence that establishes the *absence* of the exception to a degree of probability such that the probability of the *occurrence* of the exception necessarily falls short of S_2. So the prosecution does *have* to give evidence that the exception did not occur; yet this is not their 'burden' proper: it is merely their tactical burden, that which must be done in order to ensure that the burden proper is discharged.

It is equally important to stress one more time that the standard of proof for exceptions is frequently very low. In criminal law it is often the standard of making the occurrence of the exception a 'live issue' (a standard sometimes also described, as we saw, as that of *raising* a 'reasonable doubt' as to the occurrence of the exception)[57]. That means that in examples like the one we have been discussing—where the defendant has offered reliable evidence that would meet that low standard—the prosecutor *has to* (instrumental 'has to') show the non-occurrence of

[57] See the passage quoted to n 44 and the text following n 46.

the exception to be *very likely indeed*: likely, in fact, 'beyond a reasonable doubt'. In this description, however, the phrase 'beyond a reasonable doubt' relates again, of course, to the prosecutor's *tactical* burden—not to any standard of *proof*. It is simply a way of referring to the degree of probability that has (instrumental 'has') to be attained for the prosecution to make sure that the exception has not been proved.

It is unquestionably natural to employ the language of 'proof' to refer to this demanding tactical burden. It is natural to say that now that the defendant has offered evidence that would *prove* the occurrence of the exception, the prosecution has to *disprove* the exception—to *prove the absence of* the exception—beyond a reasonable doubt. And that is indeed how lawyers, courts, and even lawmakers more often than not express themselves. That is the kind of language at play in the various examples quoted at the beginning of this section.[58] For yet another example of the same kind, consider this passage from *R v Fontaine*, a decision from the Supreme Court of Canada:

> 52 In some instances, the proponent of an issue bears both the persuasive and the evidential burdens. But this is not invariably the case.
>
> 53 On the ultimate issue of guilt, the Crown bears both burdens. The Crown's persuasive burden on this issue can only be discharged by proof beyond a reasonable doubt. Accordingly . . . the case against the accused cannot go to the jury unless there is evidence in the record upon which a properly instructed jury could rationally conclude that the accused is guilty *beyond a reasonable doubt*.
>
> 54 In the case of 'reverse onus' defences, such as mental disorder automatism, it is the accused who bears both the persuasive and the evidential burdens. Here, the persuasive burden is discharged by evidence on the balance of probabilities, a lesser standard than proof beyond a reasonable doubt. Reverse onus defences will therefore go to the jury where there is any evidence upon which a properly instructed jury, acting judicially, could reasonably conclude that the defence has been established in accordance with this lesser standard.
>
> 55 With respect to all other 'affirmative' defences, including alibi, duress, provocation and others . . . the persuasive and the evidential burdens are divided.
>
> 56 As regards these 'ordinary', as opposed to 'reverse onus' defences, the accused has no persuasive burden at all. Once the issue has been 'put

[58] See the text following n 48.

> in play' . . . the defence will succeed unless it is *disproved* by the Crown beyond a reasonable doubt. Like all other disputed issues, however, defences of this sort will only be left to the jury where a sufficient evidential basis is found to exist. That foundation cannot be said to exist where its only constituent elements are of a tenuous, trifling, insignificant or manifestly unsubstantive nature: there must be evidence in the record upon which a properly instructed jury, acting judicially, could entertain a reasonable doubt as to the defence that has been raised.[59]

This standard way of putting things confounds legal burdens proper and tactical burdens. The *only* difference between what the Court calls 'reverse onus' defences and 'ordinary' defences is that in the former case the standard that has to be met is much higher. Some defences (like mental disorder automatism) are proved only if shown to have occurred *on the balance of probabilities*. Some other defences are proved if shown to have occurred to the standard (as the Court rather imprecisely puts it) of raising 'a reasonable doubt as to the defence', the standard of putting the defence 'in play'. As we already know, these are not standards of different kinds. The latter as much as the former is a standard of legal *proof*.[60] In *all* cases, moreover, the prosecution carries the burden—the burden proper—of ensuring that no defence—no exception—is actually proved. That means that if the defendant has offered evidence that would have established some exception to the applicable standard, the prosecution now *has*—instrumental 'has'—to offer further evidence to ensure that on the whole, the body of available evidence shows the *non*-occurrence of that exception to a degree of probability such that the probability correlatively assigned to the occurrence of the same exception fails to satisfy the relevant standard of proof. With exceptions like mental disorder automatism, for which the standard of proof is balance of probabilities, the prosecutor's task is lighter: in order to make it true that the exception is not proved, it is enough to show that the non-occurrence of the exception is >50% likely. With 'ordinary' defences, for which the standard of proof is much lower—it is the making-the-exception-a-live-issue standard: the standard of *raising* 'a reasonable doubt' as to the occurrence of the exception—the prosecutor will be forced, of course, to offer evidence establishing the non-occurrence of the exception *beyond a reasonable*

[59] *R* v *Fontaine* [2004] 1 SCR 702.

[60] See section 4.4.2.2., especially the text following n 42.

doubt. But again the main point is that to do that is not to 'prove' the absence of the exception—it is not to 'disprove' the exception. So when the Court asserts that 'once the issue has been put "into play" . . . the defence will succeed unless it is *disproved* by the Crown beyond a reasonable doubt', it is misusing the language of legal proof. Their point must be—it can only be—that the defendant will succeed unless the exception that has been raised is shown beyond a reasonable doubt not to have occurred. This is true: but it is a description of the Crown's tactical burden in scenarios like this, not a description of a 'persuasive' burden of proof.

And here is another example that allows us to view this point from a different perspective. We saw at the beginning of this section that the Draft Criminal Code for Scotland contains the following provisions:

(3) The prosecution need not prove the absence of any defence or exception unless there is evidence relating to the defence or exception which is sufficient to raise a reasonable doubt as to guilt.

(4) Where there is such evidence it is for the prosecution, unless legislation provides otherwise in relation to a particular matter, to prove the absence of the defence or exception beyond reasonable doubt.

Again this confuses the legal and the tactical burdens. In fact, the stipulation that if there is evidence sufficient 'to raise a reasonable doubt as to guilt' it is 'for the prosecution . . . to prove the absence of the exception beyond reasonable doubt' is inert—normatively superfluous—since in those cases *that the prosecution will have to show the absence of the defence beyond reasonable doubt* already follows from the fact that if the exception is proved (to the standard of 'raising a reasonable doubt as to guilt') the prosecution will lose. In other words, if no such statutory provision were in place, nothing would be different from the perspective of what the prosecution has to do in order to secure a conviction. The same applies to the following section from the Crown Prosecution Service's Prosecution Policy and Guidance:[61]

Burden of Proof

The burden of proof remains with the prosecution when the issue of self-defence is raised.

[61] Available at: <http://www.cps.gov.uk/legal/s_to_u/self_defence/#Burden_of_Proof>, accessed 13 January 2015.

The prosecution must adduce sufficient evidence to satisfy a jury beyond reasonable doubt that the defendant was either:

— not acting to defend himself/herself or another; or
— not acting to defend property; or not acting to prevent a crime or to apprehend an offender; or
— if he was so acting, the force used was excessive.

Prosecutors should take special care to recognise, and ensure a sufficiency of evidence in, those cases where self-defence is likely to be an issue.

It is true that if the issue of self-defence is 'raised'—that is, made a 'live issue', and therefore *proved* to that standard—'the prosecution must adduce sufficient evidence to satisfy a jury beyond reasonable doubt' that the defendant was *not* acting in self-defence. But this is the instrumental 'must': it does not mean that 'the burden of proof remains with the prosecution when the issue of self-defence is raised'.

One final, related point—a final potential source of confusion—can now be dealt with fairly quickly. Given that it is possible (and frequent, in the case of exceptions) that the legally determined standard of proof for some given material fact *F* is a degree of probability *lower* than 50%, is it not then possible that both *F and not-F* can be proved in the same decision-making context? Once again, the answer is negative. First, we have already learned that no fact is properly said to be 'proved' or 'not proved' except by reference to some legally determined standard, and that the legal determination of a standard for the proof of some fact *F* does not amount to the automatic determination of a supposed complementary 'standard' for the proof of *not-F*. Therefore in order for *both F and its negation* to be 'proved' in some decision-making context, it would have to be the case that the correct decision would depend *simultaneously* (as a matter of law) on the probability of *F* being established to some given standard *and* on the probability of *not-F* also being established to some *other* given standard (it would be *another* standard even if both standards imposed the same degree of probability). But that would be an absurd condition to have in place, a condition for which no sound normative rationale could, it seems, be given. Since a standard sets a *threshold* to be met (rather than a precise degree of probability that not only has to be met but cannot be surpassed), if there happened to be not only a standard for the proof of *F* (≥ 40% likelihood, say), but also a standard for the proof of *not-F* (≥ 40% likelihood, say), then there would always be a point—61% likelihood: a point *above* the threshold set for the proof of *F* in our example—beyond which the degree of probability of *F* on the basis of the available evidence would render impossible the satisfaction of the standard for *not-F*; and vice versa.

4.5.4 *A Square of Opposition for Legal Proof*

It can be helpful to pin down—and to visualize—the logical relations that hold between sentences (and their negations) about whether some proposition *X* is shown on the basis of the available evidence to be ≥ *n*% likely, where '≥ *n*%' is the legally applicable standard of proof.

There are four relevant types of sentence, (A), (B), (C), and (D). For any *n*, '*X* is proved' is true if

(A) On the basis of the available evidence, the probability of *X* is ≥ *n*%.
(This is equivalent to 'On the basis of the available evidence, the probability of *not-X* is ≤ (100 – *n*%)'.)

Therefore '*X* is not proved' is true if

(C) It is not the case that on the basis of the available evidence, the probability of *X* is ≥ *n*%.
(This is equivalent to 'It is not the case that on the basis of the available evidence, the probability of *not-X* is ≤ (100 – *n*%)'.)

(A) and (C) are *contradictories*: necessarily, if one is true, the other is false. When is (C) true? Either when there is simply no evidence either way (that is, no evidence for *X* and no evidence for *not-X*), or when

(B) On the basis of the available evidence, the probability of *X* is < *n*%.
(This is equivalent to 'On the basis of the available evidence, the probability of *not-X* is > (100 – *n*%)'.)

(A) and (B) are *contraries*: they cannot both be true (though they can both be false—which is the case precisely when there is no evidence either way). And (C) is *subaltern* to (B): if (B) is true, then (C) is true, but not vice versa.

Finally, whenever (B) is true, (D)—its *contradictory*—is false, and vice versa:

(D) It is not the case that on the basis of the available evidence, the probability of *X* is < *n*%.

(This is equivalent to 'It is not the case that on the basis of the available evidence, the probability of *not-X* is > (100 – *n*%)'.)

And (D), in turn, is *subaltern* to (A): (D) is true whenever (A) is true, but not vice versa.

So we can put together the following square of opposition:

On the basis of the available evidence, the probability of *X* is ≥ *n*%.

On the basis of the available evidence, the probability of *X* is < *n*%.

A B

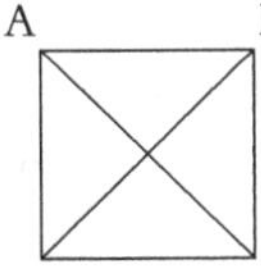

D C

It is not the case that on the basis of the available evidence, the probability of *X* is < *n*%.

It is not the case that on the basis of the available evidence, the probability of *X* is ≥ *n*%.

So again: (A) and (C) are contradictories (when one is true, the other is false); (B) and (D) are contradictories as well; (A) and (B) are contraries (they cannot both be true, though they can both be false); (C) and (D) are subcontraries (they cannot both be false, though they can both be true); (D) is the subaltern of (A) (if (A) is true, then (D) is also true, but not vice versa); and (C) is the subaltern of (B).

The reason the square has to be constructed with statements of this sort, rather than statements about what is and is not *proved*, is that not all four kinds of statements (A), (B), (C), and (D), can be translated into statements about what is and is not proved. (A) does make it true—though it is not synonymous with the assertion—that *X* is proved, and correspondingly (C) makes it false—though it is not synonymous with the denial—that *X* is proved (and thus makes it true that *it is not the case that X* is proved). (B), which is the contrary of (A), also makes it false that *X* is proved. But (D) is compatible with it being the case either that *X* is proved (since (D) is compatible with

(A) being true) or that *X* is *not* proved (since (D) is compatible with (C) being true).

4.6 The 'Logic' of Exceptions

4.6.1 The Third Objection

The third and final of the objections listed in section 4.1 was that the proof-based account matches only one of two ways in which the burden of proof relative to exceptions can be allocated. It is also possible, the objection goes, for the burden of disproving exceptions to be imposed on the prosecution—as English criminal law has done, as a rule, since *Woolmington*.

This objection is vitiated by *petitio principii*. It assumes that we are able to identify exceptions independently of and previously to any allocation of burdens of proof. In other words, the objection assumes that the question 'Who should carry the burden of proving exceptions?' can be intelligibly asked, and that the answer may vary according to context. If the proof-based account is sound, however, this question is ill conceived. For my main claim is precisely that in order to discern which facts are exceptions relative to some decision-type, we need to look at what facts must and must not be ascertained for the decision to be correct. Exceptions, I argued, are *D*-facts, not *P*-facts: and I said that *P*-facts just are those facts that must be proved for the prosecutor or plaintiff to succeed, and *D*-facts those that must *not* be so proved (that is, those whose proof benefits the defendant).

It is interesting to see how the failure to acknowledge the distinction between *P*- and *D*-facts lies at the root of some persistent puzzles within the ongoing debate about *how* to allocate the burden of proof relative to exceptions in English law. As I made clear in Chapter 1, both *P*-facts and *D*-facts can be either positive or negative. Indeed, the importance of distinguishing between *P*-facts and *D*-facts becomes particularly visible when we compare a *negative P*-fact with a *positive D*-fact. What is the difference between a scenario in which *not-X* is a *P*-fact and a scenario in which *X* is a *D*-fact relative to some judgment or decision-type? In one respect there might seem to be no difference, for we have seen that either the ascertainment of the negation of a *P*-fact beyond a certain degree of probability, or the ascertainment of a *D*-fact beyond a certain degree of probability, is sufficient to prevent a defeasible judgment from being correctly issued. But it is only when *not-X* is a *P*-fact—not when *X* is a *D*-fact—that it is necessary that *not-X be proved* for the decision to be correct. We have also seen in Chapter 3 that this difference cannot be made explicit if we concentrate—as legal theorists traditionally do—on the facts *P* and *D* themselves, rather than on whether or not they are proved. The structural distinction between a scenario in which *not-X* is a *P-fact* and one in which *X* is a *D*-fact is lost in traditional, 'substantive' representations of the conditions of judicial decisions, which in both cases will represent *not-X* as a negative condition of a correctly issued decision. Traditional representations have no viable way to distinguish between these two scenarios. At the same time, no one denies that there *are* distinctions worth drawing between such negative conditions. Many theorists think—to return to an example I have already used—that *absence of consent* in a criminal case of rape is in one respect significantly different from, say, *absence of self-defence* in a criminal case of murder. These theorists would find it ludicrous to maintain that for someone to be rightly convicted of rape no proof should be required that sexual intercourse was *not* consensual, but at the same time they do not find it all that implausible to suggest that a murder conviction should *not* be made to depend on it actually being proved that there was *no* self-defence. Yet if both absence of consent and absence of self-defence are, in their view, logically equivalent—if both have the status of negative conditions—what is it that explains this difference? Are there two different *kinds* of negative conditions?

It is a mistake to think that the problem can be solved simply by saying that self-defence, unlike consent, is a proper 'exception' to criminal conviction. Consider, for example, the following provision, section 101 of the English Magistrates' Courts Act 1980:

> *Where the defendant to any information or complaint relies for his defence on any exception*, exemption, proviso, excuse or qualification, whether or not it accompanies the description of the offence or matter of complaint in the enactment creating the offence or on which the complaint is founded, *the burden of proving the exception*, exemption, proviso, excuse or qualification *shall be on him*; and this notwithstanding that the information of complaint contains an allegation negativing the exception, exemption, proviso, excuse, or qualification.[62]

[62] Emphasis added.

This provision relies on a contrast between an 'offence' and an 'exception, exemption, proviso, excuse or qualification'. Clearly, the contrast is not meant to imply that offences are made up of *positive* elements only. The thought behind this provision, then, is that if a certain fact—such as absence of consent in rape—is properly classified as an element of the offence, *then* the burden of proving should remain on the prosecution; whereas if a fact—such as self-defence—is properly classified as an exception, then the burden of proving it should be placed on the defendant. But all is not well. Think of a court having to determine whether this provision applies to some given fact *X* that would, if established, prevent the conviction. The first task the court is being asked to perform is one of classification. Is *X* to be counted as an 'exception, exemption, proviso, excuse or qualification'? Or is *not-X* to be counted as a negative offence element instead? Before the court can answer this question, it is unable to determine whether section 101 will apply—it is unable to determine whether the burden of proving *X* should be placed on the defendant. But how is the court to go about answering the classificatory question? My point, of course, is that it is a self-defeating question; it is rendered unanswerable by the very assumption that allows it to be asked.

To see this more clearly, let us survey some of the arguments that legal scholars have been exchanging on the topic. It is telling that the debate—which has been going on for decades—is yet to generate a satisfactory criterion.

4.6.2 Williams's 'Logical' Point

The debate has not been restricted to this particular provision. In *Edwards*, for example, the Court of Appeal held that (a) the question of how to distinguish negative qualifications that are true exceptions from those that are not is a matter of statutory construction; and that (b) the common law has 'evolved', 'over the centuries', an 'exception to the fundamental rule of our criminal law that the prosecution must prove every element of the offence charged'. This exception, 'limited to offences arising under enactments which prohibit the doing of an act save in specified circumstances or by persons of specified classes or with specified qualifications or with the licence or permission of specified authorities', establishes that *if* the 'true construction' is in those cases 'that the enactment prohibits the doing of acts, subject to provisos, exemptions and the like', then 'the prosecution can rely upon the exception'.[63] Thus in step (b), a rule similar to the one in section 101 of the English Magistrates' Courts Act 1980[64] is asserted as a general rule of common law.[65] *Edwards* concerned the offence of selling liquor without a licence contrary to section 160(1)(a) of the Licensing Act 1964. The Court of Appeal found the 'true construction' to be that the provision prohibited the act of selling intoxicating liquor, and that possession of a licence was to be counted as an 'exception' proper. The burden of proving that they had a licence could *therefore* be placed upon defendants.

Not all of the many objections directed at this ruling are equally interesting for our present purposes. Take Glanville Williams's 'argument from absurdity', purporting to establish that the general 'rule as to licences is nonsensical':

If having a licence is a defence, the remaining words must state the offence. So the offence of *driving a vehicle without a licence* becomes simply an *offence of driving a vehicle*. But to express the offence in this way would misstate the law. The offence is *not* aimed against people who drive vehicles; it is aimed against those who *drive them without licences*. The absence of a licence is, in common sense, an integral part of the offence.[66]

This does not go to the heart of the matter. It leaves points (a) and (b) untouched, and questions only their applicability to the case at hand. And Williams himself remarks that there may be decisions against which this argument 'misses its fire':

Take a statute making it an offence for an employer to fail in his duty to take safety precautions 'so far as reasonably practicable'. Some may think it reasonable to treat the qualifying phrase as an exception, because leaving it

[63] *R* v *Edwards* [1975] 1 QB 39-40 (CA).

[64] Or rather to the one in section 81 of the Magistrates' Courts Act 1952, then in force, but whose content and language are retained *verbatim* in section 101 of the 1980 Act currently in force.

[65] *Edwards* is but a conspicuous example of the sort of approach I mean to discuss. In 1944, Julius Stone was able to offer the following as a 'brief but substantially accurate statement of accepted [though, in Stone's view, ill-founded] legal principles': '[W]hich party has the burden of proof of Fact A depends upon whether Fact A is included among the facts defining the scope of the general rule, or is merely contained in an exception to that rule'. See Stone (1944: 280).

[66] Williams (1988: 273–4).

out still makes the offence one of failing to take safety precautions, which is an intelligible charge.[67]

But Williams has another, stronger argument targeting the assumption—which underlies both (a) and (b)—that some distinction can 'rationally' be drawn between exceptions and (negative) elements of an offence. His argument has been influential, and is worth reviewing in some detail. As I remarked in Chapter 3, Williams adopts what I proposed to call an 'incorporationist' approach to exceptions. He makes the 'general', 'logical' point that 'there are no exceptions as self-subsisting concepts', 'no intrinsic difference between the elements of an offence and an exception or defence to that offence'. I already quoted the following passage:[68]

> A rule that is subject to an exception is only partly true if it is stated without the exception . . . The exception is, rationally regarded, part and parcel of the rule. Hence looking for the line between a rule and an exception is, to use the proverbial simile, like looking in a dark room for a black cat that isn't there.[69]

Given that 'all the exceptions (or defences) can be stated in negative form as part of the offence, instead of as something outside the offences',[70] the 'offence package', consisting of 'the offence elements and the negative of defences', forms 'an indivisible whole'.[71] So if Williams is right, both *Edwards* and section 101 of the Magistrates' Courts Act fallaciously suppose 'a distinction between the offence and the exception'.[72] But according to Williams, this is not the fundamental flaw of section 101 or any other similar rule. For even though Parliament 'did not venture to define an exception, but assumed that everyone knew what an exception was',[73] the truth is that Parliament 'could define exceptions for us: it could say that such and such shall be exceptions to the rule'.[74] The fundamental problem lies instead in the 'injustice of using a rule about exceptions', *however* defined, 'to shift

[67] Williams (1988: 276–7).
[68] See Williams (1988: 276–7, 279–80).
[69] Williams (1988: 278).
[70] Williams (1988: 277).
[71] Williams (1988: 280).
[72] Williams (1988: 280).
[73] Williams (1988: 273).
[74] Williams (1988: 279).

the burden of proof'.[75] If an 'exception', 'rationally regarded', 'merely states the limits of an offence',[76] then there is no difference between burdening defendants with the proof of 'exceptions' and burdening them with the proof that any other element of the offence is not verified. In other words, the mere fact that some qualification is deemed an 'exception' rather than an element of a 'rule' or 'offence' can have no argumentative import in determining who should bear the burden of proof.

There are two further points worth highlighting about Williams's general argument. The first is that his 'logical' remarks are motivated by a preoccupation with the integrity of the *Woolmington* rule, which, Williams believes, ought to be 'unconditionally accepted'.[77] His particular concern is with the allocation of the *persuasive* burden of proof. 'Evidential burdens', he says, 'should be readily placed on the defendant',[78] and section 101 of the Magistrates' Courts Act 1980 'would be acceptable' if 'it were merely a statement of the evidential burden'.[79] After all, he observes, while 'the allocation of burdens of proof goes to the heart of our notion of justice', evidential burdens 'are not matters of great moment', and are 'settled largely for practical reasons':

> The principle is that the prosecution might give evidence on the bare bones of the charge, while the defendant must normally offer evidence on matters of justification or excuse on which he wishes to rely.[80]

The second point is that although Williams rightly indicates Julius Stone as the pioneer of the 'logical' argument,[81] he nonetheless rebukes Stone by remarking that

> having discovered that it is quite arbitrary to try to spell out exceptions from the arrangement of the words of a law, he [Stone] proposed to get over the difficulty by looking for exceptions by the test of policy; we can then place the burden of proving exceptions, so discovered, on the defendant to a civil action.[82]

[75] Williams (1988: 280); compare Stone (1944: 281).
[76] Williams (1988: 262).
[77] Williams (1988: 281).
[78] Williams (1988: 281).
[79] Williams (1988: 272).
[80] Williams (1988: 269).
[81] See Williams (1988: 277); Stone (1944: 278–84).
[82] Williams (1988: 280).

'This will not do', William says: 'neither in the civil nor in the criminal law can a distinction between rules and exceptions properly be used in allocating the burden of proof'.[83] He then moves on to briefly consider Zuckerman's 1976 essay 'The Third Exception to the *Woolmington* Rule'. Zuckerman, says Williams,

> accepted Stone's point that exceptions cannot be gathered from the arrangement of wording in statutes, but argued that the criminal burden should be distributed according to policy (as Stone had done for the civil burden).[84]

Williams remarks that it might 'at first sight' seem 'that [Zuckerman's] proposal is open to the same objection as Stone's'; but the fact is, he says, that 'earlier in his article Zuckerman had announced an intention of using "burden of proof" to cover both persuasive and evidential burdens', and it appears 'that he intended to propose *only* that the distribution of *evidential* burdens should be settled according to policy'.[85] So perhaps Zuckerman 'intended that his "policy" proposal was to be conditional on acceptance of his proposal that criminal burdens on the defendant should be evidential only'[86]—in which case, Williams suggests, the objection made to Stone would not hold against Zuckerman as well.

4.6.3 A Circular Impasse

But it is hard to see why not. We can begin to assess Williams's argument by noting that in the two passages just excerpted, he states Julius Stone's proposal in two rather different ways. The first attributes to Stone the claim that it is possible to *look for exceptions* by the 'test of policy' in order *then* to 'place the burden of proving exceptions, so discovered, on the defendant to a civil action'. The second attributes to Stone the claim that the 'burden should be distributed according to policy'. But these are two distinct proposals, each one addressing a very different question.[87] The second is a proposal about *how to*

[83] Williams (1988: 280).

[84] Williams (1988: 281 n 45).

[85] Williams (1988: 281 n 45); and see Zuckerman (1976: 403).

[86] Williams (1988: 281 n 45).

[87] It is in fact the second, rather than the first, that matches Stone's actual proposal: see Stone (1944: 282–3). MacCormick also misses the relevant point. Discussing Stone's argument, MacCormick (1995: 105–6) insists that 'in its proper setting the difference between

allocate the burden of proof relative to any given relevant circumstance; it applies a 'test of policy', however devised, to determine whether or not, given any circumstance *X*, the corresponding burden of proof should be placed on the defendant. Here whether *X* is to be counted as an exception (according to any conceivable criterion) is completely irrelevant. The first proposal, in turn, is a proposal about *how to identify exceptions*. It applies a test of policy to determine whether, given any circumstance *X*, *X* counts as an exception. And here, as both Williams's rendition of this proposal and his objection to it make perfectly clear, the allocation of the corresponding burden of proof is but a *consequence* of the fact that *X* is classified as an exception.

Why is this distinction important in the context of our discussion? Recall that Williams takes no issue with the possibility that 'evidential burdens' be placed on the defendant. On the contrary, he says, there are sound 'practical reasons' for defendants to be made to offer evidence on matters of justification or excuse.[88] Surely, however, he wouldn't require defendants to discharge a similar evidential burden

[negative] qualification and exception is far from illusory'; 'understood in terms of pragmatics', he says, the difference is 'real'; see also MacCormick (2005: 245–6). Stone's point, however, is not that no 'real' distinction (whatever that means) can be drawn between exceptions and negative qualifications. Stone's point is that there is no intelligible pre-existing distinction between exceptions and negative qualifications by reference to which—ie on the grounds of which—any particular distribution of burdens of proof can be justified. Moreover, MacCormick's equivocal claim (1995: 106) that 'if a rule is [expressly] formulated in the terms that a right vests on conditions c_1, c_2, c_3, but this is subject to exceptions in case e_1, e_2 . . ., we are to take that express formulation as one conventionally used to signal one allocation of the burden of proof, while the other formulation, in terms of positive (and qualification) negative conditions of vesting signals the opposite allocation' leaves the issue completely unsettled. MacCormick seems to think, mistakenly, that there is no 'logical' obstacle to the law's proclaiming that a 'differential burden of proof' is '*dependent* on exactly this differentiation' (1995: 105, emphasis added) and that a conditional such as 'If . . . *A* has a right upon certain conditions, but the vesting of the right is expressly subject to a certain exception, then the evidentiary burden shifts to the other interested party or parties to show that the exception does obtain' (1995: 104) can be non-tautologically true. Claire Finkelstein incurs in comparable confusion. She thinks that a differential allocation of burdens of proof is only a 'typical' and by no means a necessary feature or 'implication' of the offence/defence divide; and yet she construes our 'intuitions' about how to allocate probative burdens relative to some negative circumstance *X* as intuitions as to whether *X* 'should be regarded as an affirmative defence or as a negative offence element': see Finkelstein (1999: 160, 166). Even Gordon, who at one point states very clearly that 'general rules with exceptions . . . are one way of dividing up the burden of proof', seems inconsistently to believe that exceptions can be identified on the grounds of the 'substantive' law alone—ie irrespective of any allocation of 'burdens of proof': see Gordon (1995: 40, 115).

[88] Williams (1988: 269); and compare his earlier discussions in Williams (1977a) and Williams (1977b).

relative to the (absence of the) elements of the offence. He therefore needs some criterion to distinguish between, on the one hand, circumstances—and, particularly, *negative* circumstances such as lack of consent in rape—which, constituting elements of the offence, are to be proved by the prosecution without it being necessary for the defendant to bring them into issue; and on the other hand, circumstances that are to be brought into issue by the defendant.

Williams refers to the latter as 'matters of justification or excuse';[89] but how is the task of looking for the dividing line between 'offences' and 'justifications', for example, any less misguided, by Williams's own 'logical' standard, than that of looking for the dividing line between offences and exceptions? Take self-defence once again. This is a circumstance that Williams would doubtless classify as a 'justification or excuse'. But self-defence, Williams insists, 'perhaps the most plausible example of a [supposed] free-standing "exception" in the criminal law',[90] is in fact no 'exception' at all—for 'there are no exceptions as self-subsisting concepts'.[91] Self-defence 'is impliedly incorporated' into each crime 'as (in negative form) an offence element'; it is 'a negative element of the crime, just as the woman's non-consent is a negative element of rape'.[92] Hence Williams's inconsistency is manifest. For if his rejoinder to Stone that 'neither in the civil nor in the criminal law can a distinction between rules and exceptions properly be used in allocating the burden of proof'[93] is sound, then his own contention that the equivalent distinction between rules and justifications be used in allocating the evidential burden (and that section 101 of the Magistrates' Courts Act 1980 would be 'acceptable' if 'it were merely a statement of the evidential burden') is wrong—and vice versa. Therefore, contrary to Williams's suggestion in the last excerpted passage, it should make no difference that Stone happened to be concerned with the 'persuasive' rather than the evidential burden. Williams simultaneously adopts two incompatible claims: first, that no rule relying on the distinction between offences and exceptions can ever be applied, as it supposes an non-existent distinction; and second, that evidential burdens ought to be placed on the defendant relative to exceptions,

89 Williams (1988: 269).

90 Williams (1988: 278).

91 Williams (1988: 279).

92 Williams (1988: 278–9); and see also an earlier statement of this very same point, explicitly addressing 'justifications', in Williams (1982: 247–9).

93 Williams (1988: 280).

but not offence elements. The second claim endorses a rule of the kind that the first claim declares inapplicable, and a distinction that the first claim declares nonsensical.

It might be submitted that perhaps what Williams actually meant was not that evidentiary burdens be allocated *on the basis of* any distinction between 'offences' and 'justifications or excuses', or between 'rules' and 'exceptions'. Perhaps he did not really mean to maintain that what justifies placing on the defendant the evidential burden relative to, for example, self-defence is the fact that it is a 'justification'. Perhaps what he meant—in spite of his unfortunate phrasing—was that there may be reason for placing on the defendant the evidential burden relative to self-defence. This interpretation, however, would only allow us to approach the very same inconsistency from the other end. If the reason for burdening the defendant with bringing self-defence into issue has nothing to do with self-defence's supposed status as an 'exception' or a 'justification', then Williams's 'logical point' about the equivalence of offences and exceptions is immaterial; any such reason for so allocating the evidential burden will remain unaffected whether or not the 'logical point' is sound. And the same must hold for any proposal that—like Stone's proposal, according to Williams's *second* statement of it—maintains that there may be a 'policy' reason to place on the defendant the *persuasive* burden of some relevant negative circumstances. To maintain that 'neither in the civil nor in the criminal law can a distinction between rules and exceptions properly be used in allocating the burden of proof' is simply beside the point.[94]

Not only is Williams's 'logical point' immaterial for the soundness of the claim that there may be reason for placing on the defendant the evidential burden relative to some relevant circumstance, but this claim actually implies that Williams's point is wrong. We already know why. If one accepts, as Williams (as well as most anyone) does,[95] that the evidential burden relative to self-defence is to be placed on the defendant, then it is possible for the defendant to be rightly convicted

[94] This does not mean that there *is* reason—a reason of policy or, for that matter, of any other kind—to allocate in such a manner the persuasive burden relative to self-defence. It means only that the debate whether or not such reason exists is unaffected by the 'logical' issue. It is worth noting that Williams (1988: 281) himself endorses an argument of policy in favour of his preferred allocation of the persuasive burden.

[95] Williams (1988: 279).

without the absence of self-defence being ascertained. And this means that the 'logical point' must be wrong. For the logical point asserts that absence of self-defence is but an element of the offence, with the implication that a conviction necessarily depends on its ascertainment.[96]

At the root of Williams's impasse is his inability to conceive of the relevant circumstances as anything other than 'conditions' or 'elements' whose occurrence is needed for conviction. My point can now be restated more generally. In accepting that there is reason to burden the defendant with the proof of self-defence in a case of murder, but not with the proof of consent in a case of rape, one is surely accepting a distinction between kinds of circumstances. One is accepting that *absence of self-defence* is not something that has to be ascertained for someone to be properly convicted of murder, while *absence of consent* does have to be ascertained to a given standard for someone to be properly convicted of rape. These are both, in a sense, 'negative' circumstances; but each behaves differently. Williams's problem is that his misguided assumption that these circumstances count as 'conditions' or 'elements' of liability commits him to viewing both *absence of self-defence* and *absence of consent* as having the same kind of 'logical' role: the role of *conditions*, respectively, of murder and rape. But this is wrong, I suggested, not because there is some 'logical' difference between absence of self-defence and absence of consent, but simply because neither circumstance is to be represented as a condition of liability.[97]

[96] An additional factor of confusion in Williams's essay is that he also mistakes (unsurprisingly) the prosecution's 'burden of disproving' self-defence 'if the defendant raises the issue' for a burden of *proving the absence* of self defence: see Williams (1988: 279). That is why, in fact, he wrongly believes that he can agree that the evidential burden should be placed on the defendant and go on maintaining that the rule in *Woolmington* should be 'unconditionally' applied in relation to all the elements of the 'offence package', lest the defendant 'be condemned on a cause of action that has not been proved against him': see Williams (1988: 280, 281). This is the exact same common confusion that was discussed and dispelled in section 4.4.

[97] Huigens (2009: 651–2) claims that Williams's 'negative elements' view of justification defences would imply that 'the prosecution would have to prove every aspect of the defendant's not being justified' (ie that the prosecution would have to prove *every element* of *every admissible justification defence*). Thus Williams is wrong (argues Huigens) since 'in all jurisdictions . . . [p]roof of one non-justification element, along with fault as to that element, will suffice' to convict. Despite my lack of sympathy for Williams's 'negative elements' account of defences, I believe Huigens's particular criticism is unwarranted. The view that the prosecution needs to 'disprove' self-defence (for example) is fully consistent with the claim that if self-defence is analysable as a conjunction of elements x *and* y *and* z, then the prosecution needs to disprove only x *or* y *or* z in order to discharge its burden.

What our discussion shows is that the question 'Should the burden of proof relative to justifications be placed on the defendant?' is unintelligible and unanswerable. The right question is, for example, 'Should the burden of proof relative to self-defence be placed on the defendant?', or, in the case of rape, 'Should the burden of proof relative to consent be placed on the defendant?' These are questions to be tackled by appeal to reasons of different sorts (including reasons of policy), though certainly not by appeal to any 'logical' distinction. Indeed, any 'logical' distinction will be the product rather than the ground of a disparate allocation of the burden of proof. If a law-making authority answers the first question affirmatively, and the second negatively, this means in my terminology that self-defence is *thereby* made a *D*-fact, and absence of consent a *P*-fact. *In that case*—given that there *is* a 'logical' or 'structural' difference between *P*- and *D*-facts, and that *D*-facts are aptly called 'exceptions'—it can be said that self-defence is an 'exception', and that lack of consent is not. This, however, is a consequence of the way in which the burdens were allocated. To make proof of self-defence burden the defendant *is* to make self-defence a *D*-fact; and being a *D*-fact just *is* what it means being an exception.

It is no wonder that rules like the one in section 101 of the Magistrates' Courts Act 1980 or the similar one in *Edwards*[98] have been found to have caused nothing but 'uncertainty, confusion, and inconsistency',[99] nor that courts may have taken 'Parliament's foolish formula' in that statutory provision 'as allowing them to pick any words out of the definition of an offence and to call the negatives of these words "exceptions" carrying a reverse onus'.[100] Section 101 functions differently from express statutory 'reverse onus clauses'. The latter concern certain specified circumstances—'absence of consent' in section 75 of the Sexual Offences Act 2003, for example—and *make* those circumstances 'exceptions' by stipulating that the corresponding burden of proof is to be placed on the defendant. But section 101 instructs the courts to look for the exception in order *then* to burden the defendant with the corresponding proof. It thereby turns logical priority on its head, and is impossible to apply. In *Hunt*, Lord Griffiths spoke of the

98 Or, for another example, section 13.3(3) of the Commonwealth *Criminal Code*.

99 See Roberts and Zuckerman (2010: 268).

100 Williams (1988: 273).

'construction of the particular legislation to determine whether the defence is an exception within the meaning of section 101 of the Act of 1980'.[101] But if—as some claim—this requires us to ponder whether *there is reason* to place the corresponding burden on the defendant[102] (on the basis of such familiar considerations as the defendant's 'peculiar knowledge' of the circumstance at stake, the comparatively greater ease with which she might give evidence on it, or even the 'seriousness' of the offence[103]), then we will simply be bypassing, rather than applying, section 101.[104]

[101] *R* v *Hunt* [1987] 1 AC 375-6 (HL).

[102] This seems to be the suggestion made in Birch (1988: 223).

[103] See Ashworth (2006: 259–70) for a discussion of 'reasons that tend to be advanced to justify imposing a burden (exceptionally) on the defendant'.

[104] Compare Zuckerman (1976: 413–22), as well as Zuckerman (1987); Husak (1987: 207–11); Smith (1987: esp. at 227–36); Mirfield (1988: esp. at 26–7); Stein (1991); Ashworth and Horder (2013: 72–3); Simester and others (2013: 61–2). See also Fletcher's account of the issues and problems raised by what has been, since the end of the 19th century, the dominant model for the allocation of persuasive burdens in private litigation in German law: Fletcher (1968: 894–910); Fletcher (1978/2000: 519–52).

5

Implicit Exceptions

5.1 The Problem

So far we have been concerned with so-called 'explicit' exceptions only. This common label picks out those facts that are classified as exceptions as a matter of general law: facts that can be identified as exceptions as part of the process of identifying the relevant legal rules on any given matter. 'Implicit' exceptions, in turn, are those circumstances of particular cases—actual cases before a judge—which a court may decide to classify and admit as exceptions, immediately operative in the case at hand. Their classification as exceptions therefore involves, as Neil MacCormick puts it, 'an exercise of discretionary judgment by a deciding official or judge'.[1]

It was MacCormick who popularized the use of these adjectives, 'explicit' (or 'express') and 'implicit', to refer to the two kinds. That the labels are imprecise can be seen from the definitions just given. There may be no canonical or otherwise explicit statutory formulation on which to ground the identification of 'express' exceptions. The point is that it is possible to identify those circumstances *as* exceptions in advance and independently of any particular case; but this identification may itself be the outcome of complex interpretative procedures not based on any statutory provision or on any explicitly formulated catalogue of admissible exceptions. Nor are 'implicit' exceptions *implicit*—'in' the law—in the common sense of the term. But there would be little point in coining new labels simply for the purpose of

[1] MacCormick (1995: 102); see also MacCormick (2005: 240–2).

the present discussion. The definitions just given should leave no room for confusion as to the phenomena referred to by these terms.

Our proof-based account of explicit exceptions, then, is not a complete account of exceptions and defeasibility in law. We need to see whether implicit exceptions can also be accounted for in proof-based terms. But that is not the only challenge we face. The phenomenon of implicit exceptions gives rise to a deeper worry: the worry that one line of argument defended in previous chapters may actually be wrong-headed. I have argued against the thesis that

(T1') The circumstances on which the correctness of a defeasible decision depends cannot be specified by a set of necessary and sufficient conditions.

The worry is that the phenomenon of implicit exceptions seems to bring (T1') into play once again. Remember the incorporationist view of explicit exceptions. This is the view that exceptions can simply be represented as negative conditions in more accurately formulated rules. I argued in Chapter 3 that though incorporationism is inadequate as an account of explicit exceptions, theorists who adopt it are right to reject (T1'). For what the proof-based account proposes is that we represent explicit exceptions, not as negative rule-conditions themselves, but as the content of '*not proved that . . .*' rule-conditions; and that gives us no reason to adopt (T1'). When it comes to implicit exceptions, however, it may be thought that (T1') is actually correct. And, in fact, that is the view endorsed by many who think that incorporationism *does* give us a satisfactory picture of explicit exceptions. For explicit and implicit exceptions, they say, are very different phenomena. After all, how could incorporationism ever be true of the latter? If implicit exceptions cannot—by definition—be identified in advance of any actual case, then they cannot be incorporated as parts of any previously identifiable rules.

MacCormick held this view. Whenever implicit exceptions are allowed, 'the problem', he said,

> is in one aspect that of the limits to accuracy or exhaustiveness in statements of the law, and in another aspect that of the reliability with which one can draw inferences from the express statements in which the law is formulated.[2]

[2] MacCormick (1995: 103).

Let us try to set out this challenge in greater detail. When judges are authorized to classify and admit as exceptions facts not previously identified or identifiable as such, they are thereby authorized to set aside an otherwise applicable legal rule *even though* the case may clearly fall under the rule's scope. Such powers are normally granted in the name of justice or some other principle or value. Here is an example. Section 111(2) of the Powers of Criminal Courts (Sentencing) Act 2000 stipulates that

> The court shall impose an appropriate custodial sentence for a term of at least three years except where the court is of the opinion that there are particular circumstances which—
>
> (a) relate to any of the offences or to the offender; and
> (b) would make it unjust to do so in all the circumstances.[3]

There is no closed list of the circumstances that classify as exceptions under this provision. Any list of such exceptions would be, as MacCormick (1974: 125) puts it, 'open-ended'. And his claim is that this is quite simply 'fatal to any attempt to represent the express institutive rules as containing necessary and sufficient conditions for valid adjudication by tribunals or whatever'. In cases like this, no formulation of the relevant rule can be given with 'the logician's precision as an "if and only if . . ." rule laying down necessary and sufficient conditions':[4]

> Even if, for any given . . . institution, we were to write out the statutory rules, including in them all the exceptions hitherto imposed by the courts in that and analogous cases, we could not be confident that we had succeeded in listing the sufficient conditions for validity of a determination or an act of delegated legislation or whatever . . . [N]o formulation, however detailed, of the institutive rule of an institution can be taken as giving a complete list of sufficient conditions for the validity of a purported instance of the institution, any more than stating conditions each of which is in all cases necessary. Any such formulation of a rule has to be read as subject to further exceptions [.][5]

[3] For other examples of similar provisions, see Section 2(3) of the Crime and Punishment (Scotland) Act 1997; or Sections 225(2) and 226(2) of the Armed Forces Act 2006.

[4] MacCormick (1974: 123).

[5] MacCormick (1974: 125–6). Although he concentrates on 'institutive rules of institutions', MacCormick explicitly notes that 'the same may be said in relation to . . . other types of rule . . . and indeed of "rules of law" generally': see MacCormick (1974: 127).

In other words, (T1') is true. Whenever implicit exceptions are allowed, we may know the applicable legal rule, know what the relevant standards of proof are, and know exactly what facts have and have not been ascertained and become part of the accepted body of evidence—and we still won't be able to tell what the correct decision should be.

This is a popular line of argument.[6] Is it sound? We will see that the answer is negative. But first we need to acquire a firmer grasp on the very notion of an implicit exception, and to examine more closely the widespread view—let us call it the 'common view'—that explicit and implicit exceptions are essentially different phenomena.

5.2 The Common View

With regard to explicit exceptions, as I noted, the common view is that incorporationism is right. Given that explicit exceptions can be identified in advance of any particular case, they can always be restated as part of more rigorously articulated rules. Explicit exceptions are nothing more than negative delimitations of the scope of the applicable rules; there is nothing particularly interesting about the phenomenon.

Implicit exceptions, on the other hand, are according to the common view both interesting and problematic. They are interesting and problematic not simply because they seem to bring thesis (T1') back into play, but also because of the nature of the court's power whenever

There appears to be general agreement that the admissibility of implicit exceptions is a contingent, if widespread, phenomenon: see eg Schauer (1998: 237); Rodríguez (2000: 166); Bayón (2001: 340–1); Schauer (2013: 212–13); Navarro and Rodríguez (2014: 189). As Tur remarks, however, meta-theoretical discussions of what features of legal systems should be counted as ('conceptually') 'necessary' for the purposes of jurisprudential theorizing should not too swiftly discard as merely 'contingent' certain features which are—as the admission of implicit exceptions may well be—so ubiquitous and salient that any 'conceptual' account that fails to take them into account may in some sense be said to be *descriptively* unsound: see Tur (2001b: 130); Tur (2012: 363); and Tur (2013: 246); and the remarks in Hage (2005: 21–3). It is also agreed that the admission of implicit exceptions, being an expression of sensitivity to the demands of equity, is, within limits, a desirable feature of well-ordered legal systems: see eg Moore (1981: 238–9), and compare Raz (1979/2009: 31–2). For a doctrinal approach to the 'equitable forces' underlying the granting or denying of exceptions to administrative rules, see Aman (1982).

[6] Compare eg Patton (1956: 524–30); Singer (1958: 165); Honoré (1977: 78–9); Susskind (1987: 193–8); Prakken (1997: 33–5, 47–9); Bayón (2000: 195–7); Tur (2003: 798); Godden and Walton (2008: 8–9).

implicit exceptions are admitted. How is this power to be described? The answer is not obvious; we seem to have conflicting thoughts on this issue. Implicit exceptions emerge only when the moment comes to actually *apply* the relevant rule. If they do emerge, then the court will be justified in *not* applying that rule. It seems, however, that we still want to say that this rule, the rule that the decision-maker is authorized not to follow even though the particular case may unequivocally fall within its scope, *remains* a 'rule'—it remains 'the' rule on the matter—and indeed that it remains, *qua* rule, unchanged. This is true of exceptions in extra-legal domains as well. In *The Concept of Law*, for instance, H. L. A. Hart illustrates this phenomenon of exceptions 'not exhaustively specifiable in advance' by a non-legal example:

> We promise to visit a friend the next day. When the day comes it turns out that keeping the promise would involve neglecting someone dangerously ill. The fact that this is accepted as an adequate reason for not keeping the promise surely does not mean that there is no rule requiring promises to be kept, only a certain regularity in keeping them. It does not follow from the fact that rules have exceptions incapable of exhaustive statement, that in every situation we are left to our discretion and are never bound to keep a promise. A rule that ends with the word 'unless . . .' is still a rule.[7]

So even though there may be exceptions; even though these exceptions are 'incapable of exhaustive statement'; and even though whenever an exception occurs one will be justified in not following or applying the 'rule' that promises are to be kept; *that rule*, Hart says, is 'still a rule'—it is still *the* rule on promises. But is this not puzzling? How can the 'rule' that promises are to be kept still be a 'rule'—how can it be *the* rule that governs promises—if it fails to dispose of the case even though all its elements are satisfied? Is Hart's claim not self-contradictory?

Authors like Frederick Schauer—who defends a well-known version of the common view—believe so. Schauer thinks that the idea that decision-makers can be allowed to add exceptions to any given rule 'at the moment of application' is inconsistent. He gives the example of a 'No Dogs Allowed' rule in a restaurant. This rule might reflect 'the background purpose of preventing disturbance of the patrons in the restaurant'.[8] But suppose that the decision-maker—the restaurant

[7] Hart (1961/2012: 139).

[8] Schauer (1991a: 893).

porter—is authorized to allow dogs in the restaurant 'in the name' of that background purpose: she is authorized to allow dogs in the restaurant if she finds them well behaved and unlikely to be boisterous or annoying. This is the sort of power that would commonly be described as a power to *exceptionally* allow well-behaved dogs in the restaurant: a power to create exceptions if the 'application of the [rule's] literal language would not serve the rule's purpose'.[9] But that, Schauer says, misdescribes the situation. What we have in a situation like this is actually a different rule. The restaurant porter's supposedly 'exception-creating' power is really 'identical to the power to apply the purpose rather than the [putative] rule, or to take the purpose as in fact being the rule'.[10] For rules are, relative to their background purposes or justifications, 'hardened' or 'entrenched' generalizations,[11] and rule-based decision-making involves treating such generalizations 'as supplying reasons for decision independent of those supplied by the generalization's underlying justification'.[12] Rule-based decision-making 'exists only insofar as the instantiation resists continuous modification in the service of its generating justification'.[13] So 'when a [putative] rule is not applicable in those cases in which the justification *for that* [putative] *rule* is inapplicable', then it becomes inapplicable 'because of internal failure', as it were—'and a rule that is inapplicable in every case of internal failure is in an important way no rule at all':[14]

> If, because the justification behind the exclusion of all dogs was the desire to exclude boisterous and annoying dogs, we were to *exclude* under the 'No dogs allowed' rule *only* boisterous and annoying dogs, we would in effect be unentrenching the generalization, causing the rule to collapse into its justification.[15]

So in a case like this 'it is the purpose rather than the rule-formulation that in fact *is* the rule'.[16] The 'No Dogs Allowed' formulation is simply devoid of any strength *qua* rule; it is but a 'weightless rule of thumb'.[17]

9 Schauer (1991a: 894).
10 Schauer (1991a: 895).
11 Schauer (1991b: 43–52).
12 Schauer (1991b: 51).
13 Schauer (1991b: 84).
14 Schauer (1991b: 117).
15 See Schauer (1991b: 63).
16 Schauer (1991a: 894–5).
17 See Schauer (1991b: 77, 109).

And a similar argument applies to 'implicit' exceptions in law. When 'the reason for creating an exception is equity or justice rather than the single purpose behind a single [putative] rule', then 'the power to create an exception to a rule when required by justice is equivalent', says Schauer (1991a: 895), 'to the power to do justice simpliciter'.

Schauer's broader point is that it is wrong to think that 'exceptions are epiphenomenal adjuncts to the rules they are exceptions to, such that the power to append an exception does not undercut the primary force of the rule itself'.[18] In fact 'the very definition of an exception . . . presupposes that what is excepted is otherwise within the scope of the broader rule'; exceptions are by definition 'continuous with the rules they are exceptions to'.[19] So any decision-maker's supposed 'power to create an ad hoc exception' is actually a 'power to change the rule'[20]—it is a power to treat some putative rule-formulation as nothing more than a transparent rule of thumb, a 'defeasible marker of a deeper reality'.[21]

Taken literally, then, a claim like Hart's, that 'rules may be subject to exceptions added at the moment of application' and 'still be rules', appears to be misguided. Perhaps, however, hypothesizes Schauer, Hart's description is meant to refer, not to 'exceptions' in the sense just explained, but to a different phenomenon:

> [Hart] confuses and conflates two distinct phenomena—creating an exception to a rule and overriding a rule. The phenomenon Hart describes . . . is that some rules or principles are not absolute, but rather are capable of being overridden in particularly exigent circumstances . . . Hart wants to capture the way in which rules can be overridden in particularly exigent circumstances and still be rules, even if it is impossible to predict or specify in advance what those exigent circumstances will be.[22]

To treat rules—rule-formulations—as 'transparent rules of thumb rather than mandatory rules' is something different, says Schauer (1991b: 128), from treating rules as overridable rather than absolute. The fact, which is the hallmark of rules, that 'even in the face of a recalcitrant experience, an entrenched generalization would still

[18] Schauer (1991a: 873).

[19] Schauer (1991a: 874, 893); see also Schauer (1991b: 45 n 7); Schauer (1998: 226–8).

[20] Schauer (1991a: 897).

[21] Schauer (1991b: 51, 127).

[22] Schauer (1991a: 896–7); compare Boonin (1966: 375).

qua generalization control the decision'[23] does not entail that the entrenched generalization *conclusively* determines that decision.[24] Rules can be overridden by stronger reasons that happen to be present in any given case: overridden 'by particularly exigent factors *external* both to the rule and to *its* justification'.[25] But rules, *qua* rules, 'have a dimension of weight, a degree of resistance to being overcome, that can also be expressed in terms of a rule not being completely defeasible':[26]

> In the case of override, we are reluctant to say that the rule (or the justification behind it) evaporates when it is overridden by a reason of sufficient exigency. The rule's insufficiency in this case is neither inconsistent with its sufficiency in others, nor with its possessing some ongoing force, or residue, even in the cases in which it is overridden. In some domains this residue triggers remorse, even as we correctly override the strictures of the rule, and in other domains it may trigger compensation. But there is something still left over when a rule is (properly) overridden.[27]

What Schauer gives us, then, is a detailed elaboration of the common view that 'explicit' and 'implicit' exceptions are significantly different phenomena. The latter—Schauer's 'overrides'—are *genuine* or 'true' exceptions *to* the rule, as some authors put it.[28] In such cases, the decision-maker's power is not a power to add exceptions to the rule's antecedent at the moment of application; it is not a power to modify the applicable rules. Rather, it is a power not to apply an 'applicable' rule while treating it *as a rule* nonetheless.[29] And that is exactly what makes implicit exceptions—as contrasted with explicit ones—a particularly interesting topic. For a precise account must be given of how it is that a rule can possibly retain its 'ruleness'[30], its 'rulehood',[31] even when an implicit

[23] Schauer (1991b: 45).

[24] No connotation of 'conclusive effect' is meant to attach to Schauer's use of the term 'control': see Schauer (1991b: 4–6, 45 n 8).

[25] Schauer (1991b: 118, emphasis added).

[26] Schauer (1991b: 117).

[27] Schauer (1991b: 110); and see also Schauer (1991a: 896–7); Schauer (1998: 228–31, 237–9); and Schauer (2012: 79–81).

[28] See Celano (2012: 280–3).

[29] See Miller (1956: 262, 269).

[30] Schauer (1991a: 897).

[31] Susskind (1987: 195).

exception emerges and the rule is eventually *not* followed. We need an account that can make sense of the idea that a rule can remain 'intact and available to be applied again and again even though trumped or defeated by equitable considerations in a particular case'.[32]

That is also why Hart's reference to 'a rule that ends with the word "unless. . ."' may appear confused. If we are concerned with explaining how it is that a rule may be subject to 'exceptions incapable of exhaustive statement' and 'still [be] a rule', then—as Atria (who also adopts the common view) points out—Hart seems to be 'miss[ing] the whole point', for 'what we are dealing with' are 'rules that *do not*, as a matter of fact, end with "unless. . ."'.[33]

To summarize, the view that implicit and explicit exceptions are not cut from the same cloth is widespread. The former—Schauer's 'overrides'—are 'external' to the rule, as it were, whereas explicit exceptions, being nothing more than negative delimitations of the rule's scope, are in that sense 'internal'. As Susskind—yet another endorser of the common view—puts it,

> an implied exception is not the same as an exceptive qualification: the latter can always, in principle, be articulated in any statement of the contents of a momentary legal system and is an integral part of the [legal] production itself, whereas the former, by definition, cannot be so expressed, but emerges in the process of solving legal problems.[34]

This common view, I will now argue, is fundamentally mistaken.

5.3 Two Senses of 'Rules'

5.3.1 *'Applying' Legal Rules*

I begin with some general remarks about the language of 'rules' and their 'application', which is prevalent in discussions of implicit exceptions. Here is a representative sample of how the subject is usually talked about:

[32] Tur (2001a: 359).

[33] Atria (2001: 125); compare Schauer (1991b: 115).

[34] Susskind (1987: 196). For recent endorsements of the common view, see Ferrer and Ratti (2012: 1, 15); Guastini (2012: 183); and Rodríguez (2012: 89).

> There is a *legislative* moment, in which the rule is posited, and then an *adjudicative* moment, in which it is applied. There is nothing particularly interesting about exceptions introduced at the legislative moment: they are simply part of the rule, and limit its scope. The interesting problem . . . is that of exceptions introduced to the rule at the moment of application.[35]

> We do not speak of an action as an exception to a rule, of course, unless we believe or assume that the rule applies to the action. If the rule does not apply, there can be no question of an exception; if the rule applies, there could be a question about an exception; and if the rule applies but we are justified in not following it, an exception is allowed.[36]

> To argue that legal rules are defeasible is not to make the obvious point that legal rules have exceptions, but the stronger one that it is theoretically impossible to enumerate all the exceptions and state all the sufficient conditions for the rule's application.[37]

> The issue is not whether rules may have exceptions and still be rules, for of course they may. It is whether rules may be subject to exceptions added at the moment of application in light of the full range of otherwise applicable factors and still be rules . . . and the answer to that question is no.[38]

This talk of 'applying' legal rules is, I think, is a periphrastic or circumlocutory idiom, and we had better do away with it in the context of our discussion. Take once again Schauer's example of a 'No Dogs Allowed' rule in a restaurant. It seems to me that there is no difference between saying that the restaurant porter is required to 'apply the "No Dogs Allowed" rule' and saying that she is required not to allow dogs in the restaurant. There is no further requirement to 'apply the "No Dogs Allowed" rule', over and above the requirement not to allow dogs in the restaurant.

To put matters more clearly, consider a simple scenario, which I will call '*Situation 1*', in which the restaurant porter is required not to allow *any* dog in the restaurant. She has no power that can possibly be described as a power to 'create' or 'fashion' exceptions; she is required not to allow dogs *no matter what*:

[35] Atria (2001: 124).
[36] Miller (1956: 262).
[37] Boonin (1966: 372).
[38] Schauer (1991b: 116).

Situation 1

> The porter is required not to allow dogs in the restaurant, no matter what. No exceptions are admitted.

In *Situation 1* the porter's position would be accurately and completely described by saying plainly that she is required not to allow dogs in the restaurant. We could phrase this in conditional form as follows:

(1a) For every *x*: if *x* is a dog, then the porter is required not to allow *x* in the restaurant.[39]

Should we choose in this case to speak of the applicable 'rule', and say that the porter is required to 'apply' it, we would be saying nothing more than (1a) is already saying. We would simply be restating—albeit less straightforwardly—the content of the requirement in (1a). The point is that in any true description of *Situation 1* in terms of the 'application' of 'rules', the content of the relevant 'rule' would have to match exactly—as in formulation (1b) below—the content of the requirement in (1a). What then would the relevant 'rule' in *Situation 1* be? It would be the 'No Dogs Allowed' rule; or, to give it a conditional formulation, the rule 'For every *x*: if *x* is a dog, then *x* ought not to be allowed in the restaurant':

(1b) The porter is required to apply the rule 'For every *x*: if *x* is a dog, then *x* ought not to be allowed in the restaurant'.[40]

The restaurant porter in *Situation 1* could then be said, in the ordinary language of 'rules' and their 'application', to be required to 'apply' such a rule. But with (1b) we would be saying nothing that (1a) does not already convey.[41]

[39] It would also be idiomatic to formulate the consequent in (1a) with 'normative' terminology, for example in terms of 'duties' and/or 'powers'. In order to avoid the kind of equivocation I discuss in Duarte d'Almeida (2011: 167–99), however, I prefer in these formulations to employ the more clearly prescriptive vocabulary of 'requirements'.

[40] Throughout this chapter, because I am discussing the common view *in its own terms*, I make use of 'substantive' formulations of rules and requirements. I resume my proof-based formulations in Chapter 6, where I offer my own account of implicit exceptions.

[41] My suggestion is not that there is nothing more to our ordinary notion of what it is to 'apply' a 'rule' than simply coming to do (for whatever reason) whatever it is the rule prescribes. My point is a specific point about the use of the term 'rule'—in contexts like *Situation 1*, but also in the legal domain—to refer to the content of authoritatively issued prescriptions.

This point is, I suppose, a fairly trivial one. Why bother making it? Because the common view on implicit exceptions appears to fail to take it into account. Proponents of the common view hold, as we saw in section 5.2, that when courts are allowed to admit *as* exceptions certain facts of the case at hand not previously identified as such, they are thereby allowed to disregard the applicable 'rule'; they are allowed not to 'apply' the 'applicable' rule to the particular case. But this way of putting things seems to involve a contradiction. Notice that what is at issue is not whether courts may happen to be *morally* allowed, or even required, not to 'apply' the 'applicable' legal rules. The answer to this question is evidently affirmative. The kind of situation with which we are concerned, rather, is one where courts are *legally* allowed, or even required, to take such exceptions into account. But as we have just seen, to say that a judge is—all *legal* things considered—required to 'apply' a legal rule to the effect that 'if *P*, then obligatory *Q*' is but a circuitous way of saying that the judge is legally required to Q whenever *P*. Hence if there is any situation *R* where the judge is legally allowed not to Q even if *P*, then *R* can certainly *not* be described as a situation in which the judge is allowed *not* to apply the 'rule' 'if *P*, then obligatory *Q*'. In that scenario, rather, the 'applicable' 'rule', if we choose to employ this language, would be 'if *P*, then obligatory Q, unless *R*'. In other words: *R*, whatever its content, will constitute an element whose non-verification is certainly a part of what must be true for the consequence (the requirement to Q) to follow. Strictly speaking, therefore, the received view that it can ever be the case that a court may be legally allowed not to apply the relevant legal 'rule' would appear to be mistaken.

Of course, this would be too simple and even superficial a way of refuting the common view. And indeed my impression is that when endorsers of the common view speak of 'rules' in the context of the debate on implicit exceptions, they are often using the term in a very different sense, and have fallen prey to a surreptitious ambiguity.

5.3.2 Disambiguating 'Rules'

To see this, let us work through a couple of variations of Schauer's 'No Dogs Allowed' example.

The basic scenario is the one just described, in section 5.3.1, as *Situation 1*. In *Situation 1*, as we saw, the porter is required not to allow dogs in the restaurant—no matter what. But let us now bring exceptions into the picture. Consider *Situation 2*:

Situation 2

> The restaurant owner explicitly tells the porter that an exception is to be made for seeing-eye dogs, which the porter is authorized and required to allow in the restaurant. No other exceptions are admitted.

How should we describe the porter's position in *Situation 2*? We could simply say that

(2a) For every *x*: if *x* is a dog, then the porter is required not to allow *x* in the restaurant, unless *x* is a seeing-eye dog.

A partisan of the roundabout language of 'rules' and their 'application' might accordingly prefer to say (equivalently) that

(2b) The porter is required to apply the rule 'For every *x*: if *x* is a dog, then *x* ought not to be allowed in the restaurant, unless *x* is a seeing-eye dog'.

To be clear: the term 'rule' in (2b)—as in (1b) above—designates a conditional formulation that is reconstructed or abstracted from the actual circumstances on which the porter's normative position actually depends. Since the porter's position is different in *Situation 1* and in *Situation 2*—the porter's position in each case depends on a different set of conditions—we have different 'rules', 'rules' with different contents, in (1b) and (2b) (though, of course, the term 'rule' means the same in both cases).

In *Situation 2* we have what is usually called an 'explicit' exception. The exception, in this case, would be the fact that a dog is a seeing-eye dog. But the notion of an exception, as commonly employed, is a relational notion; a statement that some given fact *D* is an 'exception' is an incomplete statement. If *D* is an exception, it is an exception *to* something else. It is, we would naturally and colloquially say, an exception to—some *rule*. But it should be clear that by 'rule', here, we would be meaning a very different thing from what we mean when speaking, as we did in (1b) and (2b), of the applicable 'rule'.

In (1b) or (2b), it bears repeating, we use 'rule' to refer to what the porter is required to do. Let me call this a 'rule$_R$'. But when we say that in *Situation 2* the fact that a seeing-eye dog is an exception *to* a 'rule', we are not using 'rule' to refer to what the porter is required to do. We are using the term to refer to what the porter is required to do *when no exception is present*. In this sense, in *Situation 2* the 'rule'—the rule *to which* the fact that a seeing-eye dog is an exception—is *not* the $rule_R$ described in (2b), but the 'No Dogs Allowed' rule. Let me use '$rule_D$', then, to speak of rules in this second, colloquial sense.

I want to argue that these two senses of the term 'rule' are systematically conflated in common accounts of exceptions, and that this confusion has been the cause of some grave mistakes. But you may remain unconvinced by my claim to have distinguished between two senses of the term 'rule'. And it is true that the difference between a $rule_R$ and a $rule_D$ can be difficult to make manifest in contexts, like *Situation 2*, in which only explicit exceptions are admitted.[42] So let us consider a different scenario that will further clarify the distinction:

Situation 3

> The restaurant owner decides not to mark out any particular circumstance as an exception. Instead, she allows the porter to assess and determine for herself whether any of the particular features of each case is sufficiently relevant to be recognized as an exception (and, in that event, to allow the dog in the restaurant).

In contrast to *Situation 2*, in which the one admissible exception could be identified in advance, in *Situation 3* the decision-maker is authorized to decide by herself—'at the moment of application'—whether any given circumstance is to be admitted as an exception in the case at hand. In *Situation 3*, then, we come across the phenomenon of implicit exceptions.

Now, if and when the porter does decide to classify some particular fact as an exception, the same question can be asked that was raised

[42] I find it preferable to attempt to make the distinction visible, rather than to rehearse a precise definition of the second sense of the term. I could nonetheless very cursorily remark that the second, colloquial notion—the notion of a $rule_D$—is a notion with which we try in some way to capture the particular connection that exists between the fact that something is a dog and the fact that it ought not to be allowed in the restaurant. This is a connection that we might also try to characterize (though not rigorously) in terms of what 'normally', 'ordinarily' or perhaps 'regularly' happens or ought to happen—in terms of what happens *as a rule*—by contrast with the 'extraordinary' or 'exceptional' character of—well, *exceptions* to that 'rule'. Ultimately, however, I don't think that these are satisfactory ways of putting the point; and there is a reason, as we shall see, that the notion of a $rule_D$ is particularly resistant to such attempts at definition.

about the explicit exception in *Situation 2*. If the porter recognizes some fact as an exception, she recognizes it as an exception *to* something. To what, exactly? The answer is the same as in *Situation 2*. She recognizes it as an exception to the relevant *rule*—in the sense of what I called a 'rule$_D$'.

Indeed, in order to meaningfully contrast *Situations 2* and *3* in terms of the distinction between explicit and implicit exceptions—by saying, as is usually said, that a 'closed' list of exceptions can be specified 'in advance' in the former case, but not in the latter—we must mean the same thing by an 'exception' in both cases. (Nor would the 'explicit'/'implicit' classification be intelligible otherwise: 'explicit' and 'implicit' exceptions are 'exceptions' in the same sense of the term.) So Table 1 shows how such a contrast might be displayed if we were to restrict ourselves to what we are able to say 'in advance of application':

Table 1

	Rule$_D$	**Exceptions to the rule$_D$**
Situation 2	No Dogs Allowed.	The fact that a dog is a seeing-eye dog.
Situation 3	No Dogs Allowed.	. . .

The important point to notice is the ellipsis in the section corresponding to the list of exceptions to the rule$_D$ in *Situation 3*. The reason we are unable to specify its content is that it is up to the decision-maker, the porter, to decide for herself which facts to classify as exceptions. To say this does not commit us to any view about the nature of such decisions, or about the kind of reasoning involved in classifying a fact as an exception to a rule$_D$. I will return to these knotty issues very shortly. For now, I simply wish to make clear that the entry corresponding to *Situation 3* cannot actually be completed 'in advance of application' precisely because the column of exceptions to the relevant rule$_D$ is to be completed with the *actual circumstances that count as exceptions*. In other words, the porter is not really authorized to classify particular facts *as* 'implicit exceptions'. Rather, the porter is authorized to classify particular facts *as exceptions*. These are dubbed 'implicit' only in the sense that they cannot be identified unless and until the porter actually classifies them as such.

In pointing this out, I am saying nothing new. It is precisely what the endorsers of the common view maintain. This is how their distinction between explicit and implicit exceptions is drawn: in terms of exceptions that can, and exceptions that cannot, be listed or specified beforehand. That is why, they claim, the list of exceptions in situations like *Situation 3* must be left open-ended.

We would have no comparable difficulty, however, in describing the porter's position in *Situation 3* in the straightforward language that was used in formulations (1a) or (2a). We would be able to say something along the following lines:

> (3a) For every *x*: if *x* is a dog, the porter is required not to allow *x* in the restaurant, unless she judges any one of the features of the particular case to be sufficiently relevant to be admitted as an exception.

I hasten to stress that my point is not that (3a) is a suitably *precise* description of the porter's position in *Situation 3*. It is not. In fact, it is particularly difficult to provide an accurate description of the content of a decision-maker's power to recognize particular facts of the case at hand as exceptions (as opposed to a power simply to decide at one's discretion).[43] I will try in Chapter 6 to make some progress in this regard. My point at this stage is simply that any true statement of the conditions under which, in *Situation 3*, the porter is required not to allow dogs in the restaurant, will include a reference to the *fact* that, in her judgment, no feature of the particular case constitutes an exception. (This judgment of hers, of course, is a distinct event from her decision that this particular dog should not be allowed in the restaurant: the former is a precondition of the correctness of the latter.[44])

Accordingly, if one should wish to speak, relative to *Situation 3*, of the applicable 'rule' *in the sense of a rule*$_R$—that is, in that same familiar sense in which the term is used in (1b) or (2b)—one would quite simply say that

[43] For the same reason, my working description of *Situation 3* is also imprecise or unclear in some respects, though not more so than the scenarios and narratives commonly found in the literature.

[44] If this is not immediately evident, imagine a variant case in which porter A is required not to allow dogs in the restaurant unless porter B judges any of the features of the particular case to be sufficiently relevant to be admitted as an exception. This intelligible scenario helps to bring out more clearly the distinction between these two judgments—which simply happen, in the original version of *Situation 3*, to be expected of the same agent.

(3b) The porter is required to apply the rule 'For every *x*: if *x* is a dog, then *x* ought not to be allowed in the restaurant, unless the porter judges any of the features of the particular case to be sufficiently relevant to be admitted as an exception'.

I can now more vividly restate my case for discerning two senses of the term 'rule'. In (3b), as in (1b) or (2b) above, the language of 'rules' is employed, as I explained, as one way of describing the conditions on whose satisfaction the decision-maker's requirement not to allow dogs in the restaurant depends. We have a different set of conditions in each of the three situations; we have in each case, as Table 2 shows, a different rule$_R$ (as I proposed to call them):

Table 2

	Rule$_R$
Situation 1	For every *x*: if *x* is a dog, then *x* ought not to be allowed in the restaurant.
Situation 2	For every *x*: if *x* is a dog, then *x* ought not to be allowed in the restaurant, unless *x* is a seeing-eye dog.
Situation 3	For every *x*: if *x* is a dog, then *x* ought not to be allowed in the restaurant, unless the porter judges any of the features of the particular case to be sufficiently relevant to be admitted as an exception.

You will recall, however, from our previous contrast (depicted in Table 1) between *Situations 2* and *3* in terms of the distinction between explicit and implicit exceptions, that the relevant rules$_D$—that is, the 'rules' to which we allude when we speak of exceptions *to* 'rules'—were not only the same in both cases, but different in each case from the rule$_R$ just identified for the same situations. This should suffice, I trust, to convince you of the need for disambiguation along the lines that I have proposed.

5.4 The Common View Dismissed

The effort involved in throwing this distinction into relief shows how easy it could be to miss. Why does it matter? Because the endorsers of the common view on exceptions have become irretrievably entangled in a confusion of rules$_D$ and rules$_R$; and because once the confusion is dissolved we can see that *none* of the common view's characteristic theses is correct. Recall what these theses were:

1. Explicit exceptions are neither problematic nor particularly interesting, since, unlike implicit ones, they can simply be incorporated, as negative conditions, in more accurately formulated rules.
2. In contrast, what makes implicit exceptions theoretically interesting is the challenge of explaining how it can be that a rule whose antecedent is fully satisfied in some given case can simultaneously *fail* to apply to that case and still be said to be a rule (thus remaining, *qua* rule, unchanged).
3. Whenever implicit exceptions are allowed—that is, whenever decision-makers are empowered to classify as exceptions particular facts of the case not previously identified as such—no list of conditions necessary and sufficient for the correct decision can be given in advance of application.

Not only are all three claims wrong; the first two cannot really be consistently endorsed at the same time. Whatever semblance of plausibility they may have derives solely from a failure to distinguish between our two senses of 'rule'—or so I will now argue. Let us consider these common theses one by one.

5.4.1 *The First Thesis*

In maintaining that explicit exceptions can simply be incorporated, as negative conditions, in more accurate statements of the rule, what sense of 'rule' would endorsers of the common view have in mind? Take, for example, Ronald Dworkin's matter-of-fact contention that

> [o]f course, a rule may have exceptions . . . However, an accurate statement of the rule would take [its] exception[s] into account, and any that did not would be incomplete.[45]

The first part of this passage seems to refer to a rule$_D$. It draws a distinction between a rule and *its* exceptions; and when we speak

[45] See Dworkin (1967: 24–6); Dworkin contrasts 'exceptions', which 'in theory, at least . . . could all be listed', with 'counter-instances', which 'are not, even in theory, subject to enumeration'; and he holds that, as a 'logical' matter, rules—unlike principles—cannot have counter-instances. See also Dworkin (1972: 74, 76).

of exceptions to rules it is the notion of a rule$_D$, as we saw, that we employ. One would charitably assume that the passage does not equivocate, and that the term 'rule' takes the same meaning in its two occurrences. Yet how could an exception possibly be incorporated in a statement of the rule$_D$ *to which* it is an exception? The very definition of a rule$_D$ seems to preclude any such incorporation. Still, let us set this worry aside for a moment (though the worry is symptomatic of a deeper problem in the received view) and grant the point that, for any rule$_D$ *R*, the negation of its explicit exceptions can indeed be incorporated in more fine-grained statements of *R*. What this reveals, say the endorsers of the common view, is that explicit exceptions are equivalent to negative conditions in the antecedent of a rule. Very well: but in that case the endorsers of the common view are bound by their own standards to acknowledge that, contrary to what they also characteristically deny, *implicit* exceptions, too, must be equivalent to negative rule-conditions. Why so? The incorporationist's claim (that is, the claim we are momentarily granting) is clearly not a claim about the incorporation of this or that particular exception in this or that particular rule$_D$. It is a general claim about the relation between exceptions and rules$_D$. It must therefore be the claim that

(M) If some fact *F* is an exception to some conditional rule$_D$ *R*, then it is possible to represent *F* as a negative element in the antecedent of *R*.

Now in order actually to carry out the incorporation of some particular exception *F* as a negative element in the antecedent of some particular rule$_D$, we need to be able to identify that fact as an exception to that rule$_D$. We need to be able to state that

(m) Fact *F* is an exception to rule$_D$ *R*.

Evidently, statements of this kind form no part of thesis (M). Statements of this kind would be necessary—as minor premises, as it were: hence the lowercase 'm'—to justify the actual incorporation of some particular fact in some particular rule. But they are merely statements about whether some particular fact *is* an exception to some particular rule$_D$. Unlike (M), they tell us nothing about the status of exceptions or the relation of exceptions to rules$_D$. They do nothing to establish the common view's claim that explicit exceptions are equivalent to negative rule-conditions.

So now recall *Situation 2*, our simple one-exception scenario, where the fact that a dog is a seeing-eye dog is an explicit exception *to* the 'No Dogs Allowed' rule$_D$:

Table 3[1]

	Rule$_D$	Exceptions to the rule$_D$
Situation 2	No Dogs Allowed.	The fact that a dog is a seeing-eye dog.

[1]Table 3 repeats the relevant row from Table 1.

Here, claims the incorporationist, the negation of the fact that a dog is a seeing-eye dog can be incorporated in a more accurate statement of the 'No Dogs Allowed' rule$_D$. Given that we are for the moment granting the incorporationist her theoretical claim (M), we must certainly agree, for we are also able to identify that fact as an exception to the 'No Dogs Allowed' rule$_D$, and thus able to produce a statement with the form of (m). What is it that enables us to identify this fact as an exception to the rule$_D$? It is the fact that the restaurant owner has decided to *make* it an exception. That is why the fact that a dog is a seeing-eye dog can be said in *Situation 2* to amount to an explicit exception. What this means, again, is that we are able to identify it *as* an exception 'in advance of application' (not that we are able to identify it *as* an 'explicit exception', which makes no sense) and so that we are able, relative to it, and likewise 'in advance of application', to produce a statement with the form of (m).

What, then, of the common claim that implicit exceptions *cannot* be incorporated as negative elements in more 'accurate' statements of the rule? It must surely be true—by definition—that no actual implicit exception can in effect be incorporated as a part of any actual rule$_D$ 'in advance of application'. For implicit exceptions are those facts that a decision-maker decides to classify *as* exceptions to some rule$_D$, and thus facts that can only be identified *as* exceptions to the relevant rule$_D$ if (and after) the decision-maker decides to *make* them exceptions to the rule$_D$. We are therefore prevented from making any statement of the (m) kind relative to any such fact 'in advance of application'. Notice, however, that this is a purely epistemic problem about the identification of exceptions. Indeed, the distinction between explicit and implicit exceptions is explicable in purely epistemic terms. But the fact that we may not know, or be able to know, at a given moment in time (namely 'in advance of application') what the full list of exceptions to any rule$_D$ is (or will be) has no bearing on the incorporationist's theoretical claim, which is thesis (M). For when a decision-maker validly decides to admit as an exception any particular fact *F* of the case not previously recognized as such, *F becomes* an exception to the relevant rule$_D$ *R*, which must mean, if thesis (M) is right, that *F* is now equivalent to a negative condition in a more accurate formulation of *R*.

If this seems unclear, here is another way of making the point. The common view maintains that the explicit exception in *Situation 2* can be incorporated in a more accurate formulation of the 'No Dogs Allowed' rule$_D$. This more fine-grained formulation would presumably read as follows:

(R2) No dogs allowed, unless they are seeing-eye dogs.

If the same exercise were attempted, 'in advance of application', for *Situation 3*, the resulting formulation could only be the incomplete or 'open-ended' (R3):

(R3) No dogs allowed, unless . . .

But what this again shows is that from the incorporationist's point of view, implicit exceptions pose a merely epistemic difficulty. The incorporationist is unable to determine the content of the 'unless'-clause in (R3) in advance of application: the ellipsis stands for whatever facts a decision-maker may come to accept as exceptions. But the incorporationist believes that it is *as the content of such an 'unless'-clause* that those facts are to be understood. Because she endorses thesis (M), she has to agree—even though she is known for denying it—that the status of implicit exceptions to rules$_D$ (the status, that is, of whatever circumstances come to be validly classified as exceptions by decision-makers 'at the moment of application') is that of negative conditions in more accurate formulations of the respective rule$_D$. If, as the incorporationist says, explicit exceptions are equivalent to negative rule-conditions, then, by the same token, so are 'implicit' ones.

Of course, the problem remains, as we saw at the beginning of this section, that the incorporationist claim is indefensible if taken as the view that exceptions to any given rule$_D$ can be recast as negative conditions in a more fine-grained formulation *of that rule*$_D$. (The formulation in (R2), for instance, does not capture the relevant rule$_D$ in the situation—*Situation 2*—to which it refers.) This suffices to disprove thesis (M), which we had only provisionally granted; and my impression, as I said, is that the claim that explicit exceptions can be recast as parts of more precisely formulated 'rules' confuses and oscillates between the two senses of 'rule' that I have tried to discern. Their insistence that only explicit exceptions, not implicit ones, can be 'incorporated' in the relevant 'rules' seems to suggest that Dworkin and the many other endorsers of the common view may be thinking of rules$_R$, not rules$_D$. For when, as in *Situation 2*, an exception can be identified as such 'in advance of application', the fact which constitutes such an explicit exception can indeed be 'incorporated' as a negative element in the fully formulated rule$_R$. The relevant rule$_R$ in *Situation 2*, recall, was the rule mentioned in (2b) (which I now reproduce with the explicit indication that we are dealing with a 'rule$_R$'):

(2b) The porter is required to apply the rule$_R$ 'For every *x*: if *x* is a dog, then *x* ought not to be allowed in the restaurant, unless *x* is a seeing-eye dog'.

So it is true—if we grant thesis (M)—that the explicit exception in *Situation 2*, the fact that a dog is a seeing-eye dog, can be represented as the content of an 'unless'-clause, and thus as a negative condition, in the full formulation of the relevant rule$_R$. And it is also true that no similar representation is possible for implicit exceptions: in *Situation 3*, there is no place in the formulation of the relevant rule$_R$ (the one described in (3b)) for any of the facts that the decision-maker may come to classify as exceptions:

(3b) The porter is required to apply the rule$_R$ 'For every *x*: if *x* is a dog, then *x* ought not to be allowed in the restaurant, unless the porter judges any of the features of the particular case to be sufficiently relevant to be admitted as an exception'.

However, if this is how the common view is to be understood—and keep in mind that the common view has no reason to dispute that (2b) and (3b) are apt (if general) descriptions of the porter's position in the respective situations—then its endorsers will have to concede (once again against what they characteristically deny) that explicit exceptions are *not* the same as negative conditions in rule-antecedents. Notice that the rules$_R$ described in (2b) and (3b) are identical in form. Both are conditional formulations; both include 'unless'-clauses. For our present purposes, we can simplify their common form as:

(F1) If *P*, then A ought to φ, unless *D*.

The endorser of the common view will maintain, we know, that the fact described in the content of the 'unless'-clause in (2b) is an explicit exception. Yet she will balk at making a similar claim about the content of the 'unless'-clause in (3b). Indeed, while the notion of an exception *occurs in* the description of the fact that figures as the content of the 'unless'-clause in (3b), this fact—that the porter admits any of the particular circumstances of the case *as an exception*—is itself no 'exception'. ('To which rule$_D$?' would be the test-question.) That means that in spite of her protests to the contrary, the endorser of the common view *is* drawing a distinction between what she characterizes (or would have to agree to characterize) as a mere negative rule-condition, and what she classifies as an ('explicit') exception. (It also means that no actual 'incorporation' of exceptions into rules is actually taking place. It just *happens* to be the case that sometimes a fact described as a condition in the applicable rule$_R$ coincides with what the common view would also be willing to recognize as an 'exception'. The incorporationist claim would thus have to be reformulated as the claim that whenever explicit exceptions—which are 'exceptions' *to* 'rules' *in the sense of rules$_D$*—are allowed, then the facts that constitute such exceptions will also figure as the content of 'unless'-clauses, and thus as negative conditions, in the relevant 'rule' *in the different sense of a rule$_R$*.)[46]

This argument can now be generalized as follows. The more accurately formulated 'rule' in which explicit exceptions can supposedly be incorporated is to be understood as either a rule$_R$ or as a rule$_D$. If the former is the apt reading, then (as argued in the previous paragraph) it

[46] Perhaps underlying the errors of the common view there is also an equivocation between two senses of 'exception'. The prominent sense, as we saw, is the one that supports the 'express'/'implicit' distinction. It is in this sense that one may say that whereas in (R2) the list of exceptions was 'closed', in (R3) it is 'open-ended'; or that in *Situation 2*, but not in *Situation 3*, the relevant exceptions could be identified 'in advance of application'. An exception, in this sense, is a particular kind of fact identified by its function or role. It is a fact whose emergence will justify not 'following' or 'applying' the 'rule'—the rule$_D$—*to which* it is an exception. We could call this an exception$_D$. Yet there is a second sense of 'exception' in which the term simply designates the *content of an unless-clause* in the formulation of some rule or other. We could call this an exception$_R$. In *Situation 2*, therefore, both senses coincide in content: the fact that a dog is a seeing-eye dog can be said to be both an exception$_D$ and an exception$_R$. In *Situation 3*, however, as we can now see, the two senses come apart: the relevant exception$_R$ is the fact that the porter judges any of the features of the particular case to be sufficiently relevant to be *admitted as an exception$_D$*. But there is no need to press this point any further. Throughout the text, the term is always used in the sense of an exception$_D$.

follows that endorsers of the common view are in fact committed to recognizing a distinction between explicit exceptions and mere negative conditions in rules$_R$. But the same conclusion can be established if by that more accurate formulation the endorser of the common view does mean a rule$_D$. For she would accept that the rule$_D$ in *Situation* 2—that is, the 'No Dogs Allowed' rule$_D$ *to* which the fact that a dog is a seeing-eye dog is, she would say, an 'explicit' exception—could be restated in conditional form: 'For every *x*: If *x* is a dog, then *x* ought not to be allowed in the restaurant'.[47] This rule has the structure 'If *P*, then A ought to φ'. Now, it is surely possible, one would think, that the antecedent of any given rule$_D$ includes positive as well as negative conditions, and thus that it displays—*qua* rule$_D$—the following structure (a restatement of (F1)):

(F2) If *P* and *not-D*, then A ought to φ.

The endorser of the common view would therefore need to explain how it is that she draws the distinction between a rule$_D$ interpretation of (F2) in which '*D*' stands for a mere negative condition, and a rule$_D$ interpretation of (F2) in which '*D*' stands for an explicit exception to some less accurate, compressed version of the relevant rule$_D$.[48]

Either way, then, endorsers of the common view are by their own standards committed to maintaining that there *is* indeed a material difference between a mere negative condition and what they would recognize as an 'explicit' exception proper. The problem, of course, is that this is also precisely what they insistently and characteristically deny.

5.4.2 *An Aside on the 'Individuation' of Laws*

Let me note, as a brief aside, that the common incorporationist proposal should not be mistaken for a position on the so-called problem of the 'individuation' of laws. In particular, it should not be mistaken for a position against the autonomous individuation of exception-creating laws.

[47] The point now is not whether or not a conditional formulation of rules$_D$ is possible whose antecedent states a *sufficient* condition for the consequent; the formulation in the text is meant to be neutral in this respect. I return to the point later.

[48] Moreover, no fact is in virtue of its own 'nature', as it were, an exception. By the endorser of the common view's own standards, there is no reason why the fact that a dog is a seeing-eye dog could not conceivably figure, in some scenario, as a negative condition *in* some rule$_D$ rather than as an exception *to* a rule$_D$.

Whereas the incorporationist's is a conceptual claim about the bare possibility of representing exceptions as parts of more accurately formulated rules, the individuation of exceptions as independent laws concerns the issue of how the content of a legal system ought to be represented in view of some expository purpose. In fact, the very question of how to individuate exceptions is predicated on the possibility of incorporation; those who argue for the autonomous representation of all or some exception-creating laws would at any rate agree that all-*legal*-things-considered statements of what the law is on any given matter—presupposing, as such statements do, the resolution of any relevant and resoluble conflicts of laws—are necessarily to 'incorporate' whatever 'express' exceptions there may be.

These distinctions are sometimes glossed over.[49] But Joseph Raz's remarks on the general, meta-theoretical 'requirements by which the adequacy of every proposed set of individuating principles will be tested' give us an explicit enunciation of the relevant issues.[50] Raz's preferred set of requirements admittedly reflects a normative judgment to the effect that law's specific function of 'regulating human behaviour by guiding it' should be made clear in its theoretical exposition.[51] His particular views in favour of the autonomous individuation of exceptions (or rather of *some* exceptions[52]) are also

[49] Claire Finkelstein, for example, argues that 'to eliminate [exceptions] by thinking of them as *already* implicit in the rules they qualify is to *misconceive the nature of rules of prohibition*' (emphasis added), and that 'it is in fact more *accurate* to omit certain kinds of conditions from the statement of a rule of prohibition'. She defines an exception as 'a qualification of a rule that stands in a certain relation to it, namely it stands *outside* the rule it qualifies'. See Finkelstein (1999: 149–50). This seems to me to misconceive the stakes in this debate, running together a normative claim (on the individuation of exceptions) and a conceptual one (on the supposed 'nature' of exceptions).

[50] See Raz (1980: 143, 146).

[51] See Raz (1980: 145, 223). Raz maintains that 'every act situation . . . that is guided by a legal system' should, as a rule, 'be the core of a law' (1980: 143, 147); but, against the Benthamite view that 'conflicts of laws are [to be] resolved before the representation of the law in its proper form' (1980: 76), he finds it preferable that 'the laws individuated by the principles of individuation should, as far as possible, make clear important connections between various parts of a legal system' (1980: 145).

[52] Raz (1980: 172) holds that 'some statements of the form "X is permitted to do A in C" are to be regarded as describing laws'; his individuation principles allow for permission-granting as well as duty-imposing laws, in such a way that each of the former will be 'internally' related to at least one of the latter, whose application it modifies (1980: 172, 174). Yet not all permissions should be represented as autonomous laws. Raz's proposal extends only to permissions that can be regarded as *representing an exception* to one or more duty-imposing laws. And even those are not all envisaged: some exceptions are to be incorporated as parts of rules rather than admitted as separate laws. ('The fact that a true statement describing a permission describes an exception to a prohibition', says Raz (1980: 173), 'is only a

transparently set against the background presupposition that incorporation remains a possibility in all cases.[53]

5.4.3 The Second Thesis

What of the common view's second thesis—the thesis that implicit exceptions, unlike explicit ones, pose an interesting theoretical challenge?

Perhaps it is helpful to recall just what this challenge is supposed to be. When decision-makers happen to be permitted to classify certain facts as exceptions immediately operative in the case at hand, they are correspondingly permitted, say the endorsers of the common view, not to 'apply' or 'follow' the relevant rule. Yet we would still wish to maintain that this rule remains a rule, and indeed that it remains 'the' rule on the matter. Remember, for example, Hart's insistence that the 'rule requiring promises to be kept' is not affected, *qua* rule, by the fact that exceptional circumstances may emerge that give us 'adequate reasons' for not fulfilling a promise.[54] The challenge is to explain how, exactly—if at all—a view like this can be consistently maintained. If by a power to classify as exceptions to the applicable 'rule' circumstances not exhaustively specified in advance as such, one means something other than a power simply to *change* the applicable rule, then an account is needed of how even though a decision-maker is justified in *not* following it,

necessary, and not a sufficient condition, for regarding it as describing a separate law. It may be regarded as a consequence of a statement describing a more narrowly defined prohibition.') Hence further reasons are needed to justify the autonomous representation of an exception. One reason might be, for example, 'that the permission is an exception to each one of a group' of duty-imposing laws and that 'it reveals an important feature common to them, thereby pointing out an important connection between laws' (as is the case, in Raz's view, with self-defence): see Raz (1980: 174).

[53] See also Raz (1972: 831). This is why, incidentally, there seems to me to be no real disagreement with Dworkin on this particular point. Dworkin (1967: 23) had suggested, as we saw, that 'of course, a rule may have exceptions', and that any 'accurate statement' of a rule would take exceptions into account (see the passage quoted to n 45); and this is certainly compatible with his assertions, in Dworkin (1972: 76), that 'an exception *can* be stated in the form of a distinct rule, like the rule about self-defence, as well as in the form of a revised statement of the original rule', and that the difference 'is largely a matter of exposition' (my emphasis). On the principles that should govern the exposition of the law—that is, on Raz's topic—Dworkin can simply profess to be agnostic.

[54] See the passage quoted to n 7.

this rule can nevertheless be 'still a rule'. I noted in section 5.2 that what Schauer and others suggest is that it is in terms of the notion of an *override* that this phenomenon has to be characterized. An override is a factor of greater 'weight' or 'exigency' than that of the rule that it correspondingly displaces in some particular case. Therefore a power not to apply an applicable rule in the presence of such overriding circumstances is not the same as a power to add negative conditions *to*, and thereby modify, some putative rule-formulation. So overriding circumstances—'true' exceptions—operate 'externally' rather than 'internally', as opposed to those supposed 'exceptions' which (like all explicit ones) are really to be understood, we are told, as negative rule-qualifications. It is accordingly possible to maintain, say the defenders of the common view, that a rule remains unchanged in the presence of an overriding circumstance. Indeed, they claim, though the rule may fail to determine the outcome in the particular case at hand, it still 'controls' this outcome to some extent, and it controls it *qua* rule—namely, by offering a certain degree of 'resistance' that makes a difference in the decision-maker's reasoning process.[55]

Now it must be in the sense of a 'rule_D' that a decision-maker can be said to be legally permitted (and perhaps also required) not to apply the relevant 'rule'. In the sense of a 'rule_R', it would be self-contradictory to speak of a permission not to apply the relevant 'rule'. Think again of the law: the formulation of any legal rule_R just tracks, as we saw, and recasts in 'rule'-language, the complete, all-legal-things-considered normative position of a decision-maker in a given decision-making context. So if, all-legal-things-considered, you are legally required to φ in situation X, then there is no legal rule_R permitting you not to φ in X. It is only in the sense of a 'rule_D', moreover, that it can plausibly be said that the relevant rule remains 'unchanged' even when the decision-maker recognizes as exceptional any particular circumstance of the case at hand.

But then it is inconsistent to insist on the need for such an 'override'-based account of implicit exceptions while maintaining that no similar account is required for explicit exceptions. The need to explain *how* it is that a rule_D can be 'overridden' by an implicit exception

[55] See the text following n 22.

while remaining a rule has to do with the notion of an exception *to* a rule$_D$, not with whether any given exception happens to be implicit or explicit. If implicit exceptions are to be theorized in terms of overrides, then so are explicit ones. Exceptions, to use Schauer's spatial metaphor, are *always* 'external' relative to the corresponding rule$_D$. Explicit and implicit exceptions, theoretically speaking, stand or fall together.

The common view rejects this, of course, because of its incorporationist approach to explicit exceptions; but we have already dealt with *that* argument, and seen how it is grounded on a confusion of the ideas of a rule$_D$ and a rule$_R$. Because of their equivocation, endorsers of the common view find themselves in a paradox of sorts. They are committed to both affirming and denying that exceptions are distinct from negative rule-conditions. Explicit exceptions, they say, are equivalent to such conditions: but then they must accept that so are implicit ones. Yet they claim that the latter are different from negative rule-conditions, and must be accounted for in terms of overrides: but then so are, and so must, explicit exceptions.

Which of their two inconsistent theses must be retracted? The answer, I will eventually conclude, is 'both'.

5.4.4 *The Third Thesis*

Before we directly address the third of the common view's theses, let me point out that the fundamental problem with the common view does not lie in the fact that it confuses the two senses of 'rules' with which it actually operates. The fundamental problem with the common view lies, I think, in the fact that it operates with the notion of a rule$_D$ to begin with.

Once the notion of a rule$_D$ is introduced and in use, one can see just how easily it may be confused with a rule$_R$. It may seem natural to suppose, for example, that *Situation 1* (our 'no matter what' scenario) and *Situation 2* can be correctly contrasted by saying that the relevant 'rule' is the same in both instances; and that this rule has no exception in the former situation, and one exception in the latter. This would be a mistake, as we now know: the fact that any given rule$_R$ may have a similar content ('No Dogs Allowed') to any given rule$_D$ is a matter of coincidence, not an indication that they must be 'rules' in the same sense of the term. If one fails to notice the two senses, however, one may find oneself thinking and speaking of rules$_D$ as if they were rules$_R$

(rather more than the reverse: in the context of our discussion, the risk of confusion is for the most part one-way); and one may be led to think, as some do, that the admissibility of defeating circumstances in legal decision-making contexts gives rise to the conflicting intuitions that on the one hand, every legal rule 'imputes a legal consequence to a generic case described through a list of fixed properties', and on the other hand, 'context-sensitive' considerations may justify not applying 'the [instantiated rule's] consequence to particular cases';[56] for one may not detect the equivocation in this way of putting things. For the same reason, one may see no way around what some construe as a dilemma:

> [either] there are exceptions to norms . . . which are not already included in the formulation of the norm, with the consequence that it will no longer be possible to deduce from a norm what we have to do . . . or we do not accept the possibility of exceptions (in other words: we only accept exceptions which are already included in the formulation of the norm); the question then is, however, whether we are indeed capable of formulating valid norms.[57]

And one will also naturally speak of decision-makers 'applying' or 'following' (or 'not applying' or 'not following') the relevant rules$_D$, not realizing that this vocabulary—characteristically and intelligibly employed in connection with rules$_R$—is actually nonsense in regard to rules$_D$, which are not the sort of thing that we can 'apply' or 'follow'. This conceptual and terminological blunder will in turn feed back into, and reinforce, one's original confusion of the two senses of the term 'rule'. For one will then find it unobjectionable to describe *Situation 2* by saying—with what is actually a rule$_D$ in mind—for example, that

(2c) The porter is required to apply the rule 'For every *x*: if *x* is a dog, then *x* ought not to be allowed in the restaurant', except in the case of seeing-eye dogs;

[56] See Pérez Bermejo (2012: 288).

[57] Soeteman (1989: 195–6). Soeteman chooses the 'second alternative'—'if exceptions exist, why then should they not be included in the formulation of the norm?'—and finds it preferable to 'proceed on a norm which, if necessary, can be altered'. Compare Ramsey (1968: esp. 79–81); and see, for discussion, Rodríguez (2012: 97–8); Navarro and Rodríguez (2014: 108–14).

and, continuing to treat this 'rule' as if it were or behaved like a $rule_R$, one will then take (2c) to be synonymous with

(2a) For every *x*: if *x* is a dog, the porter is required not to allow *x* in the restaurant, unless *x* is a seeing-eye dog,

and thus also with

(2b) The porter is required to apply the rule 'For every *x*: if *x* is a dog, then *x* ought not to be allowed in the restaurant, *unless x* is a seeing-eye dog'.

One will thus not simply have missed the distinction between the notion of a $rule_R$ and a $rule_D$, but found further cause to ignore it.

But the fundamental error of the common view lies, as I said, in the very fact that it operates with the very notion of a $rule_D$. Why is this an error?

The notion of a $rule_D$ is but the colloquial, pre-theoretical articulation of the idea that decision-makers must preoccupy themselves only with those exceptions that *actually happen to come up* in the relevant decision-making contexts. Otherwise—if no exception happens to emerge—decision-makers need not concern themselves with exceptions in the process of deliberating about what to do. In the context of our discussion, this is by now a familiar idea. Think again of Hart's rule on promises;[58] it is (as we now see) a rule in this sense of a $rule_D$. 'If I have promised you to φ', one would naturally say, 'then I have a duty to φ'. Of course, we would add, there can be exceptions—but *that* is the rule. This common use of 'rule', in this sense of a $rule_D$, tracks a particular kind of connection between some fact or facts (in our example, the fact that I have promised you to φ) and some consequence or conclusion (my duty to φ), a connection that holds, we seem to think, despite the fact that there can be exceptions. Even though the occurrence of an exception, we would agree, exonerates the agent from the duty to φ in the particular case, we would still deny that the non-occurrence of the exception is (or can be recast as) just another condition of the $rule_D$. (Or think—for the idea is precisely the same—of Hart's example of a legal case of contract, which we have discussed in previous chapters. Hart's discussion suggests that those facts 'required' for the judge to decide for the plaintiff—offer,

[58] See the text accompanying n 7.

acceptance, consideration, and so on, together with, say, the fact that the contract has been breached—are not merely 'necessary' but *normally* sufficient: they will suffice *unless* some exception emerges; and yet, Hart (1951: 152) insists, the non-occurrence of the exception is not itself aptly represented as a 'negative condition' of what we might now call the 'rule$_D$' on contracts.)

There is no denying that we do ordinarily employ the term 'rule' to refer to what I called a 'rule$_D$'. But what I want to claim is that this common notion of a rule$_D$ is no necessary part of the conceptual and terminological tools with which the phenomenon of exceptions, implicit as well as explicit, is to be analysed. On the contrary, this colloquial notion of a rule$_D$ is part of what is to be elucidated by a theory of defeasibility. It is part of our *explananda*, not part of our explanation. And now that we have a general understanding of the notion of an exception—that was the object of Chapters 3 and 4—we are able not only to explain the idea of a rule$_D$, but also to identify the root of the common view's paradoxical claims. It is the familiar but erroneous assumption that 'substantive' representations can be given of defeating circumstances—an assumption that was already discussed and discarded in previous chapters.

The difference between exceptions and what the common view characterizes as negative rule-conditions—a difference, we saw, that the common view cannot but acknowledge—is none other than the difference between what I have proposed to call *D*-facts and (negative) *P*-facts. So we need the proof-based account if we want to be able to accommodate our intuitive resistance to the representation of *D*-facts as negative elements in the antecedents of the relevant rules (in the sense of 'rules$_R$') without that preventing us from saying, as we also want to, that the 'absence' of *D*-facts is itself an element in the antecedent of those rules. The proof-based account allows us to retain, in our rule-formulations, the distinction between explicit *D*-facts and (negative) *P*-facts. Accordingly, the need to employ the language of rules$_D$ disappears—and the notion of a rule$_D$ can be simply explained away. For what this colloquial notion purports to track is that particular 'strength' of *P*-facts which is often mistaken, as we learned in Chapter 3, for sufficiency (or for 'presumptive' sufficiency, or for their sufficiency in 'normal' cases, as some authors have also attempted to put it[59]). This strength boils down to the fact

[59] Compare Baker (1977: 32); MacCormick (1974: 126–7); MacCormick (1994: 245); and MacCormick (1995: 103–4).

that *P*-facts are all that must be established for a defeasible decision to be correctly issued.

But if, as a theorist engaged with the topic of legal exceptions, you attempt to explain this very point while remaining committed to 'substantive' representations, you will be trapped between abandoning your (sound) pre-theoretical resistance to the thought that exceptions are really no different from negative conditions, and introducing *in* your theory, as part of the apparatus with which you try to make sense of the issue, something like the colloquial notion of a rule$_D$. Thus in any decision-making scenario where *D* is an exception, given that you (rightly) reject formulating the relevant 'rule' as

(F2) If *P*, and *not D*, then A ought to φ,

and given also that you remain committed to a 'substantive' representation of legal rules, you will find no other option than to say that the applicable 'rule' must therefore be

(F3) If *P*, then A ought to φ.

This move is not only explanatorily infertile; it also has considerable theoretical costs. Because the (F3) 'rule' is meant to be compatible with the possibility of exceptions, it would be impossible to treat *P*, in (F3), as a sufficient condition. To introduce in our theory the notion of a 'rule' like (F3) would therefore require us to develop and defend some weaker notion of implication which would not invariably (but only, say, *generally*, or *normally*) allow the detachment of the consequent when the antecedent is verified. We would need to develop a notion of a 'defeasible' rule: a rule 'to which', as Richard Holton has recently put it, 'exceptions can be made without rejection'; and which cannot have the form of a 'simple universal generalization', or of a conditional specifying sufficient conditions for the consequent.[60] One problem with any such 'defeasible' conditional is its weak inferential power; we would

[60] Holton (2010: 369–70). For an early example of an approach of this sort, see Toulmin's reconstruction of argumentative patterns, in which the fact that any 'exception or rebuttal' R is admitted is taken to be incompatible with an *unequivocally* legitimate step from our *data* (ie from 'the facts we appeal to as a foundation for [our] claim') to the '*claim* or conclusion we are seeking to establish'; if a rebuttal R is admitted, then the 'step from data to conclusion' is authorized (or 'warranted') only *presumably* or *probably*: see Toulmin (1958/2004: 90–4, 131–2). Toulmin's version of the ordinary mistake lies in the fact that he thinks that the *data* is restricted to what I call *P*-facts.

not be able to avail ourselves of *modus ponens*, and to conclude that A ought to φ whenever *P* is the case.[61]

My suggestion, however, is not that no sound, apt, and useful, account of 'defeasible' conditionals and 'defeasible' rules can be put forth. My suggestion is that no such effort is needed to account for the phenomenon of defeasibility in law. It is only their substantivist bias that prevents the endorsers of the common view from seeing that a non-'defeasible' rule-formulation can be given that captures exactly what we want to capture, and excludes exactly what we wish to exclude, regarding the behaviour of legal exceptions. It is, as we now know, the proof-based formulation

(F4) If *proved that P*, and *not proved that D*, then A ought to φ.

And a rule like (F4), of course, is no $rule_D$. (F4) is a $rule_R$ like any other. It is the rule that the decision-maker is required to 'apply'. It has no exceptions. In fact, $rules_R$ are not the kind of thing *to which* there can be exceptions. The idea of a '$rule_D$', in turn, can serve us merely as a handy summary reference to the fact that *P*-facts are all that needs to be established for a correct defeasible decision. But a '$rule_D$' is not normative; it requires nothing; it cannot be 'applied'; it is no $rule_R$; it is *no rule*. To have it in our theory even as a mere auxiliary expository device is to run too high a risk of confusion. So I shall simply discard the notion—and, with it, the common view's inadequate account of exceptions explicit and implicit.

But what of *Situation 3*? What of implicit exceptions? How are *those* to be represented along the lines I have proposed? Can a sound proof-based account of implicit exceptions be given? These, at last, are the right questions to ask. My description of the porter's position in (3b) was not meant, as I noted,[62] to stand as a sufficiently perspicuous account of a decision-maker's power to classify as exceptions facts not previously identified as such. So this is the problem before us: *how is a decision-maker's power to classify particular facts as exceptions to be described*—and how, particularly, does it differ from a power simply to decide the case discretionally? I discuss this problem in Chapter 6. Before, however, let me briefly comment on the last of the three commonly endorsed

[61] See Alchourrón (1986: 176-9); Alchourrón (1993: 64–9); Soeteman (2003: 200–2); Redondo (2005: 47); Holton (2011: 173–6); and Rodríguez (2012: 97–8). For a helpful summary of the debate in the jurisprudential context, with references, see also Bayón (2000).

[62] See the text accompanying n 43.

theses which we haven't yet explicitly refuted—the claim that whenever implicit exceptions are allowed, no list of necessary and sufficient conditions for the correct conclusion can be specified in advance of application, and so that (T1') is true in those contexts after all:

(T1') The circumstances on which the correctness of a defeasible decision depends cannot be specified by a set of necessary and sufficient conditions.

That third thesis can now be swiftly dismissed. Whatever the best description of a decision-maker's power to classify particular facts as exceptions is, it is now clear that the *fact* that *the decision-maker does not exercise that power* will figure in the relevant rule—in the relevant rule$_R$—as one of the elements on which the correctness of the defeasible judgment *J* depends. The fact that the decision-maker classifies some particular circumstance as an exception, conversely, is an element in the antecedent of the correlative rule$_R$ whose consequent determines that it is *not* correct to issue the defeasible judgment *J*. *These* facts, the facts that the decision-maker does or does not classify some particular circumstance as an exception—rather than the facts actually classified as exceptions—are the relevant facts whose occurrence satisfies the rules' antecedents. So we are *not* prevented from stating, 'in advance of application', the list of jointly sufficient conditions for the defeasible decision to be correctly made. It is just that at least one such condition describes an act of the decision-maker. This act is part of what must be the case for the antecedent of the applicable rule to be verified, and for the conclusion to *then* follow—deductively—that the decision-maker is authorized to decide in some particular way. Therefore the phenomenon of implicit exceptions gives us no reason to accept (T1').

6

Ceteris Ignotis Clauses

6.1 Completing the Proof-Based Account

So how, exactly, are we to characterize and describe a decision-maker's power to classify as exceptions facts not previously identified as such? How are we to express the fact that such a decision-maker is still constrained to decide in a certain way when no exception emerges, and does not enjoy the discretion simply to decide the case on the balance of reasons or according to what she thinks is just? This is the question that arose from our discussion, in Chapter 5, of the common view on implicit exceptions.

We saw that endorsers of the common view often attempt to account for this difference by saying that the decision-maker's final judgment is still 'rule-based' to some extent, even if the relevant 'rule'—in the sense of what I proposed to call a 'rule$_D$'—may ultimately be 'overridden' and fail to determine the outcome. I have criticized the very notion of a rule$_D$ on which this common approach relies. But we still need to be able to clarify the idea that the common view is trying to capture. It is the idea that underlies, for example, a passage like the following (regarding implicit exceptions in testamentary validity cases):

> [A] judge cannot consistently maintain that a will has been signed by the appropriate number of witnesses and *on that account alone* hold that the will is not valid. What he can do is hold that the will, *though* properly attested, is to be deprived of the force of a valid testament on the grounds that some *other* condition has not been fulfilled.[1]

[1] See Tur (1977: 57, 76 n 46).

The thought, then, is that to authorize decision-makers to classify as exceptions particular circumstances of the case at hand does *not* amount to granting them unconstrained discretion to decide the case as they see fit.[2] So what is the difference?

6.1.1 Accounting for Implicit Exceptions

Let us begin by comparing a situation where *no* exceptions (explicit or implicit) are allowed with the sort of scenario that we now want to characterize. Explicit exceptions can then be introduced to complete our picture. The contrast to be drawn at first is therefore that between

(1) If *P is proved*, issue judgment *J*,

and a scheme like

(2) If *P is proved*, issue judgment *J*, unless . . .

where the ellipsis is to be replaced by the description of the kind of power that we have in mind. The task at hand is to fill in the ellipsis in (2).

Take any requirement, like (1) above, that a judge issue judgment *J* whenever *P* is proved, and put yourself in the position of a law-making authority—a legislator—who so instructs a judge. Such an authority must suppose that *J* is the correct judgment to issue whenever *P* is proved. Does this mean that the law-making authority must also suppose that *J* is (or would be) the correct decision to issue whenever *P* is actually the case? It might seem so. Even though epistemic and pragmatic constraints may require that our decisions be grounded on what we have been able to ascertain, it might seem that we cannot hold that a decision issued on the grounds of a set *P* of proved propositions is

[2] Tur proposes to account for scenarios like the one described in the passage just quoted in terms of his 'third canonical form': '*If A is, then B ought to be, unless there is an overriding reason to the contrary*'. This form purports to 'transcend closure without embracing absolute (or scorer's) discretion': see Tur (2001a: 360–2). It seems to me, however, that the 'third canonical form' fails to achieve its goal: the decision-maker's lack of evaluative assent to the prescribed course of conduct is in Tur's formula a *sufficient* condition for her not to be bound to perform it. The root of the problem lies, I think, in the fact that Tur seems to believe that the formula '*If a + b + c exist, and neither x, y,* or *z is present, then a contract ought to be recognised to exist, unless it would be unconscionable (or otherwise intolerably unjust) to do so*' is an 'unpacked' version ('applied to the law of contracts') of the 'third canonical form', '*If A is, then B ought to be, unless there is an overriding reason to the contrary*': see Tur 2001a: 362. Yet the former, 'unpacked' formula fails to preserve the notion of an override—which notion, moreover, does not really seem to be a 'formal' notion at all.

justified unless we would also be willing to issue it—or to issue some decision that would include or entail it—if we knew for sure that the propositions in *P* were true. (This is not to say that our decisions cannot be justified unless the proved propositions that ground them *are* true; that is not the case.)

The thought seems plausible, but it is too loosely stated. It cannot strictly be the case that when we think that *J* is the correct judgment to issue *whenever P is proved* we are committed to the claim that *J* is the correct judgment to issue *whenever P is the case*. On the contrary, we may be aware that our epistemic and pragmatic constraints can generate not only false positives, so that false propositions are deemed proved, but also, and particularly, false negatives, so that true *relevant* propositions may happen not be proved. No matter how extensive our investigations have been, the possibility always remains that some proposition is true which, had it been proved, would have led us to decide differently than we now must on the grounds of the body of propositions that we have been able to ascertain. When we deem correct any judgment *J* issued on the grounds of some given set *P* of proved facts, then, we are not exactly committed to the claim that *J* is the correct judgment to issue in *any* conceivable situation in which *P* is the case (or that *J* is included in or entailed by the correct decision to issue in any conceivable situation in which *P* is the case; but I shall henceforth omit this qualification). What we are committed to is the claim that *J* is the correct judgment to issue in any conceivable situation in which *P* is the case *and we have no information about any further circumstance*. What we claim, then, to coin a phrase, is that, *ceteris ignotis*—that is, all else being unknown, or unproved—if *P* is the case, then *J* is the correct judgment to issue.

Nor is this all that we are committed to when we judge *in advance of any actual case* that *J* is the judgment to issue *whenever P is proved*. If we agree (for some interpretation of '*P*' and '*J*') that the sound requirement to make or have as a matter of general law is indeed a requirement like (1) above—a requirement that if *P is proved*, then judges issue judgment *J no matter what*—then we must not only believe that

(A) *Ceteris ignotis*, if *P* is the case, *J* is the correct judgment to issue;

we must also believe either that

(B1) No further relevant facts can ever possibly occur: that is, no other circumstance or set of circumstances Q can possibly occur which would lead us to maintain that, *ceteris ignotis*, if *P* and *Q*, then *J* is not the correct judgment to issue;[3]

or that

(B2) We are justified, all things considered, in ruling out of consideration, in advance, any possible further *relevant* fact that may happen also to be established in any particular case.

Rarely, if ever, will one be in a position to justifiably hold a belief like (B1). But there may often be good reason to hold a belief like (B2). It would be mistaken to suppose, as some theorists do, that it is irrational to accept as justified, in advance of any actual case, a requirement that a decision-maker issue judgment *J whenever* certain pre-identified facts or properties *P* are established.[4]

With this in mind, let us now consider how to complete our 'unless'-clause in that scenario—scenario (2)—in which, instead of being required to issue judgment *J whenever P* is proved, a judge is authorized to identify particular circumstances as exceptions immediately operative in the case at hand. This is the scenario in which implicit exceptions are at play. The exercise of such a power involves an evaluative assessment of the relevant circumstances: the decision-maker is being called to assess whether to issue judgment *J* in the particular case would be (un)warranted or (in)correct according to some evaluative standard. She will have to assess whether to issue judgment *J* in the case at hand would be unjust, for example, or absurd, or whether it would contravene or fail to satisfy some other standard or principle.[5]

I gave one example of this in Chapter 5; here is another. Sections 103(1) and 103(2) of the Criminal Justice Act 2003 read as follows:

[3] In which case we effectively believe that *J* is the correct decision to issue *whenever P* is the case—a belief that subsumes (A).

[4] Bayón (1991: 348–9) appears to make this unwarranted supposition. Hart (1961/2012: 133–4) also seems to think that we can only have reason to adopt, for example, 'a rule against killing' if (even though 'the circumstances in which human beings kill others are very various') 'very few factors appear to us to outweigh or make us revise our estimate of the importance of protecting life', so that 'we are not blindingly prejudging issues which require to be weighed against each other'.

[5] There is room for further distinctions—'contravene' is arguably not the same as 'not satisfy', for example; nor is 'not to contravene' the same as to 'satisfy'. To keep things manageable (and readable) I skip over these complications.

(1) For the purposes of section 101(1)(d) the matters in issue between the defendant and the prosecution include—
   (a) the question whether the defendant has a propensity to commit offences of the kind with which he is charged, except where his having such a propensity makes it no more likely that he is guilty of the offence;
   (b) the question whether the defendant has a propensity to be untruthful, except where it is not suggested that the defendant's case is untruthful in any respect.

(2) Where subsection (1)(a) applies, a defendant's propensity to commit offences of the kind with which he is charged may (without prejudice to any other way of doing so) be established by evidence that he has been convicted of—
   (a) an offence of the same description as the one with which he is charged, or
   (b) an offence of the same category as the one with which he is charged.

Subsection (3) then provides (emphases added) that

(3) Subsection (2) does not apply in the case of a particular defendant *if the court is satisfied*, by reason of the length of time since the conviction *or for any other reason*, that *it would be unjust for it to apply in his case.*

In situations like this, then, decision-makers have to assess whether to issue a certain decision in the case at hand would fail to satisfy some given principle or evaluative standard *S*.

Notice, however, that what I am calling the 'case at hand' is defined and described by reference to what has been proved in the particular decision-making context; it is defined by reference to the total set of proved propositions in that context. Call the conjunction of these propositions '*P+*'. Can we then say that what the decision-maker is called to evaluate is whether it would contravene some given evaluative standard *S* to issue judgment *J* whenever *P+* is proved? Would the following formulation, (2'), adequately capture our understanding of a decision-maker's power to classify as exceptions circumstances not previously identified as such?

(2') *If P is proved, issue judgment J, unless* you think that, *ceteris ignotis*, to issue *J* if *P+* is the case would contravene standard *S* (where '*P+*' is the conjunction of the propositions proved in the particular decision-making context).

Clearly, (2') is not a satisfactory rendition of the sort of power that we are trying to articulate. A formulation like (2') would authorize the decision-maker *not* to issue judgment *J* even when *only* *P* has been proved (that is, when {*P*} and {*P*+} are co-extensive), since the decision-maker may well be of the opinion that to issue judgment *J* in *any* situation where *P* is true contravenes standard *S*. (To put it more vividly, if less rigorously: the judge may be convinced that it is *always* unjust, absurd, and so on, to recognize as valid *that* sort of contract; to convict agents who performed *this* sort of action; etc.) In effect, (2') is no different from an authorization to simply decide in accordance with standard *S*—and this is precisely what we want to distinguish from a power not to issue judgment *J* only if an exception is deemed to be present. In the sort of situation with which we are concerned, it is on the grounds of *further* proved circumstances—of proved circumstances *other than P*—that the judge is allowed not to issue *J* if she finds that such a judgment would contravene the relevant evaluative standard *S*. Otherwise, she is certainly required to issue judgment *J*, whether or not she finds such a judgment to live up to standard *S*.

Our previous analysis of the claims involved in 'no matter what' requirements to issue a judgment *J* whenever *P* is proved will help us to see how that simpler scenario differs from the kind of situation that we are now attempting to characterize. Here is formulation (1) again—the formulation displaying the scheme of such 'no matter what' requirements:

(1) If *P is proved*, issue judgment *J*.

We saw that a legislative authority that issues (for some interpretation of '*P*' and '*J*') a 'no matter what' requirement of this sort is committed to two joint claims: that (A) *ceteris ignotis*, if *P* is the case, *J* is the correct judgment to issue; and either that (B1) no further relevant facts can ever possibly occur, or that (B2) we are justified, all things considered, in ruling out of consideration, in advance, any possible further relevant fact that may happen also to be established in any particular case. Now, an authority that chooses instead to allow for implicit exceptions is clearly committed to *neither* (B1) nor (B2). On the contrary, the point of allowing judges to classify and admit as exceptions particular facts of the case at hand is to enable them to take into consideration any further possibly relevant facts, and not to issue judgment *J* if they find that on the grounds of these further facts such a decision would contravene some standard *S*. It is as though the law-making authority is aware that other circumstances relevant to the question of whether or not to issue judgment *J* may conceivably occur, and that these circumstances can never be satisfactorily thought up and enumerated in advance. Thus—instead of attempting to put together a closed catalogue of exceptions, thereby risking over- and under-inclusion—the authority decides to delegate such an assessment to judicial decision-makers. The corresponding evaluative standard or standards *S* will be explicitly or implicitly specified in advance, as will the ways in which possible circumstances stand to be assessed relative to *S*.

But notice that this does *not* prevent the law-making authority from remaining fully committed to the claim in (A). In the absence of further relevant circumstances, the judge is required to issue judgment *J* irrespective of whether she judges that decision to conform to standard *S*: *that* is an assessment definitively made beforehand, a judgment not delegated to adjudicators. The relevance of the set of facts described in *P*, in other words, is authoritatively pre-assessed and fixed.[6] (I assume that if it is by reference to standard *S* that the judicial decision-maker is authorized to recognize exceptions, then the criterion of correctness employed in (A) implies correctness according to *S*.) And this is precisely the feature that distinguishes the judge's position in the sort of situations with which we are concerned, from decision-making contexts in which judges have discretion to decide in accordance with some evaluative standard or other.

It is for ease of exposition that I speak of legislative 'authorities' making 'requirements' of judicial decision-makers. I do not mean to suggest that the kind of decision-making context in which a judge

[6] See Rodríguez's discussions of normative relevance in connection with the topic of implicit defeasibility in Rodríguez and Sucar (1998: 135–42) and Rodríguez (2000: 166); and the developments in Navarro and Rodríguez (2000); Rodríguez (2003: 227–34); and Navarro and Rodríguez (2014: 185–95). Rodríguez attempts to characterize the phenomenon of implicit defeasibility in terms of the (non-)existence, in any given normative system, of a second-level 'rule of closure for relevance' preventing decision-makers to attribute relevance to properties of the case not explicitly marked as relevant in the applicable norms. In drawing this contrast between applicable first-level rules and second-level closure-rules, however, Rodríguez too conflates the notions of a rule_D and a rule_R—the mistake I sought to dissolve in Chapter 5. What he treats as applicable legal rules or norms are in fact the formulations of those supposed 'rules_D' *to* which exceptions may happen to be allowed. Rodríguez (2000: 166) himself affirms that a system in which such a 'closure rule' happens to exist corresponds to what Schauer would call a fully 'entrenched' model of rule-application. For discussion (albeit sharing Rodríguez's basic assumptions), see Bayón (2000: 186–94).

can be said to enjoy the power to classify particular facts of the case at hand as exceptions necessarily presupposes the existence of any *actual* legislator issuing requirements and conferring powers upon decision-makers. Nor is my 'delegation' metaphor intended to imply that such an exception-classifying power can only be described in dispositional terms (for example, by reference to what the relevant legislative authority, had it anticipated the facts of the case, would have accepted *as* an exception[7]). So here is how the sort of decision-making context with which we are concerned can be described:

(2'') If *P is proved, issue judgment J, unless*:

(2.1) you think that, *ceteris ignotis*, to issue *J* if *P+* is the case would contravene standard *S* (where '*P+*' is the conjunction of the propositions proved in the particular decision-making context),

and

(2.2) this judgment of yours described in (2.1) could consistently be accepted by someone who thinks that, *ceteris ignotis*, to issue *J* if *P* is the case would *not* contravene standard *S*.

These two requisites, (2.1) and (2.2), are jointly satisfied in only one scenario: when the body *P+* of proved propositions includes some fact *other than P*—a *further* relevant fact—that is taken by the decision-maker to make a difference. Such a fact is thus taken to be a *D*-fact: it is taken to be an *exception* to judgment *J*, precisely as I have defined it in this book. It is a fact whose ascertainment or proof is taken to render *J* incorrect, but ascertainment of the negation of which is not necessary for *J* to be correct. And this, I suggest, is how we should reconstruct the notion of an implicit exception.

6.1.2 Combining Explicit and Implicit Exceptions

Combined scenarios in which both explicit and implicit exceptions happen to be admitted can now be easily characterized. Let us begin by briefly contrasting our 'no matter what' situation in (1) with a context where only explicit exceptions are allowed. So we have on the one hand

(1) If *P is proved*, issue judgment *J*,

[7] Compare Alchourrón (1996: 341–2).

and on the other, the conjunction of (3a) and (3b) (taken both as all-legal-things-considered formulations):

(3a) If P *is proved* and it is *not proved that* D, issue judgment J_P (e.g. a judgment for the plaintiff or prosecutor);

(3b) If P *is proved* and D *is proved*, issue judgment J_D (e.g. a judgment for the defendant).

The justification for (1) would be (as we have seen) that

(A) *ceteris ignotis*, J would be the correct judgment to issue in a situation where P is the case,

coupled with either the claim that

(B1) nothing else matters,

or the claim that

(B2) nothing else that matters ought to be taken into account.

In (3a) and (3b), that first claim—the claim in (A)—remains unchanged. Not the second, though: the law-making authority (or whoever agrees that (3a) and (3b) are the correct provisions to have in some context) does *not* claim that no *further* circumstance apart from P can matter. In (3a) and (3b), on the contrary, the authority believes that, *ceteris ignotis*, in a situation where P *and* D are the case, J_P is actually *not* the correct decision to make. The judge is accordingly instructed, in (3b), to decide in a certain way—against the plaintiff, for example—when D is proved; and correspondingly instructed, in (3a), to decide for the plaintiff only if *that* circumstance, D, is not proved. It is precisely because that first claim, in (A), remains unchanged—the law-making authority remains committed to it—that we are able to classify D as an exception. (So in a criminal case of rape, the claim is *not* made that, *ceteris ignotis*, if X has sexual intercourse with Y, the correct decision to issue is to convict either agent of rape. There is something else that has to be *known*—or proved—namely, whether there was consent, before we agree that, *ceteris ignotis*, a conviction for rape is the correct decision to issue.)

So the full justification for (3a)—which is itself, as is (3b), a 'no matter what' requirement—will be the conjunction of three claims: that

(A) *ceteris ignotis*, if P, then J_P is the correct decision to issue;

that

(B) *ceteris ignotis*, if P and D, then J_P is *not* the correct decision to make;

and either that

(C1) no other circumstance (that is, no circumstance apart from P and D) matters,

or that

(C2) no other circumstance that matters is to be taken into account.[8]

In (3b), more simply, the underlying claims are that (A) *ceteris ignotis*, if P and D, then the correct decision to make is J_D (for example, a decision for the defendant) and either that (B1) no other circumstance matters, or that (B2) no other circumstance that matters is to be taken into account.

Obviously, then, both (3a) and (3b) can be supplemented with 'unless'-clauses of the kind that have been discussed. Both can be converted from 'no-matter-what' formulations into formulations that allow the decision-maker to identify new exceptions. The full specification of the underlying claims in the corresponding scenarios—call them (3a') and (3b')—would thus simply combine the analysis just offered with the one given above (in section 6.1.1) of the phenomenon of 'implicit' exceptions:

(3a') If P *is proved* and it is *not proved that D, issue judgment* J_P, unless:

(3a'1) you think that, *ceteris ignotis*, to issue J_P if $P+$ is the case would contravene standard S (where '$P+$' is the conjunction of the propositions proved in the particular decision-making context),

and

(3a'2) this judgment of yours described in (3a'1) could consistently be accepted by someone who simultaneously thinks that

(i) *ceteris ignotis*, if P, then J_P would *not* contravene standard S;

and that

[8] It would be an error to suppose that the joint endorsement of (A) and (B) implies non-monotonicity. In (A) '*ceteris*' refers to *everything that is not P* (that is, the '*ceteris ignotis*' clause can be paraphrased as 'if apart from P we know nothing else'); in (B), '*ceteris*' refers to *everything that is neither P nor D* (and the clause can be paraphrased as 'if apart from P and D we know nothing else').

(ii) *ceteris ignotis*, if P and D, then J_P *would* contravene standard S.

(3b') If P *is proved* and D *is proved*, issue judgment J_D, unless:

(3b'1) you think that, *ceteris ignotis*, to issue judgment J_D if $P+$ is the case would contravene standard S (where '$P+$' is the conjunction of the propositions proved in the particular decision-making context),

and

(3b'2) this judgment of yours described in (3b'1) could consistently be accepted by someone who thinks that, *ceteris ignotis*, if P and D, then J_D would *not* contravene standard S.

6.2 On Overrides

As we saw in Chapter 5, endorsers of the common view on implicit exceptions frequently suggest that it is in terms of the idea of an *override* that we should characterize a decision-maker's power to recognize as exceptions particular facts—facts of the case at hand—not previously identified as such. They think there is no other way of accounting for the 'ruleness' of the 'rule' that the decision-maker is entitled not to 'follow' or 'apply'. I have already sought to discredit this common approach to exceptions in law. But now that we have a positive characterization of the phenomenon of implicit exceptions, we can add some remarks on the notion of an override to our criticisms of the common view.

The idea of an override is neither necessary nor sufficient to explain the operation of legal exceptions, explicit or implicit. In fact, it does not allow us to draw the fundamental contrast with which a theory of exceptions is concerned. This is the contrast understood by the common view as a distinction between exceptions proper and mere negative rule-conditions, and which I have rendered as the distinction between D-facts and negative P-facts.

Think of a case in which a legislator decides to make a given fact an exception—a D-fact—in some decision-making context: think, once again, of the D-fact of self-defence in a criminal case of murder. Simplifying a bit, the judicial decision-maker will be instructed to convict if some facts P are proved (the facts of the actual killing) and the occurrence of self-defence is not proved. This is an instruction of the kind captured in our (3a) formulation:

(3a) If *P is proved* and it is *not proved that D,* issue judgment J_P.

Now it *may* be, of course, that behind the legislator's decision for making self-defence a *D*-fact in murder there lies an understanding of the relation between *P* and *D*—between the fact of killing and the fact of self-defence—that can be cast in the language of overrides. Maybe the legislator believes that there is always reason not to kill another person, a reason that is outweighed or overridden when self-defence happens also to have occurred.[9] Perhaps; but my point is that this sort of justification does not necessarily lie behind any decision to make some given fact a *D*-fact. Nor is it the case that this sort of justification cannot lie behind the decision to make some given fact a negative *P*-fact (to make it, that is, from the common view's perspective, a negative rule-element). It is not necessarily absurd for someone to think with regard to rape, for example, that there is always reason not to engage in sexual intercourse, and that consent operates as a factor that outweighs such a reason. While this wouldn't be my view, it has been proposed;[10] and it is surely not incompatible—this is the point—with the claim that the *non*-occurrence of consent must be *proved* in order for a criminal conviction to be correctly issued, and thus that absence of consent should be a *P*-fact (rather than consent being a *D*-fact).[11] Conversely, it is also possible for someone to maintain that there is no reason at all against killing when the killing is done in self-defence—that there is no invariant reason against killing, irrespective of whatever other circumstances may have occurred—while simultaneously maintaining that self-defence ought to be treated as a *D*-fact, and thus that proof of its *non*-occurrence is not necessary for a correctly made conviction for murder.

So the override account is useless as a theory of exceptions. The hallmark of an exception, and the distinctive stance that a law-making authority adopts when deciding to make some fact *F* a *D*-fact, does not directly concern the normative relation between *that* fact and any other

[9] Hart, too, seems in *The Concept of Law* to assume that such weighing of facts 'against each other' must be what underlies the idea of an exception: see Hart (1961/2012: 133).

[10] See Dempsey and Herring (2007); and compare Fletcher (1978/2000: 706–7), and Westen (2008: 573–4).

[11] Indeed, Dempsey and Herring (2007: 471–2) make it clear that to argue for the 'prima facie' wrongfulness of sexual penetration is not equivalent to claiming that sexual penetration should be 'sufficient to establish the elements of a criminal offence'; and that their view on the matter is meant to be compatible 'with its conceptualization under law'.

relevant *P*- or *D*-fact. It concerns the question of how to decide a case when a fact whose ascertainment or ascertainment of whose complement *would* indeed make a difference, happens to remain uncertain. This is the question of how to decide, if, *ceteris ignotis*, all the *P*-facts are the case.

6.3 On 'That's it' Clauses

In a series of recent articles, Richard Holton has introduced and developed the idea of a '*That's it*' clause, which, like my account, supports the conclusion that the defeating or 'superseding' effect of exceptions is compatible with a deductive justification of legal verdicts.[12] His proposal, however, seems to me unsatisfactory. In a nutshell, it is as follows.

Think of the relevance of self-defence, for example, for our assessment of the moral wrongness of killing others. (Though explicitly meant to apply to legal decisions and arguments,[13] Holton's account is originally motivated by what he calls the 'supersession argument' for moral particularism.) The proper contrast to draw here, according to Holton, is not the contrast between the putative rules 'For every *x*: If *x* is a killing, then *x* is wrong' and 'For every *x*: if *x* is a killing and x is done in self-defence, then *x* is not wrong'. Rather, it is the contrast between the rules (R1) and (R2):

(R1) For every *x*: if *x* is a killing and *That's it*, then *x* is wrong.
(R2) For every *x*: if *x* is a killing and *x* is done in self-defence and *That's it*, then *x* is not wrong.

Here '*That's it*' has the partly self-referential meaning that 'there are no further relevant moral rules and non-moral facts (i.e. there is no true moral rule and set of *true* sentences that supersede those which appear in this argument)'.[14] So a conclusion that a given action of killing is wrong can be deductively derived from the conjunction of a statement of (R1) and the two premises that (P2) the action is a killing, and (P3) *That's it*. Call this 'Argument 1':

Argument 1

P1 For every *x*: if *x* is a killing and *That's it*, then *x* is wrong.
P2 This action is a killing.

[12] See Holton (2002); Holton (2010); Holton (2011).
[13] See Holton (2002: 208–9); Holton (2010: 377–8); Holton (2011).
[14] See eg Holton (2010: 375).

P3 *That's it.*
C This action is wrong.

Now Holton says that Argument 1 is 'superseded' by Argument 2, provided that Argument 2 is *sound* (that is, provided that Argument 2, besides being valid, has *true* premises):

Argument 2

P1 For every *x*: if *x* is a killing and *x* is done in self-defence and *That's it*, then *x* is not wrong.
P2 This action is a killing.
P3 This action is done in self-defence.
P4 *That's it.*
C This action is not wrong.

So Argument 1 will *not* be superseded by Argument 2 when the actual killing was *not* done in self-defence: 'If the killing was not done in self defence', says Holton, 'and there is equally no other excusing condition, then the *That's it* premise in the original argument will be true'; so Argument 1 will not be superseded, and its conclusion 'will be simply true'.[15]

It seems to me that Holton's proposal, too, fails to accommodate the distinction—which is by no means specific to the legal domain—between negative elements of rules (corresponding to what in this book I refer to as 'negative *P*-facts', such as absence of consent in rape) and the absence of exceptions (that is, the absence of what I call '*D*-facts').

In Holton's account, if the fact that a killing was done in self-defence counts as a further relevant fact, then so does the fact that a killing was *not* done in self-defence: *whether there was self-defence* becomes a 'relevant' issue. Hence, as Holton notes, the conclusion in Argument 1 is true only if *there was no self-defence*: the actual non-occurrence of self-defence—as well as the actual non-occurrence of any other conceivable exception—is part of what makes the *That's it* premise in Argument 1 true. But to propose this is in effect to treat self-defence, not as an exception proper, but simply as just another (negative) condition whose verification is necessary for the moral judgment to count as soundly made. So Holton's account does not recognize the distinction between self-defence and absence of consent

[15] Holton (2010: 376).

in rape; Holton loses sight of the sense in which we colloquially say that there is a 'rule' against killing—a rule *to which* self-defence is an exception—though not one against sexual intercourse.

A 'rule' in this sense, as we know, is what in Chapter 5 I have proposed to call a 'rule$_D$'. And Holton professes to be concerned with exceptions in this familiar sense of exceptions *to* rules: 'When we explicitly identify an exception to a rule', he says, 'we invoke *That's it*'; but 'by treating it as an exception, rather than using it to show that the rule is wrong, we thereby implicitly reaffirm the rule for the cases in which *That's it* is not triggered'.[16] The problem is that Holton, too, concentrates only on what happens to have actually been the case. He fails to notice that the peculiar behaviour of exceptions is the product of our need to make decisions, including moral and legal judgments, in the absence of information *either way* about the occurrence of certain possibly relevant further circumstances. He says at one point that 'the crucial thought is that what makes a rule apply to a case is not just what obtains: it is also what does not obtain'.[17] We should rephrase this by saying that—in particular 'from the judge's perspective'[18]—what makes a rule (a rule$_D$) 'apply' is not just what we know or have otherwise established, but also what we do not know or have not established; and that the kind of 'rules' with which we are concerned are the rules about *justified judgments that killing is wrong* (to employ Holton's example), rather than rules about when killing *is* wrong.

Thus the 'rule' corresponding to Holton's (R1) formulation should read instead, I would suggest, 'For every *x*: if *x* is a killing, and if it has been ascertained that *x*, then, *ceteris ignotis*, we are justified in judging *x* to be wrong'. It would include, not a '*That's it*' clause, but a '*That's all we know*' clause.[19]

6.4 Concluding Remarks

Introduced in Chapter 3, clarified in Chapter 4, and expanded in Chapter 5 and the present chapter, our account of legal exceptions is now complete. In the process, the argumentative programme

[16] Holton (2002: 209).
[17] Holton (2011: 168).
[18] Holton (2010: 379).
[19] I discuss Holton's account at much greater length in Duarte d'Almeida (2014a).

laid down in Chapter 1, and restated at the end of Chapter 2, has been fulfilled. To summarize our main results: the *irreducibility thesis*, introduced in Chapter 1 and refined in Chapters 2 and 3, was shown to be correct. It means that exceptions—*D*-facts—are neither to be described as (negative) elements in the antecedents of the rules that govern defeasible decision-making, nor otherwise reducible to (or explainable in terms) of *P*-facts. Whereas *P*-facts are facts whose ascertainment to a given standard of proof is a condition for a given defeasible decision to be correct, *D*-facts—explicit as well as implicit—are facts whose ascertainment to a given standard prevents the corresponding defeasible decision from being correctly issued.

Defeasible decisions, then, are decisions that depend not on the ascertainment, to any standard, of the non-occurrence of exceptions, but on the non-ascertainment, to a given standard, of their occurrence. Defeasibility in law is a by-product of the need to reach a decision in the face of uncertainty about the occurrence of relevant facts. In a world of omniscient judges there would be no exceptions.

PART III
Defeasibility in Action

7

Actions and Accusations

7.1 Introduction

Now that we have a general account of defeasibility in place, let us look at the paradigmatic field of ascriptions of responsibility. My goal is to offer an account of defeasibility in the particular kind of decision-making context that I will call 'accusatory'. It will be an opportunity to put the proof-based account to the test. In this chapter, I discuss ascriptions of responsibility in general, before turning my attention, in Chapter 8, to criminal responsibility.

We should take care to distinguish ascriptions of responsibility from ascriptions of *actions*. There is a tradition of conflating the two. It goes back to some influential work done in the 1950s by J. L. Austin, and also to the 1949 essay by H. L. A. Hart in which the problem of defeasibility in law was first raised and addressed. As I mentioned in Chapter 1, Hart's discussion of defeasibility in law was meant to support his defence of the 'ascriptivist' thesis that the 'principal function' of 'sentences of the form "He did it"' is 'to ascribe responsibility for actions'.[1] His views are remarkably similar—although the similarity has not often been noticed—to those advanced by Austin in the famous 1957 essay 'A Plea for Excuses'. I want to begin by offering a reconstruction of their theses on the relation between our everyday practices of holding each other responsible and the concept of human action. There is much to learn from the exercise. Despite their claims, I believe that both Austin and Hart were trying to characterize what I

[1] Hart (1949: 171).

will call the *domain of accusations*. In this and section 7.2, I seek to bring out what I take this domain to be. In section 7.3, I offer an account of the distinction between two kinds of replies to accusations—plain 'No' answers, and 'Yes, but . . .' answers—and explain how the distinction relates to the defeasible character of accusations. A fuller characterization of defeasibility in accusatory contexts is given in section 7.4; and section 7.5 considers some ways of developing the proposed analyses.

Perhaps it will be useful to briefly review the ascriptivist thesis. Hart presents it as the view that

> the concept of a human action is an ascriptive and defeasible one, and that many philosophical difficulties come from ignoring this and searching for its necessary and sufficient conditions. The sentences 'I did it', 'you did it', 'he did it' are . . . primarily utterances with which we *confess* or *admit* liability, make accusations, or *ascribe* responsibility; and the sense in which our actions are ours is very much like that in which property is ours, though the connection is not necessarily a *vinculum juris*, a responsibility under the positive law.[2]

I already discussed some aspects of the example Hart gives to illustrate these claims. He is concerned with sentences in the past tense in which a verb of action φ is used to say of some person X that she φ-ed. We say, for example, on the basis of certain facts that we observe, that 'Smith hit her'. Upon learning that the hitting was done in self-defence, however, we retract our judgment. We would now resist saying, without qualification, that 'He did it'.[3] But given that the occurrence of the actual facts of the hitting is not called into question, the conclusion seems to follow—claims Hart—that our initial judgment is not (or not merely) a description of those facts.

Many critics have objected to this thesis, and rightly so. It is hardly ever the case that in or by saying that some person X φ-ed one is ascribing responsibility to X. Hart's example is misleading: it illustrates, as Pitcher puts it, a 'wrongful, or at least apparently wrongful action—that of a man hitting a woman';[4] but as Geach (1965: 251) says,

[2] Hart (1949: 187–8).

[3] Hart (1949: 192).

[4] Pitcher (1960: 226).

as regards hundreds of our voluntary or intentional acts, it would in fact be absurdly solemn, not to say melodramatic, to talk of imputation and exoneration and excuse, or for that matter of praise and reward. Ascribing an action to an agent just does not in general mean taking up a quasi-legal or quasi-moral attitude, and only a bad choice of examples could make one think otherwise.

This is not to deny that certain 'legal concepts' and 'forensic action terms' may imply responsibility, as Cherry (1974: 104) suggests. And it seems that our ordinary lexicon also includes some verbs with 'censurability built into them', as Pitcher (1960: 30) puts it: verbs—such as 'to murder', 'to lie', or 'to steal'—whose use in sentences of the form '*X* φ-ed' does appear to involve the 'claim that the person deserves to be censured or punished for what he did'.[5] It may even be that such verbs belong, as Feinberg (1965: 20) says, to a larger class of verbs 'used to impute faulty actions', such as '"mis-calculate" and "stammer" [which] also have faultiness built into their meaning'.[6] And perhaps it is also true that a subclass of these 'faulty-action' verbs has 'vulnerability to defeat built into [their] meaning'.[7] So if a circumstance emerges that renders censure inappropriate, then if 'φ' is one of those 'condemnatory verbs',[8] any judgment or assertion that '*X* φ-ed' will have been rendered inappropriate, too. For example, if 'murder' by definition implies responsible performance, then, as Cherry (1974: 104) says, 'to *assert* that A murdered B *is* to claim that A's action was responsibly' done. But that would not constitute a denial of agency; indeed the 'neutral' equivalent of the corresponding condemnatory verb—'to kill', 'to tell a falsehood', 'to take'—would remain applicable.[9] And at any rate, 'in everyday contexts the statement that A did X *tout court* makes no *claim* that X has been responsibly performed'.[10] So Hart's thesis is simply 'false as a general thesis about all statements of the form "He did it"':

5 Pitcher (1960: 230); compare Brandt (1958: 22).
6 Feinberg (1965: 120).
7 Feinberg (1965: 120, 122).
8 Pitcher (1960: 230).
9 Pitcher (1960: 232).
10 Cherry (1974: 104).

> [I]n those numberless cases in which the action is not wrongful, as in 'He played the piano', 'He paid his taxes', and so on, it does not even make sense to speak of the agent [*ipso facto*] deserving censure or punishment.[11]

In these cases of 'perfectly ordinary actions'[12] it is of course 'always possible . . . to ask whether an agent was responsible for his action'.[13] But a negative answer will not make it improper to assert that the agent φ-ed. On the contrary, *X*'s responsibility for φ-ing *presupposes* that *X* did do φ. So do the available exceptions. If *X* φ-ed in self-defence, then *X* φ-ed.[14]

As sound as they may be, these common objections take Hart's statements of his views on action and responsibility a little too literally. His thesis was clearly not the product of any thoroughly considered view about the analysis of action, and can be chiselled into a more sensible shape. One important point is that Hart's remarks on the defeasibility of the 'concept of an action' are strictly analogous to those made in connection with the defeasibility of legal concepts.[15] We already know that his claims about legal concepts are but an application of his more general views on 'defeasible concepts', and I proposed in Chapter 2 to recast Hart's thesis on defeasibility in law not as a thesis about concepts, but about defeasible decisions. Can we similarly read down Hart's ill-considered statements regarding the defeasibility of the 'concept of action'?

[11] Pitcher (1960: 231).

[12] Pitcher (1960: 226).

[13] Cherry (1974: 106).

[14] See Pitcher (1960: 234); Cherry (1974: 106). With more or less detail and elaboration, this line of criticism has been continuously pursued, expanded, or simply iterated in Baier (1951: 190–1); Yolton (1957: 307–10); Rankin (1959: 89–90, 93); Stoljar (1959: 356); Mandelbaum (1960: 218); Rankin (1961: 21–32); Davis (1962: 93–4); Rankin (1963: 239–40); Chisholm (1964: 614); Ladd (1965: 636); Hall (1966: 20); Taylor (1966: 99–103); Whiteley (1966: 224); White (1968: 4–5); Holdcroft (1969: 324–9); Baier (1970: 112–13); Brand (1971: 45); Helm (1971: 428); Langford (1971: 48–53); Rayfield (1971: 40–5); Horovitz (1972: 155); Gizbert-Studnicki (1976: 136–7, 139); Moore (1980: 1569–70); Kindhäuser (1980: 164–6); Howarth (1981: 34); Harré (1982: 13); Páramo Argüelles (1984: 69 n 198); White (1985: 32–3); Nino (1987: 18–20); Bayles (1992: 231–2); Moore (1993: 62–3, 92–3); Loui (1995: 25); González Lagier (2003: 35–6); Epstein (2005: 234); Finkelstein (2005: 582–3); Garzón Valdés and others (2007: 126); Stoecker (2007: 39); Mañalich (2009: 188–9).

[15] See Hart (1949: 187). In Duarte d'Almeida (2015b) I say more about the several strands of argument (and their relative importance) in Hart's early essay, and about the influential 'Frege point' made against ascriptivism in Geach (1960) and developed in Geach (1965).

The answer is 'yes'. His claim that action is a 'defeasible' concept reads just like his claim that contract is a 'defeasible' concept. It reads as a claim about a certain domain of judgments or decisions, a domain supposed to provide another illustration of the phenomenon of defeasibility.

The problem is that the identification of this domain is done less transparently than in the case of law. Hart's references to a judge's role in a 'case of contract' allow us fairly clearly to identify the sort of situations he has in mind when speaking of the law. In the case of action, however, the domain is less helpfully described as the domain of situations in which one can be said to be 'ascribing' responsibility to someone (situations in which 'we *confess* or *admit* liability, make accusations, or *ascribe* responsibility'[16]); but this is just too superficial a description to pin down the class of decisions that Hart takes to be 'defeasible' in the relevant sense.

The difficulty is not only that 'responsibility' is a multiply ambiguous term.[17] The difficulty is also that it is not clear why this reference to ascriptions of *responsibility* is introduced at all. Is the topic under scrutiny not supposed to be that of judgments *of action*, judgments that someone φ-ed? Hart's analogy with property[18] would indeed appear to suggest that it is the ascription of *actions* that concerns him: 'the sense in which our actions are ours', he says, 'is very much like that in which property is ours'.[19] And Hart does on occasion refer to his endeavour as that of accounting for our practices of 'ascribing *an action* to a person'.[20] But then he also speaks indistinctly (while clearly intending to allude to the same problem) of the ascription of 'responsibility';[21] of the

16 Hart (1949: 187).

17 For different attempts at discerning and relating relevant senses of 'responsibility', see Haines (1955); Pennock (1960); Feinberg (1965: 130–7); Hart (1968/2008: 211–30); Baier (1970: 103–8); Baier (1972/98: 100–8); Baier (1987: 101–14); Feinberg (1988a: 74–6); Feinberg (1988b); Zimmerman (1988: 1–6); Gardner (2008). I return to this point in section 7.2.

18 See the quotation accompanying n 2.

19 Hart (1949: 188). At 185 he also compares judgments of the form 'He did it' to judgments in which 'the possessive terms "mine", "yours", "his" appear as grammatical predicates' ('This is yours', 'This is his', etc). Given that he refers to the latter as ascriptions *of rights* (namely, 'rights of possession')—see Hart (1949: 171, 172, 185, 186, 187) and, of course, the paper's title—should the former not then be characterized as ascriptions *of actions* rather than of responsibility?

20 See Hart (1949: 191, emphasis added); and his reference, on the same page, to 'cases where we recognise an action'.

21 Hart (1949: 171, 187, 189, 190, 193) as well as, again, the paper's title.

ascription of 'liability' or 'liabilities';[22] and even, more than once, of the ascription of responsibility *for actions*.[23] Does that mean that ascriptions of action and ascriptions of responsibility are equivalent or at least overlapping notions—or, perhaps, that there is some class of judgments that can equivalently be said to be ascriptions of actions *and* of responsibility?

In clarifying this point, it will prove useful to turn our attention to Austin's 'A Plea for Excuses'. As I said, his project and his claims on action are strikingly similar to Hart's. Austin, too, believed that defences—'excuses'—are directly material for the 'philosophical study of conduct'.[24] A discussion of his comparatively clearer views on this point will help us to reconstruct and make sense of what was in fact a common argument—and to make some progress of our own on this topic.

7.2 Responsibility and Action

7.2.1 Excuses

'When', asks Austin, 'are excuses proffered?' 'In general', he says,

> the situation is one where someone is *accused* of having done something, or (if that will keep it any cleaner) where someone is *said* to have done something which is bad, wrong, inept, unwelcome, or in some other of the numerous possible ways untoward. Thereupon he, or someone on his behalf, will try to defend his conduct or to get him out of it.[25]

Whoever offers an excuse is trying to get the accused 'out of it'. Out of *what*, exactly? Austin never quite pinpoints the characteristic effect of successful excuses. The omission is likely to be intentional. Apart from one or two metaphors (excuses, he tells us, get us 'out of the fire'[26]), Austin says little more than that '[i]f ordinary language is to be our guide, it is to evade responsibility, or full responsibility, that we most often make excuses'.[27] But again, 'responsibility' is an ambiguous

[22] Hart (1949: 189, 190, 193).

[23] Hart (1949: 171, and twice at 194, describing his endeavour as an attempt 'to elucidate the criteria we do in fact employ in assigning responsibility for actions').

[24] Austin (1957: 180).

[25] Austin (1957: 175–6); notice the original italics.

[26] Austin (1957: 177).

[27] Austin (1957: 181); 'blame' is also mentioned in a note. Compare Austin (1975: 155).

term, and Austin fails to employ it consistently. On the one hand, he avails himself of the notion for the purpose of distinguishing excuses from justifications. When we offer an excuse, he says, we 'admit that [that which we are '*said* to have done'[28]] was bad but don't accept full, or even any, responsibility':[29] to offer an excuse is 'to admit that it wasn't a good thing to have done, but to argue that it is not quite fair or correct to say *baldly* "X did A"':

> We may say it isn't fair just to say X did it; perhaps he was under somebody's influence, or was nudged. Or, it isn't fair to say baldly he *did* A; it may have been partly accidental, or an unintentional slip. Or, it isn't fair to say he did simply A—he was really doing something quite different and A was only incidental, or he was looking at the whole thing quite differently.[30]

If this is the hallmark of excuses, then when offering a justification, do we concede (rather than deny) that it is 'fair or correct to say *baldly* "X did A"'? So Austin tells us: in offering a justification 'we admit *flatly* that he, X, did do that very thing A'; what we argue is 'that it was a good thing, or the right or sensible thing, or a permissible thing to do, either in general or at least in the special circumstances for the occasion'.[31] The suggestion, then, is that in accepting that it *is* fair or correct to say baldly 'X did A', one accepts—and that in denying the fairness of the flat 'X did A' one correspondingly denies—'responsibility'. In Austin's well-known summary,

> In the one defence [justification], briefly, we accept responsibility but deny that it was bad: in the other [excuse], we admit that it was bad but don't accept full, or even any, responsibility.[32]

But we saw that both justifications and excuses will, if successful, get us 'out of it'. How, then, can the answer to our question (*What* is it that excuses, as well as justifications, get us 'out of'?) be 'responsibility'? It cannot. Not, at least, in the sense in which the term is

[28] Austin (1957: 176).
[29] Austin (1957: 176).
[30] Austin (1957: 176).
[31] Austin (1957: 176).
[32] Austin (1957: 176).

employed to differentiate both kinds of defences. Yet Austin makes no such distinctions, and offers no disambiguation.

On the other hand, how solid is Austin's separation of justifications and excuses on the grounds of whether 'responsibility' is accepted or denied? His pithy summary is unhelpfully imprecise. In fact, Austin immediately follows it by remarking how both kinds of defences 'can be confused, and can *seem* to go very near to each other, even if they do not perhaps actually do so':

> You dropped the tea-tray: Certainly, but an emotional storm was about to break out: or, Yes, but there was a wasp. In each case the defence, very soundly, insists on a fuller description of the event in its context; but the first is a justification, the second an excuse.[33]

But if both justifications and excuses amount to an insistence, as Austin says here, on a 'fuller description' of the event than the plain 'X did A'—if both amount, as we might put it, to a 'Yes, but . . .' sort of rejoinder—then must both kinds of defences not be said equally to deny 'responsibility' after all? Does Austin not maintain, as we have just seen, that in denying the fairness of the flat 'X did A' one is denying 'responsibility'? If that is the case, his proposed criterion for discerning excuses from justifications is flawed.

Matters are made worse by Austin's admission, some pages later, that *both* kinds of defences are in fact compatible with *either* the rejection or the acceptance of 'responsibility'. For even though he takes ordinary language to suggest that it is 'to evade responsibility' that 'we most often make excuses', he nonetheless observes that

> in fact [the term] 'responsibility' . . . seems not really apt in all cases: I do not exactly evade responsibility when I plead clumsiness or tactlessness, nor, often, when I plead that I only did it unwittingly or reluctantly, and still less if I plead that I had in the circumstances no choice: here I was constrained and have an excuse (or justification), yet may accept responsibility.[34]

We should cut through this tangle. The difference between justifications and excuses is, I think, marginal to Austin's project. Both his subject and his main thesis can be stated and discussed independently

[33] Austin (1957: 176).
[34] Austin (1957: 181).

of it. Austin himself remarks at one point that he is 'using the word "excuses" *for a title*', and that his field of enquiry includes such other terms as '"plea", "defence", "justification", and so on'.[35] Plainly, his direct domain of concern is defences or pleas that argue that 'it is not quite fair or correct to say *baldly* "X did A"', and these, as we have just seen, range similarly over excuses and justifications. There may be room for distinguishing between species of such 'Yes, but . . .' defences in terms of what they 'deny' (that is, in terms of their grounds); but all such defences are alike in terms of what they 'evade' (that is, in terms of their effects).

What, then, do they commonly 'evade'? It was not my intention to suggest that 'responsibility' cannot be the answer. But given that the term can be employed in several senses (and that Austin himself indistinctly employs it in at least two senses), careful disambiguation is in order. If there is a sense in which it can plausibly be asserted that a successful 'Yes, but . . .' reply to an accusation enables the accused to evade 'responsibility', it must be the sense in which judgments or claims of 'responsibility' can be said to be associated to the 'accusations and defences of daily life'.[36] It must therefore be the sense in which it can be said that whoever accuses someone of φ-ing is thereby, as Austin suggests in passing, 'holding' the accused 'responsible for doing it'.[37] So how is this notion to be characterized?

7.2.2 *'Holding Responsible'*

The expression 'holding others responsible' is commonly used in philosophical discourse to refer to a particular class of backward-looking practices of reacting or responding in certain ways to other people's actions or putative actions. The range of responses involved is quite diverse. It includes different 'reactive feelings and attitudes' (in Strawson's well-known expression[38]) as well as various types of action which, expressing favourable or unfavourable appraisal, are meant in some way to affect or reverberate on those whose φ-ings have prompted such responses. These can be adverse responses—such as blaming, resenting, reproaching, or punishing some agent *X* for having

[35] Austin (1957: 175).
[36] Austin (1957: 188).
[37] See Austin (1957: 181 n 1).
[38] Strawson (1974: 9).

φ-ed—as well as favourable ones—such as praising or rewarding *X* for having φ-ed.

Apart from this ostensive, open-ended, and very general description, there is little to be said of these practices of holding others responsible that is not to some extent contentious and debated. (The very assumption that such practices can adequately be taken as a discrete object of study—or even the assumption that there is, as Bennett puts it, a class of 'blame-related responses' that is, like its seemingly correlative class of 'praise-related responses', 'unified enough for philosophy to be done about it'[39]—is but a provisional, revisable pre-theoretical step.) But perhaps it is safe to note that a distinctive and unifying feature of such responses lies in the fact that they all seem to address and engage with persons in view of their actions (as opposed to being responses to actions *tout court*). When holding others responsible for their φ-ings, we suppose that the relevant φ-ings can be ascribed to an agent as something more than a mere event which can be traced back causally to a person. Otherwise it would in some sense be inappropriate or unfair to submit the individual to the particular kind of appraisal that is carried by our responses to their φ-ings. If I blame you, for example, or sincerely reprimand you, for having φ-ed, I must regard you, at least in connection with φ, as (in Watson's phrase) an 'agent in a strong sense'. I must believe that the action of φ-ing is ascribable to you in the manner required, if not sufficient, for the response to count as an appropriate one.[40]

[39] See Bennett (1980: 15); compare also Wallace's discussion of the (de)merits of broad pre-theoretical constructions of the class of moral reactive attitudes in Wallace (1994: 10–12, 25–33).

[40] Watson (2004: 263). This 'attributability' of an action 'to an individual as its agent', as Watson also puts it, is the mark of what is normally called, in a different sense of the term, 'responsible' agency. A responsible agent, in this sense, is someone whom we regard as a 'fit subject' for 'attributions of credit or discredit which are not reducible to acknowledgement of [the individual's] causal roles': see Wolf (1990: 41), and the related distinction between 'superficial' and 'deep responsibility' at Wolf (1990: 40–2). On the topic, see also Wallace (1994: 52–62) and Scanlon (1998: 248–51). The underlying thought is anything but recent; its explicit articulation can be traced back at least to Pufendorf: see Hruschka (1984: 692–702) and Hruschka (1986: 672–6). Which of the two senses of 'responsible' is explanatorily prior is also a debated issue. The standard picture treats the fact (and the corresponding belief) that someone *is* a responsible agent as an independent, necessary precondition of someone's being appropriately *held* responsible for her actions. But Strawsonians wish to maintain, to the contrary, that to believe that an individual is responsible is simply to regard her as an apt target of the range of 'reactive attitudes' and behaviours with which we respond to each other's actions, and thus that, as Wallace (1994: 5) puts it, 'we cannot establish what it is to *be* a morally responsible agent unless we first understand the stance of holding someone

We can usefully think of such responses as 'consequences' of their target subjects' φ-ings—consequences that can be assessed as appropriately or inappropriately, fairly or unfairly held or imposed, in any given context. For any such potential response *R*, and any φ-ing by a person *X*, we may intelligibly ask whether and under which conditions it is appropriate to react to *X*'s φ-ing with *R*. We are often able to indicate, for some given φ-ing by *X* in some sufficiently described context, a range of potential reactions or responses *R* associated to *X*'s φ-ing. This range will vary from context to context, and from case to case, according to various factors (such as, for example, the entitlements and expectations attached to our social positions and roles: different ranges of reactive attitudes and actions are typically available, say, to our parents, our friends, our colleagues, or our employers, as a consequence of our φ-ings). In each context or case, moreover, whether each one of the potential reactions *R* is appropriately held or imposed may itself depend on its own partially different set of conditions. (My employer may be justified in suspending me for a week, though not in terminating my contract, as a consequence of some particular φ-ing of mine.)

Yet there is also room to discern and classify, and to attempt to characterize, what may appear to be importantly different general aspects of our practices of holding others responsible. We may find it illuminating, for instance, to differentiate among *kinds* of factors on which any actual reactive response will jointly depend; and we may want to concentrate our attention on only some of those factors to the detriment of others (since not all will be equally interesting, philosophically puzzling, or difficult to characterize).

One particular attention-drawing subset is formed by those factors that enable us to say of some person that she has, in virtue of some action of hers, made herself an eligible, deserving candidate,[41] as it were, for some response or reaction. We can think of this position as a *liability* of sorts. In asking whether, and under what conditions, someone may appropriately be held liable, in this sense, to a given range of potential consequences, we are concerned only with those circumstances that bear on the evaluation of the agent's φ-ing, and of the

responsible—the stance of the moral judge, rather than of the agent who is judged'; see Strawson (1962: esp. 22–3). These are side issues in the context of my discussion; for development, see Oshana (1997); Smith (2007: esp. 469–71); Macnamara (2011: 83–7); Eshleman (2014).

41 See Fischer (1987: 63).

agent in view of her φ-ing, as meritorious or unmeritorious. That is a question we can intelligibly ask while leaving aside the further question whether the potential impending consequences may or should actually—all things considered—be imposed. This further question will turn on additional considerations, but these are considerations of a significantly different sort; one can be liable to—a deserving candidate to—certain consequences that nevertheless there is reason not to impose.[42] The point is that judgments and claims that some person *P* is in this sense liable—in some context, and in virtue of her φ-ing—to a given range of favourable or unfavourable consequences, form a salient part of our practices of holding others responsible.

7.2.3 The Domain of Accusations

Recall, then, with these general remarks in mind, the kind of situation with which Austin is concerned. He describes it indifferently as the situation 'where someone is *accused* of having done something' or 'where someone is *said* to have done something which is bad, wrong, etc'.[43] This second formulation is not fully clear; but it seems that we should take it to refer to situations in which a speaker *Y* says of some person *X* that '*X* did A', where 'A' is (or is assumed by *Y* to be) 'in

[42] Typically included in the range of potential consequences is the imposition of liabilities proper, liabilities *in the strict sense*: see Gardner (2008: 132–9). One reason why the term 'liability', as I employ it in the text, is not used in its strict sense is that even though one paradigmatic class of consequences can indeed be described in terms of the acquisition, by the agent, of liabilities proper (and therefore also in terms of the acquisition, by someone, of some set of correlative normative powers), the actual acquisition of such liabilities (and powers) may well be dependent on a set of conditions that is not equivalent to (though it includes) the narrower set of factors with which I am concerned. Another reason is that there is also one paradigmatic class of consequences that does not seem to be aptly described with the language of 'powers': the class of the reactive *attitudes* as opposed to the class of the reactive *actions* (to employ a parallel phrase). Neither class seems to be more basic than the other. I can blame you or resent you for having φ-ed without engaging in any sort of conduct related to your φ-ing; but likewise the unfavourable reactive actions do not necessarily presuppose any correspondingly unfavourable reactive attitudes. This seems clear when we consider examples that we wouldn't count as examples of moral offences. I will quite rightly rebuke you for having chosen to use Royal Gala rather than Braeburn apples in your *tarte Tatin*, and appropriately penalize you with a low score in the domestic cooking competition that the two of us decided to put on just for the fun of it. This conduct of mine fully counts, in the relevant sense, as an unfavourable consequence of your action. But using the wrong kind of apples seems not to be the kind of action that would necessarily engage any one of the unfavourable attitudes or emotions, however mild.

[43] Austin (1957: 175–8).

some [or] other of the numerous possible ways untoward'.[44] Austin's concern, in other words, is with the domain of *accusations*.

Now, a natural way of performing the speech act—the illocutionary act—of accusing someone of something is indeed by uttering a sentence of the form '*X* did A': by saying, that is, that person *X* φ-ed. But, of course, an accusation is not a mere description of someone's action. If I sincerely accuse someone of having φ-ed, I am doing something more than simply stating that the accused did do φ. I am singling or pointing the accused out as an appropriate candidate, in virtue of her φ-ing, for the range of unfavourable consequences that may happen to be associated to φ-ings of that kind. I am claiming that the agent is *liable* to such consequences, in the sense of 'liability' introduced at the end of section 7.2.2.

But it may be convenient to allow for a partly stipulated use of 'accusation' in the context of our discussion. For Austin is concerned with *any* case in which, by saying that '*X* φ-ed', one claims that *X* can be deemed liable to a given range of unfavourable consequences in virtue of her φ-ing. His range of examples is notably undiscriminating. It includes killing others as well as dropping tea-trays; pushing people over cliffs and shooting donkeys, but also eating one's soup or knocking over cream-jugs; treading on babies and treading on snails.[45] Arguably not all such cases would count as *accusations* in the ordinary meaning of the term, which seems to apply only when the action involved is a sufficiently grave or serious one, and the stakes considerably high.[46] But it is true that, given the adequate background or context, any action φ whatsoever may make its agent an appropriate candidate for criticism or some other unfavourable consequence. Moreover, there is no reason to differentiate, for our present purposes, between cases in which the 'accusation' is in the second person ('You φ-ed'), the third person ('She φ-ed'), or even the first person ('I φ-ed'). Although he works

[44] Austin (1957: 176).

[45] See Austin (1957: 176–7, 181 n 1, 185, 193, 194, 195).

[46] This is not to say that it would be senseless otherwise to apply the term, in jest, for example, or at any rate less seriously (as in the cooking example given in n 42). Austin's use of 'accusation' seems also to encompass at least some of those acts that we would ordinarily refer to as 'denunciations' and 'complaints' against someone, in so far as these can be differentiated from the speech act of accusation proper.

mainly with second- and third-person examples,[47] Austin's domain of inquiry also clearly covers all three cases.

If this is our domain, it will prove convenient to have a term to unitarily designate the relevant kind of speech act—whatever the content of 'φ', and whether or not the speaker and the accused happen to be different individuals. So this is how I will be using the noun 'accusation' for the remainder of this chapter. I will be using it, in this partly stipulated sense, to refer to any illocutionary act that, though naturally performed by the simple utterance of a locution of the form 'X φ-ed', involves and purports to communicate the claim that a given range of unfavourable consequences can appropriately be imposed on X in virtue of her φ-ing.

So now I can draw your attention to the fact that this was also Hart's domain of inquiry in his discussion of responsibility and action. He discusses situations in which, by uttering sentences of the form 'X φ-ed', we '*confess* or *admit* liability, make accusations, or *ascribe* responsibility',[48] and suggests that these three kinds of actions—confessions, accusations, and ascriptions of 'responsibility'—map onto, respectively, the first-, second-, and third-personal uses of such sentences in the past tense:

> There are in our ordinary language sentences whose primary function is not to describe things, events, or persons, or anything else, nor to express or kindle feelings or emotions, but to do such things as . . . to admit or ascribe or make accusations of responsibility ('I did it,' 'He did it,' 'You did it').[49]

Hart restricts his use of 'accusation' to the second-personal 'You φ-ed'. But the third-personal 'He φ-ed' is not untypical of accusatory contexts in the ordinary sense of the term,[50] and a first-personal 'confession' is nothing other than a self-accusation. Hart's domain of investigation is the same as Austin's: it is the domain of accusations.

Moreover, they are both concerned with the same aspect of this domain—the interplay between the 'accusations and defences of daily

[47] But see his famous example in Austin (1957: 185 n 1) for a discussion of a first-person case.

[48] Hart (1949: 187).

[49] Hart (1949: 171; see also 187).

[50] And Hart (1949: 190) does speak here of a 'charge'.

life'[51]—and both concentrate on precisely the same class of 'defences'. We have already seen that Austin, though professing to be mainly interested in 'excuses' (which, he thinks, can, if only 'in principle', be kept distinct from justifications[52]), is actually concerned with those replies to accusations that amount to a claim that 'it will not do to say simply "X did A"'[53] and that a 'fuller description of the event' is called for.[54] (That 'the verb needs modifying'—that the accused 'did it but only *in a way*, not just flatly like that'[55]—is his explanandum; and this, 'the tenor of so many excuses',[56] is likewise a mark of justifications.) And this class of 'Yes, but . . .' replies, as I proposed to call them, coincides exactly with the set of what Hart counts as 'defences' proper.

The point is easy to miss, as the critical literature on ascriptivism amply illustrates. But remember how Hart describes the example in which, having accused Smith of having 'hit her', we come to find out that the hitting was accidental. Here, says Hart (1949: 193), 'it appears that we should have said "Smith hit her accidentally"'. It is *not* that we should refuse to say—that we should deny—that Smith hit her. It is, rather, that we should 'refus[e] to say "He did it" without qualification'.[57] Our judgment needs 'to be qualified'[58]—or 'modified', as Austin would put it. It won't do to say 'Smith hit her' *sans phrase*—or 'flatly', as Austin would put it. Both Austin and Hart are working with, and attempting to account for, the same body of linguistic data.

Interestingly, both are also committed to the view that defences are directly relevant to what Hart (1949: 179) calls the 'philosophical analysis of action' and Austin (1957: 180) the 'philosophical study of conduct'.[59] They use 'action' in precisely the same sense, though it

[51] See Austin (1957: 188), and also Hart's endnote on 'different senses of responsibility' in Hart (1968/2008: 264–5), where he asserts that there is a 'very direct connection' between 'liability-responsibility' (which he takes to be 'the primary sense of responsibility'), and the notion of 'answering or rebutting accusations or charges': 'a person who fails to rebut a charge is liable to punishment or blame for what he has done, and a person who is liable to punishment or blame has had a charge to rebut and failed to rebut it'.

[52] Austin (1957: 177).

[53] Austin (1957: 180).

[54] Austin (1957: 176).

[55] Austin (1957: 187).

[56] Austin (1957: 187).

[57] Hart (1949: 192).

[58] Hart (1949: 193).

[59] Austin (1957: 180).

is again Austin who makes the relevant point more clearly. '"Doing an action", as used in philosophy', Austin (1957: 178) remarks, 'is a highly abstract expression—it is a stand-in used in place of any (or almost any?) verb with a personal subject'. We should beware 'the myth of the verb', he says, and avoid treating

> the expression 'doing an action' no longer as a stand-in for a verb with a personal subject . . . but as a self-explanatory, ground-level description, one which brings adequately into the open the essential features of everything that comes, by simple inspection, under it.[60]

This remark reflects Austin's own view on the proper subject-matter of philosophy of action. 'Philosophical study of conduct' ought to occupy itself, not with the notion of an *action* itself, but with all and each of the verbs for which the phrase 'doing an action' operates as a stand-in.[61] This is why Austin focuses, not on situations in which someone is actually said to have 'done an action', but on situations in which a speaker can be described as having said that someone has 'done A'—has 'φ-ed'—where 'A' (or 'φ') is in each particular case to be replaced by a given verb of action.

But this was Hart's approach, too. It is true that more often than not Hart speaks of the 'concept of an action',[62] or of 'the concept of a human action'.[63] But it is 'verbs of action',[64] rather than the concept of action, that form his actual topic. He makes it plain, as I have already pointed out, that his remarks are confined to simple sentences in the past tense in which a verb of action is used to accuse someone of having φ-ed,[65] and his references to situations in which someone says 'He did it' are, of course, not *oratio recta* pointers, but shorthand allusions to uses of sentences of the *form* 'X φ-ed'—'sentences of the *form* "He did it"'—as he states at the outset of his essay.[66]

[60] Austin (1957: 178).

[61] See Austin (1957: 179).

[62] Hart (1949: 176–7, 188, 189).

[63] Hart (1949: 171, 187, 189).

[64] See Hart (1949: 188, 192, 193).

[65] See Hart (1949: 188).

[66] See Hart (1949: 171–2, emphasis added; and also 189—'"He did it" (*e.g.*, "He hit her")'—or 190—'"He did it" ("He hit her")'). Hart uses 'He did it' to indicate the *form* of actions sentences, and 'He hit her' as an example of an actual sentence—an actual interpretation—*of* that form. The symmetry between Hart's and Austin's essays, though little noticed, is not surprising; both articles stemmed from a seminar jointly conducted by Austin and Hart on the topic of excuses. See Austin's reference to the 'class that Hart used to

So both Hart and Austin maintain that when, in the face of an accusation, someone argues that 'it is not quite fair or correct to say *baldly* "X did A"',[67] one is thereby claiming that some 'qualification' is required.[68] One is claiming that some 'modifying expression', viz. some 'adverb of excuse, such as "unwittingly" or "spontaneously" or "impulsively"', is in order.[69] These must *therefore* be cases—or so they seem to think—that 'pick out the internal detail of the machinery of doing actions'.[70] They must be cases in which 'there has been some abnormality or failure' in the doing of the corresponding action.[71] Why else would the qualification be called for? How else would we 'explain our refusal to say "He did it" without qualification'?[72]

One of the 'lessons to be learned from the study of Excuses', says Austin (1957: 189), is that there is 'no modification without aberration':

> The natural economy of language dictates that for the *standard* case covered by any normal verb . . . no modifying expression is required or even permissible. Only if we do the action named in some *special* way or circumstances, different from which such an act is *naturally* done (and of course both the normal and the abnormal differ according to what verb in particular is in question) is a modifying expression called for, or even in order.[73]

Hence any occasion in which the unqualified 'X φ-ed' *is* appropriate must be a 'natural' or 'normal' case of conduct: a case of 'normal action', as Hart (1949: 193) says. And precisely because 'as so often, the abnormal will throw light on the normal', the study of excuses—helping us 'to penetrate the mechanisms of the natural successful act'—may throw light on the 'philosophical study of conduct' and get it off to a 'positive fresh start'.[74]

This, then, is their argument. Is it sound?

conduct with me in the years soon after the war' in Austin (1957: 195 n 1); and see also Šimenc (1991: 68); Lacey (2004: 144–5); Sugarman (2005: 276); Yeager (2006: 132, 190 n 19); and MacCormick (2008: 218).

67 Austin (1957: 176).

68 Hart (1949: 192).

69 Austin (1957: 190).

70 Austin (1957: 193).

71 Austin (1957: 179–80).

72 Hart (1949: 192).

73 Austin (1957: 190, emphases in the original, except for 'naturally').

74 Austin (1957: 180).

7.3 'Yes, but . . .'

Let us pay closer attention to the kind of 'Yes, but . . .' rejoinders to accusations that interest both Austin and Hart. Suppose that someone faced with an accusation successfully objects 'Yes, but there was a wasp', as in one of Austin's examples,[75] or, as in one of Hart's, '[Yes], but he [or 'I'] was forced to by a bully'.[76] What, exactly, is the import of this reply?

In attempting a general explanation, I adopt the working assumption that whoever sincerely accuses *X* of having φ-ed must believe that the accused did in fact do φ. I assume therefore that whether or not *X* performed action φ is a matter of fact, one that can in principle be ascertained and form the truth-apt propositional content of other people's beliefs. (This is not to prejudge any relevant issue.[77] If it turns out that as a result of this assumption we find ourselves unable to explain some central feature of the interplay of 'X φ-ed' accusations and 'Yes, but . . .' replies, the resulting impasse will have given us reason to revise and discard this starting point of our inquiry.)

Faced with an accusation, one may oppose it or object to it in various ways. The accuser's belief that *X*—the accused—φ-ed will have been formed on the grounds of a given body *E* of evidence or information, and one way of objecting to the accusation is to deny that some or all of the evidence in *E* is sound. Or one may deny that the accuser's belief that the accused did in fact do φ is justified or warranted relative to *E*. Or one can adduce further evidence about the events, and claim that the accuser's belief that *X* φ-ed is not justified relative to the expanded body of evidence *E*+. But these are not the sort of replies with which we are directly concerned. These are plain 'No' objections, rather than 'Yes, but . . .' replies. It is true, of course, that anyone who puts forth a 'Yes, but . . . reply' is *objecting* to something. But by contrast to straightforward, unqualified 'No' replies, there is also something—the 'Yes'

[75] See the passage accompanying n 33 above.

[76] Hart (1949: 191).

[77] Austin does not ever deny that one's past actions *can* be the object of true descriptions; after all he refers to excuses as insistences on 'a fuller *description* of the event': see Austin (1957: 176). Hart (1949: 183) too at one point characterizes the sentence 'Smith put arsenic in his wife's coffee on May 1st, 1994' as a 'statement of temporal fact'.

element—that whoever voices a 'Yes, but . . .' reply concedes or grants.

What one grants, it seems, is precisely that the accuser's belief that the accused φ-ed is true, or at least justified relative to *E* (or, as far as the objector knows, to any superset *E*+ of material evidence). Yet if by pressing a 'Yes, but. . .' objection one is nonetheless insisting, as Austin (1957: 176) says, on a 'fuller description of the events', the point of doing so must surely be to draw the accuser's attention to some further feature(s) of those events, features that (the objector implicitly claims) the accuser ought also to consider. What one is claiming, in other words, is that the body of relevant evidence (be it *E* or *E*+) happens also to establish some circumstance or set of circumstances which are relevant for the accusation's discernible purpose. (The 'purpose' of an accusation, in the sense in which I am using the word, is to single out the accused as liable, in a given and identifiable context, to a given and identifiable range of unfavourable consequences—as explained in section 7.2.2.)

Hence two things are assumed in such a reply. First, and given that judgments of relevance are relative to some context and purpose, a 'Yes, but . . .' reply assumes some particular purpose *p* as being the purpose of the accusation that it purports to oppose. Second, it assumes that in phrasing her accusation by saying that *X* φ-ed, the accuser (conforming to the rules of communicational pragmatics) has made reference to all and only those features that she deems relevant for *p*. Thus a 'Yes, but . . .' reply involves a claim that some further circumstance disregarded by the accuser is also relevant, and may well make a difference, and ought therefore to be taken into account.

The accuser may in turn reply that such a circumstance is *not* in fact reliably established by the pertinent body of evidence, *E* or *E*+. Or she may point out that the objector has misidentified *p* as the purpose of the accusation, and that for her actual purpose p_2 the circumstance alluded to by the objector happens to be irrelevant. Or she might acknowledge both that the circumstance is established and that the objector has correctly discerned the purpose of the accusation, but disagree that, for that commonly assumed purpose, that circumstance makes a difference; or agree that it makes a difference, but disagree about what exactly that difference is. Let us imagine, however, a situation in which the accuser acknowledges that the circumstance pointed to by the objector is indeed both reliably established and relevant for the purpose of the accusation—a situation, that is, in which the 'Yes, but . . .' reply is a successful one. The accuser must then recognize that the accusation is not, or is no longer,[78] warranted, at least in the precise terms in which it was formulated. She should then abandon her original purpose—and withdraw her accusation.

Now if an accusation is in this sense withdrawn, it seems safe to say that it wouldn't have been sincerely made if the would-be accuser had known about the relevant circumstance. So given our running supposition that the accuser had originally verbalized her accusation, as one naturally would, by uttering a locution with the form 'X φ-ed', it does seems to be true, in a sense, that in view of a successful 'Yes, but . . .' objection the accuser would not be 'willing', as Hart and Austin are fond of saying, to 'repeat' it—to say it again. But it is wrong to conclude from this that the concept of action is not 'descriptive'. Hart reasoned, as we saw, that if the accusation is withdrawn even though none of the facts upon which it was originally made is contested by the objector, the accuser's 'X φ-ed' sentence is not withdrawn as *false*.[79] Nevertheless it *is* withdrawn. So that must mean that 'X φ-ed' does not—or not merely—describe those facts; after all, 'if it were "descriptive" of [such] facts' why should the accuser 'not willingly repeat it'?[80] But this reasoning is flawed, and in fact the view that 'X φ-ed' is not descriptive is unable to account for the *conceding* aspect—the 'Yes' aspect—of a 'Yes, but . . .' reply. How then are we to explain that an accuser faced with a succesful 'Yes, but . . .' answer will refuse to repeat that X φ-ed?

Here we can profit from our previous discussion of defeasibility in law. In Chapter 2, when criticizing the idea that the role of a judge in a case of contract can be adequately described as that of having to 'apply' the 'concept' of a contract, I drew a distinction between what I called a 'CONTRACT$_{P}$' and a 'CONTRACT$_{V}$'.[81] As I then explained, 'CONTRACT$_{V}$' stands for a CONTRACT$_{P}$ that is, in a given context, and for a given purpose, a valid one. So there is a difference between the plain denial, by a defendant, that there ever was a CONTRACT$_{P}$ between her

[78] Recall the brief discussion of 'no longer' in section 2.1.1.

[79] It is 'not withdrawn', says Hart (1949: 193) 'as a false statement of fact'.

[80] Hart (1949: 186).

[81] See section 2.3.

and the plaintiff, and the submission that *yes*, there is a CONTRACT$_P$ between them, as the plaintiff claims, *but* that CONTRACT$_P$ is not valid—that it is not a CONTRACT$_V$ in the relevant context. A submission of the latter kind does not imply that there is no CONTRACT$_P$—to the contrary, it grants that there is one—nor does it entail that the claim that there is a CONTRACT$_P$ between the parties is false, let alone that such a claim cannot be descriptive, or truth-apt.

How does this distinction bear on our present discussion? We saw in Chapter 2 that it is an error to suppose that the content of a judicial decision for the plaintiff in a case of contract is correctly described by saying that 'there is a CONTRACT'; nor is that how the judge herself would naturally phrase it. But it does appear to be true that one natural way of phrasing accusations will be by saying that '*X* φ-ed'. And it seems that the accuser who withdraws her accusation, when it is brought to her attention that *X*'s φ-ing was, say, done in self-defence, is acknowledging a distinction analogous to the CONTRACT$_P$/CONTRACT$_V$ distinction. What she acknowledges is not that *X* did not φ; that *X did* φ is accepted by both accuser and objector. What she acknowledges, rather, is that if *X*'s φ-ing was done in self-defence, then *X*'s φ-ing is not the sort of φ-ing (or the sort of φ-ing by *X*) that matters for the purpose of her accusation—that it is not the sort of φ-ing with which she is concerned. She acknowledges, in other words, that *X*'s φ-ing is not what she *counts as* a φ-ing: that it is not a *relevant* φ-ing in the context.

This notion of a relevant φ-ing, which parallels the notion of a valid CONTRACT, can be characterized as one possible sense of 'φ-ing'. Let us mark it out as 'φ-ing$_R$'. We need a matching marker with which to represent the other sense of 'φ-ing' that happens also to be at play: the sense of 'φ-ing' that—just as 'CONTRACT$_P$' says nothing about its validity—implies nothing about its relevance. Since we have no reason to treat this sense of 'φ-ing' in any other way than as straightforwardly 'descriptive', I shall employ the scheme 'φ-ing$_D$'.

Hart's and Austin's argument can now be tackled head on. Is there anything particularly puzzling about the fact that, in view of a successful 'Yes, but . . .' reply, the accuser would not now willingly say, or repeat, that *X* φ-ed? Whichever of the two senses of 'φ-ing' just distinguished one happens to have in mind, the answer is clearly negative. The accuser would certainly not repeat *the accusation* and insist that *X* φ-ed$_R$, for that is precisely what the successful 'Yes, but . . .' reply has shown not to be in order. But she would also not say, or repeat, that X φ-ed$_D$. Not that there would be any sort of deep inappropriateness about it. (It is because of his failure to distinguish both senses of 'φ-ing' that Hart mistakes the inappropriateness of repeating 'X φ-ed$_R$' for a supposed inappropriateness of repeating 'X φ-ed$_D$'.) The accuser would not now say that X φ-ed$_D$ simply because she would no longer have any reason to care about X's φ-ing; the mere fact that a proposition is true does not give us reason actually to go about asserting it.[82] As for Austin, he makes the same mistake of confusing φ-ings$_D$ and φ-ings$_R$. That is why he concludes that defences bear on the 'philosophical study of conduct'. It is also why both he and Hart so confidently draw a direct connection between responsibility and the concept of action.[83]

[82] See Searle (1966: 48–9) for a different take on Austin's 'no modification without aberration' slogan, which Searle interprets as 'a point about what it is to make an assertion' (suggesting that it should be rewritten as 'no remark without remarkableness'). See also Searle's discussion of the 'assertion fallacy' ('the fallacy of confusing the conditions of the performance of the speech act of assertion with the analysis of the meaning of particular words occurring in certain assertions') in Searle (1969: 141–6); Graham's discussion of Austin's 'doctrine of the standard case' in Graham (1977: 234–9); Grice (1989: 8–13); and Warnock (1991: 65–76).

[83] For a recent account of 'defeasible ascriptions of responsibility' and their 'default-and-challenge' patterns (an account inspired by a critical reading of Hart's views) see Blöser (2013). My discussion says nothing about the general viability of what Paprzycka (2008: 69–88; 2013: 161, 167–73; 2014: 323–4, 330–6) calls 'responsibilist' accounts of action: accounts that (compatible with more literal readings of Hart's claims than mine) treat the notion of responsibility, in some carefully defined sense, as explanatorily prior to that of an action. For more or less systematic discussions along such lines, some of which in explicit 'neo-ascriptivist' vein, see Rayfield (1968: 131); Rayfield (1971: 39–58); Coval, Smith and Burns (1980); Coval and Smith (1986: 1–26), on which see Duff (1988); Cruz (1990); Sneddon (2006: 19–47), on which see, very critically, Paprzycka (2008); Stoecker (2007); and Denaro (2012). Contrast, also, Duff's take on ascriptions of intentional agency, and particularly his views on when foreseen but not directly intended effects can properly be said to have been brought about intentionally, in Duff (1982: 3–6); Duff (1990: 76–82), on which see Hornsby (1993) and Duff (1996: 301–5); and Arena's reinterpretation of ascriptivism as essentially connected to the fallibility and revisability of ascriptions of mental states on the grounds of empirical evidence in Arena (2008). I should point out that Hart's conflation of φ-ings$_D$ and φ-ings$_R$ was compounded by the fact that he also believed, mistakenly, that the facts that ground ascriptions of responsibility are exhausted by bodily movements and include no mental factors. He thought that 'when we are ascribing an action to a person, the question whether a psychological "event" occurs' comes up only 'in the form of an inquiry as to whether any of [the] extenuating defences cover the case': see Hart (1949: 188, 191, and, with regard to *mens rea* in criminal law, 180). To see why this is a mistake, just think of accusations that someone

7.4 Defeasibility in Accusatory Contexts

So we have identified a domain in which defeasibility happens to be at play. It is not the broad domain of claims that someone φ-ed. It is not even the domain of claims that someone φ-ed as set forth in accusatory contexts. Our domain, rather, is that of accusations—or, more precisely, of judgments or claims that φ-ed$_R$ as set forth in the making of accusations. Accusations are at once ascriptions of actions$_R$ and ascriptions of liability. The claim that defeasibility *is* at play in this domain is, accordingly, not a claim about 'concepts' and their 'applications'. It is a claim about the kinds of elements on which appropriately made accusations depend.

Should we then avail ourselves of the distinction between *P*-facts and *D*-facts—the distinction on which this book's proof-based account of legal exceptions is rooted—in order better to understand what it is to make an accusation? Is the distinction between *P*-facts and *D*-facts even *applicable* to extra-legal decision-making contexts like this one? It may seem at first that the answer is negative. The difference between *P*-facts and *D*-facts, I argued in Chapter 3, is a difference between two kinds of facts whose presence or absence bears on the correctness of defeasible

φ-ed where 'φ' is any verb that semantically implies intentionality, such as 'to plan', 'to cheat', 'to lie'—or, of course, 'to try': 'He tried to hit her'. This mistake seems to me the product of a confusion of the question of how to characterize the content of an accuser's justified belief that someone φ-ed$_D$ with the rather different set of issues involved in explaining just how it is that other people's actions$_D$ can come to form the object of justified beliefs (as well as, in the legal domain, the object of proof). That other people's actions can form the object of justified beliefs does not mean, of course, that actions, in so far as they involve some 'subjective' or 'mental' aspect, are directly perceivable or observable; we should not confuse *that* which we may observe (for example, that *Smith's body moved in conjunction with another person* in such and such manner), and which constitutes our evidence, with *that* which ('on the strength', as Hart puts it, of such evidence) we come to believe (namely, that *Smith hit*$_D$ *her*). On this point, see Chisholm (1964: 614 and n 2); and also Williams's protest (absent from the second edition) in Williams (1953: 29 n 4); the attempt to differentiate 'two main types' of defences in Mackie (1955: 39–42); the 'logical ledger' in Stoljar (1959: 357); the complaint in Houlgate (1968: 116); and Golding (2005: 227–8). In his later writings on the topic, however, Hart avoids this mistake: he acknowledges *mens rea* as a 'condition' proper—a 'subjective element'—of criminal liability, and asserts repeatedly throughout his articles on the subject that in 'all advanced legal systems' an 'individual's liability to punishment' is 'made by law to depend, among other things on certain mental conditions'. See Hart (1957: 28, 31, 35); Hampshire and Hart (1958: 5–7); Hart (1961/2012: 90, 95, 97, 101, 104; 1961: 178); Hart (1961b: 139–40, 152); Hart (1965: 187); Hart (1967: 113–14); Hart (1968/2008: 210); Hart (1969: 39–40, 46).

legal decisions. In this context, we saw, 'presence' and 'absence' are equivocal terms. What matters, I suggested, is not whether some given circumstance actually *is* (or *is not*) *the case*, but whether a given circumstance has been ascertained or proved in the relevant decision-making context. In particular we should be alert to the distinction between saying of a given fact *X* that it is *proved that not-X*, and saying that *it is not proved that X*. Defeating circumstances—*D*-facts—are facts that must not be proved, rather than facts whose negation must be proved, for the corresponding defeasible decision to be correctly issued. But if this is right—if the phenomenon of defeasibility does hinge on such a distinction—how can our non-legal, everyday accusations, which are not constrained by institutionalized evidentiary rules and standards and procedures of proof, possibly be said to be defeasible? Some, like Baker, are sceptical:

> Outside courtrooms there are no similar rules to settle questions of onus of proof. This obstructs the extension of the concept of defeasibility to any non-legal concepts; in particular to the concept of a human action.[84]

But these doubts are misguided. The fact that there are no institutionalized mechanisms of proof in the kinds of context with which we are now concerned does not mean that defeasible decision-making is confined to the realm of the law. Quite the contrary; we can plausibly think of defeasible decision-making in legal contexts as being modelled after its non-legal counterparts.

To clarify the point, take the simple scenario of a non-legal accusation that somebody, Smith, hit somebody else—this is Hart's 'He hit her' example—in a context in which self-defence is indisputably the sort of circumstance we would be prepared to count as an exception or 'defence'. How is the underlying rule of correctly made accusations to be reconstructed? We can begin by availing ourselves of the general account of accusations offered in sections 7.2 and 7.3. One first point we can stress is that my accusation that Smith hit_R someone else will not be appropriate unless my belief that Smith did_D it is justified on the grounds of the available

[84] See Baker (1977: 33); and compare Patton (1956: 528–30) and Feinberg (1965: 121–2).

evidence. In other words, if my body of evidence does not warrant the belief that Smith hit_D her—or if it actually warrants the contrary belief that Smith did *not* hit_D her—it will be incorrect for me to accuse him of having hit_R her. So suppose that I have directly observed some fact or facts that do warrant my belief that Smith did hit_D someone else. By hypothesis, however, *that Smith* hit_D *someone else* is not the only relevant fact in our example. If my body of evidence happens to warrant the belief that Smith's $hitting_D$ was done in self-defence, then even though I will be justified in believing that Smith hit_D her, it will still be inappropriate for me to accuse him of having hit_R her. This is not to say that my accusation is properly made only if I justifiably believe (on the grounds of the available evidence) that Smith's $hitting_D$ was *not* done in self defence. That is clearly not the case.[85] I must have no reason to believe that the $hitting_D$ was done in self-defence; but it is not necessary that I have reason to believe that the $hitting_D$ was not done in self-defence.

If this is right, the analogy with the legal domain is straightforward. What we need to take into account when assessing the correctness of an accusation that Smith hit_R someone is not whether Smith hit_D her or whether the $hitting_D$ was done in self-defence. Instead of operating for each relevant circumstance X with this binary alternative which attends only to whether or not X is the case, we need to factor in a reference to justified beliefs, and to operate with the following quaternary distinction (where 'E' stands for the available body of evidence):

A. E warrants the belief that X;
B. E warrants the belief that *not*-X;
C. E does not warrant the belief that X;
D. E does not warrant the belief that *not*-X.

85 This point, which is the crucial one, is easily mishandled. See, for some examples, Beardsley's analysis of the constitutive conditions (and 'the agency condition' in particular) of several kinds of illocutionary act whose performances can be said to amount, in a sense, to an act of 'blaming', in Beardsley (1969: 36–40) and Beardsley (1970: 169–71), and the related discussion in Beardsley (1979). See also Kauffeld (1998: 252–5); Fritz (2005: 153); and Tiersma's analysis of the illocutionary act of accusing (characterizing the propositional content of accusations as the proposition 'that someone has done or is doing something blameworthy or discreditable') in Tiersma (1987: 312–16).

We need to take into account this fourfold range of possibilities for precisely the same reason that, when discussing defeasible decision-making in judicial contexts, we had to look into the symmetrical proof-related range. Then as now, we needed to differentiate between two senses in which some given fact *X* can be said to be 'absent' or ('not present').

In accusatory contexts, then, some facts are such that they have to be justifiably believed in order for a sincere accusation to be correctly made. The 'presence' (in this sense) of such facts is a condition of a correct accusation. We may accordingly call them, as in the legal domain, '*P*-facts'. In our example, the fact that Smith hit_{D} her is a *P*-fact. Likewise, if I properly accuse Smith of having raped_{R} someone, then the fact that the victim did not consent is also a *P*-fact: it is only appropriate to accuse Smith of having committed rape if I justifiably believe that Smith raped_{D} his victim (which means that the fact that Smith raped_{D} his victim is itself a complex *P*-fact), and *that the victim did not consent* is part of the definition of rape_{D}. But compare this circumstance that *the victim did not consent* with the circumstance, in our previous example, that *the* $\textit{hitting}_{\text{D}}$ *was not done in self-defence.* Both are, in a sense, 'negative' circumstances; both are circumstances that have to be 'absent' if the accusation is to go through. In both cases, moreover, if the respective complements are 'present'—that is, if their complements are justifiably believed on the grounds of the available evidence—the corresponding accusations will not be appropriately made. But *absence of self-defence* in the hitting example, unlike *absence of consent* in the rape example, does not have to be 'present'—does not have to be justifiably believed—in order for the respective accusation to count as properly made. And what this means is that *absence of self-defence* is not a *P*-fact.

There is therefore in accusatory contexts a relevant difference between circumstances that must be 'absent' in the sense that *their complements* must be 'present'; and circumstances that must be 'absent' in the sense that *they* have *not* to be 'present'. The latter are genuine exceptions—genuine *D*-facts. So we can speak of 'defeasible' accusations in precisely the same sense in which we speak of 'defeasible' judicial decisions. The distinction between *P*- and *D*-facts is the same in both domains. For what mattered in the legal domain was not that the distinction was drawn in terms of institutionalized rules and set standards and procedures for 'proof' in some uniquely legal sense.[86] What mattered was that we had to consider whether or not the relevant facts were properly ascertained as being the case in the respective decision-making context. And this is a distinction that is equally in place—a distinction that we actually draw—in the non-legal domain of everyday accusations.

This also enables us to explain more rigorously the difference between 'Yes, but . . .' and plain 'No' replies to accusations—between qualifications and plain denials, as one might also put it.[87] So far we have been using these labels to convey the idea that there are two interestingly different kinds of relevant facts. These two kinds have now been more precisely presented in terms of the distinction between *P*- and *D*-facts. So now that it has been shown that an accusation is appropriately made only if the accuser (a) justifiably believes that all the relevant *P*-facts are the case; and also (b) has no sufficient reason to believe that any relevant *D*-fact is the case, those two sorts of answer can be more simply and accurately characterized as follows. A plain 'No' reply denies that all the relevant *P*-facts are correctly ascertained: it denies that the relevant body of evidence warrants the belief that *P*.[88] By contrast, a 'Yes, but . . .' reply, granting that the relevant *P*-facts are correctly ascertained, claims that at least one *D*-fact happens also to be established by the relevant body of evidence. Hence each of these replies denies a necessary condition for the accusation to be correctly made—which is precisely what allows them both to operate as *objections* to accusations.[89]

[86] Compare Cane's discussion, in Cane (2002: 44–9 and 92), of 'judgments of responsibility that result from the application of techniques to deal with epistemological uncertainty' in 'any normative domain [ie not solely the legal one] where adverse consequences are attached to holding a person responsible'. But Cane's claim that the distinction between what I call *P*-facts and *D*-facts 'provides a technique for distributing . . . the burden of proof . . . as to whether particular components of relevant responsibility criteria were present in particular circumstances', in Cane (2002: 91), is yet another instance of that ordinary view that in Chapter 3 we have seen to be untenable.

[87] See Gardner (2007a: 169); but under the 'Yes, but . . .' rubric Gardner runs together, to some extent at least, two contrasts which are, I think, independent: the denial/qualification contrast, and the not-an-X/not-a-paradigmatic-X contrast.

[88] As noted in section 7.3, this can be achieved by different (and not mutually exclusive) means: by directly questioning that the accuser's beliefs are warranted by what she took as *her* body of evidence, for example, but also by questioning the soundness of that body of evidence, or by adducing new evidence.

[89] To be clear, I do not mean to suggest that as a matter of ordinary language, our actual use of these expressions, ('No', and 'Yes, but . . .') in replying to accusations, necessarily or characteristically maps onto the two kinds of objections just distinguished. It is not unimaginable that denials of *P*-facts be phrased with 'Yes, but . . .' locutions, nor that the invocation of an exception be preceded by a plain 'No'.

7.5 Lines of Development

The results from our discussion can be refined and expanded, I should now like to suggest, into a more general model of ascriptions of φ-ings$_R$.

So far the focus has been on what I called the 'domain of accusations': the domain of first-, second- or third-personal claims that some person *X* φ-ed$_D$ which simultaneously single out or indicate *X* as being an appropriate candidate, in virtue of having φ-ed$_D$, for a given class of unfavourable responses. I claimed that appropriately made accusations do not depend solely on the fact that the body of evidence *E* on which the accuser relies warrants her belief that *X* φ-ed$_D$. They depend also on the fact that *E* does not warrant the belief in any other fact *D* such that *D* would make a difference to the judgment that *X* is indeed, as the accuser claims, an apt candidate for the given set *R* of responses that the accuser has in mind. So these *D*-facts are exceptions proper, in the sense clarified in Part II of this book; and accusations, I said, are defeasible claims that some person *X* φ-ed$_R$, not just claims that *X* φ-ed$_D$. Accusations amount to defeasible claims that *X*'s φ-ing$_D$ is just the sort of φ-ing$_D$ that matters for the purposes of liability to a given range of unfavourable reactions in a given context.

But we can now easily see that the analysis is not essentially or even characteristically connected with liability to *unfavourable* responses or reactions. Ascriptions of φ-ings$_R$ that single out the agent as an apt candidate for any given set of favourable, welcome responses seem to be characteristically defeasible in exactly the same sense. ('He cooked a wonderful codfish *vol-au-vent*'; 'Yes, but he bought the puff pastry already made'.) It would be too much of a stretch, of course, to go on speaking of 'accusations' in these cases. We might perhaps, in order to refer to the common genus, speak of 'designations' or 'indications' of persons as liable to given ranges of consequences in virtue of their φ-ings: or indeed—why not?—of 'ascriptions' of φ-ings$_R$. But the main point is that by generalizing our analysis of accusations, a common model might be constructed of these ascriptions of φ-ings$_R$. These are claims, made at some point in time *T* on the grounds of an available body of evidence *E*, that some person *X* φ-ed$_D$ in just the way that matters for the purpose *P* of judging *X* liable to some range *R* of reactions in a given context *C*. The task would then be to make explicit the various issues that each one of these interacting variables may raise, and the corresponding range of cross-cutting possibilities. That is not a task to be pursued in this book; but one or two very general remarks may be profitably tacked together expanding on some aspects of our previous discussion.

A first point concerns the proper understanding or interpretation of the possible descriptive scope of 'φ'—as employed to refer to any φ-ing$_D$ that can ground a correctly made ascription, to the agent, of a φ-ing$_R$. Even though our illustrations so far of correctly made ascriptions that someone φ-ed$_R$ have come from examples (such as the 'He hit her' hypothetical) in which the person doing the ascription—the 'ascriber', we might say—would naturally voice it by the *unqualified* use of a verb of action, there is of course no reason why adverbial modifications ('He hit him below the belt') cannot constitute the basic description of the φ-ing$_D$ that forms the ground of any given ascription. It may be, in other words, that for the purpose of the ascription—for the purpose of singling out a person, in a given context, to a given range of consequences—the relevant action-description should include such modifications or qualifications. (In such cases, of course, the facts that make the adverbially modified description true are all *P*-facts.) Thus even though it may be said (as we saw that Hart and Austin would) that to offer a 'Yes, but . . .' reply to an ascription of a φ-ing$_R$ is to claim that 'it is not quite fair or correct to say *baldly* "X did A"' and so that some 'qualification' is called for, the reverse is not the case: the 'qualification' of action is neither exclusively nor even primarily the domain of 'Yes, but . . .' replies. Indeed, 'qualification' is here a relative notion: 'He did it accidentally' is qualified relative to 'He did it'; but 'He did it accidentally' will be correctly used *sans phrase* in a range of ascriptive situations, and may itself require (further) qualification in some others.

A second, related point is that there is also no reason that a successful 'Yes, but . . .' reply to an ascription to *X* of a φ-ing$_R$ should have the effect of *fully* extenuating *X*'s liability—instead of only mitigating, or indeed aggravating, the range of responses for which *X* may aptly be singled out as a candidate.[90] This point can be made

90 Compare Austin's passing remarks on 'expressions that aggravate' or 'words of aggravation' in (1957: 176) and Austin (1966: 272); and Hart's references to the fact that that defences may either 'defeat the claim or accusation or to "reduce" it so that only a weaker claim can be sustained': see Hart (1949: 174, 179, 181, 190).

clear by combining different elements of the foregoing discussions. There is nothing extraordinary about contexts in which a person may be liable not only to a given set R_1 of reactions or responses by virtue of having done an action$_{R1}$ of some description, but liable also to a set R_2 of reactions by virtue of having done an action$_{R2}$ of some other description—where the two action$_R$-descriptions are related in such a way that one corresponds to an adverbial qualification of the other.

Suppose, for example, that (a) whoever φ-ed is appropriately held liable to R_1; but that (b) whoever φ-ed *insidiously*, say, is liable instead to R_2; whereas (c) whoever φ-ed *in the heat of the moment* is liable only to R_3—where R_2 is worse overall, and R_3 is less bad overall, than R_1. The facts that X φ-ed$_D$ *insidiously* or that X φ-ed$_D$ *in the heat of the moment* are defeating circumstances—*D*-facts—relative to accusations (or ascriptions) that X φ-ed$_R$ that single X out as liable to R_1. (The facts that X φ-ed$_D$ insidiously or that X φ-ed$_D$ in the heat of the moment are also, of course, *P*-facts, or parts of the corresponding *P*-facts, relative to, respectively, accusations that X φ-ed-insidiously$_R$ and is therefore an apt candidate for R_2, and accusations that X φ-ed-in-the-heat-of-the-moment$_R$ and is accordingly liable to R_3.) Suppose, moreover, that at a given point in time T_1, an accusation that X φ-ed$_R$ is properly made: the relevant body of evidence E warrants the belief that X φ-ed$_D$ and does not warrant the belief in any of the admissible *D*-facts (including the fact that X φ-ed$_D$ insidiously, or that X φ-ed$_D$ in the heat of the moment). Then if at T_2 a 'Yes, but . . .' rejoinder is successfully put forth (on the grounds, for example, of further evidence meanwhile acquired) that X's φ-ing$_D$ was done in the heat of the moment, the original accusation that X φ-ed$_R$ is now shown to be unwarranted: it is unwarranted relative to the expanded evidential body $E+$ relative to which its correctness is to be assessed at T_2. $E+$ is such, however, that it now warrants a distinct accusation. It now warrants the accusation (itself potentially defeasible) that X φ-ed-in-the-heat-of-the-moment$_R$.

Because R_3, the set of consequences to which X is thereby held to be liable, is less bad overall than the original set R_1, one could also say, though less precisely, that 'the' original charge has been 'reduced'. This is because the circumstance that counts as a *D*-fact relative to the former accusation also counts as a *P*-fact relative to the latter, and both accusations can be described as serving some common purpose in a shared context. (The parallel analysis can evidently be given of the 'aggravating' effect of successful exceptions: in our example, the emergence of the fact that *X* φ-ed-insidiously$_R$ would 'aggravate' the charge in precisely the same sense.) *D*-facts are fully extenuating only when such a scenario is not the case.

And other interesting lines of development suggest themselves. It is possible, for example, that the same φ-ing$_D$ by *X* is differently evaluated from the first- and the second- or third-personal standpoints. There may be, say, some fact that is counted as a relevant *D*-fact by a third-party judge, though not by the agent herself (or vice versa) for comparable purposes. There also seems to be room, for example, not only to discern and contrast various degrees of belief that, similarly to the legally adopted standards of proof, attach differently to *P*- and *D*-facts in different contexts, but also to observe that these degrees may differ according to other variables. (For instance, the degree to which a belief in a relevant *D*-fact must be warranted in order for the exception to produce its characteristic effect seems in general to be higher when the agent is being singled out as an apt candidate for a given range of favourable reactions than when the reactions are unfavourable.)

Yet another issue concerns the fact that even in everyday, extra-legal contexts, we seem to have content-independent, non-qualitative standards of what counts as a correctly formed body of evidence, one on the grounds of which ascriptions of φ-ings$_R$ can properly be made. We will normally suspend our judgment that *X* φ-ed$_R$ when, even though the evidence that we already have warrants the belief that *X* φ-ed$_D$, we have no further evidential information *at all* about the circumstances in which X's φ-ing$_D$ was done. One colloquial way of putting the point would perhaps be to say that we tend not to draw conclusions about other people's φ-ings$_R$ 'until we know all the facts'; but this issue is not to be explained in terms of a lack of *P*-facts—for there is no further particular fact that we must know (or in whose occurrence we must justifiably believe) in order for the ascription of a φ-ing$_R$ to count as properly made. It is, rather, a matter of gathering a sufficient (perhaps a sufficiently fair?) share of the available evidence; though plainly such suspensions of judgment are regulated by many concurring and possibly conflicting factors. But I will pursue this exercise no further. I draw attention to these aspects merely as a way of rounding up the discussion on action, accusations, and responsibility that occupied us in this chapter.

8

Criminal Answerability and the Offence/Defence Distinction

In Chapter 7 we were concerned with ascriptions of responsibility and with the interplay of accusations and answers in extra-legal, everyday contexts. Can our discussion also illuminate any aspect of our *legal* practices of holding people responsible for their actions? It is criminal responsibility that I have particularly in mind. Criminal accusations and convictions everywhere are markedly defeasible, in the relevant sense of the term. But the distinction between offences and defences, long recognized as a central issue in criminal law theory, has yet to be satisfactorily explained. Making use of results from previous chapters to cast light on this issue, this final chapter illustrates the application of the analyses set forth in the book to a specific domain of the law.

Let us look first into the dominant Continental theoretical approach to criminal law—the German *Verbrechenslehre* ('doctrine of crime')—before turning our attention to some recent attempts at elucidating the notion of a criminal defence by authors working in the Anglo-American tradition.

8.1 Criminal Defences in the German Model

Criminal law theorists working in the German tradition take themselves to be primarily engaged in a definitional enquiry on the concept of a crime. They seek to articulate the substantive 'conditions' or 'elements' that are both necessary and sufficient for an action to count as a crime. The shared product and template of many decades of theorization is a 'tripartite' analysis of the concept of a crime. I will refer to this analysis as 'the German model'.

The German model purports to give us a representation of the set of general substantive conditions on which correct criminal convictions actually depend. Its development is an exercise in 'legal science' (or 'legal dogmatics'); descriptive fit with the positive criminal law is a self-imposed test of adequacy.[1] Keep in mind, then, as we examine the German model, that defences operate in German criminal procedure very much like anywhere else. Courts do not need to satisfy themselves that the *absence* of each one of the admissible defences has been ascertained before they correctly convict someone. There is therefore an immediately discernible division—a bipartite division—between kinds of circumstances that bear on the legal correctness of criminal convictions. It is the division between circumstances that *must* and circumstances that *must not* be ascertained for the conviction to be legally correct. It is the division between what throughout this book I have referred to as '*P*-facts' and '*D*-facts'. Our question, then, is this: how is this division accounted for by the German model? The surprising answer is that it is not. Not directly, at least, and certainly not satisfactorily. Let us see why.

8.1.1 Can the German Model Account for Criminal Defences?

According to the German model there are three jointly necessary conditions that someone's action (or omission) must meet if it is to be correctly classified as a crime. First, the action must satisfy the description of a legally defined '*Tatbestand*'. The notion of a *Tatbestand* is similar, in content and function, to the Anglo-American notion of a criminal offence.[2] It refers to the types of conduct (characterized in both 'objective' and 'subjective' terms) that form the core of the so-called 'special part' of the criminal law: homicide, theft, rape, burglary, larceny, and so on. These types of conduct are the focus of criminal liability.

But an action's correspondence to some legally defined *Tabestand* (an action's '*Tatbestandsmäßigkeit*') is not sufficient for it to count as a crime (as a criminal *infraction*, a criminal '*Verbrechen*'). For

[1] On the methods of legal dogmatics, see Alexy (1978/89: 250–74).

[2] See Fletcher (1978/2000: 553); Duff (2007: 205); Bohlander (2009: 29–36).

one, only legally wrongful actions—impermissible actions—can count as crimes, and the mere fact that someone's action satisfies a *Tatbestand* does not suffice to establish its legal wrongfulness (its '*Rechtswidrigkeit*'). For example, an intentional killing done in self-defence satisfies the *Tatbestand* of homicide; but the law permits rather than forbids it. Hence legal wrongfulness is a further 'element' of crime. But that an action both satisfies a *Tatbestand* and is legally wrongful is still not enough for it to count as a criminal *Verbrechen*. There is a third condition to be met: the agent must be culpable of performing the legally wrongful action. Her culpability (her '*Schuld*') is the third 'element' of crime. So the concept of a crime is given a tripartite definition. Someone's action is criminal if and only if these elements of *Tatbestandsmäßigkeit*, *Rechtswidrigkeit*, and *Schuld* are jointly satisfied.

This formula is only a very general frame within which many generations of scholars have been carrying out efforts to reconstruct and systematize the criminal law. I cannot even hint at the myriad ways in which those three elements and their interrelations have been understood, or at the many schools and methodological trends that have shaped and continue to shape German criminal law theory.[3] But there are important questions that can be raised even at this most general of levels. Here is one. Consider again the example of self-defence in a case of homicide. If it is established that the agent killed her victim as a necessary means of defending herself from the victim's aggression, then as a matter of law the accused is to be acquitted.[4] This would appear to suggest that *absence* of self-defence is a necessary condition of a correct conviction in homicide. Yet in its definition of a crime the German model recognizes only 'positive' elements, as we just saw. How does self-defence—how do defeating circumstances—fit in?

It is generally agreed among endorsers of the German model that defeating circumstances have no bearing on an action's *Tatbestandsmäßigkeit*—the first element of the definition of a crime. But when any one of the admissible defeating circumstances is

[3] For variously informative overviews, see Naucke (1984); Hassemer (1990: 200–48); Brito (1995); Jescheck and Weigend (1996: 195–9); Jung (2002: 370–6); Krey (2003: 3–25); Dubber (2005); Roxin (2006: 190–9); Duff (2007: 204–6); Bohlander (2009: 16–17).

[4] §32 of the German Criminal Code.

present, then one of the other two elements is consequently absent. A defeating circumstance negates either legal wrongfulness or culpability. Self-defence, for example, negates wrongfulness. So it 'excludes' or 'rules out', as German theorists say, a necessary element of the crime of murder.[5] Defeating circumstances that exclude legal wrongfulness are said to *justify* the act. So self-defence is an example of a justificatory defence. Necessity—'justificatory necessity' ('*rechtfertigender Notstand*')—is another.[6] As to defences that exclude culpability, they are said to *exculpate* the agent. An example of an exculpatory defence is duress, or 'exculpatory necessity' ('*entschuldigender Notstand*').[7]

That, then, is how the German model purports to accommodate defeating circumstances. But is the account plausible? If an action can be legally wrongful only when no justificatory defences are present, and if an agent is culpable only when no exculpatory defence is present, then are those two 'positive' terms—'wrongfulness' and 'culpability', '*Rechtswidrigkeit*' and '*Schuld*'—anything other than mere summary markers of the fact that none of the admissible defences is present?[8] Though the fact is little known nowadays, there were discussions of similar worries during the earlier stages of the German model's development. In his groundbreaking 1906 monograph *Die Lehre vom Verbrechen*, Ernst Beling, the author to whom the introduction of the notion of the *Tatbestand* as a definitional element of crime is owed, considers a claim which we may now—at this point in the present book—find familiar. It is the claim that legal wrongfulness ought not to be recognized as a 'positive' element in the definition of crime, and that we should instead regard the *absence* of wrongfulness as ruling out the existence of a crime. In other words, we should think of criminal conduct not as being *legally wrongful*, but rather as being incompatible with *there being a justification*.[9]

Beling believes he can swiftly dismiss this suggestion as logically untenable:

[5] See eg Roxin (2006: 600).

[6] §34 of the German Criminal Code.

[7] §35 of the German Criminal Code.

[8] See Nino (1980: 49); and a parallel objection in Hart (1949: 177–80).

[9] See Beling (1906: 36–7); Beling also describes it as the 'opinion that *Rechtswidrigkeit* [legal wrongfulness] does not belong to the concept of a crime; rather, its absence eliminates the presence of a crime' (my translation). For historical background, see Hirsch (1960).

> Legal wrongfulness and absence of legal wrongfulness are contradictory notions. The statement 'There is no punishable action [that is, no *crime*] when the fact is not legally wrongful' is logically identical to the statement 'There is a punishable action just in case the fact is legally wrongful'. From the point of view of their content, there is no difference at all; any one of the two statements implies the other.[10]

Whoever insists that absence of legal wrongfulness is a 'negative element' of crime is bound by the 'laws of logic', says Beling (1906: 37–8), to accept that legal wrongfulness is a 'positive' element, and vice versa: 'it is impossible to deny one and affirm the other'.

That is true, but beside the point. What Beling's opponents maintained was not that we should speak of 'absence of wrongfulness' and call *it* a 'negative' element, instead of speaking of 'wrongfulness' and calling it a 'positive' element. In fact, they could agree with Beling on his 'logical' claim. What they meant—what they must have meant—was that justificatory defeating circumstances are not the sort of circumstances that can be accounted for in terms of 'elements' *at all*.

Another way of putting this is by noting—recalling a point we discussed in Chapter 1—that there are two different senses in which we can speak of an 'element' of crime as being either 'positive' or 'negative'. In one sense of the contrast, an element is 'positive' if it describes of refers to something that must *be the case*, and 'negative' if it refers to something that must *not* be the case. But that is not the sense in which Beling's opponents used the distinction. What they suggested was not that *absence* of justifications should be seen as being on a par with the criminal offence, as another 'element' to be added to the components of the *Tatbestand*. Their claim was not the claim (which other authors had made[11]) that there is no important evaluative distinction to draw between (a) actions that do not satisfy the strict definition of a criminal *Tatbestand*, and (b) actions that, though they do satisfy some such definition, happen to have been performed under 'justificatory' circumstances. (Whoever holds *this* view will deny, to give a famous example, that criminal law theory should acknowledge an evaluative distinction between the killing of a mosquito and the killing of

[10] See Beling (1906: 38, my translation); and compare Mezger (1949: 183–4).

[11] See also Beling (1906: 148–9).

a man in self-defence.[12]) Rather, their claim was that the fact that an action is legally wrongful—which *they would agree* can be equivalently described as *the fact that the action is not justified*—is itself not a fact or 'element' that *must be established* in order for the agent to be properly convicted.

The contrast they meant to draw, then, is a contrast between elements (regardless of whether they are described in 'positive' or 'negative' terms) that *must*, and elements (also regardless of whether they are described in 'positive' or 'negative' terms) that *must not* be established for there to be a crime—which gives us a second, different sense of the 'positive'/'negative' contrast. And matters pertaining to wrongfulness and justificatory defences fell, they said, under the latter category. In short, they seemed to be after something like the distinction between our *P*-facts and *D*-facts—and Beling simply fails to address their views.

Interestingly, however, Beling (1906: 38–9) refrains from extending his 'logical' point to the domain of private law. There, he grants, it *would* indeed matter—for the purpose of allocating the burden of proof between the parties in civil procedures—whether the relevant circumstances are understood in 'positive' or 'negative' terms.[13] This acknowledgement should have sufficed to alert him to the inappositeness of his 'logical' point in the context of the criminal law. For the 'positive'/'negative' divide that governs the allocation of burdens of proof has nothing to do with the fact that the relevant circumstances are *described* in positive or negative terms. So Beling should have seen that what his opponents were suggesting was that the fact *that self-defence is absent* in a case of murder should be understood as a 'negative' element in the sense that *it* is a fact that does *not* have to be established for the conviction to be correct, whereas the *fact that consent is absent* in a case of rape is a 'positive' element in the sense that *it* does have to be established for the conviction to be correct. *This* is the contrast that parallels the distinction upheld in the civil domain.

[12] It was Welzel who made the example popular (his view was that the two cases *are* indeed relevantly different): see Welzel (1955: 211); Welzel (1969: 81); and Hirsch (1960: 278–80). Fletcher (1978/2000: 561) presses a similar point (though it is with 'killing a coyote' that he contrasts 'killing a human being in self-defence'). In German criminal law theory the view is now overwhelmingly prevalent that the commission of the *Tatbestand does* ground an autonomous and negative evaluative assessment, which is not undone even when the fact is rendered permissible by the presence of 'justificatory' circumstances.

[13] See Beling (1906: 38–9).

Beling should have realized that 'logical' remarks on interdefinability of contradictories were neither here nor there.

He might still see no reason to abandon his position: 'There is' after all 'in the criminal process', he exclaims at one point, 'no distribution of the burden of proof!'[14] We know from our discussion in Chapter 4, however, that this is false as a general claim; and it is false also as a claim about German criminal procedure in particular, where (as I already noted) it is not the case that the actual non-occurrence of each admissible defence must be established before a conviction is properly issued. The exact same contrast between 'positive' and 'negative' circumstances that we find in the civil context can be drawn in the criminal one. Thus Beling would have to agree that, by his own standards, a theory of crime needs to be able to account for the bipartite distinction between those kinds of circumstances. It follows that either the tripartite German model is capable of performing that task, or it must on those grounds be found wanting.

I have been taking Beling as a representative of the views of German criminal law theorists, but other endorsers of the German model could no doubt protest that they have the resources to account for how defeating circumstances operate. They know how criminal procedure works. But what it comes down to, they would say, is two different ways of establishing whether the elements of a crime are satisfied. As another prominent theorist, Hans Welzel, puts it, legal wrongfulness is an element to be ascertained 'in *purely negative manner*, namely by determining that no justificatory grounds are present'.[15] And Beling himself observes that of the three definitional 'elements' of crime, only the first—the action's conformity to a *Tatbestand*—is to be positively ascertained.[16] The ascertainment of an action's legal wrongfulness, he says, is 'in practice' confined to verifying whether any justificatory circumstance is present.[17] But this reply leaves something to be explained. What is the point of insisting that legal wrongfulness is a definitional 'element' in crime—an element that necessarily *has* to be established[18]—if 'in practice' an action's wrongfulness is actually *not* ascertained?

[14] See Beling (1906: 39).

[15] See Welzel (1969: 82, emphasis added); and compare Roxin (1970: 54–61); Jescheck and Weigend (1996: 247); or Bohlander (2009: 16–17, 77).

[16] Beling (1906: 164)

[17] See Beling (1930a: 123).

[18] See Beling (1930b: 20).

The answer that German theorists usually give is that legal wrongfulness, though not directly established, is *presumed*. What grounds this presumption is the fact that an offence definition—a *Tatbestand*—has been satisfied; this fact, they say, is an indication, an *indicium*, that the action is legally wrongful.[19] And the presumption stands unless some justificatory defence emerges. *As a rule*, then, an action that satisfies an offence definition is a legally wrongful action; justificatory circumstances are *exceptions* to this rule.[20]

But this is an equivocal claim. It can be understood either as a claim regarding the action-types described as legal offences, or as a claim regarding particular actions that happen to satisfy a *Tatbestand* definition. Sometimes it seems that German theorists mean the former. They argue, for example, that the fact that the legislative authority chose to formulate the description of any given *Tatbestand* in a certain way indicates that it views actions of that type as being 'in principle' impermissible.[21] Whether or not these theorists are right about that, this argument does not address the relevant point. Endorsers of the German model all acknowledge that any particular action that meets a *Tatbestand* definition may well be legally permissible or even required. And they are very clear that 'the bare assessment of an action's satisfaction of a *Tatbestand never* dispenses us from the particular assessment of its legal wrongfulness'.[22] But the supposed fact that the corresponding *Tatbestand* describes an action-type φ that the authority sees as being 'in principle' impermissible (whatever that means) tells us nothing about whether any particular action—any token of the type—should be regarded as impermissible. Moreover, any judge deciding a case will also be aware of a range of justificatory circumstances that the very same legislative authority will have decided to allow. The judge will know that *as a matter of general law* self-defence is allowed as a

[19] The *locus classicus* is perhaps Mayer (1923: 10 n 21, 51–2, and 182–8); but see also Mezger (1926: 191) explicitly affirming that 'the judgment of legal wrongfulness' is here 'but a provisional, *prima facie* assessment ['eine Prima-Facie-Bestimmung'] that does not preclude the intervention of justificatory circumstances' (my translation). Compare Welzel (1969: 80–1); Brito (1995: 84); Jescheck and Weigend (1996: 324); Roxin (2006: 197, 300); Wessels, Beulke, and Satzger (2013: 37, 49–50).

[20] See Beling (1906: 39–40); Welzel (1969: 83); Roxin (2006: 292, 377); Wessels, Beulke, and Satzger (2013: 107). This presumptive establishment of wrongfulness is understood at least partly in epistemic terms; the fact that an action satisfies a *Tatbestand* definition is sometimes said to be the '*ratio cognoscendi*' (as opposed to the '*ratio essendi*') of that action's legal wrongfulness: see eg Mezger (1949: 182–5).

[21] See Beling (1906: 125); Mezger (1926: 194–5); Mezger (1949: 184).

[22] See Beling (1906: 161, my translation and emphasis).

justificatory defence in homicide. Hence if she adopts the German model and takes self-defence to 'rule out' legal wrongfulness, why should she think that the sphere of what the legislative authority views as impermissible 'in principle' is uniquely determined by the formulation of the *Tatbestand*?[23]

At the level of determining whether any particular action satisfies the 'element' of legal wrongfulness, furthermore, the German model's 'presumptive' account is at odds with judicial practice. It is not the case that self-defence in a case of murder is treated as cancelling a presumption that some circumstance is missing whose ascertainment is required for a criminal conviction. Nor do judges take themselves as having in any way—presumptively or otherwise—to establish an element called 'wrongfulness'. In court, no fact or 'element' must be presumed that must not be proved or otherwise ascertained; and 'wrongfulness' is *not* something that needs to be ascertained.

My broader point can be made as follows. That an action satisfies an offence definition is what is sometimes called an 'operative' or 'constitutive' fact.[24] In contrast to evidentiary facts, whose ascertainment is required only instrumentally, the ascertainment of the fact that an action satisfies an offence definition is relevant in its own terms. This fact is something that *must*, as a matter of law, be ascertained; it is the determinate point of reference of whatever evidential facts may happen to ground its ascertainment. And it seems that it is with facts of this sort—operative facts—that we should concern ourselves when constructing a general model of crime. We must look to the relevant operative facts if we want to isolate the 'elements' on whose presence and absence criminal convictions depend.[25] This does not mean that it is not also the job of criminal law theorists to ask and answer further questions—questions of all sorts—*about*

[23] Not to mention, of course, the possibility of second-order defeating circumstances targeting the admissible first-order defences. Take, for example, the fact, in self-defence, that the aggression was intentionally provoked by the defendant precisely so that she would then be able to claim to have acted in self-defence; in this case, the defendant's action is not justified: see eg Roxin (2006: 687–95). Does that fact, one that clearly does not belong to the relevant *Tatbestand*, fall under the scope of what is 'in principle' forbidden? If so, the received view is falsified. If not—why not?

[24] See Corbin (1919: 164); Hohfeld (1923: 32–4).

[25] See Engisch's remark that doctrinal definitions of crime profess to be 'real' rather than 'nominal' definitions, and that any definition of crime is accordingly open to criticism if it fails to track the actual conditions on which the imposition of criminal punishment depends: Engisch (1974: esp. 351–2).

such constitutive 'elements' of crimes. For example, one might try to reconstruct the reasons that underlie the legislative classification *as* criminal offences of some larger or smaller group of action-types; one could suggest that *all* recognized criminal offences are related in some interesting sense (or ought to be related) to descriptions of harmful action-types; and one might even intelligibly phrase that conclusion by saying that harmfulness is something that must be 'present' for there to be a crime, perhaps even that harmfulness is *in some sense* an 'element' of all crimes. It should be obvious, however, that harmfulness—whatever the theoretical usefulness of the notion for our understanding of the law—would not thereby become, in the relevant sense, a constitutive element in a criminal case.

If this is clear, consider now that defeating circumstances stand precisely *at the same level* as the fact that an action satisfies an offence definition. Any one of the admissible criminal defences is a 'constitutive' fact in the strict sense that its ascertainment is relevant, not instrumentally, but in its own terms. Compare the fact that a killing was done in self-defence with, say, the fact that a person's death came about as a consequence of someone's muscular automatism with no prior fault. Both kinds of circumstance will prevent conviction for murder. So they produce a similar effect. But the ways in which this effect is produced are very different. There is no constitutive fact to which that latter circumstance—the agent's automatism (or its negation)—directly corresponds. *Absence of automatism* is no constitutive fact in homicide. The relevance of this circumstance derives from its evidential effect: it disproves voluntary killing, which itself is a relevant operative fact in homicide. With self-defence the picture is different. Its conviction-preventing effect is not explained by pointing to some *other* fact whose occurrence is disproved by the fact that the killer was defending herself. Rather, the conviction depends directly on the 'absence' of self-defence; the fact of self-defence (or its negation) is not an evidential fact, but is itself placed at the constitutive level. My point then is that a model that purports—as the German model does—to represent the 'substantive' conditions on which a successful conviction depends ought *in its own terms* to operate, at the level of what *it* recognizes as the relevant 'elements', with the defeating circumstances actually admitted as a matter of law. Again, this is not to say that there can be no useful or important discussions about what it is that explains or justifies the fact that any given set of the admissible defences is actually admitted. Perhaps there is a notion of 'legal wrongfulness' that can be fleshed out at a sufficiently general level of discourse and which helps us to understand several of the admissible defences as in some sense 'denying' or 'excluding' wrongfulness. Yet 'wrongfulness'—like 'harmfulness' in the example from the previous paragraph—would certainly not thereby become a constitutive 'element' of all crimes. It would be a methodological mistake to suppose otherwise.[26]

The German model seems to me to rely on just this sort of methodological confusion, with its insistence on accounting for the characteristic effect of justificatory defences in terms of some *other* definitional 'element', namely legal wrongfulness, that is supposedly shown not to be present whenever a defeating circumstance is ascertained. In doing so, the model conflates the object-level of constitutive facts and the meta-level of the theoretical notions introduced to account for certain interesting aspects of constitutive facts.[27] This is the root of the putative and self-inflicted problem of the 'ascertainment of legal wrongfulness'.[28] It is also what gives rise to the need to come up with some ad hoc way of rendering the account compatible with what everyone agrees is the actual 'negative' behaviour of criminal defences.[29] The tripartite German model of such 'elements' of crime is unwarrantedly superimposed on the (actually operative) bipartite divide, which the model superficially ignores, between 'positive' and

[26] Whoever denies that absence of self-defence is required for a murder conviction to be correct makes a descriptive mistake about law—a mistake about what the law in fact is. Whoever denies that self-defence 'excludes' legal 'wrongfulness' makes no such mistake; she rather questions—and this is a normative, meta-theoretical claim—the soundness of any theoretical account of murder that insists on the explanatory necessity or importance of the notion of 'wrongfulness'.

[27] The German model's commitment to the idea that a crime is necessarily legally wrongful seems to be grounded on a conceptual argument rather more than on an attempt to account for any aspect of the actual practice of criminal law. The argument can perhaps be traced back to Karl Binding's distinction between the penal *law* (the '*Strafgesetz*') specifying the conditions on which the legitimate application of criminal sanctions depends, and the prescriptive *norm*, addressed to the legal subjects, and whose violation the *Strafgesetz* is thought to conceptually presuppose: see Binding (1872: 6–14, 23–31).

[28] Welzel (1969: 80).

[29] Notably, it is to detailed examinations of each one of the admissible defeating circumstances—self-defence, necessity, consent (in the sense of '*Einwiligung*', not of '*Einverständnis*'), etc—that textbooks and treatises of German criminal law devote almost the entirety of their chapters on legal wrongfulness.

'negative' relevant circumstances—between offences and defences, *P*- and *D*-facts.

8.1.2 Criminal Defences and 'Comprehensive' Rules of Liability

I say 'superficially ignores', but perhaps I should say that the German model *professes* to ignore the offence/defence distinction. This, at least, is Fletcher's suggestion, in a study of the historical origins of contemporary German criminal law theory. It was by design rather than by accident, Fletcher (1968: 901) says, that the German model came not to include a general classificatory term that captures the notion of a 'defence' as contrasted with that of a criminal offence. Indeed, it was precisely the denial of the very applicability in criminal law theory of the 'concept of "defense"' that set German theory on its track to developing a distinctive, 'comprehensive' understanding of the rules of criminal liability. According to Fletcher, this marked a 'paradigmatic shift' from the nineteenth-century private-law-style view of such rules as 'rules subject to exceptions'.[30] The point is worth a moment's attention.

What exactly is the difference between each kind of approach to rules of liability? This last-mentioned view of the criminal law, which German theorists are said to have outgrown, is a 'dualistic' view. It sees 'rules of criminal liability' along the same lines that rules of private law are normally understood. It sees them as 'incomplete' (though 'well-formed') 'statements of the relevant substantive issues'; and it draws a distinction between these rules, on the one hand, and the available defences or 'exceptions' on the other hand.[31] Under the competing approach, by contrast, rules of criminal liability are understood as encompassing '*all* relevant substantive issues'; criminal law is seen as 'a system of *comprehensive* rules expressing the *necessary and sufficient conditions* for justifying the use of criminal sanctions:'[32]

> The difference between rules subject to exceptions and comprehensive rules is reflected in the structures they impose on the issues relevant to criminal liability. If rules of liability must be supplemented by exceptions, the concept of liability they express is unavoidably dualistic: some issues comprise rules and other issues constitute exceptions. Comprehensive

[30] See Fletcher (1968: 892); Fletcher (2007: 51).

[31] Fletcher (1968: 892).

[32] Fletcher (1968: 892–3, emphases added).

rules, on the other hand, impose a unified structure on the issues related to the blameworthiness of the defendant's conduct. The virtue of this unified structure is that all substantive issues thus encompassed, be they affirmative or negative in form, be they inculpatory or exculpatory in effect, play the same functional role in determining the defendant's liability for crime. This functional parity derives from the one factor unifying the issues so structured: they all relate to the defendant's moral guilt in acting contrary to law.[33]

'Comprehensive rules of liability emerged in their most systematic form', says Fletcher, 'as a by-product of advances in German criminal theory in the late 19th century'.[34] Fletcher credits theorists like Paul Anselm von Feuerbach and Mittermaier with the insights that rules of criminal liability are not to be regarded 'as functional analogues to rules for settling criminal disputes',[35] and that 'defensive criminal issues' in particular are not to be treated like 'defensive issues at private law':[36]

Mittermaier challenged the applicability of the private law concept of 'defense' (*Einrede*) in criminal theory. 'The claim of self-defence', he argued, 'is not to be treated as a defense (*Einrede*) but rather as a denial that the killing is a criminal act'.[37]

Now to hold this view is not to deny that 'criminal disputes' can be 'reduced to an inculpatory case for the state and an exculpatory case'.[38] But Feuerbach's and Mittermaier's point was that both kinds of issues are, *qua substantive* issues, equivalent. In contrast to private law, where a 'defensive burden'[39] prevails, in criminal law 'all substantive

[33] Fletcher (1968: 892–3).

[34] Fletcher (1968: 893).

[35] Fletcher (1968: 892).

[36] Fletcher (1968: 901).

[37] Fletcher (1968: 901). It is instructive, however, to look directly at Mittermaier's own full sentence (which Fletcher does not reproduce), and to notice that what is at stake is actually rather unclear: is it the concept of a defence (and the associated idea that the 'burden' of proving exculpatory circumstances is the defendant's to bear)? Or merely the comparatively lower standard that has to be met for the criminal defendant's burden to be discharged? The sentence reads as follows: 'The concept of a defence in its civil-procedural sense has no application in criminal procedures, given that the mere likelihood of the fact upon which the defendant relies is sufficient [to warrant an acquittal]': see Mittermaier (1846: 365, my translation).

[38] Fletcher (1968: 900).

[39] Fletcher (1968: 901).

issues bearing on criminal guilt'[40] are to be proved by the state against the accused.[41] Therefore, the argument goes, if all the relevant 'exculpatory issues' operate as 'denial[s] of one of the elements of the prosecutor's case',[42] then exculpatory issues play the same 'functional role' as any other substantive issues 'in determining the defendant's liability for crime'.[43] So the relevant substantive issues ought *all* to be understood as issues bearing on a single material question, namely, 'Are the conditions of criminal guilt satisfied?'[44] It must thus be in terms of 'comprehensive rules'—rules enumerating all 'necessary and sufficient substantive conditions for the justified use of criminal sanctions'—that criminal law theory should undertake the 'structuring and categorization of the issues pertaining to criminal liability'.[45]

The German model's characteristic tripartite structure builds on this thought that 'all defences bearing on guilt function as challenges to a comprehensive rule of liability' and particularly that 'one need never characterize an issue as an exception'.[46] As I said, Fletcher (2007: 51) thinks that this was a 'paradigmatic shift'. As he recently once again put it:

> The consequence of the German system of analysis is that three positive concepts (definition, wrongdoing, culpability) replaced the old mode of classification distinguishing between positive (or inculpatory) and negative (or exculpatory) issues. Nineteenth-century German criminal lawyers wrote of 'defenses' (*Einwände* or *Einwendungen*), just as common lawyers do today. But when the theory took the step of insisting that the entire offense [that is, all substantive issues relevant for criminal liability] be analysed under a single theory . . . the term for 'defenses' disappeared from the language of German criminal lawyers. The logic of 'defenses' was replaced by a model for subsuming all issues under the three dimensions of liability. Virtually every 'defensive' question came to be treated as a denial of one of the three affirmative dimensions of the crime: definition, wrongdoing, and culpability.[47]

[40] Fletcher (1968: 892).
[41] Fletcher (1968: 902).
[42] Fletcher (1968: 916).
[43] Fletcher (1968: 893).
[44] Fletcher (1968: 892).
[45] Fletcher (1968: 892–3).
[46] Fletcher (1968: 917).
[47] Fletcher (2007: 50); see also, similarly, Fletcher (2001: 272).

But we are now—at this point in the book—able to detect the flaw in this line of reasoning. *Pace* Fletcher, the inference is unwarranted from the (true) premise that, ultimately, exculpatory and inculpatory issues alike 'all bear on the defendant's guilt or innocence',[48] to the (false) conclusion that 'there is no *significant* difference between causing harm, intending it, intending it in self-defence, and intending it under duress'[49]—or to the further conclusion (also false) that 'that some of these issues may appear in the affirmative and some in the negative is irrelevant'.[50] It is also not true, as we have seen in section 8.1.1, that the German model managed to successfully overcome 'the image of exculpatory issues as exceptions to rules of liability', as Fletcher claims on its behalf.[51] Nor is it true that 'by ordering the defences under affirmative inquiries', modern German criminal theory somehow managed to 'convert [. . .] exceptions into denials [of necessary 'elements of the prosecutor's case']'.[52]

In fact the very contrast between 'rules subject to exceptions' and 'comprehensive rules' is ill-drawn. Exculpatory and inculpatory issues alike are indeed equally material for the judgment of criminal liability, and this point does suggest that a 'comprehensive' picture of the necessary and sufficient conditions of criminal liability can be given that articulates *both* kinds of issues. But it is *as inculpatory* and *exculpatory* issues that they must be articulated. 'Comprehensiveness' does not entail, as Fletcher claims it does, 'functional parity'.[53]

The 'inculpatory'/'exculpatory' divide is no mere 'theoretical structure' with which we may choose to represent how the law actually works. Rather, the 'inculpatory'/'exculpatory' divide—or as we may also call it, the offence/defence divide, the *P*-fact/*D*-fact divide, or even the rule/exception divide[54]—is a characteristic structure of our actual legal systems, in civil law and common law systems alike, and in private as well as criminal law. And that is precisely why, despite its efforts to model criminal liability in terms of

48 Fletcher (1968: 917).
49 Fletcher (1968: 917, emphasis added).
50 Fletcher (1968: 917).
51 Fletcher (1968: 916).
52 Fletcher (1968: 916).
53 Fletcher (1968: 893).
54 In the particular sense of the term 'rule' that in section 5.3 I labelled a 'rule_D'.

an all-'positive', tripartite structure, German criminal theory displays the unresolved internal tensions discussed in section 8.1.1.[55]

These are tensions that criminal law theorists working in the Anglo-American tradition do not face. Here the offence/defence distinction looms large in doctrinal and philosophical discussions of criminal liability. It is true that in this context, too, theorists might for the most part agree that, as Duff (2007: 263–4) has recently put it, defences can be 'usually divided into justifications and excuses, in line with the German framework: justifications deny *Rechtswidrigkeit* or wrongfulness, excuses deny *Schuld* or culpability'; and perhaps also that, as Duff goes on to affirm, 'justifications do claim, and if successful *show*, that the action was all things considered at least permissible' and that '[c]omplete excuses do *show* that the agent was not blameworthy'. But we should not take Duff to be suggesting that 'wrongfulness' or 'blameworthiness' are to be counted as definitional 'elements' of crime in any particularly strong or important sense. He certainly does not mean to imply that there is no significant distinction to be drawn between offences and defences.

But have theorists working in the Anglo-American tradition been able to satisfactorily explain what, exactly, the distinction is? Taking some prominent recent attempts as my exemplars, I should now like to suggest that they have not.

8.2 Offences and Crimes

The offence/defence divide, Victor Tadros (2005: 102) claims, communicates 'morally significant distinctions'. In a sense, as we will see, this must be correct—just not in the sense that Tadros and others have in mind.

[55] It is no wonder that Mittermaier himself, whose 'remarkable claim' it was, in Fletcher's words, that self-defence 'is not to be treated as a defense (*Einrede*) but rather as a denial that the killing is a criminal act', nonetheless maintained—inconsistently, as Fletcher (1968: 901) also notes—that though the 'state should bear the full risk of non-persuasion' relative to *in*culpatory issues, the criminal defendant was burdened with the proof (to the 'showing of probability' standard) of self-defence and other *ex*culpatory issues: see Fletcher (1968: 913), and recall n 37. Compare, incidentally, Fletcher's own insistence on the 'important structural and substantive difference between the inculpatory and exculpatory dimensions of wrongdoing' in Fletcher (1978/2000: 554, 576–7); or in Fletcher (1993: 177).

Tadros thinks that in order to understand the distinction between offences and defences we ought to 'focus on the nature of criminal conviction'.[56] Defences 'operate', he says, 'when it is inappropriate to impose criminal responsibility on the defendant even though he has fulfilled the conditions of the offence'.[57] But he is struck by the fact that '[w]hen an individual is held criminally responsible for his conduct he is convicted of a particular offence':

> The absence of defences do[es] not normally play a part in the description of the conviction. Consider a defendant who is charged with assault and raises the defence of coercion. His defence fails and he is convicted. His conviction is for assault. That he was not coerced does not play a role in the nature of his conviction. The offence definition ought to describe the defendant's conduct in the appropriate way. The nature of *what he has been convicted of* is intentionally attacking another. It is only that description that captures the nature of his wrongful conduct accurately. The absence of a defence is not part of the proper description.[58]

What this suggests, he thinks, is that the offence/defence distinction is primarily to be explained in terms of the contrast between 'elements that are constitutive of the proper description of the wrong' and 'elements which, in their absence, are not morally significant to that description':[59]

> [A]n offence definition ought to include within it the central features of the conduct of which it is appropriate to convict the defendant. Defences describe the conditions under which such conduct is not worthy of the attribution of criminal responsibility. But they do not constitute essential features of conduct which express why the defendant's conduct is worthy of conviction where the defence is unavailable.[60]

But is this not self-contradictory? Tadros (2005: 105) acknowledges that when a defence is present 'criminal responsibility ought not to be imposed even if the conditions of an offence have been fulfilled'. The implication, as he notes, is that

[56] Tadros (2005: 102).
[57] Tadros (2005: 105).
[58] Tadros (2005: 109).
[59] Tadros (2005: 110).
[60] Tadros (2005: 109).

offences, at least as they are defined in law, do not contain all of the necessary conditions for a defendant to be criminally responsible for his actions.[61]

That must mean that the conditions on which a properly made conviction depends are not exhausted by the elements of any given offence. Absence of each of the admissible defences is a necessary condition of a correctly made conviction. But then what can it mean to say that defences play no role in the 'nature' of criminal convictions, as Tadros puts it in the first of the excerpted passages? How can the fact that an agent was not coerced be simultaneously deemed 'necessary' for, but play no role in the 'description' of, a criminal conviction? Tadros further defends his example:

> Of course it is true, in a sense, that [that] the defence of coercion was not available to the defendant is morally significant. If he was coerced, a criminal conviction would not have been warranted . . . However, that fact in itself does not show that the absence of the defence is an important part of the conduct for which [the agent] is appropriately convicted, worthy of description in the context of criminal offences.[62]

But again, what does it mean to say that warranted criminal convictions *necessarily* depend on the agent's *not* having φ-ed under coercion, but that absence of coercion is not 'an important part' of the conduct for which the agent is appropriately convicted?

What Tadros appears to find decisive is that it is merely in terms of having performed a given action φ, where 'φ' satisfies the relevant offence definition, that we ordinarily speak of that of which people are criminally convicted. The agent in Tadros's example, if appropriately convicted, would be convicted, we would say, of *assault*—not of *assault not done under coercion*. But this linguistic aspect does not warrant Tadros's claim that the fact that the agent was not coerced does not 'play a part' in the 'description' (or the 'nature') of the conviction. If we do say that the agent is properly convicted of 'assault', making no reference to the absence of the available defences in describing the conviction; and if the performance of the act of assault (that is, the satisfaction, by the agent's conduct, of the offence definition of

[61] Tadros (2005: 106).
[62] Tadros (2005: 110).

assault) is not a sufficient condition of the conviction—since in order for the agent to be properly convicted 'of assault' it is not enough that the offence definition of 'assault' is satisfied: it must also be that no defence is present—then when we speak of the 'assault' of which the agent was properly convicted we cannot mean to refer exclusively to the definitional offence-elements of assault. We must be speaking, not strictly of the *offence*, but of what we may refer to as the *crime* of assault. And there is no *crime* unless, together with the satisfaction of the corresponding offence elements, all the other material conditions that must be in place for the conviction to be warranted—including, of course, the absence of any of the admissible defences—are actually verified.[63]

Perhaps there is a wider sense of 'offence' in which the term can be used to refer to what I have now called a 'crime'. But it is only in its strict sense—in the sense that is the correlate of the German model's '*Tatbestand*', not of its '*Verbrechen*', as we saw in section 8.1—that 'offence' can plausibly be *contrasted*, as Tadros means to, with 'defence'. Yet to focus, as Tadros (2005: 109) does, on 'the moment of *conviction*' is to focus on crimes rather than on offences in the strict sense.

Should we then be puzzled that in describing crimes we make no explicit mention of the necessary absence of defences? How can we explain the fact that in order to refer to the crime of which an agent is convicted we speak of the crime of 'φ', where 'φ' is the same noun or verb of action ('assault', for example) used in describing or referring to the corresponding offence, and that we omit from the relevant 'description' any mention of the admissible defences? This is by now a familiar issue. We discussed it in Chapter 7. In fact, it is not a specifically legal puzzle. This linguistic feature is equally at play in the domain of extra-legal ascriptions of responsibility—the domain of accusations, as I then called it—which we often verbalize by the use of sentences of simple form '*X* φ-ed'. We saw in section 7.2 that this was precisely the linguistic datum that motivated Austin's and Hart's claims about human action and its relation to defences. They too had noticed that even though it is only when no defeating circumstances are present that we are warranted in using such '*X* φ-ed'

[63] I take this to track standard usage; see, for example, Simester and others (2013: 18–19), identifying, in addition to the 'external' and the 'mental' elements of an offence, a 'third basic element of every crime: the absence of a valid defence'; and compare Husak (1987: 192).

sentences to assign liability, it is still the bare, unqualified '*X* φ-ed' that we employ. When accusing someone of hitting someone else, for example, we use the unqualified 'He hit her', rather than, say, the qualified 'He hit her and the hitting was not done in self-defence, not done under coercion [etc]'. But they did not conclude from this, as Tadros would seem to want to, that the unqualified '*X* φ-ed' must refer to or 'describe' *only* the actual performance by *X*, irrespective of circumstances, of the action of φ-ing. This hypothesis patently fails to account for the relevant aspects of the data. Rather, Austin and Hart correctly saw that we ought to recognize that those *unqualified* 'X φ-ed' judgments or utterances cannot be reduced to mere descriptions of φ-ings.

How then are we to explain such utterances? I already tried to answer this question. In section 7.3 I introduced the distinction between (a) the purely descriptive notion of a φ-ing$_D$; and (b) the notion of a φ-ing$_R$, which refers to a *relevant* φ-ing$_D$ in some given decision-making context and for some given purpose. I also explained how ascriptions of φ-ings$_R$ depend on the absence of defences. The analogues of those two notions in the context of criminal liability are, respectively, the notion of a criminal offence understood in its strict sense, and the notion of a crime. Criminal convictions are convictions *of* φ-ings$_R$, not φ-ings$_D$, and there is no support for the claim that the absence of defences is no part (or no 'important' part) of the 'nature' of a crime—a φ-ing$_R$—or of a criminal conviction.

That does not mean that the distinction between criminal offences and defences does not communicate, as Tadros (2005: 102) thinks it does, 'morally significant distinctions'. I shall return to this idea in section 8.5. But it does mean that Tadros's claims that an 'offence definition ought to include within it the central features of the conduct of which it is appropriate to convict the defendant', and that defences 'do not constitute essential features of conduct which express why the defendant's conduct is worthy of conviction where the defence is unavailable',[64] make no progress towards explaining the offence/defence distinction. Such claims merely restate, and imprecisely at that, what stands in need of explanation. We already *know* that 'descriptions' of crimes—of criminal φ-ings$_R$—do not

[64] Tadros (2005: 109).

explicitly mention the necessary absence of each one of the admissible defences. That is a manifest aspect of our notion of a crime, a notion that presupposes absence of defences as well as the ascertainment of the relevant offence elements. The fact that someone has been properly convicted of having committed a crime we describe as the crime of 'φ-ing', tells us nothing about how to distinguish between the two classes of relevant circumstances, offences and defences, φ-ings$_D$ and φ-ings$_R$.[65]

Nor is there any explanatory advantage in focusing on 'the moment of *conviction*' rather than, say, on the moment of the making of a criminal charge or accusation. Indeed, criminal accusations should also be understood as ascriptions of φ-ings$_R$ rather than φ-ings$_D$. Let me elaborate on this point as I consider a different kind of attempt to make sense of the offence/defence divide.

8.3 Defences, Convictions, and Accusations

Antony Duff (2007: 18) has suggested that the distinction between offences and defences reflects the distinction between responsibility and liability to criminal punishment. 'Responsibility' stands here for criminal answerability: 'to be responsible is to be answerable'—'*for* something, *to* some person or body, within a responsibility-ascribing practice'.[66] In what sense, then, can it be said that the offence/defence contrast 'maps that between responsibility and liability'?[67]

[65] Tadros at one point entertains the thought that perhaps 'the important distinction is that between positive features of the world, features that positively describe the conduct of the defendant, and morally significant absences', that is, 'features of the situation which are not present, but which, if present, would have moral significance'. He casts this in terms of the difference between 'features which are constitutive of the moral nature of conduct' and 'features whose absence is not constitutive of the moral nature of conduct, but whose presence would be morally significant': see Tadros (2005: 110–11). This is on the right track; yet Tadros's unexamined substantivist bias—he too takes 'presence' and 'absence' to stand, respectively, for what is and is not the case—prevents him from convincingly explaining how it can be simultaneously said of any given circumstance *F* that its 'presence' is morally significant, but its 'absence' is not. Surely if it makes a difference whether a fact *F* is the case, it makes a difference whether *F* is not the case; and Tadros's occasional references to the 'exceptional' character of defeating circumstances (for example at 111–12) are left undeveloped.

[66] Duff (2007: 15, 23).

[67] Duff (2007: 207).

It is *for* offences, says Duff, that people are held criminally responsible: it is for the commission of offences that they are charged and called to answer in criminal courts. Yet responsibility 'is a necessary but not a sufficient condition of liability'.[68] Anyone properly held responsible for the commission of an offence may still 'avert liability by offering a suitable exculpatory answer':[69]

> The distinction between responsibility and liability is reflected in the distinction between offences and defences: proof that the defendant committed an offence is proof that there is something for which he is criminally responsible—something for which he must answer in a criminal court; but he can then avoid conviction, blocking the transition from responsibility to liability, by offering a defence.[70]

To offer a defence is therefore something 'distinct from marking the absence of an element of the offence'.[71] To deny that the offence was committed is to deny responsibility: it is to deny that there is something for which one must answer in a criminal court. Defences, by contrast, 'admit responsibility';[72] it is liability that they deny.

Duff notes further that it is not strictly speaking sufficient for a defendant to *offer* an exculpatory answer. She must also provide 'evidential support' for it. In other words, the 'substantial' distinction between criminal answerability and liability to criminal punishment is reflected in a 'procedural' distinction between two kinds of circumstances: those—the offences—'as to which the prosecution bears the full burden of proof'; and those—the admissible defences—'as to which the defence bears at least an evidential burden'.[73] 'To place this evidential burden on the defendant', says Duff,

> is to claim that she owes it to the court (and to the polity in whose name the court acts) either to admit her guilt, or to offer an explanation of why she committed the offence which will exculpate her; but to admit guilt or to offer an exculpatory explanation of why she committed the offence is to answer for the offence. This is why the Presumption of Innocence requires

[68] Duff (2007: 20).
[69] Duff (2007: 16).
[70] Duff (2007: 18).
[71] Duff (2007: 21 n 7).
[72] Duff (2007: 21).
[73] Duff (2007: 207).

only that citizens be presumed innocent until it is proved that they committed an offence, ie until it is proved that there is an offence for which they are criminally responsible: once criminal responsibility is proved, it is up to them to rebut the presumption that they are guilty by providing a suitably exculpatory answer that will block the transition—the presumptive inference—from responsibility to liability.[74]

Thus the distinction between offences and defences is no mere 'expository device'.[75] It marks, Duff (2007: 208) says, 'a significant distinction between different aspects of criminal liability and different logical stages in the construction of criminal liability'. Offence definitions are—or ought to be—those action-types 'for which a defence is needed',[76] those actions 'for which a defendant can properly be called to answer in a criminal court on pain of conviction and condemnation if she cannot offer an exculpatory answer'.[77]

I should stress that Duff means this not only as a descriptive claim about the distinction between offences and defences, but also, in a sense, as a normative claim about how this distinction ought to be regarded in our systems of criminal liability. It is with the reconstruction of the 'principles and values that do or should structure our criminal law' that Duff is concerned—where the phrase 'our criminal law' stands for the criminal law 'in a modern or liberal democracy', not for the criminal law 'as it ought to be at all times and places'.[78] That means that, even though Duff's task is not exactly expository or doctrinal, the correctness of his account is dependent on some degree of fit with the materials that make up the law and the practice of our actual criminal law systems. The goal, in Duff's own words, is 'the excavation and reconstruction of norms that can be shown to be implicit *in the system of law as it is applied by the courts*'.[79]

74 Duff (2007: 207).

75 Duff (2007: 207–8).

76 Duff (2007: 211).

77 Duff (2007: 260).

78 Duff (2007: 6, 10).

79 Duff (2007: 5, 7, emphasis added). This also means, in what particularly concerns the issue of how to differentiate offences and defences, that the criterion that governs the distinction as it is *actually* drawn in our criminal systems and by our criminal courts will be the relevant criterion when addressing the normative question of whether any given circumstance *ought* to be recognized as an defence or, instead, as a (negative) element of an offence. Thus in relation to 'the victim's lack of consent' in rape, for example, the question to ask—the issue to submit to our normative judgments 'as citizens of contemporary

Why do I emphasize this methodological point? Because I think that Duff's account of the distinction between offences and defences is inadequate at both the descriptive and the normative level. I could summarize my view, which I develop in the following paragraphs, by saying the following. Duff believes that

> [w]e will gain a clearer understanding (both analytical and critical) of the structure of the criminal law, and of the principles of criminal liability, if we distinguish two sets of questions: one concerns the conditions under which agents can be held criminally responsible, ie be called to answer in a criminal court; the other concerns the further conditions that must be satisfied if they are to be criminally liable for that for which they are criminally responsible.[80]

My view is the opposite. The set of conditions under which agents can be held criminally liable mirrors the set of conditions under which they can be held criminally responsible. Both questions are governed—and ought to be governed—by the very same set of material conditions. Let me elaborate.

A central aspect of Duff's account is his contention that the question of whether some offence was committed and the question of whether the agent has a valid defence are sequentially related. Criminal responsibility, which is concerned with offences, is seen as a prior logical 'stage' to that of criminal liability, and the effect of defences is described as that of 'blocking the transition' from the first stage to the second.[81] This contention is, I think, mistaken—and several points and distinctions made in previous chapters may now assist us in seeing where the mistake lies.

One useful distinction to keep in mind at this point is a distinction between two equally common senses of the term 'defence'. As we saw in Chapter 2, the term 'defence' can be used, first, to refer to certain *facts*—our '*D*-facts'—whose presence in a given decision-making context brings about the particular sort of 'defeating' effect (of preventing decisions of certain kinds from being correctly issued) that

liberal democracies'—is, thinks Duff, whether we should 'have to answer, to our fellow citizens through the criminal courts, for every act of sexual penetration'; see Duff (2007: 80, 208–9).

[80] Duff (2007: 22).

[81] See Duff (2007: 18, 21, 22, 73, 74, 119, 175–6, 178, 179, 207–8, 216, 223, 229, 260, 263, 284, 296–7); and also more compressed presentations in Duff (2008) or Duff (2009).

Part II of this book characterized in detail. To speak of defences in this first sense I have primarily used the term 'exception'. But 'defence' can also be used to refer to a way of bringing relevant facts to the attention of the court. A defendant charged with murder may thus invoke, *as* a 'defence' in this second sense (as a defence *to* the charge) the fact that the killing was done in self-defence.

In this latter sense, of course, the notion of a defence is necessarily a second-'stage' notion. 'Defences' in that sense are necessarily posterior to claims and charges, in the way that answers are posterior to questions, acceptances to offers or invitations, glosses to their corresponding verses.

In the first sense, however, the notion of a defence—of an exception, of a *D*-fact—is completely independent of the fact that the relevant defeasible decision can be said to mark one of several stages (and namely some non-final stage) in any diachronically structured procedure. That self-defence is a *D*-fact in murder does not imply that defendants enjoy the procedural opportunity to claim it—to put it forth as a 'defence' in the second sense—in reply to any relevant decision whose correctness depends on that *D*-fact's absence. *To* unappealable murder convictions, which by definition are procedurally final, there can be no defence; nevertheless they are defeasible decisions: their correctness depends on exceptions not being present.

The first sense of the term is clearly the one that matters in explaining the offence/defence distinction. It is in this first sense that we can consistently say that whereas self-defence is a 'defence' in murder, consent in rape is the complement of a negative offence-element instead (and thus that it constitutes the denial of an offence-element *rather than* a 'defence'), even though both circumstances can with equal plausibility be put forth as answers (as 'defences' in the second sense) to the corresponding accusations.

Duff should agree. He finds it important to differentiate, within the general class of answers *to* criminal *charges* ('which is what any defendant is summoned to' offer), the subclass of answers *for* criminal *offences* ('which only a defendant who is proved to have committed the offence must' provide).[82] Duff refers to answers in this subclass as 'defences', contrasting them with denials of offence-elements (although he nevertheless admits such denials as members of that general class of answers to criminal charges). But in order to define these

[82] See Duff (2007: 175–6, 177–9; but also 21–2, 206, 224, 263).

two subclasses of potentially successful answers to charges—in order, that is, to distinguish answers that invoke defeating circumstances from answers that do not—one needs first to be able to draw the contrast between (negative) offence-elements and the necessary absence of *D*-facts.

Yet Duff never clearly acknowledges this distinction between the substantial notion of a defeating circumstance and the procedural, diachronic notion of a defence. He indifferently uses 'defence' to speak both of a subclass of 'conviction-averting pleas'[83] that can be entered in reply to criminal charges,[84] and (though less frequently) of the actual *facts* the occurrence of which is claimed by whoever enters such a plea.[85]

But then he may believe that all defences in the first sense—all admissible defeating circumstances—are allowed only *as* defences in the second sense. He may believe, that is, that the potential exonerating effect of defeating circumstances is confined to the second 'stage' of criminal liability, the stage at which the defendant, having been formally charged, is given the procedural opportunity to offer her answer *to* such charge.

Whether this is so, however, is a purely contingent matter. It is a matter of how criminal procedures happen to be structured in our actual legal systems. So the relevant question becomes the following: is it the case, as a matter of positive law, that the characteristic effect of the admissible defeating circumstances manifests itself exclusively at the post-accusatory stages of criminal procedures? Is it the case, in other words, that criminal charges—as opposed to criminal convictions—are not defeasible in the relevant sense? Is Duff's account *descriptively* sound?

The answer is negative. In English criminal law, to go no further, the decision to prosecute does not rest solely on there being evidence 'on the main points that need to be proved' (as Ashworth and Redmayne recently put it) for a defendant to 'be brought to court to answer the charge'.[86] Such a test, failing to make 'explicit reference' to

[83] Duff (2007: 22).

[84] See Duff (2007: 180, 260, 263, 264 n 10).

[85] As when the fact of self-defence, for example, is said to be a defence: Duff (2007: 21 n 7, 211, 219); or when agents are said to '*have* a justification', eg on the grounds of the *facts* of the case rather than on what they may have happened to have pleaded in answering any charges: Duff (2007: 21, 218).

[86] See Ashworth and Redmayne (2010: 200).

'probable lines of defence', has been publicly and officially denounced as inadequate;[87] and the 2013 *Code for Crown Prosecutors*, in accordance with which decisions whether to prosecute are to be made, now provides in Section 4 that:

> 4.4 Prosecutors must be satisfied that there is sufficient evidence to provide a realistic prospect of conviction against each suspect on each charge. They must consider what the defence case may be, and how it is likely to affect the prospects of conviction. A case which does not pass the evidential stage must not proceed, no matter how serious or sensitive it may be.
>
> 4.5 The finding that there is a realistic prospect of conviction is based on the prosecutor's objective assessment of the evidence, including the impact of any defence and any other information that the suspect has put forward or on which he or she might rely. It means that an objective, impartial and reasonable jury or bench of magistrates or judge hearing a case alone, properly directed and acting in accordance with the law, is more likely than not to convict the defendant of the charge alleged. This is a different test from the one that the criminal courts themselves must apply. A court may only convict if it is sure that the defendant is guilty.

Sufficient evidence of a defence—sufficient evidence, that is, of an admissible defeating *fact*, of an exception—will prevent a decision to prosecute from being correctly made. Prosecutions, thus, are *defeasible* decisions in the sense that has occupied us throughout this book. For what the paragraphs just quoted stipulate is *not* that a decision to prosecute is not correctly made unless the actual non-occurrence of the admissible defeating circumstances is established by the relevant body of evidence. There must be sufficient evidence, of course, relative to all the constitutive elements of the offence. As to the admissible defeating circumstances, the requirement is plainly to be understood as the requirement that the relevant body of evidence does not establish the occurrence of any such circumstances to the prescribed standard of proof.

Hence we need first to be able to grasp and explain the distinction between offences and defences in order to fully understand the conditions under which a decision to prosecute is correctly made, and thus before (and independently) of any answers that the person actually

[87] See Ashworth and Redmayne (2010: 200).

charged may successfully come to offer *in* her defence. Defences, in other words, operate already at the first 'stage' of criminal liability. Any account that proposes to explain the offence/defence divide by suggesting that criminal answerability depends only on the commission of an offence being proved to the relevant standard,[88] and that defences are then 'answers to a criminal charge that seek to block the transition from responsibility to liability',[89] is wrong.

Underneath Duff's flawed characterization of the offence/defence distinction there seem to lie some of the typical and interrelated mistakes that we have dissolved in previous chapters. One such mistake, discussed in Chapter 3, is the unwarranted conflation of the notion of *all that has to be to be proved* for any given decision to be correctly made, and the notion of a *sufficient condition* for any given decision to be correctly made.[90] This may explain why Duff appears to think that correctly made prosecutions depend only on there being sufficient evidence that the offence was committed,[91] when in effect they also depend on there being no evidence of any admissible defeating circumstance. Elsewhere Duff discusses the 2004 version of the *Code for Crown Prosecutors*, whose paragraph 5.2 (similarly to paragraph 4.4, quoted above, of the 2013 version) reads:

> 5.2 Crown prosecutors must be satisfied that there is enough evidence to provide a 'realistic prospect of conviction' against each defendant on each charge. They must consider what the defence case may be, and how that is likely to affect the prosecution case.

Nevertheless, Duff and others maintain that the prosecution's 'case to answer' is constituted solely on the grounds of 'sufficient evidence' that the offence is committed.[92] He insists, in other words, that sufficient evidence of an offence is a sufficient condition of there being a properly constituted 'case to answer'.

What is the root of this mistake? It is, quite possibly, the received, but unwarranted 'substantivist' approach to judicial decision-making in law, complemented by a purely instrumental conception of legal proof as an activity directed at the ascertainment of the factual antecedents of 'substantive' legal norms. We saw in Chapters 3 and 4 that

[88] See Duff (2007: 198, 207).

[89] See Duff (2007: 179, 260).

[90] See sections 3.2 and 3.5.

[91] See Duff (2007: 182).

[92] See Duff and others (2007: 184–5; and also 140, 147–9).

this conception of legal proof rests on the erroneous notion that we should think of legal consequences as being attached to the actual occurrence of such facts rather than to their ascertainment in court. And when one mistakes the actual occurrence of the material facts (including not only those facts that make up the criminal offences, but also the facts admitted as exceptions) for the relevant conditions of correctly made prosecutions, then the only apparent alternative to Duff's view is the picture according to which prosecutors must '*prove the absence* of any plausible defence, as well as the commission of the offence'[93]—which is not only false as a matter of law, but evidently unviable. (To put it differently: if one represents the conditions of correctly made prosecutions in terms of what facts were and were not the case—rather than in terms of what facts were and were not proved to be the case—and if one correspondingly thinks of legal proof as an activity whose function is that of determining when each such condition can be accepted as true by the decision-maker, then one will be led to say that for a decision to prosecute to be correctly made, the occurrence of the offence is a sufficient condition: for the occurrence of the offence, as a matter of law, is indeed *all* that has to be proved.) One must discard that common substantivist bias in order to see that correctly made prosecutions, similarly to correctly made convictions, are dependent on it being the case that the commission of the offence *is* proved, and that *no* admissible defeating circumstance is proved.

A related mistake concerns Duff's views on what he refers to as 'the formal allocation of responsibilities and burdens between defence and prosecution'.[94] Never does he depart from the ordinary misconception—which I criticized in Chapter 4—that the prosecutor has an 'initial' burden which is simply that of proving the offence, and that it is *if* (and *after*) the defendant has discharged the evidential burden (the burden she is said to bear 'in relation to any defence on which he wants to rely') that the prosecution will have to disprove any defence thus raised.[95] Burdens, however, as we saw in section 4.3, do not actually 'shift'[96] in any such manner: the prosecution's 'initial' burden is no different from its final one. Not only is the prosecution

[93] See Duff (2007: 231, emphasis added).

[94] Duff (2007: 231).

[95] See Duff (2007: 198, 206–7, 217–18, 223, 229, 236); Duff and others (2007: 145, 147–8); and Duff (2009: 281).

[96] See Duff (2007: 198, 208).

burdened, at all stages of the criminal process, with the *absence of proof* of defeating circumstances, it also *never* carries the burden of disproving any defeating circumstance—it never has, *pace* Duff (2008: 198), to 'prove the absence of' *D*-facts—no matter how persuasively it may have been established by the defendant's evidence at an earlier stage of the criminal process.[97]

A third mistake, regarding the notion of a criminal *charge*, replicates the mistake that Tadros makes in connection with the notion of a criminal *conviction*. As we saw in section 8.2, Tadros is impressed by the fact that when we speak of what we are convicted *of*, we seem to employ the same action-description that constitutes the definition of the relevant offence. He suggests, accordingly, that offence definitions exhaust the description of the 'conduct which is worthy of conviction',[98] and that the absence of defences 'does not play a role' in the 'nature' of criminal convictions.[99] I argued that this confuses the notion of a criminal offence (in the sense in which it can be contrasted with that of a defence) and the notion of a *crime*. It is for φ-ings$_R$, not for φ-ings$_D$—it is for the commission of crimes, not strictly speaking for the performance of actions described as offences—that we are convicted. The very same is true of criminal accusations. It is not for the commission of offences, in the strict sense, that we are charged and called to answer. It is for the commission of crimes.[100] Criminal accusations and criminal convictions are substantially equivalent. Both are defeasible judgments or claims that some person X φ-ed$_R$. Both

[97] Nor is the effect of the successful ascertainment of a defeating circumstance at the liability 'stage' to be explained in terms of any 'presumption of guilt' (supposedly grounded on the bare proof of elements of an offence) that the defeating circumstance 'cancels'. Duff's views about a 'presumptive inference from responsibility to liability', and his idiosyncratic reading of the presumption of innocence, strike me as ad hoc—just as ad hoc, indeed, as the German model's similar (and similarly motivated) insistence that the fact than an action satisfies the definition of a *Tatbestand* grounds a presumption that it is legally wrongful. See Duff (2007: 196, 198, 207, 216, 236, 263).

[98] Tadros (2005: 111).

[99] Tadros (2005: 109); see the passage accompanying n 58.

[100] It is not for the commission of the *Tatbestand*, if one were to employ the German notion that Duff (2007: 206) thinks 'might be a better way of capturing the idea of a criminal offence', that we are charged; it is for the commission of the *Verbrechen*. In spite of his insistence that it is 'offences' (in the strict sense) that we are criminally responsible *for*, Duff's terminology oscillates. We often find him also speaking of 'crimes' (or 'criminal conduct') as that which prosecutors must 'prove', and for which we must answer: see Duff (2007: 177–9, 191, 198); Duff and others (2007: 101, 108, 113, 132, 142, 144–5, 147), as well as, of course, the very title of his monograph, '*Answering for Crime*.' See the remarks in Westen (2008: 568–9).

are correctly made only if it is simultaneously the case that (a) it has been ascertained that *X* φ-ed$_D$ and (b) none of the admissible defeating circumstances has been ascertained.

Duff proposes, as I noted, to distinguish 'two sets of questions', one concerning 'the conditions under which agents can be held criminally responsible', the other 'the *further* conditions that must be satisfied if they are to be criminally liable for that for which they are criminally responsible'.[101] But as we now see, these two sets are substantially identical. Even though the dialectic interplay of charges and answers can be seen as a characteristic feature of the way in which the criminal process is structured, the diachronic distinction of procedural 'stages' does not map onto any (content-relative) difference between the sets of facts that are relevant at each stage.[102] It has no 'logical' counterpart: there is no correlate distinction of 'logical stages'[103] that can usefully be delineated. The reason that a successful defence—in the procedural sense of the term—is able to 'block the transition from criminal responsibility to liability'[104] can now be straightforwardly explained, not in terms of any 'further' substantial condition that distinguishes correctly made charges from correctly made convictions, but by reference to the uniform set of substantial conditions (or lack thereof) that govern the criminal process at all stages.

It is quite easy, of course, to make the slip of supposing that the characteristic effect of defences—of *D*-facts—is inextricably connected to some kind of sequential or logical ordering of offences and defences. In the domain of criminal responsibility, as in that of the everyday, non-institutional accusations discussed in Chapter 7, the natural and most vivid way of thinking of the operation of *D*-facts is in terms of the expansion of the body of relevant

[101] Duff (2007: 22, my emphasis); see the passage accompanying n 80.

[102] Duff (2007: 18, 21, 73, 179). There are many differences between accusations and convictions. The point, however, is whether the content of an accusation, in the sense of that *of which* one is properly charged in the criminal process, is different from the content of a criminal conviction; whether, more precisely, the set of relevant circumstances on which *the judgment or claim that someone* 'φ-ed' *that is a proper part of any criminal accusation* depends is different from the set of relevant circumstances on which *the judgment or claim that someone* 'φ-ed' *that is a proper part of any criminal conviction in the same procedural context* depends. And the answer, I suggested, is negative.

[103] Duff (2007: 208).

[104] Duff (2007: 179).

evidence *after* some charge or accusation has already been made. The literature on legal defeasibility abounds with instances of that mistake, starting with Hart's own misguided association of legal defeasibility to 'the ways in which legal utterances can be challenged'.[105] Many authors take the view, discussed in Chapter 2, that *P*-facts must enjoy some sort of procedural or structural precedence over *D*-facts—that 'rules' are sequentially prior to their exceptions.[106] Indeed, we can immediately see the point in examples like the following:

> Certain *discoveries* about why a regretted action was performed will lead any civilized person to regard blame-related responses as inappropriate. Suppose someone commits a murder, and *it turns out that* he had a brain tumour which had a crucial role in the causation of the murderous act: every victim of such a tumour would be virtually certain to commit hostile and violent acts, and this man will become a mild and reliably law-abiding citizen once his tumour is removed. In that case it would be *inappropriate* to respond to the murder with reproaches etc., or to seek revenge or demand punishment.[107]

Yet the reason that these 'discoveries' make it inappropriate to respond in certain ways to the agent's action has nothing to do with the fact that they are discoveries made *after* the charge or accusation. The fact that the agent had the described brain tumour is relevant per se, independently of the point in time at which it happens to be discovered. Does this then mean that the original charge was incorrectly made? Certainly not, as we already know. It was correctly made relative to the body of evidence then available. If the fact that the agent had the brain tumour is relevant *as an exception*, as a *D*-fact, then the charge depends only on the available evidence *not*

105 Hart (1949: 175).

106 See the references given in Chapter 2, n 16; and see also Nakhnikian (1957: 26); Baier (1970: 101); Heinz (1981: 243); Howarth (1981: 36); Tur (2001a: 358, 360), contrasting his 'defeasibilist' approach, which 'seeks to reconstruct the data in structured, conceptually sequenced manner', with the 'unsequenced logic of closure'; and Husak's hesitation in Husak (2005: 291 n 26). But see also Campbell's rightly drawn distinction between 'things [that] are correctly regarded as defences [*lato sensu*] in the context of planning and conducting a defence against legal proceedings, but are not to be so regarded at the level of the formulation of the relevant legal rules' in Campbell (1987: 77, 82).

107 Bennett (1980: 15, emphases added).

establishing that the agent had such a tumour (which is, by hypothesis, the case).

This was the central argument in Chapter 2, where I sketched a general model of the diachronic 'defeasibility' (defeasibility$_{NF}$) of claims and accusations. The non-procedural defeasibility of accusations (their defeasibility$_{P}$—their defeasibility *proper*[108]) was then discussed in Chapter 7. Similar models might be developed with criminal liability specifically in mind. But they would take into account the lessons that can now be gleaned about the relation between criminal answerability and criminal liability. The first lesson is that the defeasibility$_{NF}$ of any given decision *Y* to hold someone criminally liable, either by charging or convicting her, on the grounds of having φ-ed$_{R}$—where 'φ' stands for the corresponding crime—is absolutely independent of its defeasibility$_{P}$. Defendants might (and indeed should) equally be called publicly to answer non-defeasible$_{P}$ criminal charges—which would mean that the range of potentially successful defences would not include the offering or ascertainment of a defeating circumstance.

Of course, in our actual legal systems, criminal accusations *are* for the most part defeasible$_{P}$ decisions. But conversely—and this is the second lesson—this common feature of criminal charges is not dependent on the fact that charges are not, in the context of the procedure, final judgments that someone φ-ed$_{R}$, nor on the fact that the later-stage, final decision may happen to be an acquittal rather than a conviction.[109] The corollary lesson is that if we wish to understand the particular class of *answers*—of defences—that does consist in the offering or ascertainment of a defeating circumstance—of a *D*-fact—we need to grasp defeasibility$_{P}$, not defeasibility$_{NF}$. The study of defeating circumstances (and, accordingly, of the distinction between *P*- and *D*-facts) must thus precede that of defences. In this respect, differently from what Duff suggests,[110] criminal liability is prior (explanatorily, at least) to criminal answerability.[111]

108 See section 2.1.2.

109 It does seem to be the case that accusations (or, more precisely, the claims that someone φ-ed$_{R}$ that form part of the complex act of accusation) must be defeasible$_{NF}$; on the issue see eg Kauffeld (1998: 247–8, 252–9); Fritz (2005: 152–3); Yeager (2006: 115). But the point made in the text is that their possible defeasibility$_{P}$ is not connected to their defeasibility$_{NF}$ in any necessary or interesting way.

110 See Duff (2007: 18, 20).

111 I stress 'in this respect'. There may be dimensions in which answerability or accountability—legal or extra-legal—can plausibly be said to be primary relative to other senses of

The foregoing establishes the descriptive inadequacy of an answerability-based account of the offence/defence along the lines that Duff proposes. Yet as I emphasized, Duff seems independently to believe that a system of criminal liability structured in accordance with his view of the distinction between offences and defences divide would also be normatively agreeable. Is this the case? I will now briefly suggest otherwise.

8.4 'O Call Me Not to Justify the Wrong'[112]

Should individuals be criminally charged, and called to publicly answer such charges, and convicted and punished whenever they 'cannot offer an adequately exculpatory answer',[113] if there is sufficient evidence that they performed an action described as a criminal offence?

Duff seems to think that this question should be answered affirmatively; and so does John Gardner, whose account of the distinction between offences and defences is similar to Duff's in some important respects, and whose ideas we may also bring into discussion. Both see the criminal trial as 'primarily' a 'vehicle' for responsible agents to answer for their alleged offences, and 'only secondarily [as] a vehicle for condemnation, deterrence, and punishment'.[114] And both appear to believe that the fact that a person has committed a criminal offence—in the strict sense of the term, the sense compatible with both the occurrence (or the ascertainment) and the non-occurrence (or the non-ascertainment) of any one of the admissible defeating circumstances—is sufficient reason for that person to have to publicly account for her action in a court of law 'on pain of formal condemnation and punishment' if she fails to provide an 'exculpatory answer'.[115]

We may be called, and 'must be ready', to answer for our conduct:[116] one ought to explain one's actions—giving an answer to the question 'Why did you do that?'—whenever one has done any

'responsibility'. See eg Nowell-Smith (1976: 315); Lucas (1993: 5–6); Watson (2004: 262–4); Garzón Valdés (1997: 113–14); Oshana (1997: 77–9).

112 Shakespeare, Sonnet 139.

113 See Duff (2007: 77).

114 Gardner (2002: 80); contrast Duff (2009: 129–30).

115 Duff (2007: 147, and also 214, 238, 252, 260).

116 See Duff (2007: 24, 25, 27, 32, 213–14).

action that one had reason not to do;[117] and in classifying an action-type φ as a criminal offence the law 'declares' or 'asserts' that there is sufficient reason against φ-ing 'to make its performance prima facie wrongful'.[118]

Here the phrase 'prima facie' is used, along lines first suggested (in connection with the criminal law) by Kenneth Campbell,[119] 'to identify an *actual* wrong, not just an apparent or putative wrong'.[120] The phrase refers to 'conduct that we have, in the law's eyes, reason not to engage in',[121] conduct against which there are 'legally recognized reasons'.[122] It may be that an agent had, all things considered, good reason to φ; it may be that the reasons for which she acted 'outweighed or defeated' the reasons against φ-ing.[123] But 'that a reason is defeated does not mean that it is undermined or cancelled', that it 'dropped out of the picture'.[124] A 'genuine reason', even when defeated on the balance of reasons, remains 'relevant to an understanding and assessment' of our actions.[125] And in any case, 'proof that the defendant committed the offence charged' is proof that, 'in the law's eyes', the agent 'had reason not to act'.[126]

For the sake of argument, let us now assume that the commission of a criminal offence is always 'prima facie wrongful' in this sense, and thus that there is always reason against doing it. Does it follow that one should have to answer, should be called to answer, for it? Is it the case that, as Gardner puts it, 'an answer to the question "Why did you do that?"' is 'called for *whenever* anyone does anything she has any reason not to do'?[127]

I think not. To answer for my action is for me to 'explain' it, to 'explain why I acted as I did': it is to 'explain my action by reference to the reasons that I take, or that I reasonably took, to be good reasons for acting thus'.[128] Not just any explanation, even if sincere,

[117] Gardner (2003: 196); Duff (2007: 63–4).

[118] See Gardner (1996: 96); Gardner (2007a: 239); Duff (2007: 59); Duff (2009: 127).

[119] See Campbell (1987: 79).

[120] Gardner (1996: 96), and also Gardner (2002: 77–9); Gardner (2004: 144–5); and Duff (2007: 216–17).

[121] Duff (2007: 218).

[122] Gardner (1996: 96); and compare Campbell (1987: 80).

[123] See Duff (2007: 35).

[124] Gardner (1996: 96).

[125] Duff (2007: 219).

[126] Duff (2007: 218).

[127] Gardner (2003: 196, emphasis added); compare Duff (2007: 63–4).

[128] See Duff (2007: 279).

will count as an 'adequately exculpatory' answer.[129] It all depends, first, on the content of the explanation, and, second, on the agent's ability to convincingly establish the facts that make up the explanation of her action (or at least to raise a reasonable doubt as to their occurrence). But then—and this is the simple point that I wish to press against both Duff and Gardner—why would we insist on calling a person to publicly answer for her action in a criminal court when we *already* know, as it were (that is, when we already have sufficient evidence), that the action was all things considered permissible or done for the right reason?

Suppose, for example, that as a result of police investigation, sufficient evidence has been gathered that establishes beyond any reasonable doubt that a certain killing was done in self-defence. Why should the state nonetheless charge the agent with having committed the offence, and call her to publicly explain in a criminal court *why she did it*, and—worse—convict her and punish her if no such explanatory answer is actually offered? What reason, more generally, do we have to ask her 'Why did you do that?' if and when we already know the answer?

It is not my intention to deny the value of a criminal process that allows us to 'have structured explanatory dialogues in public, in which the object of explanation is ourselves', as Gardner puts it.[130] Nor do I mean to question the claim that in calling us to answer for our actions the state is treating us, and respecting us, as 'responsible agents' in an important sense of the term.[131] My issue, rather, is with Gardner's and Duff's suggestion that I must still be called to answer for an action, the performance of which has already been shown to have been permissible or even obligatory; and that, accordingly, I should be charged with having committed the criminal offence, and called to defend myself from that charge *on pain of conviction if I fail to do so*, even if the state has sufficient evidence that one of the admissible (and fully exculpatory) defeating circumstances is verified.

I do not see how these counter-intuitive propositions can be defended. Nor do I really think that Duff and Gardner would insist that these contentions are indeed correct.[132] Can it be that they are

[129] Duff (2007: 17, 37, 77, 80, 84, 216, 238).

[130] See Gardner (2003: 189); Duff (2007: 89).

[131] See Gardner (2002: 80, 84–6); Duff (2007: 88); Duff and others (2007: 113).

[132] Does Gardner (2003: 197) not explicitly agree that 'anyone who threateningly asks "Why did you do that?" is claiming to have a reasonable *suspicion* that the person she is addressing is a wrongdoer' (emphasis added)? Does Duff (2007: 197) not stress that if

misled into overstating their claims by one of the familiar mistakes that most theorists happen to commit regarding the notion of a defence?

That is my impression. As we have seen in section 8.3, such a scenario in which people are accused, and summoned to offer their answers, whenever they are suspected of having committed a criminal offence, whether or not there is sufficient evidence of defeating circumstances, is not a scenario that we ordinarily encounter in our legal systems. Our practice, rather, is that of charging people with having committed *crimes* rather than criminal offences (in the strict sense); and as we saw in section 8.2, it is only if no defeating circumstance is present that we can speak of a crime. Now I do think that people *should* be called to answer criminal charges in these circumstances, and at any rate that they should not be convicted and punished unless they have had the opportunity to publicly explain themselves and their actions. And I would not deny that the value of having the defendant intervene, and explain herself, in the criminal process is not reducible to the mere instrumental value of gathering as much information as possible about the circumstances of her actions. So I can agree that this feature of our criminal systems is, at least at the intuitive level, normatively attractive.

The difficulty, however, lies in discerning what *particular* aspects of our actual criminal systems are responsible for such normatively appealing features. And it is at this juncture that a descriptively marred understanding of our own systems will prevent us from making good sense of our normative intuitions. We saw that when we point out, as I just have, that a criminal charge is correctly made only if no defeating circumstance is present, what we mean is that it must not be established that any *D*-fact was the case (and not that it must be established that no *D*-fact was the case). But we also saw that it can be easy to confuse the (true) proposition that all that has to be proved for a criminal charge to be correctly made is the commission of a criminal offence, with the (false) proposition that a correctly made criminal charge depends only on proof that a criminal offence has been committed. Given, moreover, that we would also agree that when there is no sufficient evidence of the commission of an offence no charge will be correctly made, we may therefore come to think, mistakenly, that the (ascertainment of the)

defendants are brought to trial they are 'suspected' to be guilty of criminal conduct? But 'suspicion' is an epistemic term: if I know or believe that you are innocent, that you acted permissibly, I do not suspect that you are guilty of a crime.

commission of a criminal offence is as a matter of fact—that is, as a matter of how our systems actually operate—both necessary and sufficient for someone to be correctly charged and called to answer in a criminal trial.

Having thus come to misdescribe our own systems, we will likely misrepresent those of its features that happen to muster our normative adhesion, becoming convinced, perhaps, that what we find intuitively agreeable is indeed a practice of calling people to answer for the commission of criminal offences in the strict sense. But we will have failed in the task of rendering explicit the factors that underlie our evaluative intuitions about answerability and about the circumstances under which there is reason to call persons to answer publicly for their actions.

(Nor is the risk of misinterpretation confined to the legal domain; take this example of Duff's:

> I knock over your treasured vase, which breaks. This was, let us suppose, an accident in which I was in no way at fault: the vase was just behind the door that I opened, and I had no reason to believe that it had been moved there; or the doorknob unexpectedly fell off onto the vase as I opened the door. Nonetheless, when we see what has happened, you might properly hold me responsible for breaking the vase, and I should accept that responsibility . . . *[I]f you say, in challenging tones that accuse me of breaking your vase, 'Look what you did!'*, a proper response would not be to deny that I broke it, or to claim that I do not have to answer to you for breaking it. I should instead recognise that you have the right to call me to answer for breaking your vase, and offer the exculpatory answer that I have: that I was taking all due care (which is to say that it would have been unreasonable to expect me to take the kind of care that would have averted the harm), and broke the vase through non-culpable accident.[133]

Yes; but you will only say 'Look what you did!' in 'challenging tones that accuse me of breaking your vase'—you will only have me 'explain how I came to break the vase'[134]—if you *don't know* that 'I was taking all due care' and that I 'broke the vase through non-culpable accident'. This is clearly an implied feature of the example, which would not be

[133] Duff (2007: 73–4, emphasis added).

[134] Duff (2007: 74).

plausible otherwise. But in leaving this feature implicit we risk missing its centrality in our responsibility-ascribing practices.)

Labouring under such skewed descriptions of our actual systems, we will be prone to misstating any general theses about criminal answerability with which we may try to capture or reconstruct our intuitions. This is the sort of flaw that I have tried to expose. For if we also agree that agents ought *not* to be charged, and called to answer for their conduct, when from the very beginning we already have sufficient evidence of the occurrence of defeating circumstances—then it cannot be the case that what strikes us as meritorious about our legal systems is the fact that they summon defendants to answer for their actions *whenever* a criminal offence has been established.

This point can be made in a different way. To propose (as Duff in particular does) that people should have to answer for the commission of a criminal offence 'on pain of conviction if they cannot offer an exculpatory answer'[135] is to suggest that the mere fact that an explanatory answer is offered is a factor to be weighed in the balance of reasons that determine whether 'all things considered' the agent can be said to have acted wrongly. And this cannot be right. Even if we were to accept Duff's and Gardner's reason-based approach to the offence/defence distinction, and to concede that there is always reason not to commit an action described as a criminal offence, it would still be the case that no aspect of our 'all things considered' judgments (that is, our judgments whether 'in the final analysis'[136] there were reasons *for* the agent's action that outweighed the reasons against it and rendered it permissible or maybe even required) would turn on the fact that the agent had (or had not) *offered* an explanation of her actions. This fact is not part of the 'things' that should constitute the object of our 'all-things-considered' judgment. What matters, to repeat a point made in Chapter 2, is whether the relevant circumstances—those pertaining to the offence, and those pertaining to the relevant *D*-facts—were present or absent; not the way by which we may have come to learn of their presence or absence.[137]

[135] Duff (2007: 237).

[136] Gardner (1996: 96).

[137] For another example: we can agree with Duff (2007: 2014–15) both that the criminal offence in murder is to be described as 'killing a human being', rather than as 'killing a human being without his (free, informed) request', and that the fact that the killing was done at the victim's free and informed request ought to 'function as a defence' in murder;

It is interesting in this respect to look into Douglas Husak's recent efforts to establish whether *de minimis* is to be counted 'as a true defence' or whether 'its contrary' appears 'as an element of a criminal offence'.[138] Given that 'according to Duff', as Husak (2011: 341) says, 'persons are responsible for that for which they may be made to answer', how is the relevant question to be phrased? Here is Husak's formulation: 'Should a defendant be required to answer in criminal court for his de minimis wrongs?'[139] The answer appears to be negative: 'If someone engages in conduct that causes a trivial harm', says Husak (2011, 341–2), 'it seems unjust to deem him responsible (in Duff's sense) and to require him to respond by pleading a defence on pain of liability'. And then:

> [S]uppose our bubble-gum thief is arrested and prosecuted. If his conduct should not be punished, as I have tentatively claimed it is intuitively correct, it must be because he should not be required to answer for it in a criminal court. *What could this defendant possibly say to a judge that was not already known?*[140]

This hits the nail on the head, though Husak does not take the point to its full argumentative consequences. The reason that the answer to Husak's Duffian question is negative is that the question is formulated by reference to an action-description that already includes mention of the *de minimis* circumstance. It is, in other words, the sort of question that we are able to ask of actions *we already know* to have been performed under the relevant circumstance. Now if the circumstance is a *D*-fact, of course, the answer will *always* be negative (consider: 'Should a defendant be required to answer in criminal court for a killing done permissibly in self-defence?'). But then how can Duff's should-I-have-to-answer-for-it test allow us to decide

but it certainly does not follow (nor would we agree) that '"I killed *V* at *V*'s free and informed request and to spare him the intolerable suffering of his terminal illness" is . . . an answer that [the] *D*[efendant] *should have to offer the polity if she is to avoid conviction*': see Duff (2007: 216, emphasis added). Yet this last passage, in which the fact that a defence or answer is actually offered is explicitly presented as a *necessary condition* for the defendant to avoid conviction, is exemplary of the kind of language that Duff consistently employs: see Duff (2007: 31, 77, 80, 84, 147, 211).

138 Husak (2011: 339).

139 Husak (2011: 341).

140 Husak (2011: 342, emphasis added).

whether self-defence is a defence, rather than a negative element of an offence?[141]

I have not suggested that there is no reason for an agent to answer for her conduct when defeating circumstances have been shown to have occurred.[142] I have only maintained that we—our criminal systems—ought not to call such agents to answer for their conduct if and when we already know (or justifiably believe, or have sufficient evidence) that defeating circumstances have occurred. So the question is left open whether a defendant should be allowed to face a trial, and publicly state her innocence, even when the prosecutors are satisfied that she ought to be acquitted. But they should not be—and fortunately they are not—made to answer for such conduct.

8.5 Prima Facie Wrongs and Prima Facie Judgments

To recapitulate and conclude, I now want to cast a quick glance at an issue that will allow us to bring together some strands of argument developed in the previous sections, and to highlight some points of similarity between the German and the Anglo-American approaches to the offence/defence distinction.

The language of 'prima facie' judgments, reasons, or wrongs is often used, though not always clearly, in connection with the topic of criminal defences. Lawyers, in particular, speak of a prosecutor's 'prima facie' case. Yet the expression is notably ambiguous.[143] Is there some sense in which it captures an important or interesting aspect of the interplay between offences and defences?

So believe Gardner and Duff, who, following Campbell (as I noted in section 8.4), speak of 'prima facie' reasons (and of 'prima facie' wrongs) in connection with the commission of criminal offences. They use the expression in a carefully defined sense. Their idea is that there are 'legally recognised reasons'[144] against the performance

[141] Compare, indeed, on the topic of rape and the role of the victim's lack of consent as an 'element' of the offence, Duff (2007: 209): 'we should not have to answer, to our fellow citizens through the criminal courts, for every act of sexual penetration'.

[142] See Gardner (2007b: 277).

[143] See Searle (1980), and Kramer's useful discussion in Kramer (2005: 345–9); or Kramer (2012: 473–5).

[144] Gardner (1996: 96).

of actions described as criminal offences. These are 'genuine' reasons, if 'not conclusive' ones, which even when they happen in the particular case to be outweighed by other reasons, remain 'relevant to an understanding and assessment' of our actions.[145] Here is Campbell's characterization:

In referring to *prima facie* reasons I am not using '*prima facie*' in an evidential sense. I do not mean 'that which at first blush looks like a reason, but may turn out not to be'. Nor [am I using it] to mean 'a reason which may be expected to apply generally but not always'. I am using it in the sense in which it is used by most philosophers of practical reasoning, namely to indicate a reason which is not necessarily a conclusive one. Within its defined scope the reason always applies, but it may be outweighed, or at least balanced, by opposing reasons.[146]

And here is Gardner:

Calling an action 'prima facie wrong' is intended to affirm that the action really is wrong, while leaving open the further question of whether the wrongdoing is justified. By the same token, an action that is 'all things considered wrong' is not merely a wrong action. It is a wrong action and also (a quite separate matter) an unjustified one.[147]

This is a view that Gardner (2002: 77) contrasts with what he calls 'the "closure" view': the view that 'no action is wrong' that is not 'wrong *all things considered*, i.e. taking account of both the reasons in favour of performing it (the pros) and the reasons against performing it (the cons)'. 'According to the closure view', says Gardner, 'talk of "justified wrongdoing"'

turns out to be oxymoronic. Naturally one may still say something more circumspect. Even on the closure view, one may say that an action was 'prima facie' wrong, and yet justified. But the words 'prima facie', as used by supporters of the closure view, carry the connotation that the action was not really wrong at all. It only seemed to be wrong, on the strength of incomplete information. When all the pros and cons of performing it were known, it turned out not to be wrong at all.[148]

[145] Campbell (1987: 79-80); Duff (2007: 219); and see the text accompanying n 118.
[146] Campbell (1987: 79).
[147] Gardner (2002: 78).
[148] Gardner (2002: 77–8).

Thus 'the contrast between the two views could be brought out nicely', Gardner (2002: 78–9) remarks, 'by saying that on the closure view, one cannot understand what a "prima facie" wrong is without first understanding what an "all things considered" wrong is', whereas 'on the rival view', one 'cannot understand what an "all things considered" wrong is without first understanding what a "prima facie" wrong is'.

Duff draws a similar contrast:

> [I]s a prima facie wrong or duty something that we have reason to believe is a wrong or a duty, but that could turn out on further inquiry not to be a wrong or a duty at all; or is it something that really is a wrong or a duty, but that could turn out on further inquiry not to be an all-things-considered wrong or duty—not to be something that, all things considered, we should not do, or must do? In other words, is a prima facie wrong or duty only prima facie a wrong or duty; or is it a genuine, albeit only prima facie, wrong or duty?[149]

To ask, as Gardner does, 'Which view is right?', and to answer, as Duff (2007: 18) does, that 'it is the second reading that is appropriate here', is to suggest that the two views are inconsistent. But that is not the case. Notice how Gardner (2002: 79) describes the claim endorsed by the opponent of the closure view as the claim that '[a] prima facie wrong is just a wrong, while an all things considered wrong is a wrong *with an added feature*, namely absence of justification'. This sentence leaves some room for equivocation: the term 'wrong' means different things in the phrases 'prima facie wrong' and 'all things considered wrong'. So let me replace this last phrase with 'impermissible'.[150] What the closure view, it appears, denies, and its opponents correspondingly maintain, is that the permissibility of an action is compatible with there being 'genuine' reasons against it.[151] This is indeed a real disagreement. But both views can surely agree that it may well happen that an action *seems* permissible—'on the strength' say, 'of incomplete information'—and yet that 'when all the pros and cons of performing it were known' it 'turn[s] out' not to be permissible at all.[152] In other words, the sense in which the endorser of the closure view employs

149 Duff (2007: 217).

150 See Gardner (1996: 106); Gardner (2004: 148); Duff (2007: 225, 264–7).

151 See Gardner (1996: 96).

152 See Gardner (2002: 78).

the 'prima facie' label—which is the 'lawyer's evidential sense'[153]—is in fact available to both views. (Similarly, opponents of the closure view must be prepared to recognize that some actions may only *seem* 'on the strength of incomplete information' *to be*—that is, that some actions may be, in the evidential sense of the term, only 'prima facie'—'prima facie wrongs' in *their* sense of the term.) And Duff, at least, as we will shortly see, appears to make use of the *evidential* notion of a 'prima facie' judgment as a central part of his account of the offence/defence distinction. It seems to me, however, that neither of these readings of the words 'prima facie' provides us with any interesting or useful notion with which to describe the relation between offences and defences.

On this issue, Gardner and Duff are essentially in line with what is the received view among those working under the German model. Most theorists in the German tradition would maintain that the commission of the action described in a legal *Tatbestand* is already to be negatively evaluated, irrespective of the intervention of justificatory circumstances. There *is* a substantive, normative difference, they say, between killing a mosquito and killing a person in self-defence, even though neither conduct is ultimately forbidden.[154] So they reject the closure view. Like Campbell or Duff or Gardner, they maintain that justifications are substantially 'distinct from, and additional to, a mere denial of the offence'.[155]

As I observed in section 8.1, however, this discussion is collateral to the problem that interests us. Both endorsers and opponents of the closure view may accept—since they hold nothing that discredits it—the idea that justifications are negative elements of crimes, and thus *structurally* similar to negative elements of offences. So the discussion simply fails to address the distinction between offences and defeating circumstances—between inculpatory and exculpatory circumstances, between *P*- and *D*-facts. This distinction, as we know, marks a structural or functional contrast, rather than a substantive one. It marks a difference about the way in which the presence or absence of different kinds of relevant circumstances bears on the final decision whether or not to convict. To explain the offence/defence distinction is to explain the *defeating* character—the 'exceptional' character—of defeating

[153] See Gardner (1996: 96, 105 n 26).

[154] See n 12.

[155] See Gardner (2002: 79).

circumstances: it is to explain, in Welzel's phrase, their 'purely negative' behaviour.[156] But there is nothing that we can learn about this topic from discussions about the soundness of the so-called '*Lehre von den negative Tatbestandsmerkmalen*'—the 'closure' doctrine according to which justifications are but negative elements of the *Tatbestand*. In the context of our discussion, then, Campbell's, Gardner's, and Duff's proposed idea of a 'prima facie reason' or a 'prima facie wrong' seems devoid of explanatory power.[157] It captures no distinctive feature of the notion of a criminal offence, as opposed to that of a criminal defence.[158]

What of the evidential reading of the 'prima facie' phrase? We saw in section 8.1 how theorists working in the German tradition have tried—and failed—to account for the 'negative' behaviour of justificatory defeating circumstances. Their stock claim is that *unless* a justification happens to be present, the commission of a *Tatbestand* warrants a presumption that the action is legally impermissible. Duff himself has a summary:

> A *Tatbestand* involves the violation of (or an attack on or threat to) a *Rechtsgut*, a legally protected good or interest; such a violation, attack or threat is presumptively wrongful—it presumptively constitutes *Rechtswidrigkeit*, criminal wrongfulness all things considered. But that presumption can be defeated by a justification (*Rechtfertigung*). A justification appeals to a permissive norm specifying an exception to the proscriptive norms found in the special part: for instance that the action protected a *Rechtsgut* more important than the *Rechtsgut* that it violated; or that the person whose *Rechtsgut* was violated consented to the violation.[159]

Duff, as we also saw, follows a similar strategy (acknowledging the similarity).[160] The commission of a criminal offence should justify,

156 See text to n 15.

157 Recall, also, from section 6.2, the more general conclusion that in order to correctly explain the relation between *P*- and *D*-facts the idea of an *override* is neither necessary nor sufficient.

158 This is not to say that Gardner's and Duff's (and Welzel's) reconstruction of the substantive relation between the *facts* that should be described as criminal offences and the *facts* that should be described as criminal defences is unsound. (Nor is it to say the opposite: but although I tend to find that reconstruction unsatisfactory, my reasons are not specifically related to the topic of exceptions.)

159 Duff (2007: 205).

160 See Duff (2007: 206). Gardner leaves the point untouched. He seems to think that references to the exceptional character of justifications are but reassertions of the closure view: see Gardner (1996: 146, 148–9); Gardner (2002: 79).

he says, the 'presumption that [the defendant] committed it culpably unless he offers a defence that rebuts that presumption'.[161] Offences 'are, or should be' what he calls 'presumptive wrongs'.[162] Though Duff is not always clear about the point, it seems that the notion of a 'presumptive wrong' is not the same as that of a 'prima facie' wrong, in the non-evidential sense of 'prima facie' that we have just examined. Consider:

> We might understand a presumptive wrong as a wrong that justifies the presumption that the defendant is guilty—a presumption that she can defeat by offering a defence; or as conduct that a court can presume to be a wrong unless the defendant rebuts that presumption by offering a defence.[163]

So in Duff's view, it seems, offences are not only 'prima facie wrongs'. 'Proof that the defendant committed the offence' is 'proof that he acted as he had in the law's eyes reason not to act'.[164] But it also constitutes the presumption—the 'defeasible' presumption—that 'the defendant is guilty':

> Proof that the defendant committed the offence charged is then proof that she is criminally responsible for committing a presumptive wrong for which she can be called to answer in the criminal court. Such proof creates a presumption of guilt or liability: the court is entitled to presume that she committed the offence culpably, and is thus liable to conviction and punishment for it.[165]

Now no agent is guilty whose action is justified. So given that a justified action is 'all things considered permissible',[166] it seems to follow that such a 'presumption' of guilt (and thus of 'all things considered' wrongdoing) is not considerably different from what, in the *evidential* sense of the term, one would call a 'prima facie' judgment of impermissibility and guilt. Which is, of course, how German theorists would also characterize the judgment of legal wrongfulness—of

[161] Duff (2007: 223).
[162] Duff (2007: 260).
[163] Duff (2007: 242).
[164] Duff (2007: 218).
[165] Duff (2007: 229). See also Duff (2012: 55, 57).
[166] Duff (2007: 264–5).

Rechtswidrigkeit—which, they say, is indicated or suggested by the commission of the *Tatbestand*.[167]

I have already rehearsed my criticism of this view, arguing that it is not descriptively accurate as an account of our actual practices. In any case, why should the bare knowledge or proof of the fact that a person killed another, for example, ground the 'presumption' that the killing was *not* done permissibly, rather than the contrary presumption—or no presumption at all? Even if one grants that killing is 'prima facie' wrong in Duff's non-evidential sense, that presumption seems to be unwarranted. To insist that killing is 'normally' impermissible, and justifications 'exceptional',[168] is to make no progress at all, for what we need is to understand precisely what 'exceptional' and 'normally' *mean* in this context, and we already know that these notions cannot be characterized in purely substantive terms. If Duff's normative claim were right that

> [o]ffence definitions should be such that if the prosecution discharges its initial persuasive burden by proving that the defendant committed the offence, the court can legitimately presume that he committed it culpably unless he offers a defence that rebuts that presumption. Proof that he committed the offence should be such as to justify replacing the Presumption of Innocence by a Presumption of Guilt,[169]

then it seems that no offence definition could ever be justified.[170]

[167] Recall the passage by Mezger quoted in n 19.

[168] See Duff (2007: 223), as well as the text accompanying n 20 above; and Tadros (2005: 102).

[169] Duff (2007: 223).

[170] We can see, of course, that given the German model's independent commitment to the idea that legal wrongfulness is an 'element' of crime (see section 8.1), something along the lines of this 'presumptive' account must be offered (from the point of view of the model) to explain how such an 'element' is to be ascertained—it being acknowledged that defeating circumstances behave 'in purely negative manner' (see the text accompanying n 15). And we can likewise see that given Duff's conflation of the notions of an offence and a crime (see the text following n 97), and his insistence that the set of substantive conditions under which one is appropriately charged and brought to trial is only a subset of the substantive conditions that must be in place if a defendant is to be properly convicted (see the text accompanying n 101), there may seem to be no other way of accounting for what he calls the 'transition from responsibility to liability', and for the effect of defences in 'blocking' it, than maintaining that the transition is 'presumptive': see Duff (2007: 216, 223, 260, 263, 296). In both cases, as I remarked (see the text accompanying n 29, as well as n 97), the 'presumptive' account has the feel of an ad hoc solution—to a false problem. On this point of Duff's account, see also Leader-Elliott (2010: 62–3).

Is there no role, then, for the idea of a 'prima facie' judgment in connection with our topic? There is, but only in a third, and much less robust, sense of the phrase, one which roughly tracks our procedural notion of a defeasible$_{NF}$ judgment. A prosecutorial decision to charge someone with the commission of a crime is substantially equivalent, as we have seen, to an eventual decision to convict. Both are defeasible judgments whose correctness depends on comparable sets of conditions. In a sense, in fact, the conviction *repeats*, in the same procedural context, the judgment made at the prosecutorial stage. Thus if by 'prima facie' we mean simply 'at first glance'—not in the sense that the 'glance' is not sufficiently thorough or careful, or that it fails to take into account all that it could or should, but simply in the sense that it is the *first* of possibly several 'glances' in the context of the same process—we may refer to the prosecutorial decision to charge a defendant as a 'prima facie' judgment that the defendant φ-ed$_R$. In order to contrast it with the second-stage decision to convict, however, we should here speak, not of an 'all things considered' judgment, but of a *secunda facie* (or an *altera facie*) one. Of course, depending on the contingent features of the relevant process (such as, for example, the levels of appeal that it allows), we might accordingly have to speak of a *tertia facie* judgment, a *quarta facie* judgment (each relative to the body of relevant evidence then available), and so on—until the *ultima facie* judgment is eventually issued.

8.6 In Conclusion

The view that the distinction between *P*-facts and *D*-facts cannot be substantively drawn has been my main theme. My concern throughout this book has been descriptive, not normative. The goal has been to clarify the notion of an exception, to explain what it is for a fact to *be* an exception in law. I said nothing about *which facts* ought to be classified as exceptions, and which ought not to be. But that does not mean that the distinction between *P*-facts and *D*-facts is not normatively significant. To the contrary, a clear understanding of the distinction may assist us in making some progress on a pair of important normative issues—or so, by way of general conclusion, I should now like to suggest.

First, our proof-based account may help us to see how to formulate criteria for assessing whether any given fact *ought* to count as a *P*- or a

D-fact—as an offence (or offence element) or as a defence, if discussing the criminal law—in any given context. We learned in Chapter 2 that these notions are always to be grasped relative to some given decision-type in some given decision-making context. The relevant normative queries should therefore also be formulated in view of some decision-type in some sufficiently described context. If, together with the substance of our proof-based account, developed in Part II, we also recall the notion of a *ceteris ignotis* judgment, introduced and discussed in Chapter 6, then the suggestion is that we might be able to say that (a) no fact *F* ought to be a *P*-fact relative to some given decision *C* unless *F* is a member of a set *F*+ of facts such that, *ceteris ignotis*, *C* is the right decision to issue whenever the facts in *F*+ are the case; and that (b) for any such set *F*+ and the decision *C* to which it is relative, a fact *E* ought to be a *D*-fact relative to *C* if, *ceteris ignotis*, *C* ought *not* to be issued whenever *F* and *E*.

Second, if the proposed proof-based account is sound, it might point to a richer appreciation and reconstruction of the sort of normative message that law-making authorities may be thought to be communicating to their norm-subjects by selecting which facts are to count as *P*- or *D*-facts in different decision-making contexts. In criminal law, in particular, this may lead to an account very different from the traditional and received view that offence definitions must express or communicate normative judgments about what one always has reason not to do.

The exploration of these possibilities, however, would take us beyond the elucidation and defence of the proof-based account of exceptions in law, which was the driving purpose of this book.

Bibliography

Alchourrón, C. E. (1986). 'Conditionality and the Representation of Legal Norms' in A. A. Martino and F. S. Natali (eds), *Automated Analysis of Legal Texts: Logic, Informatics, Law*. Amsterdam: North-Holland, 175–86.

Alchourrón, C. E. (1991). 'Defeasibility'. Unpublished typescript.

Alchourrón, C. E. (1993). 'Philosophical Foundations of Deontic Logic and the Logic of Defeasible Conditionals' in J. C. Meyer and R. J. Wieringa (eds), *Deontic Logic in Computer Science: Normative System Specification*. Chichester: John Wiley & Sons, 43–84.

Alchourrón, C. E. (1996). 'On Law and Logic', *Ratio Juris* 9: 331–48.

Alchourrón, C. E. (2010). *Fundamentos para una Teoría General de Los Deberes*. Madrid: Marcial Pons.

Alchourrón, C. E. and Bulygin, E. (1971). *Normative Systems*. New York: Springer.

Alchourrón, C. E. and Bulygin, E. (1992). 'Limits of Logic and Legal Reasoning' in A. Martino (ed.), *Expert Systems in Law*. Amsterdam: Elsevier, 9–27.

Alexy, R. (1978/89). *A Theory of Legal Argumentation: The Theory of Rational Discourse as a Theory of Legal Justification*. Tr. R. Adler and N. MacCormick. Oxford: Oxford University Press (1989).

Aman, A. C. (1982). 'Administrative Equity: An Analysis of Exceptions to Administrative Rules', *Duke Law Journal* 31: 277–331.

Arena, F. J. (2008). 'La Identificación de la Acción Individual', *Analisi e Diritto* 203–27.

Ashford, H. A. and Risinger, D. M. (1969). 'Presumptions, Assumptions, and Due Process in Criminal Cases: A Theoretical Overview', *The Yale Law Journal* 79: 165–208.

Ashworth, A. (2006). 'Four Threats to the Presumption of Innocence', *The International Journal of Evidence & Proof* 10: 241–79.

Ashworth, A. and Horder, J. (2013). *Principles of Criminal Law*. Seventh edition. Oxford: Oxford University Press.

Ashworth, A. and Redmayne, M. (2010). *The Criminal Process*. Fourth edition. Oxford: Oxford University Press.

Atria, F. (2001). *On Law and Legal Reasoning*. Oxford: Hart Publishing.

Austin, J. L. (1957). 'A Plea for Excuses', reprinted in Austin (1979).

Austin, J. L. (1966). 'Three Ways of Spilling Ink', reprinted in Austin (1979).

Austin, J. L. (1975). *How to Do Things with Words*. Second edition. Oxford: Oxford University Press.

Austin, J. L. (1979). *Philosophical Papers*. Third edition. Oxford: Oxford University Press.

Baier, K. (1951). 'Decisions and Descriptions', *Mind* 60: 181–204.

Baier, K. (1970). 'Responsibility and Action' in M. Brand (ed.), *The Nature of Human Action*. Glenview: Scott, Foresman, 100–16.

Baier, K. (1972/98). 'Guilt and Responsibility' in P. A. French (ed.), *Individual and Collective Responsibility*. Second edition. Rochester: Schenkman Books, 93–116 (1998).

Baier, K. (1987). 'Moral and Legal Responsibility' in M. Siegler, S. Toulmin, F. E. Zimring, and K. F. Schaffner (eds), *Medical Innovation and Bad Outcomes: Legal, Social, and Ethical Responses*. Ann Arbor: Health Administration Press, 101–29.

Baker, G. P. (1977). 'Defeasibility and Meaning' in P. M. S. Hacker and J. Raz (eds), *Law, Morality, and Society: Essays in Honour of H. L. A. Hart*. Oxford: Clarendon Press, 26–57.

Bańkowski, Z. (1981). 'The Value of Truth: Fact Scepticism Revisited', *Legal Studies* 1: 257–66.

Bayles, M. D. (1992). *Hart's Legal Philosophy: An Examination*. Dordrecht: Kluwer.

Bayón. J. C. (1991). *La Normatividad del Derecho: Deber Jurídico y Razones para la Acción*. Madrid: Centro de Estudios Constitucionales.

Bayón, J. C. (2000). 'Derrotabilidad, Indeterminación del Derecho y Positivismo Jurídico', reprinted in Bayón and Rodríguez (2003).

Bayón, J. C. (2001). 'Why is Legal Reasoning Defeasible?' in A. Soeteman (ed.), *Pluralism and Law*. Dordrecht: Kluwer, 327–46.

Bayón, J. C. and Rodríguez, J. L. (2003). *Relevancia Normativa en la Justificación de las Decisiones Judiciales*. Ed. P. Gaido, R. Sánchez Brígido, and H. O. Seleme. Bogotá: Universidad Externado de Colombia.

Beardsley, E. L. (1969). 'A Plea for Deserts', *American Philosophical Quarterly* 6: 33–42.

Beardsley, E. L. (1970). 'Moral Disapproval and Moral Indignation', *Philosophy and Phenomenological Research* 31: 161–76.

Beardsley, E. L. (1979). 'Blaming', *Philosophia* 8: 573–83.

Beling, E. (1906). *Die Lehre vom Verbrechen*. Tübingen: J. C. B. Mohr.

Beling, E. (1930a). *Grundzüge des Strafrechts*. Tübingen: J. C. B. Mohr.

Beling, E. (1930b). *Die Lehre vom Tatbestand*. Tübingen: J. C. B. Mohr.

Belton, R. (1981). 'Burdens of Pleading and Proof in Discrimination Cases: Toward a Theory of Procedural Justice', *Vanderbilt Law Review* 34: 1205–87.

Bennett, J. (1980). 'Accountability' in Z. van Straaten (ed.), *Philosophical Subjects: Essays Presented to P. F. Strawson*. Oxford: Clarendon Press, 14–47.

Binding, K. (1872). *Die Normen und ihre Übertretung: Eine Untersuchung über die Rechtsmässige Handlung und die Arten des Delikts. Erster Band: Normen und Strafgesetze*. Leipzig: Wilhelm Engelmann.

Birch, D. J. (1988). 'Hunting the Snark: The Elusive Statutory Exception', *The Criminal Law Review* 221–32.

Bix, B. H. (2012). 'Defeasibility and Open Texture' in J. Ferrer Beltrán and G. B. Ratti (eds), *The Logic of Legal Requirements: Essays on Defeasibility*. Oxford: Oxford University Press, 193–201.

Blöser, C. (2013). 'The Defeasible Structure of Ascription of Responsibility', *Grazer Philosophische Studien* 87: 129–50.

Bohlander, M. (2009). *Principles of German Criminal Law*. Oxford: Hart Publishing.

Bolding, P. O. (1960). 'Aspects of the Burden of Proof', *Scandinavian Studies in Law* 4: 11–27.

Boonin, L. G. (1966). 'Concerning the Defeasibility of Legal Rules', *Philosophy and Phenomenological Research* 26: 371–8.

Brand, M. (1971). 'The Language of Not Doing', *American Philosophical Quarterly* 8: 45–53.

Brandt, R. B. (1958). 'Blameworthiness and Obligation' in A. I. Melden (ed.), *Essays in Moral Philosophy*. Seattle: University of Washington Press, 3–39.

Brito, J. S. (1995). 'Etablierung des Strafrechtssystems zwischen formaler Begriffsjurisprudenz und funktionalistischer Auflösung' in B. Schünemann and J. F. Dias (eds), *Bausteine des europäischen Strafrechts*. Cologne: Carl Heymann, 71–86.

Brożek, B. (2004). *Defeasibility of Legal Reasoning*. Krakow: Zakamycze.

Brożek, B. (2005). 'Law, Defeasibility, and Logical Consequence' in S. Eng (ed.), *Proceedings of the 21st IVR World Congress, Part 2: Law and Practice*. Stuttgart: Franz Steiner, 69–78.

Brożek, B. (2008). 'Revisability versus Defeasibility', *Northern Ireland Legal Quarterly* 59: 139–47.

Bulygin, E. (1985). 'Norms and Logic', *Law and Philosophy* 4: 145–63.

Bulygin, E. (1994). 'On Legal Interpretation' in H. J. Koch and U. Neumann (eds), *Praktische Vernunft und Rechtsanwendung*. Stuttgart: Franz Steiner, 11–22.

Bulygin, E. (1995). 'Cognition and Interpretation of Law' in L. Gianformaggio and S. L. Paulson (eds), *Cognition and Interpretation of Law*. Torino: Giappichelli, 11–35.

Bulygin, E. (2003). 'Review of Jaap Hage's Law and Defeasibility', *Artificial Intelligence and Law* 11: 245–50.

Campbell, K. (1987). 'Offence and Defence' in I. H. Dennis (ed.), *Criminal Law and Justice*. London: Sweet and Maxwell, 73–86.

Cane, P. (2002). *Responsibility in Law and Morality*. Oxford: Hart Publishing.

Caracciolo, R. (1988). 'Justificación Normativa y Pertenencia', reprinted in Caracciolo (2009).

Caracciolo, R. (2009). *El Derecho desde la Filosofía: Ensayos*. Madrid: Centro de Estudios Políticos y Constitucionales.

Carnota, R. J. (1995). 'Lógica e Inteligencia Artificial' in C. E. Alchourrón, J. M. Méndez, and R. Orayen (eds), *Enciclopedia Iberoamericana de Filosofía, Volume 7: Lógica*. Madrid: Trotta, 143–83.

Celano, B. (2012). 'True Exceptions: Defeasibility and Particularism' in J. Ferrer Beltrán and G. B. Ratti (eds), *The Logic of Legal Requirements: Essays on Defeasibility*. Oxford: Oxford University Press, 268–87.

Chapman, B. (1998a). 'Law Games: Defeasible Rules and Revisable Rationality', *Law and Philosophy* 17: 443–80.

Chapman, B. (1998b). 'Law, Incommensurability, and Conceptually Sequenced Argument', *University of Pennsylvania Law Review* 146: 1487–528.

Chapman, B. (1998c). 'More Easily Done Than Said: Rules, Reasons, and Rational Choice', *Oxford Journal of Legal Studies* 18: 293–329.

Chapman, B. (2012). 'Defeasible Legal Rules' in J. Ferrer Beltrán and G. B. Ratti (eds), *The Logic of Legal Requirements: Essays on Defeasibility*. Oxford: Oxford University Press, 401–15.

Cherry, C. (1974). 'The Limits of Defeasibility', *Analysis* 34: 101–7.

Chesñevar, C. I., Maguitman, A. G., and Loui, R. P. (2001). 'Logical Models of Argument', *ACM Computer Surveys* 32: 337–83.

Chiassoni, P. (2012). 'Defeasibility and Legal Indeterminacy' in J. Ferrer Beltrán and G. B. Ratti (eds), *The Logic of Legal Requirements: Essays on Defeasibility*. Oxford: Oxford University Press, 151–92.

Chisholm, R. M. (1964). 'The Descriptive Element in the Concept of Action', *The Journal of Philosophy* 61: 613–25.

Coetzee, J. M. (1990). *Age of Iron*. London: Martin Secker & Warburg.

Coetzee, J. M. (2009). *Summertime*. London: Harvill Secker.

Coetzee, J. M. (2013). *The Childhood of Jesus*. London: Harvill Secker.

Cohen, L. J. (1991). 'Should a Jury Say What it Believes or What it Accepts?', *Cardozo Law Review* 13: 465–83.

Cohen, L. J. (1992). *An Essay on Belief and Acceptance*. Oxford: Clarendon Press.

Comanducci, P. (2010). 'Alcuni Problemi Concettuali Relativi alla Aplicazione del Diritto', *Diritto e Questioni Pubbliche* 10: 121–34.

Corbin, A. L. (1919). 'Legal Analysis and Terminology', *The Yale Law Journal* 29: 163–73.

Coval, S. and Smith, J. C. (1986). *Law and its Presuppositions: Actions, Agents, and Rules*. London: Routledge and Kegan Paul.

Coval, S., Smith, J. C., and Burns, P. (1980). 'The Concept of Action and its Juridical Significance', *The University of Toronto Law Journal* 30: 199–224.

Crown Prosecution Service. (2004). *The Code for Crown Prosecutors*. London: CPS Communication Division.

Crown Prosecution Service. (2013). *The Code for Crown Prosecutors*. London: CPS Communication Division.

Cruz, M. (1990). 'Origen y Desembocadura de la Acción: El Sujeto Inevitable', *Crítica. Revista Hispanoamericana de Filosofía* 22: 97–120.

Davis, P. E. (1962). '"Action" and "Cause of Action"', *Mind* 71: 93–5.

Dempsey, M. M. and Herring, J. (2007). 'Why Sexual Penetration Requires Justification', *Oxford Journal of Legal Studies* 27: 467–91.

Denaro, P. (2012). 'Moral Harm and Moral Responsibility: A Defence of Ascriptivism', *Ratio Juris* 25: 149–79.

Duarte d'Almeida, L. (2011). 'Legal Statements and Normative Language', *Law and Philosophy* 30: 167–99.

Duarte d'Almeida, L. (2012). '"O Call Me Not to Justify the Wrong": Criminal Answerability and the Offence/Defence Distinction', *Criminal Law and Philosophy* 6: 227–45.

Duarte d'Almeida, L. (2013). 'A Proof-Based Account of Legal Exceptions', *Oxford Journal of Legal Studies* 33: 133–68.

Duarte d'Almeida, L. (2014a). 'Exceptions and Supersession', *Ragion Pratica* 42: 187–203.

Duarte d'Almeida, L. (2014b). 'The Problem of Defeasibility and the Problems of "Defeasibility"', *Jurisprudence* 5: 401–08.

Duarte d'Almeida, L. (2014c). 'Substantive Norms and Substantive Questions', *Analisi e Diritto*: 11–27.

Duarte d'Almeida, L. (2015a). 'Defining "Defences"' in A. Dyson, J. Goudkamp, and F. Wilmot-Smith (eds), *Defences in Tort*. Oxford: Hart Publishing, 35–52.

Duarte d'Almeida, L. (2015b). 'Geach on Ascriptivism: Beside the "Point"' (typescript, on file with the author).

Dubber, M. D. (2005). 'The Promise of German Criminal Law: A Science of Crime and Punishment', *German Law Journal* 6: 1049–71.

Duff, R. A. (1982). 'Intention, Responsibility, and Double Effect', *The Philosophical Quarterly* 32: 1–16.

Duff, R. A. (1988). [Review of Coval and Smith (1986)], *The Philosophical Quarterly* 152: 378–81.

Duff, R. A. (1990). *Intention, Agency, and Criminal Liability: Philosophy of Action and the Criminal Law*. Oxford: Blackwell.

Duff, R. A. (1996). *Criminal Attempts*. Oxford: Oxford University Press.

Duff, R. A. (2005). 'Strict Liability, Legal Presumptions, and the Presumption of Innocence' in A. P. Simester (ed.), *Appraising Strict Liability*. Oxford: Oxford University Press, 125–49.

Duff, R. A. (2007). *Answering for Crime: Responsibility and Liability in the Criminal Law*. Oxford: Hart Publishing.

Duff, R. A. (2008). 'Responsibility and Liability in Criminal Law' in M. H. Kramer, C. Grant, B. Colburn, and A. Hatzistavrou (eds), *The Legacy of H.L.A. Hart: Legal, Political, and Moral Philosophy*. Oxford: Oxford University Press, 101–19.

Duff, R. A. (2009). 'Legal and Moral Responsibility', *Philosophy Compass* 4: 978–86.

Duff, R. A. (2012). 'Presuming Innocence' in L. Zedner and J. V. Roberts (eds), *Principles and Values in Criminal Law and Criminal Justice: Essays in Honour of Andrew Ashworth*. Oxford: Oxford University Press, 51–66.

Duff, R. A., Farmer, L., Marshall, S., and Tadros, V. (2007). *The Trial on Trial, Volume Three: Towards a Normative Theory of the Criminal Trial*. Oxford: Hart Publishing.

Dworkin, R. (1967). 'The Model of Rules I', reprinted in Dworkin (1977).

Dworkin, R. (1972). 'The Model of Rules II', reprinted in Dworkin (1977).

Dworkin, R. (1977). *Taking Rights Seriously*. Cambridge, Mass.: Harvard University Press.

Engisch, K. (1974). 'Logische Überlegungen zur Verbrechensdefinition' in G. Stratenwerth, A. Kaufmann, G. Geilen, H.-J. Hirsch, H. L. Schreiber, G. Jakobs, and F. Loos (eds), *Festschrift für Hans Welzel zum 70. Geburtstag*, Berlin: Walter de Gruyter, 343–78.

Epstein, R. A. (1973). 'Pleadings and Presumptions', *The University of Chicago Law Review* 40: 556–82.

Epstein, R. A. (2005). 'The Not So Minimum Content of Natural Law', *Oxford Journal of Legal Studies* 25: 219–55.

Eshleman, A. (2014). 'Moral Responsibility' in E. N. Zalta (ed.), *The Stanford Enciclopedia of Philosophy*. Summer 2014 edition, available at: <http://plato.stanford.edu/archives/sum2014/entries/moral-responsibility/>, accessed 13 January 2015.

Feinberg, J. (1965). 'Action and Responsibility', reprinted in Feinberg (1970).

Feinberg, J. (1970). *Doing and Deserving: Essays in the Theory of Responsibility*. Princeton: Princeton University Press.

Feinberg, J. (1988a). 'Responsibility *Tout Court*', *Philosophy Research Archives* 14: 73–92.

Feinberg, J. (1988b). 'Responsibility for the Future', *Philosophy Research Archives* 14: 93–113.

Ferrer Beltrán, J. (2005). *Prueba y Verdad en el Derecho*. Second edition. Madrid: Marcial Pons.

Ferrer Beltrán, J. (2006). 'Legal Proof and Fact Finders' Beliefs', *Legal Theory* 12: 293–314.

Ferrer Beltrán, J. (2007). *La Valoración Racional de la Prueba*. Madrid: Marcial Pons.

Ferrer Beltrán, J. and Ratti, G. B. (2012). 'Legal Defeasibility: An Introduction' in J. Ferrer Beltrán and G. B. Ratti (eds), *The Logic of Legal Requirements: Essays on Defeasibility*. Oxford: Oxford University Press, 1–7.

Finkelstein, C. O. (1999). 'When the Rule Swallows the Exception' in L. Meyer (ed.), *Rules and Reasoning: Essays in Honour of Fred Schauer*. Oxford: Hart Publishing, 145–75.

Finkelstein, C. O. (2005). 'Responsibility for Unintended Consequences', *Ohio State Journal of Criminal Responsibility* 2: 579–99.

Fischer, J. M. (1987). 'Responsiveness and Moral Responsibility', reprinted in Fischer (2006).

Fischer, J. M. (2006). *My Way: Essays on Moral Responsibility*. Oxford: Oxford University Press.

Fletcher, G. P. (1968). 'Two Kinds of Legal Rules: A Comparative Study of Burden-of-Persuasion Practices in Criminal Cases', *The Yale Law Journal* 70: 880–935.

Fletcher, G. P. (1978/2000). *Rethinking Criminal Law*. Oxford: Oxford University Press (2000).

Fletcher, G. P. (1993). 'The Nature of Justification' in S. Shute, J. Gardner, and J. Horder (eds), *Action and Value in Criminal Law*. Oxford: Clarendon Press, 175–86.

Fletcher, G. P. (2001). 'Criminal Theory in the Twentieth Century', *Theoretical Inquiries in Law* 2: 265–86.

Fletcher, G. P. (2007). *The Grammar of The Criminal Law, Volume 1: Foundations*. Oxford: Oxford University Press.

Freeman, J. B. (1991). *Dialectics and the Macrostructure of Arguments: A Theory of Argument Structure*. Berlin: Foris.

Fritz, G. (2005). 'On Answering Accusations in Controversies', *Studies in Communication Sciences* 5: 151–62.

Gardner, J. (1996). 'Justifications and Reasons', reprinted in Gardner (2007b).

Gardner, J. (2002). 'In Defence of Defences', reprinted in Gardner (2007b).

Gardner, J. (2003). 'The Mark of Responsibility', reprinted in Gardner (2007b).

Gardner, J. (2004). 'Fletcher on Offences and Defences', reprinted in Gardner (2007b).

Gardner, J. (2007a). 'Nearly Natural Law', reprinted in Gardner (2012).

Gardner, J. (2007b). *Offences and Defences: Selected Essays in the Philosophy of Criminal Law*. Oxford: Oxford University Press.

Gardner, J. (2008). 'Hart and Feinberg on Responsibility' in M. H. Kramer, C. Grant, B. Colburn, and A. Hatzistavrou (eds), *The Legacy of H.L.A. Hart: Legal, Political, and Moral Philosophy*. Oxford: Oxford University Press, 121–40.

Gardner, J. (2012). *Law as a Leap of Faith: Essays on Law in General*. Oxford University Press.

Garzón Valdés, E. (1997). 'Über Verantwortungssätze' in E. Garzón Valdés, W. Krawietz, G. H. von Wright, and R. Zimmerling (eds), *Normative Systems in Legal and Moral Theory*. Berlin: Duncker & Humblot, 111–40.

Garzón Valdés, E., Spolanski, N. E., Nino, C. S., and Urquijo, M. E. (2007). *Lenguaje y Acción Humana*. Buenos Aires: Ad Hoc.

Geach, P. T. (1960). 'Ascriptivism', reprinted in Geach (1972).

Geach, P. T. (1965). 'Assertion', reprinted in Geach (1972).

Geach, P. T. (1972). *Logic Matters*. Oxford: Blackwell.

Giesen, I. (2009). 'The Burden of Proof and other Procedural Devices in Tort Law' in H. Koziol and B. C. Steininger (eds), *European Tort Law 2008*. Vienna: Springer, 49–67.

Gizbert-Studnicki, T. (1976). 'Hart on Ascription of Responsibility', *Archivum Iuridicum Cracoviense* 9: 133–40.

Godden, D. M. and Walton, D. (2008). 'Defeasibility in Judicial Opinion: Logical or Procedural?', *Informal Logic* 28: 6–19.

Golding, M. P. (2005). 'Responsibility' in M. P. Golding and W. A. Edmundson (eds), *The Blackwell Guide to Philosophy of Law and Legal Theory*. Malden: Blackwell, 221–35.

González Lagier, D. (2003). *The Paradoxes of Human Action: Human Action, Law, and Philosophy*. Dordrecht: Kluwer.

Gordon, T. F. (1987). 'OBLOG-2: A Hybrid Knowledge Representation System for Defeasible Reasoning' in *Proceedings of the First International Conference on Artificial Intelligence and Law*. New York: ACM Press, 231–9.

Gordon, T. F. (1988). 'The Importance of Nonmonotonicity for Legal Reasoning' in H. Fiedler, F. Haft, and R. Traunmüller (eds), *Expert Systems in Law: Impacts on Legal Theory and Computer Law*. Tübingen: Attempto, 111–26.

Gordon, T. F. (1995). *The Pleadings Game: An Artificial Intelligence Model of Procedural Justice*. Dordrecht: Kluwer.

Goudkamp, J. (2013). *Tort Law Defences*. Oxford: Hart Publishing.

Graham, K. (1977). *J. L. Austin: A Critique of Ordinary Language Philosophy*. Sussex: The Harvester Press.

Grice, P. (1989). *Studies in the Way of Words*. Cambridge, Mass.: Harvard University Press.

Guastini, R. (2012). 'Defeasibility, Axiological Gaps, and Interpretation' in J. Ferrer Beltrán and G. B. Ratti (eds), *The Logic of Legal Requirements: Essays on Defeasibility*. Oxford: Oxford University Press, 182–92.

Hage, J. (2003). 'Law and Defeasibility', *Artificial Intelligence and Law* 11: 221–43.

Hage, J. (2005). *Studies in Legal Logic*. Dordrecht: Springer.

Haines, N. (1955). 'Responsibility and Accountability', *Philosophy* 30: 141–63.

Hall, J. (1966). 'Analytic Philosophy and Jurisprudence', *Ethics* 77: 14–28.

Hampshire, S. and Hart, H. L. A. (1958). 'Decision, Intention, and Certainty', *Mind* 67: 1–12.

Harré, R. (1982). 'Theoretical Preliminaries to the Study of Action' in M. von Cranach and R. Harré (eds), *The Analysis of Action: Recent Theoretical and Empirical Advances*. Cambridge: Cambridge University Press, 5–33.

Hart, H. L. A. (1949). 'The Ascription of Responsibility and Rights', *Proceedings of the Aristotelian Society* 49: 171–94.

Hart, H. L. A. (1951). 'The Ascription of Responsibility and Rights' in A. Flew (ed.), *Logic and Language: First Series*. Oxford: Basil Blackwell, 145–66.

Hart, H. L. A. (1957). 'Legal Responsibility and Excuses', reprinted in Hart (1968/2008).

Hart, H. L. A. (1961/2012). *The Concept of Law*. Third edition. Oxford: Oxford University Press (2012).

Hart, H. L. A. (1961b). 'Negligence, *Mens Rea*, and Criminal Responsibility', reprinted in Hart (1968/2008).

Hart, H. L. A. (1965). 'Changing Conceptions of Responsibility', reprinted in Hart (1968/2008).

Hart, H. L. A. (1967). 'Intention and Punishment', reprinted in Hart (1968/2008).

Hart, H. L. A. (1968/2008). *Punishment and Responsibility: Essays in the Philosophy of Law*. Second edition. Oxford: Oxford University Press (2008).

Hart, H. L. A. (1969). 'Acts of Will and Legal Responsibility' in D. F. Pears (ed.), *Freedom and the Will*. London: MacMillan, 38–47.

Hassemer, W. (1990). *Einführung in die Grundlagen des Strafrechts*. Second edition. Munich: Beck.

Heinz, L. L. (1981). 'The Logic of Defenses', *American Philosophical Quarterly* 18: 243–8.

Helm, P. (1968). 'Defeasibility and Open Texture', *Analysis* 28: 173–5.

Helm, P. (1971). 'Professor Hart on Action and Property', *Mind* 80: 427–31.

Hirsch, H. J. (1960). *Die Lehre von den negative Tatbestandsmerkmalen*. Bonn: Ludwig Röhrscheid.

Ho, H. L. (2008). *A Philosophy of Evidence Law: Justice in the Search for Truth*. Oxford: Oxford University Press.

Ho, H. L. (2011). 'Comparative Observations on the Burden of Proof for Criminal Defences', *International Commentary on Evidence* 9:2, Article 2.

Hohfeld, W. N. (1923). *Fundamental Legal Conceptions as Applied in Judicial Reasoning and Other Essays*. Ed. W. W. Cook. New Haven: Yale University Press.

Holdcroft, D. (1969). 'A Plea for Excuses?', *Philosophy* 44: 314–30.

Holton, R. (2002). 'Principles and Particularisms', *Proceedings of the Aristotelian Society: Supplementary Volumes* 67: 191–209.

Holton, R. (2010). 'The Exception Proves the Rule', *The Journal of Political Philosophy* 18: 369–88.

Holton, R. (2011). 'Modeling Legal Rules' in A. Marmor and S. Soames (eds), *Philosophical Foundations of Language in the Law*. Oxford: Oxford University Press, 165–83.

Honoré, A. M. (1977). 'Real Laws', reprinted in Honoré (1987).

Honoré, A. M. (1987). *Making Law Bind: Essays Legal and Philosophical*. Oxford: Clarendon Press.

Hornsby, J. (1993). 'On What is Intentionally Done' in S. Shute, J. Gardner, and J. Horder (eds), *Action and Value in Criminal Law*. Oxford: Oxford University Press, 55–74.

Horovitz, J. (1972). *Law and Logic: A Critical Account of Legal Argument*. Vienna: Springer.

Houlgate, L. D. (1968). 'Knowledge and Responsibility', *American Philosophical Quarterly* 5: 109–16.

Howarth, W. (1981). 'The Feasibility of Defeasibility', *The Cambrian Law Review* 12: 33–41.

Hruschka, J. (1984). 'Ordentliche und außerordentliche Zurechnung bei Pufendorf', *Zeitschrift für die gesamte Strafrechtswissenschaft* 96: 661–702.

Hruschka, J. (1986). 'Imputation', *Brigham Young University Law Review* 669–710.

Huigens, K. (2009). 'The Continuity of Justification Defenses', *University of Illinois Law Review* 3: 627–95.

Husak, D. (1987). *Philosophy of Criminal Law*. New Jersey: Rowman and Littlefield.

Husak, D. (2005). 'On the Supposed Priority of Justification to Excuse', reprinted in Husak (2010).

Husak, D. (2010). *The Philosophy of Criminal Law: Selected Essays* Oxford: Oxford University Press.

Husak, D. (2011). 'The De Minimis "Defence" to Criminal Liability' in R. A. Duff and S. P. Green (eds), *Philosophical Foundations of Criminal Law*. Oxford: Oxford University Press, 328–51.

Jackson, B. S. (1998). 'Truth or Proof? The Criminal Verdict', *International Journal for the Semiotics of Law* 11: 227–73.

Jackson, J. (1983). 'Questions of Fact and Questions of Law' in W. Twining (ed.), *Facts in Law*. Wiesbaden: Franz Steiner, 85–100.

Jackson, J. D. (2004). 'Managing Uncertainty and Finality: The Function of the Criminal Trial in Legal Inquiry' in R. A. Duff, L. Farmer, S. Marshall, and V. Tadros (eds), *The Trial on Trial, Volume One: Truth and Due Process*. Oxford: Hart Publishing, 121–45.

James, F. Jr (1961). 'Burdens of Proof', *Virginia Law Review* 47: 51–70.

Jeffries, J. C. and Stephan, P. B. III (1979). 'Defenses, Presumptions, and Burden of Proof in the Criminal Law', *The Yale Law Journal* 88: 1325–407.

Jescheck, J.-H. and Weigend, T. (1996). *Lehrburch des Strafrechts: Allgemeiner Teil*. Fifth edition. Berlin: Duncker & Humblot.

Jori, M. (1985). *Saggi di Metagiurisprudenza*. Milan: Giuffrè.

Jung, H. (2002). 'Making Sense of the German "Straftatlehre": A Personal Account' in P. Asp, C. E. Herlitz, and L. Homqvist (eds), *Flores Juris et Legum: Festskrift till Nils Jareborg*. Uppsala: Iustus Vörlag, 369–84.

Kauffeld, F. J. (1998). 'Presumptions and the Distribution of Argumentative Burdens in Acts of Proposing and Accusing', *Argumentation* 12: 245–66.

Kelsen, H. (1944a). *Peace Through Law*. Chapel Hill: The University of North Carolina Press.

Kelsen, H. (1944b). 'The Principle of Sovereign Equality of States as a Basis for International Organization', *The Yale Law Journal* 53: 207–20.

Kelsen, H. (1945). *General Theory of Law and State*. Cambridge, Mass.: Harvard University Press.

Kelsen, H. (1960/67). *Pure Theory of Law*. Tr. M. Knight. Berkeley: University of California Press.

Kelsen, H. (1979/91). *General Theory of Norms*. Tr. M. Hartney. Oxford: Clarendon Press.

Kindhäuser, U. K. (1980). *Intentionale Handlung: Sprachphilosophische Untersuchungen zum Verständnis von Handlung im Strafrecht*. Berlin: Duncker & Humblot.

Kramer, M. H. (2005). 'Moral Rights and the Limits of the Ought-Implies-Can Principle: Why Impeccable Precautions are no Excuse', *Inquiry* 48: 307–55.

Kramer, M. H. (2012). 'Michael Moore on Torture, Morality, and Law', *Ratio Juris* 25: 472–95.

Krey, V. (2003). *German Criminal Law: General Part*. Volume 2. Stuttgart: W Kolhammer.

Lacey, N. (2004). *A Life of H.L.A. Hart: The Nightmare and the Noble Dream*. Oxford: Oxford University Press.

Ladd, J. (1965). 'The Ethical Dimensions of the Concept of Action', *The Journal of Philosophy* 62: 633–45.

Langford, G. (1971). *Human Action*. Garden City: Doubleday.

Laudan, L. (2006). *Truth, Error, and Criminal Law: An Essay in Legal Epistemology*. Cambridge: Cambridge University Press.

Leader-Elliott, I. (2010). 'A Critical Reading of RA Duff, *Answering for Crime*', *Adelaide Law Review* 31: 47–78.

Loui, R. P. (1995). 'Hart's Critics on Defeasible Concepts and Ascriptivism' in *Proceedings of the Fifth International Conference on Artificial Intelligence and Law*. New York: ACM Press, 21–30.

Lucas, J. R. (1977). 'The Ascription of Actions'. Available at: <http://users.ox.ac.uk/~jrlucas/ascript.html>, accessed 13 January 2015.

Lucas, J. R. (1993). *Responsibility*. Oxford: Clarendon Press.

Luzzati, C. (1990). *La Vaghezza delle Norme: Un'Analisi del Linguaggio Giuridico*. Milan: Giuffrè.

MacCormick, N. (1974). 'Law as Institutional Fact', *The Law Quarterly Review* 90: 102–29.

MacCormick, N. (1992). 'Legal Deduction, Legal Predicates, and Expert Systems', *International Journal for the Semiotics of Law* 5: 181–202.

MacCormick, N. (1994). *Legal Reasoning and Legal Theory*. Oxford: Clarendon Press.

MacCormick, N. (1995). 'Defeasibility in Law and Logic' in Z. Bańkowski, I. White, and U. Hahn (eds), *Informatics and the Foundations of Legal Reasoning*. Dordrecht: Kluwer, 99–117.

MacCormick, N. (2005). *Rhetoric and the Rule of Law: A Theory of Legal Reasoning*. Oxford: Oxford University Press.

MacCormick, N. (2008). *H.L.A. Hart*. Second edition. Stanford: Stanford University Press.

Mackie, J. L. (1955). 'Responsibility and Language', reprinted in Mackie (1985).

Mackie, J. L. (1985). *Persons and Values: Selected Papers.* Volume II. Oxford: Clarendon Press.

Macnamara, C. (2011). 'Holding Others Responsible', *Philosophical Studies* 152: 81–102.

Mañalich, J. P. (2009). *Nötigung und Verantwortung: Rechtstheoretische Untersuchungen zum präskriptiven und askriptiven Nötigungsbegriff im Strafrecht.* Baden-Baden: Nomos.

Mandelbaum, M. (1960). 'Determinism and Moral Responsibility', *Ethics* 70: 204–19.

Martin, M. (1987). *The Legal Philosophy of H.L.A. Hart: A Critical Appraisal.* Philadelphia: Temple University Press.

Mayer, M. E. (1923). *Der Allgemeine Teil des Deutschen Strafrechts.* Heidelberg: Carl Winters.

McCarty, L. T. (1991). 'Defeasible Legal Rules'. Unpublished typescript.

McNaughton, J. T. (1955). 'Burden of Production of Evidence: A Function of the Burden of Persuasion', *Harvard Law Review* 68: 1382–91.

Mendonca, D. (2012). 'Exceptions' in J. Ferrer Beltrán and G. B. Ratti (eds), *The Logic of Legal Requirements: Essays on Defeasibility.* Oxford: Oxford University Press, 202–8.

Mezger, E. (1926). 'Vom Sinn der strafrechtlichen Tatbestände' in *Festschrift für Ludwig Traeger zum 70. Geburtstage.* Berlin: Georg Stilke, 187–230.

Mezger, E. (1949). *Strafrecht: Ein Lehrbuch.* Third edition. Berlin: Duncker & Humblot.

Miller, L. G. (1956). 'Rules and Exceptions', *Ethics* 66: 262–70.

Mirfield, P. (1988). 'The Legacy of *Hunt*', *Criminal Law Review* 19–30.

Mittermaier, C. J. A. (1846). *Das Deutsche Strafverfahren.* Volume 2. Heildelberg: JCB Mohr.

Moore, M. S. (1980). 'Responsibility and the Unconscious', *Southern California Law Review* 53: 1563–675.

Moore, M. S. (1981). 'The Semantics of Judging', *Southern California Law Review* 54: 151–294.

Moore, M. S. (1993). *Act and Crime: The Philosophy of Action and its Implications for Criminal Law.* Oxford: Oxford University Press.

Moreso, J. J. (2001). 'Principio de Legalidad y Causas de Justificación', reprinted in Moreso (2009).

Moreso, J. J. (2004). 'El Positivismo Jurídico y la Aplicación del Derecho', *Doxa: Cuadernos de Filosofía del Derecho* 24: 45–62.

Moreso, J. J. (2009). *La Constitución: Modelo Para Armar,* Madrid: Marcial Pons.

Moreso, J. J. (2012). 'Legal Defeasibility and the Connection Between Law and Morality' in J. Ferrer Beltrán and G. B. Ratti (eds), *The Logic of Legal Requirements: Essays on Defeasibility.* Oxford: Oxford University Press, 225–37.

Moreso, J. J. and Rodríguez, J. L. (2010). 'Carlos E. Alchourrón y la Máxima de la Mutilación Mínima' in Alchourrón (2010).

Múrias, P. F. (2000). *Por uma Distribuição Fundamentada do Ónus da Prova*. Lisbon: Lex.

Nakhnikian, G. (1957). 'Contemporary Ethical Theories and Jurisprudence', *Natural Law Forum* 2: 4–40.

Naucke, W. (1984). 'An Insider's Perspective on the Significance of the German Criminal Theory's General System for Analyzing Criminal Acts', *Brigham Young University Law Review* 3: 305–21.

Navarro, P. E. and Rodríguez, J. L. (2000). 'Derrotabilidad y Sistematización de Normas Jurídicas', *Isonomía* 13: 61–85.

Navarro, P. E. and Rodríguez, J. L. (2014). *Deontic Logic and Legal Systems*. Cambridge: Cambridge University Press.

Nino, C. S. (1980). *Los Límites de la Responsabilidad Penal: Una Teoria Liberal del Delito*. Buenos Aires: Astrea.

Nino, C. S. (1987). *Introducción a la Filosofía de la Acción Humana*. Buenos Aires: Eudeba.

Nowell-Smith, P. H. (1976). 'Action and Responsibility' in M. Brand and D. Walton (eds), *Action Theory*. Dordrecht: Reidel, 311–22.

Oshana, M. A. (1997). 'Ascriptions of Responsibility', *American Philosophical Quarterly* 34: 71–83.

Paprzycka, K. (2008). 'Sneddon on Action and Responsibility', *Polish Journal of Philosophy* 2: 69–88.

Paprzycka, K. (2014). 'The Social Re-Construction of Agency' in M. C. Galavotti, D. Dieks, W. J. Gonzalez, S. Hartmann, T. Uebel, and M. Weber (eds), *New Directions in the Philosophy of Science*. Cham: Springer, 323–38.

Páramo Argüelles, J. R. (1984). *H.L.A. Hart y la Teoría Analítica del Derecho*. Madrid: Centro de Estudios Constitucionales.

Patton, T. E. (1956). 'Reasoning in Moral Matters', *The Journal of Philosophy* 53: 523–31.

Pennock, J. R. (1960). 'The Problem of Responsibility' in C. Friedrich (ed.), *Nomos III: Responsibility*. New York: The Liberal Arts Press, 3–27.

Pérez Bermejo, J. M. (2009). 'Normas Jurídicas, Conflictos y Derrotas: Entre Reglas Ad Hoc y *Sub Species Aeternitatis*', *Analisi e Diritto* 11–60.

Pérez Bermejo, J. M. (2012). 'Principles, Conflicts, and Defeats: An Approach from a Coherentist Theory' in J. Ferrer Beltrán and G. B. Ratti (eds), *The Logic of Legal Requirements: Essays on Defeasibility*. Oxford: Oxford University Press, 288–308.

Pintore, A. (1990). *La Teoria Analitica dei Concetti Giuridici*. Naples: Jovene.

Pitcher, G. (1960). 'Hart on Action and Responsibility', *The Philosophical Review* 69: 226–35.

Prakken, H. (1997). *Logical Tools for Modelling Legal Argument: A Study of Defeasible Reasoning in Law*. Dordrecht: Kluwer.

Prakken, H. (2001). 'Modelling Defeasibility in Law: Logic or Procedure?', *Fundamenta Informaticae* 48: 253–71.

Prakken, H. and Sartor, G. (2004). 'The Three Faces of Defeasibility in the Law', *Ratio Juris* 17: 118–39.

Prakken, H. and Sartor, G. (2007). 'Formalising Arguments About the Burden of Persuasion' in *Proceedings of the Eleventh International Conference on Artificial Intelligence and Law*. New York: ACM Press, 97–106.

Prakken, H. and Vreeswijk, G. (2002). 'Logics for Defeasible Argumentation' in D. M. Gabbay and F. Guenther (eds), *Handbook of Philosophical Logic*. Volume 4, second edition. Dordrecht: Springer, 219–318.

Ramsey, P. (1968). 'The Case of the Curious Exception' in G. H. Outka and P. Ramsey (eds), *Norm and Context in Christian Ethics*. London: SCM Press, 67–135.

Rankin, K. W. (1959). 'Ascription and Narration', *Indian Journal of Philosophy* 1: 87–101.

Rankin, K. W. (1961). *Choice and Chance: A Libertarian Analysis*. Oxford: Basil Blackwell.

Rankin, K. W. (1963). 'A Deterministic Windmill', *Australasian Journal of Philosophy* 41: 233–45.

Rayfield, D. (1968). 'Action', *Noûs* 2: 131–45.

Rayfield, D. (1971). *Action: An Analysis of the Concept*. The Hague: Martinus Nijhoff.

Raz, J. (1972). 'Legal Principles and the Limits of Law', *The Yale Law Journal* 81: 823–54.

Raz, J. (1979/2009). *The Authority of Law*. Second edition. Oxford: Oxford University Press (2009).

Raz, J. (1980). *The Concept of a Legal System*. Second edition. Oxford: Clarendon Press.

Redondo, M. C. (2005). 'Legal Reasons: Between Universalism and Particularism', *Journal of Moral Philosophy* 2: 47–68.

Roberts, P. (2005). 'Strict Liability and the Presumption of Innocence: An Exposé of Functionalist Assumptions' in A. P. Simester (ed.), *Appraising Strict Liability*. Oxford: Oxford University Press, 151–94.

Roberts, P. and Zuckerman, A. (2010). *Criminal Evidence*. Second edition. Oxford: Oxford University Press.

Robinson, P. H. (1997). *Structure and Function in Criminal Law*. Oxford: Clarendon Press.

Rodríguez, J. L. (1997). 'La Derrotabilidad de las Normas Jurídicas', reprinted in Bayón and Rodríguez (2003).

Rodríguez, J. L. (2000). 'Axiological Gaps and Normative Relevance', *Archiv für Rechts- und Sozialphilosophie* 86: 151–67.

Rodríguez, J. L. (2002). *Lógica de los Sistemas Jurídicos*. Madrid: Centro de Estudios Políticos y Constitucionales.

Rodríguez, J. L. (2003). 'Derrotabilidad e Indeterminación del Derecho. Respuesta a Juan Carlos Bayón' in Bayón and Rodríguez (2003).

Rodríguez, J. L. (2012). 'Against Defeasibility of Legal Rules' in J. Ferrer Beltrán and G. B. Ratti (eds), *The Logic of Legal Requirements: Essays on Defeasibility*, Oxford: Oxford University Press, 89–107.

Rodríguez, J. L. and Sucar, G. (1998). 'Las Trampas de la Derrotabilidad. Niveles de Análisis de la Indeterminación del Derecho', reprinted in Bayón and Rodríguez (2003).

Rosenberg, L. (1965). *Die Beweislast auf der Grundlage der Bürgerlichen Gesetzbuchs und der Zivilprozessordnung*. Fifth edition. Munich: Beck.

Roxin, C. (1970). *Offene Tatbestände und Rechtspflichtmerkmale*. Second edition. Berlin: Walter de Gruyter.

Roxin, C. (2006). *Strafrecht: Allgemeiner Teil. Band I–Grundlagen: Der Aufbau der Verbrechenslehre*. Fourth edition. Munich: Beck.

Sánchez Brígido, R. and Seleme, H. O. (2001). 'Justificación sin Verdad'. *Analisi e Diritto* 285–94.

Sartor, G. (1991a). 'Inconsistency and Legal Reasoning' in J. A. P. J. Breuker, R. V. de Mulder, and J. C. Hage (eds), *Legal Knowledge Based Systems Jurix 91. Model-based Legal Reasoning: The Foundation for Legal Knowledge Systems*. Lelystad: Koninklijke Vermande, 92–111.

Sartor, G. (1991b). 'The Structure of Norm-Conditions and Non-Monotonic Reasoning in Law' in *The Third International Conference on Artificial Intelligence & Law. Proceedings of the Conference*. New York: ACM Press, 155–64.

Sartor, G. (1993). 'Defeasibility in Legal Reasoning', *Rechtstheorie* 24: 281–316.

Sartor, G. (1994). 'A Formal Model of Legal Argumentation', *Ratio Juris* 7: 177–211.

Sartor, G. (1995). 'Defeasibility in Legal Reasoning' in Z. Bańkowski, I. White, and U. Hahn (eds), *Informatics and the Foundations of Legal Reasoning*. Dordrecht: Kluwer, 119–57.

Sartor, G. (2005). *Legal Reasoning: A Cognitive Approach to the Law*. Volume 5 of E. Pattaro (ed.), *A Treatise of Legal Philosophy and General Jurisprudence*. Dordrecht: Springer.

Sartor, G. (2008). 'Syllogism and Defeasibility: A Comment on Neil MacCormick's *Rhetoric and the Rule of Law*', *Northern Ireland Legal Quarterly* 59: 21–32.

Sartor, G. (2012). 'Defeasibility in Legal Reasoning' in J. Ferrer Beltrán and G. B. Ratti (eds), *The Logic of Legal Requirements: Essays on Defeasibility*. Oxford: Oxford University Press, 108–36.

Scanlon, T. M. (1998). *What We Owe to Each Other*. Cambridge, Mass.: Harvard University Press.

Schauer, F. (1991a). 'Exceptions', *The University of Chicago Law Review* 58: 871–99.

Schauer, F. (1991b). *Playing by the Rules: A Philosophical Examination of Rule-Based Decision-Making in Law and in Life*. Oxford: Clarendon Press.

Schauer, F. (1998). 'On The Supposed Defeasibility of Legal Rules', *Current Legal Problems* 51: 223–40.

Schauer, F. (2012). 'Is Defeasibility an Essential Property of Law?' in J. Ferrer Beltrán and G. B. Ratti (eds), *The Logic of Legal Requirements: Essays on Defeasibility*. Oxford: Oxford University Press, 77–88.

Schauer, F. (2013). 'The Open Texture of Law', *Grazer Philosophische Studien* 87: 197–215.

Searle, J. R. (1966). 'Assertions and Aberrations' in B. Williams and A. Montefiore (eds), *British Analytical Philosophy*. London: Routledge & Kegan Paul, 41–54.

Searle, J. R. (1969). *Speech Acts*. Cambridge: Cambridge University Press.

Searle, J. R. (1980). 'Prima-Facie Obligations' in Z. van Straaten (ed.), *Philosophical Subjects: Essays Presented to P. F. Strawson*. Oxford: Clarendon Press, 238–59.

Silving, H. (1947) 'Law and Fact in the Light of the Pure Theory of Law' in P. Sayre (ed.), *Interpretations of Modern Legal Philosophies: Essays in Honor of Roscoe Pound*. Oxford: Oxford University Press, 642–67.

Šimenc, M. (1991). 'Austin and Defeasible Concepts', *Mesotes* 1: 67–70.

Simester, A. P., Spencer, J. R., Sullivan, G. R., and Virgo, G. J. (2013). *Simester and Sullivan's Criminal Law: Theory and Doctrine*. Fifth edition. Oxford: Hart Publishing.

Singer, M. G. (1958). 'Moral Rules and Principles' in A. I. Melden (ed.), *Essays in Moral Philosophy*. Seattle: University of Washington Press, 160–97.

Smith, A. M. (2007). 'On Being Responsible and Holding Responsible', *The Journal of Ethics* 11: 465–84.

Smith, J. C. (1987). 'The Presumption of Innocence', *Northern Ireland Legal Quarterly* 38: 223–43.

Sneddon, A. (2006). *Action and Responsibility*. Dordrecht: Springer.

Soeteman, A. (1989). *Logic in Law: Remarks on Logic and Rationality in Normative Reasoning, Especially in Law*. Dordrecht: Kluwer.

Soeteman, A. (2003). 'Legal Logic? Or Can We Do Without?', *Artificial Intelligence and Law* 11: 197–210.

Stavropoulos, N. (1996). *Objectivity in Law*. Oxford: Clarendon Press.

Stein, A. (1991). 'After *Hunt*: The Burden of Proof, Risk of Non-Persuasion, and Judicial Pragmatism', *The Modern Law Review* 54: 570–6.

Stelmach, J. and Brożek, B. (2006). *Methods of Legal Reasoning*. Dordrecht: Springer.

Stoecker, R. (2007). 'Action and Responsibility–A Second Look at Ascriptivism' in C. Lumer and S. Nannini (eds), *Intentionality, Deliberation, and Autonomy: The Action-Theoretical Basis of Practical Philosophy*. Aldershot: Ashgate, 35–46.

Stoljar, S. (1959). 'Ascriptive and Prescriptive Responsibility', *Mind* 68: 350–60.

Stone, J. (1944). 'Burden of Proof and the Judicial Process: A Commentary on *Joseph Constantine Steamship, Ltd* v *Imperial Smelting Corporation, Ltd*', *The Law Quarterly Review* 60: 262–84.

Strawson, P. F. (1962). 'Freedom and Resentment', reprinted in Strawson (1974).

Strawson, P. F. (1974). *Freedom and Resentment and Other Essays*. London: Methuen.

Stumer, A. (2010). *The Presumption of Innocence: Evidential and Human Rights Perspectives*. Oxford: Hart Publishing.

Sugarman, D. (2005). 'Hart Interviewed: H. L. A. Hart in Conversation with David Sugarman', *Journal of Law and Society* 3: 267–93.

Susskind, R. E. (1987). *Expert Systems in Law*. Oxford: Clarendon Press.

Tadros, V. (2005). *Criminal Responsibility*. Oxford: Oxford University Press.

Tapper, C. (2010). *Cross & Tapper on Evidence*. Twelfth edition. Oxford: Oxford University Press.

Taruffo, M. (1992). *La Prova dei Fatti Giuridici*. Milan: Giuffrè.

Taylor, R. (1966). *Action and Purpose*. Englewood Cliffs: Prentice Hall.

Thayer, J. B. (1928). *A Preliminary Treatise on Evidence at the Common Law*. Boston: Little, Brown.

Tiersma, P. M. (1987). 'The Language of Defamation'. *Texas Law Review* 66: 303–50.

Toulmin, S. E. (1958/2004). *The Uses of Argument*. Updated edition. Cambridge: Cambridge University Press (2004).

Tur, R. H. S. (1977). 'Positivism, Principles, and Rules' in E. Attwooll (ed.), *Perspectives in Jurisprudence*. Glasgow: University of Glasgow Press, 42–78.

Tur, R. H. S. (1993). 'Subjectivism and Objectivism: Towards Synthesis' in S. Shute, J. Gardner, and J. Horder (eds), *Action and Value in Criminal Law*. Oxford: Clarendon Press, 213–37.

Tur, R. H. S. (2001a). 'Defeasibilism', *Oxford Journal of Legal Studies* 21: 355–68.

Tur, R. H. S. (2001b). '*Res Judicata* and Theories of Law', *Oxford University Commonwealth Law Journal* 1: 123–32.

Tur, R. H. S. (2003). 'Two Theories of Criminal Law', *SMU Law Review* 56: 797–818.

Tur, R. H. S. (2012). 'Defeasibility and Adjudication' in J. Ferrer Beltrán and G. B. Ratti (eds), *The Logic of Legal Requirements: Essays on Defeasibility*. Oxford: Oxford University Press, 362–76.

Tur, R. H. S. (2013). 'The Alternative Character of the Legal Norm: Kelsen as a Defeasibilist?' in L. Duarte d'Almeida, J. Gardner, and L. Green (eds), *Kelsen Revisited: New Essays on the Pure Theory of Law*. Oxford: Hart Publishing, 245–58.

Ullman-Margalit, E. (1983). 'On Presumption', *The Journal of Philosophy* 80: 143–63.

Wallace, R. J. (1994). *Responsibility and the Moral Sentiments.* Cambridge, Mass.: Harvard University Press.

Waluchow, W. (2012). 'Defeasibility and Legal Positivism' in J. Ferrer Beltrán and G. B. Ratti (eds), *The Logic of Legal Requirements: Essays on Defeasibility.* Oxford: Oxford University Press, 254–67.

Wang, P.-H. (2003). *Defeasibility in der juristischen Begründung.* Baden-Baden: Nomos.

Warnock, G. J. (1991). *J.L. Austin.* London: Routledge.

Watson, G. (1996). 'Two Faces of Responsibility', reprinted in Watson (2004).

Watson, G. (2004). *Agency and Answerability: Selected Essays.* Oxford: Clarendon Press.

Welzel, H. (1955). 'Die Regelung von Vorsatz und Irrtum im Strafrecht als legislatorisches Problem', *Zeitschrift für die gesamte Strafrechtswissenschaft* 76: 196–228.

Welzel, H. (1969). *Das Deutsche Strafrecht: Eine Systematische Darstellung.* Eleventh edition. Berlin: Walter de Gruyter.

Wessels, J., Beulke, W. and Satzger, H. (2013). *Strafrecht: Allgemeiner Teil. Die Straftat und ihr Aufbau.* Forty-third edition. Heidelberg: C. F. Müller.

Westen, P. (2008). 'Offences and Defences Again', *Oxford Journal of Legal Studies* 3: 563–84.

White, A. R. (1968). 'Introduction' in A. R. White (ed.), *The Philosophy of Action.* Oxford: Oxford University Press, 1–18.

White, A. R. (1985). *Grounds of Liability: An Introduction to the Philosophy of Law.* Oxford: Clarendon Press.

Whiteley, C. H. (1966). 'Responsibility', *Proceedings of the Aristotelian Society: Supplementary Volumes* 40: 223–4.

Wigmore, J. H. (1940). *A Treatise on the Anglo-American System of Evidence in Trials at Common Law.* Volume 9, third edition. Boston: Little, Brown.

Williams, G. (1953). *Criminal Law: The General Part.* First edition. London: Stevens and Sons.

Williams, G. (1977a). 'The Evidential Burden: Some Common Misapprehensions', *New Law Journal* 127: 156–8.

Williams, G. (1977b). 'Evidential Burdens on the Defence', *New Law Journal* 127: 182–4.

Williams, G. (1982). 'Offences and Defences', *Legal Studies* 2: 233–56.

Williams, G. (1988). 'The Logic of "Exceptions"', *Cambridge Law Journal* 47: 261–95.

Wolf, S. (1990). *Freedom Within Reason.* Oxford: Oxford University Press.

Wróblewski, J. (1973). 'Facts in Law', *Archiv Für Rechts- und Sozialphilosophie* 59: 161–78.

Wróblewski, J. (1975). 'The Problem of the So-Called Judicial Truth', reprinted in Wróblewski (1979).

Wróblewski, J. (1979). *Meaning and Truth in Judicial Decision.* Second Edition, ed. A. Aarnio. Helsinki: A-Tieto.

Wróblewski, J. (1989). 'Proof in Law: Legal Language and Legal Institutions', *International Journal for the Semiotics of Law* 2: 3–16.

Wróblewski, J. (1992). *The Judicial Application of Law*. Ed. Z. Bańkowski and N. MacCormick. Dordrecht: Springer.

Yeager, D. (2006). *J. L. Austin and the Law: Exculpation and the Explication of Responsibility*. Lewisburg: Bucknell University Press.

Yolton, J. W. (1957). 'Ascriptions, Descriptions, and Action Sentences', *Ethics* 67: 307–10.

Zimmerman, M. J. (1988). *An Essay on Moral Responsibility*. Totowa: Rowman & Littlefeld.

Zuckerman, A. (1976). 'The Third Exception to the *Woolmington* Rule'. *The Law Quarterly Review* 92: 402–26.

Zuckerman, A. (1987). 'No Third Exception to the *Woolmington* Rule', *The Law Quarterly Review* 103: 170–6.

Index of Subjects

Index of Names

www.ingramcontent.com/pod-product-compliance
Lightning Source LLC
LaVergne TN
LVHW011916200926
848484LV00002B/641
9780199685783